The 3rd English-Waldeck Regiment in the American Revolution

Bruce E. Burgoyne

HERITAGE BOOKS
2008

HERITAGE BOOKS
AN IMPRINT OF HERITAGE BOOKS, INC.

Books, CDs, and more—Worldwide

For our listing of thousands of titles see our website
at
www.HeritageBooks.com

Published 2008 by
HERITAGE BOOKS, INC.
Publishing Division
100 Railroad Ave. #104
Westminster, Maryland 21157

Copyright © 1999 Bruce E. Burgoyne

All rights reserved. No part of this book may be reproduced or transmitted in any form or by any means, electronic or mechanical, including photocopying, recording or by any information storage and retrieval system without written permission from the author, except for the inclusion of brief quotations in a review.

International Standard Book Numbers
Paperbound: 978-0-7884-1301-8
Clothbound: 978-0-7884-7114-8

Contents

Private of the Third English-Waldeck Regiment iv
Key to Waldeck Census Report v
Waldeck Census Report (1777 to 1786) ..... between v, vi
Map of Waldeck vii
Map of New York-New Jersey Area viii
Preface ix
1776 1
1777 56
1778 79
1779 104
1780 136
1781 151
1782 188
1783 226
Summary 242
Addendum 243
Notes 246
Bibliography 255
Index 285

Private of the Third English-Waldeck Regiment
-- *reproduced from an original oil painting by Klaus P. Scholz.*

The 3rs English-Waldeck Regiment

Key to Waldeck/Pyrmont Census Report

A - Year
B - Number of families
C - Number of families with children
    1 - Males   2 - Females
D - Number of houses, farms, and occupied houses
E - Number of married persons
F - Number of unmarried persons
    1 - Males over 18
    2. Females over 16
G - Confirmed persons
    1 - Boys   2 - Girls
H - Unconfirmed persons
    1. Boys   2 - Girls
I - Emigrants
    1 - Permanent
        a - Males   2 - Females
    2 - Temporary
        a - Students and those aboard ships
        b. Journeymen trade youths on their wander year
        c. In the Waldeck regiments
        d - In foreign military service
        e - Domestics outside Waldeck
            (1) Male   (2) - Female
J - Immigrants
    1 - Permanently
        a - Males   b - Females
    2 - Temporarily
        a - Males   b - Females
K - Returned (to Waldeck)
    1 - Males   2 - Females
L - Born
    1 - Sons
    2 - Daughters
    3 - Total
    4 - Including
        a - Twins
        b - Triplets
        c - Herrnhuters
        d - Jews
    5 - Still born
        a - Boys   b - Girls
M - Deaths
    1 - Males   2 - Females   3 - Total
N - Married pairs
O - Confirmed
P - Number of living in this year
Q - Totals in 10 years

    The lower part of the chart has the same headings as listed above for the Earldom of Pyrmont from 1777 to 1786.

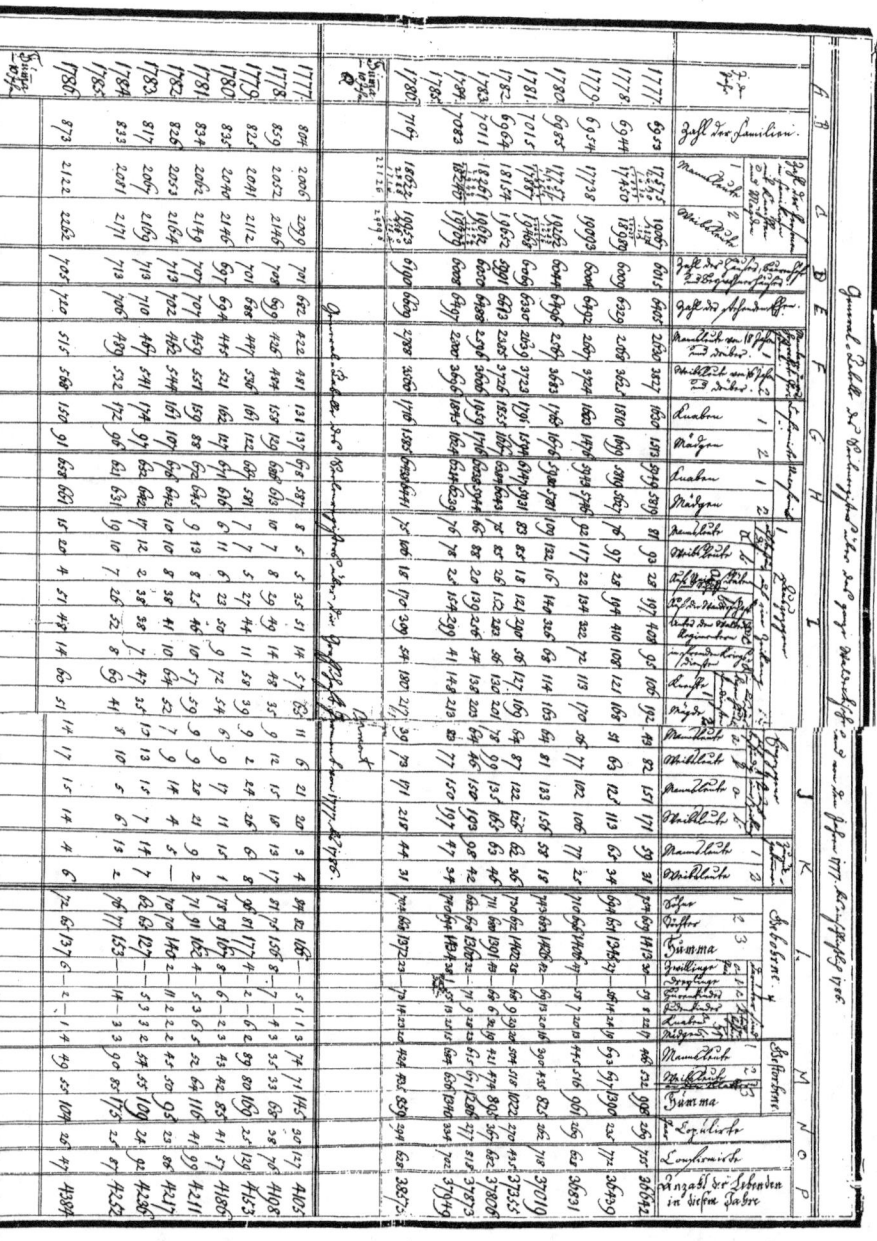

--courtesy of the author

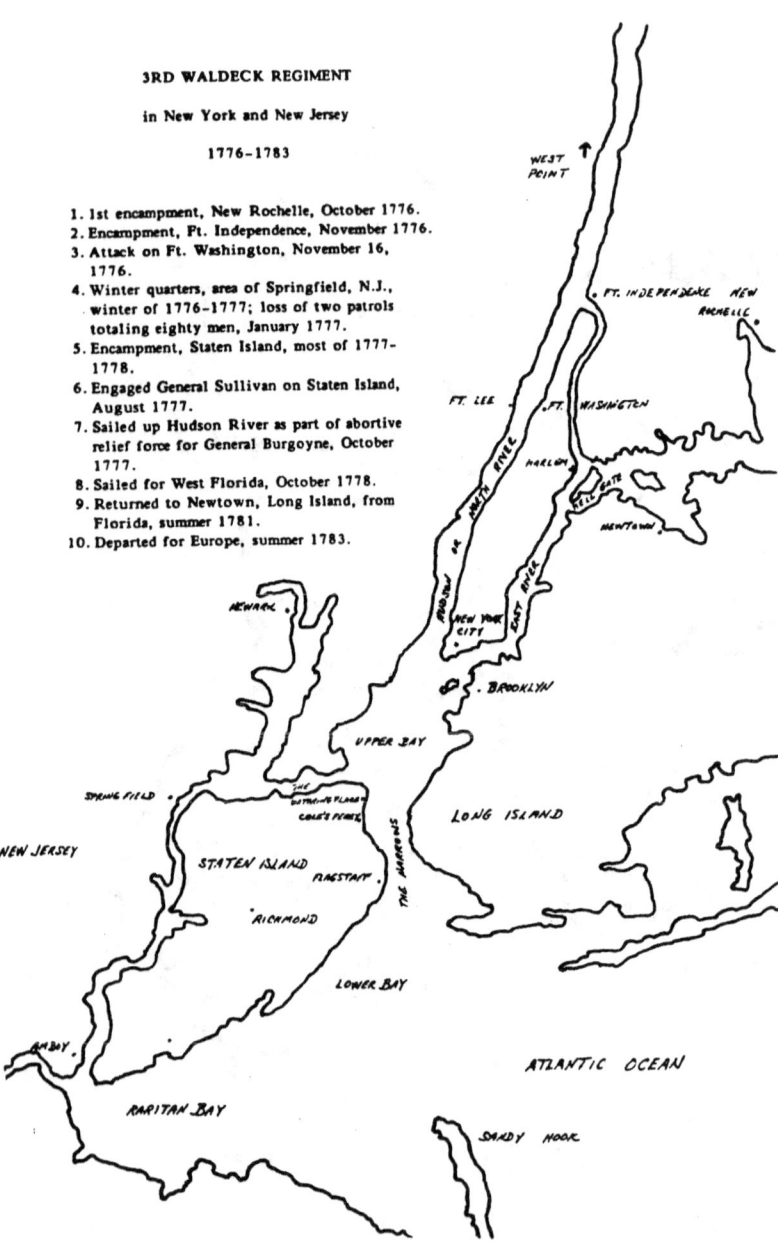

--courtesy of the author

The 3rd English-Waldeck Regiment
Preface

I first met Guenter Jedicke in the fall of 1975. At that time he was the president of the Waldeck Historical Society. The resulting friendship led to my special interest in the 3rd English-Waldeck Regiment's role in the American Revolution. After collecting considerable information on the regiment, and having translated the diary of the regimental chaplain, Philipp Waldeck, the memoir of a quartermaster sergeant, Karl Philipp Steuernagel, and an autograph book of the unit's auditor, Philipp Marc, I began to put together a history of the regiment's activities in the Revolution, 1776-1783.

The Waldeck Regiment represented the smallest contingent of troops sent to America by any of the six "Hessian" states which sent troops to the New World. Waldeck was also the smallest state and the regiment represented about one in every six men in the Waldeck population. Waldeck was so small that today it is only half a county in the German Federal Republic.

Through Guenter Jedicke and his wife, Marianne, I became acquainted, and friendships have developed, with numerous Waldeckers, who have an interest in the American Revolution. These friendships have now lasted over a quarter-century, and I have also profited from the generous donation of information, which they have provided.

In the pages which follow, I have tried to trace the activities of individuals, as well as of the regiment as a whole, because I feel that the ordinary soldier, from whatever country, is entitled to more respect. Further, no country's history can be considered complete if the "enemy soldier's" comments and conduct are not understood.

Editorial Procedures

The most distinctive feature of this volume is the assignment and use of serial numbers to aid in the identification of

The 3rd English-Waldeck Regiment

individuals. The numbers used in this volume are the same as used in *Waldeck Soldiers of the American Revolutionary War* (Bowie, MD, 1991). In lieu of umlauts for letters a, o, and u, I have added an e after the umlauted vowel. Finally, I have provided a bibliography which lists only material actually cited in the text.

Acknowledgments

In the past I have always listed my wife Marie last among the acknowledgments and as the driving force behind my literary efforts, This time I would like to put her first, where she belongs. She gives of her time, talent, and love, encouraging me to continue in a field we consider important. I can only say I am glad she is my wife, and that she works harder on my efforts than anyone else, including me.

I owe an unpayable debt to a long list of persons from Waldeck, and know of no way to list them with the respect to their contributions to this volume. Instead, I wish to thank the population of Waldeck for treating me so kindly. Frau Ingeborgg Moldenhauer archivist, and Guenter Jedicke, former President of the Waldeck Historical Society, gave and continue to give support to me and display a true attachment to the land of Waldeck. Because of his picture in the uniform of the 3rd Waldeck Regiment, and his many kindnesses and research assistance, I must give Klaus Scholz special thanks. Everyone working in the field of Hessian participation in the American Revolution is indebted to Inge Auerbach and Otto Froehlich for their compilation of *Hessische Truppen im amerikanischen Unabhaengigkeitskrieg (HETRINA)*. I have used it extensively. The Tichelaar family in The Netherlands is also the source of friendship and information - Waldeck had provided military personnel to Holland for years, a Waldeck princess had married into the Dutch royal family, and the archives at The Hague and

The 3rd English-Waldeck Regiment

the Army Museum in Delft were opened to me. The many friendships make my travels to Europe ever more enjoyable.

Personnel in the British Museum gave help in locating appropriate manuscripts, as did those of the Library of Congress, the University of Michigan Clements Library and the University of Virginia Alderman Library. It all started with the assistance of the personnel of the New York Public Library.

Individuals closer to home are Donald Londahl-Smidt and Bob Cowan, both of whom have given moral support and editorial comments in an effort to present this volume in the most favorable light. Finally, I would be neglecting the ultimate source of approval and editorial assistance , if I did not mention the ever excellent editorial assistance provided by my publisher, Heritage Books, Inc. of Bowie, Maryland. While I am still responsible for any errors, their contributions are deeply appreciated.

Bruce E. Burgoyne
Dover, DE

The 3rd English-Waldeck Regiment
1776
Introduction and Activities

"The Dogs of War are now fairly Let Loose upon us, but we are not however dismayed but expect to give a good account of the numerous Host of Foes that are coming to Slaughter us, especially your Hessians, Hanoverians, Waldeckers, etc. etc." So wrote "a gentleman of considerable distinction and influence in America," from Philadelphia on June 5, 1776.[1] The unknown American was commenting, of course, on the information recently arrived in America that the English government had engaged soldiers from a number of minor German states. These soldiers were to be shipped to America to help the English military suppress the revolution brewing in the colonies. Of the six German states - Anhalt-Zerbst, Ansbach-Bayreuth, Brunswick, Hesse-Cassel, Hesse-Hanau, and Waldeck - which eventually supplied military units for use in America, the most numerous were the Hessians from Hesse-Cassel, and the term "Hessian" was applied to men from all the German states. The Hanoverians were never sent to America in organized units, but only as individuals within the ranks of other states or of English units. The Waldeckers, on the other hand, were the smallest German contingent, and it is the 3rd English-Waldeck Regiment which is the focus of this research.

In his autobiography, Johann Gottfried Seume, who had served in the ranks of the Hesse-Cassel contingent, wrote of his experiences and criticized the use and treatment of the 'Hessians" by the petty German rulers.[2]

Joseph G. Rosengarten summarized a pamphlet published in Germany in 1879, which stated that Seume's account was taken from the diary of a Waldeck soldier (apparently an individual named Carl Philipp Steuernagel), who earlier had made the trip to America, and who was a great story-teller.[3]

At least a dozen individuals with the surname Waldeck served in the contingent of troops from Hesse-Cassel, including

The 3rd English-Waldeck Regiment

Friedrich Waldeck, surgeon of the Du Corps, or Leib Regiment, whose death was reported in a New York newspaper in October 1782.[4]

Freiherr von Dalwigk's work on the Waldeck and Hesse-Cassel mercenaries does not cite Steuernagel nor Chaplain Philipp Waldeck as sources, nor does he mention the successes or failures of the Waldeck Regiment in the American Revolution.[5] Another writer, Friedrich Kapp, at least in a condensed version of his work, also neglects the Waldeck contingent.[6]

Waldeck, a small principality located a few miles west of Cassel, had a population of 37,019 persons in 6,954 families, living in 6,004 houses in 1780.[7] The reigning prince, Carl August Friedrich, born in 1743, had ruled since 1766. Like his predecessors, he had a love of the military, and he entered Austrian service as a lieutenant colonel at the age of fifteen.

During the Seven Years' War he was wounded in a battle near Korbach, in Waldeck, and in 1772 he was made a lieutenant general in the Netherlands army. Prince Friedrich, as he was called, never married. He traveled extensively in Europe, but when at home, conducted a splendid court with no consideration or concern about financial matters.

In later life he wrote a history of the Seven Years' War as well as a series of portraits of famous men. In 1793 and 1794 Friedrich fought against the French, but later joined the Rhine Bund. He died in 1812.[8]

Indicative of both his travel and his connection with the Dutch and the Dutch military is a report of early March 1776, that the Princes of Waldeck and Hesse-Cassel, and several Dutch generals, plus the English Commissary, Colonel Charles Rainsford, had dined at the residence of the English ambassador, Sir Joseph Yorke, at the Hague.[9] Again, on May 24, 1776, the Prince of Waldeck and Colonel van der Hooven, commander of the Dutch garrison at Nijmegen, and most of the garrison's staff officers accompanied Colonel Rainsford when he visited Captain

The 3rd English-Waldeck Regiment

Georg Pausch of the Hesse-Hanau Artilllery on a small island in the Wahl. The purpose of the Rainsford visit was to inspect and muster Captain Pausch's Artillery Company, which was *en route* to Canada.[10] Edward J. Lowell's comment on the Prince of Waldeck was that "by comparison with the Margraves of Anspach the Princes of Waldeck seem almost respectable." They used their country as a stock farm for raising men for the Dutch service, but themselves fought for the Dutch with distinction.[11]

Nevertheless, Prince Friedrich, who was not related to George III of England, as were several of the other rulers who supplied troops to England, [12] was eager to sell his subjects into English service. Maybe not as eager as von Eelking indicated, i.e., April 25, 1775, as the date of the treaty signed in London,[13] but no Johnnie-come-lately. Friedrich wrote to Lord Suffolk on November 3, 1775, offering to place a 600-man regiment into English service.[14] And, although the principality had a compulsory draft for all but students,[15] it did not have eight battalions in Dutch service,[16] nor even the three regiments ready to serve anywhere for pay, which were mentioned by von Eelking.[17]

Instead, when Colonel William Faucitt, English Minister Plenipotentiary to a number of German states for the purpose of concluding treaties for the hiring of troops,[18] arrived in Waldeck, there were only about 200 men in uniform in the entire country.[19]

Faucitt negotiated a treaty, similar to those with the other German states, which provided for a 670-man regiment to be furnished to England, i.e., a bounty of 30 crowns per recruit, an annual subsidy of 20,050 crowns to the prince, and payment for men killed and wounded.[20] The result, summed up by British historian Otto Trevelyan, was that the prince received for himself 5,000 per year while "the wood-cuters and charcoal-burners of Waldeck were shooting, and being shot by the lumberers of Maine and Connecticut."[21]

The 3rd English-Waldeck Regiment

Albert Haarmann cites John Almond, editor, *Parlimentary Register*, volume III, (1775-1776), 504-507, as authority that the treaty was signed in Arolsen on April 20, 1776,[22] and this date is supported in that Faucitt was in Waldeck for "a few days from 19 April 1776".[23]

As set forth by von Eelking, the regiment supplied by Waldeck was organized with a sixteen-man staff, a grenadier company of 134 men, and four musket companies of 130 men each, for a total of 670 men. To this force, the prince added, for extra pay, a fourteen-man artillery section.[24] Haarmann has the same figures, but increases the staff size to eighteen men,[25] and other documents indicate, that according to the treaty, the staff numbered somewhere between fifteen and 21 men.[26]

However, the apparent strength of the staff which went to America seems to have had only twelve men (and possibly four officer's servants) consisting of the following positions:[27]

Lt. Col. Joh. Lud. Wm. v. Hanxleden (W100001S), Girshausen
Major Ludwig v. Dalwigk (W100002S), Dalwigksthal
Adj. & Ens. Joh. Henrich Stierlein (W100018S), Stuttgart
Regt. QM. & Lt. Karl Theodor Wiegand (W100022S)
Regt. Drummer Christian Glaentzer (W400001), Mengeringhausen
Provost Konrad Glaentzer (W400002), Mengeringhausen.
Regt. Surgeon Christian Mattern (W400004)
Commissary (Auditor) Philipp Marc (W400003), Arolsen
Chaplain Philipp Waldeck (W400005), Hemfurth, 26 yrs old
Wagon Servant Daniel Wagener (W400006), Anraff, 23 yrs old
Wagon Servant Christian Ruesel (W400007), Mengeringhausen
Povost Asst. (Not identified)

(The author has established a serial numbering system, not only for the Waldeck soldiers, but for men of all the "Hessian" units. Z prefix is used for Anhalt-Zerbst, A for Ansbach-Bayreuth, B for Brunswick, C for Hesse-Cassel, H for Hesse-Hanau, and W for Waldeck. The six digit numbers following the prefix have a first digit of 1 for officers, 2 for enlisted men, 3 for artillery, 4 for staff, and 5 for dependents. When an individual

The 3rd English-Waldeck Regiment serves in more than one category, a letter suffix is added with C denoting commissioning, S staff, A artillery, and E enlisted status. Following each name the individual's serial number, birth date and birth place, or age is indicated, if known. An underlined place of birth in this volume indicates that the birth place was in Waldeck.)

To date limited information on servants, or batmen, for the military officers on the staff has been found by this writer, but the positions seem to have been covered under provisions of the treaty. However, men may have been, and probably were, taken from the ranks to fill these duties. At least servants for the chaplain and regimental surgeon came from the ranks.[28]

The 1st or Grenadier Company of the regiment was organized with the following positions:[29]

1 - Captain	1 - Servant
1 - 1st Lieutenant	1- Servant
1 - 2nd Lieutenant	1 - Servant
3 - Sergeants	1 - QM Sergeant
1 - Captain-at-arms	1 - Surgeon's Mate
6 - Corporals	2 Fifers
3 - Drummers	110 Privates
1 - Solicitor	**134 - TOTAL**

The solicitor was apparently a fictional individual for whom pay and rations were drawn, probably to provide the company commander with a slush fund.

The following list identifies the individual members of the Grenadier Company when it marched out of Korbach on May 20, 1776. In addition to the regular positions, a volunteer and two cadets marched with the unit. These were generally individuals who were hopeful of obtaining commission status, as were most of the individuals in the musket companies who accepted the grade of free corporal.[30]

Captain Konrad Albrecht v. Horn (W100003S)
1st Lt. Augustin Christian Alberti (W100008)

The 3rd English-Waldeck Regiment

2nd Lt. Karl Henrich Strubberg (W100009)
Sgt. Henrich Schluckebier (W200002), 42 yrs old, Sachsenhausen
Sgt. Konrad Thierle (W200003), 33 yrs old, Neerdar
Sgt. Friedrich v. Axleben (W200001C), 35 yrs old, Fegebeudel, Schl.
QM Sgt. Franz Riemenschneider (W200005), 29 yrs old, Wildungen
Capt-at-arms Kaspar v. Nehm (W200004), 30 yrs old, Helmighausen
Surg. Mate Ludwig Zick (W200006), 22 yrs old, Arolsen
Cpl. Johannes Hanstein (W200007), 46 yrs old, Wildungen
Cpl. Ernst Jung (W200011), 28 yrs old, Rosdorf, Hanau
Cpl. Johannes Meisner (W200008), 30 yrs old, Rhoden
Cpl. Philipp Muus (W200009), 22 yrs old, Helsen
Cpl. Christoph Roemer (W200010), 27 yrs old, Hesperingshausen
Cpl. Christoph Weishaupt (W200012). 33 yrs old, Wrexen
Fifer Christoph Steinmeyer (W200013), 16 yrs old, Oesdorf, Pyr.
Fifer Johannes Lahm (W200557), 16 yrs old, Schweinsbuehl
Drummer Adam Knueppel (W200017), 16 yrs old, Odershausen
Drummer Jakob Matte (W200016), 25 yrs old, Rhoden
Drummer Theodor Repp (W200015), 21 yrs old, Mengeringhausen
Servant Philipp Ebe (W200622), 20 yrs old, Twiste
Servant Johannes Schaeffer (W200630), 20 yrs old, Helsen
Servant Henrich Ulenbruch (W200099), 19 yrs old, Schmillinghausen
Vol. Henr. Chrn. Karl Mueller (W200080), 23 yrs old, Korbach
Cadet Bernhard v. Canstein (W200046), 26 yrs old, Canstein, Koeln
Cadet Karl v. Rhena, (W200115), 30 yrs old, Rhena and
Grenadiers
Chrn Peter Albrecht (W200018), 18 yrs old, Barssen, Pyr.
Christoph Andre (W200019), 40 yrs old, Wildungen
Henrich Arend (W200020), 26 yrs old, Voele, Darmstadt
Ignatius Bachstaedter (W200021), 38 yrs old, Wuerzburg
Georg Backhaus (W200022), 22 yrs old, Lengefeld
Jakob Joh. Bangert (W200023), 19 yrs old, Meiningerhausen
Ludwig Bauerschmidt (W200024), 28 yrs old, Amt Gifhorn
Wilhelm Berghoever (W200026), 38 yrs old, Twiste
Georg Andreas Bock (W200027), 22 yrs old, Alt Lothheim
Johannes Braun (W200028), 36 yrs old, Giessen
Friedrich Breuninger (W200029), 24 yrs old, Neustadt, Hohen
Adam Kann (W200030), 22 yrs old, Nieder-Werbe,
Johannes Kann (W200031), 23 yrs old, Nieder-Werbe
Wilhelm Kann (W200032), 22 yrs old, Giflitz
Henrich Kaufmann (W200033), 18 yrs old, Helsen
Emanuel Kesting (W200035), 21 yrs old, Helsen

The 3rd English-Waldeck Regiment

Konrad Kleine (W200036), 22 yrs old, Reinhardshausen
Jost Stefan Kleucker (W200037), 21 yrs old, Korbach
Georg Kluss (W200038), 22 yrs old, Eichenborn, Pyr.
Philipp Andreas Knust (W200039), 17 yrs old, Meineringhausen
Friedrich Kober (W200040), 21 yrs old, Wrexen
Friedrich Koch (W200041), 30 yrs old, Hanau, Hesse
Henrich Koch (W200042), 21 yrs old, Lich, Solms
Konrad Koch (W20043), 18 yrs old, Wrexen
Wilhelm Koehler (W200044), yrs old, Helmscheid
Konrad Koenig (W200045), 30 yrs old, Korbach
Christian Koppe (W200047), 30 yrs old, Wetterburg
Franz Cramer (W200048), 26 yrs old, Landau
Joh. Jakob Kratz (W200049), 22 yrs old, Wildungen
Georg Kruhm (W200050), 30 yrs old, Wichdorf, Hesse
Joh. Josef Kuhlemann (W201195), 28 yrs old, Hermete, Pad.
Christoph Kurtze (W200052), 21 yrs old, Zimmersrode, Hesse
Thomas Dantz (W200053), 24 yrs old, Bergfreiheit
Adam Drube (W200054), 32 yrs old, Langenfeld, Hesse
Henrich Ebersbach (W200055), 26 yrs old, Sachsenhausen
Johannes Embde (W200056), 20 yrs old, Muehlhausen
Johannes Faust (W200057), 28 yrs old, Neukirchen
Jost Fischer (W200058), 19 yrs old, Leutersheim
Konrad Fischer (W200059), 23 yrs old, Braunau
Johannes Flamme (W200060), 23 yrs old, Twiste
Berthold Frede (W200061), 23 yrs old, Grossenberg, Pyr.
Henrich Giesing (W200062), 25 yrs old, Berndorf
Christian Goebel (W200063), 30 yrs old, Meineringhausen
Lorenz Goebert (W200064), 26 yrs old, Braunau
Johannes Grob (W200065), 22 yrs old, Lintefels, Kurpf.
Georg Hahne (W200067), 23 yrs old, Pyrmont
Philipp Hamel (W200068), 25 yrs old, Meineringhausen
Peter Happe (W200069), 34 yrs old, Odershausen
Daniel Hartmann (W200070), 23 yrs old, Reinhardshausen
Henrich Herbold (W200071), 30 yrs old, Rhoden
Andreas Herter (W200072), 32 yrs old, Heystrey, Wuerz.
Eberhard Leydenberg (W200073), 29 yrs old, Hameln
Valentin Linde (W200074), 22 yrs old, Mehlen
Peter Mauer (W200075), 32 yrs old, Mandern
Johannes Mertz (W200076), 50 yrs old, Wildungen
Jakob Mette (W200077), 24 yrs old, Hueddingen
Christoph Meyer (W200078), 52 yrs old, Bruhne, Hesse

The 3rd English-Waldeck Regiment

Joh. Georg Meyer (W200128), 23 yrs old, Langenscheid, Sch.
Johannes Moock (W200079), 26 yrs old, Wega
Christoph Mueller (W200081), 25 yrs old, Mandern
Konrad Mueller (W200083), 25 yrs old, Armsfeld
Philipp Mueller (W200084), 30 yrs old, Billinghausen
Johannes Neumeyer (W200086), 16 yrs old, Herbsen
Henrich Neuschaeffer (W200087), 42 yrs old, Helsen
Anton Noll (W200088), 20 yrs old, Rothenburg, Hesse
Paulus Nolle (W200089), 24 yrs old, Bergfreiheit
Chrn.. Philipp Nolte (W200090), 21 yrs old, Buehle
Hermann Ohms (W200091), 25 yrs old, Ortenstein, Br.
Wilhelm Pique (W200093), 24 yrs old, Rhoden
Fried. Joh. Phil. Pleuger (W200095), 35 yrs old, Luette, Lippe
Philipp Puettmann (W200094), 23 yrs old, Armsfeld
Andreas Reineck (W200096), 39 yrs old, Tottleben, Sach.
Henrich Riese (W200097), 19 yrs old, Beringhausen, Koeln
Johannes Schaeffer (W200098), 20 yrs old, Meineringhausen
Daniel Scheideler (W200100), 22 yrs old, Adorf
Christoph Kon. Scheuermann (W200101), 24 yrs old, Wrexen
Johannes Schleiermacher (W200102), 43 yrs old, Wildungen
Henrich Schmidt (W200103), 26 yrs old, Romersberg, Hesse
Johannes Schmidt (W200104), 24 yrs old, Wellen
Phil. Geo. Schneider (W200106), 37 yrs old, Muehlhausen
Georg Schrauff (W200107), 25 yrs old, Mandern
 Konrad Schrauff (W200627), 24 yrs old, Zueschen
Ulrich Schreiber (W200109), 28 yrs old, Hundsdor
Alexander Siegler (W200110), 39 yrs old, Falckenbourg, Koeln
Henrich Steinbach (W200111), 30 yrs old, Hanebach, Spang.
Michael Stiegler (W200112), 38 yrs old, Waltenbourg, Sach.
Henrich Striepecke (W200114), 26 yrs old, Wrexen
Wilhelm Taubert (W200116), 22 Yrs old, Korbach
Georg Thielemann (W200117), 26 yrs old, Mandern
Jakob Walter (W200118), 30 yrs old, Bassdorf, Darm.
Johannes Weber (W200120), 24 yrs old, Anraff
Karl Geo. Werbein (W200121), 21 yrs old, Holtzhausen, Pyr.
Jakob Werner (W200122), 21 yrs old, Wildungen
Stefan Wichard (W200123), 22 yrs old, Netze
Chrn. Joh. Wilhelm (W200124), 48 yrs old, Berlin
Georg Wissemann (W200125), 25 yrs old, Hoeringhausen
Friedrich Zimmermann (W200126), 26 yrs old, Pyrmont
Karl Zwick (W200127), 36 yrs old, Kosswig, A.Z.

The 3rd English-Waldeck Regiment

Two men who marched from Korbach with the Grenadiers on 20 May, but who deserted during the day, were Grenadiers Daniel Conradi, 25 yrs old, Sachsenberg, and Karl Stuhlmann, 22 yrs old, Sachsenberg. Men joining the company after the march began, included new recruits,

Ludwig Berges (W200025), 23 yrs old, Berndorf
Georg Grubert (W200066), 52 yrs old, Bertrueck, Pad. and
Leonhard Walter (W200119), 41 yrs old, Kirch Bergfort.

Three men, who had deserted on May 16, 1776, and who were returned to duty on May 31, were Grenadiers:

Johannes Kenthans (W200034), 30 yrs old, Meineringhausen
Karl Mueller (W200082), 24 yrs old, Korbach and
Johannes Stracke (W200113), 24 yrs old, Wildungen.

One man, who had gone on leave on May 6, 1776, and who returned to duty on May 22, was Gren. Ferdinand Neumann (W200065), 26 yrs old, Cuehte, Pad..

A transfer from 4 Company to 1 Company on May 21, 1776, for a man who was to have been promoted to corporal, apparently came too late. He was Grenadier Rudolph Pape, (W200092), 29 yrs old, Oesdorf, Pyr.

Fifer Lahme (W200557) transferred to 5 Company as a private on May 29, 1776, and was replaced by a transfer from 2 Company, Fifer Martin Tanner (W200014), 15 years old, Strassburg,

Two men transferred from 3 Company to 1 Company on May 29, and May 30, 1776, for further reassignment to 5 Company on June 21, 1776. They apparently sailed from Bremerlehe with 1 Company and from England with 5 Company. They were Privates Henrich Lemmering (W200559),

The 3rd English-Waldeck Regiment

35 yrs old, Wals Roden, and Johannes Mieting (W200569), 32 yrs old, Wildungen.

One hundred twenty-seven men appear to have marched with 1 Company from Korbach on May 20, 1776. Two of this total did not arrive at Bremerlehe. One hundred and thirty-five men sailed with the company to England, where two of the men were then transferred to 5 Company. One man Christoph Kuntze (W200052), died *en route* to America on August 29, 1776, so that 132 men of 1 Company have been identified as having arrived in America.

The 3rd English-Waldeck Regiment
2nd Company

The regiment's musket companies were designated 2nd, 3rd, 4th, and 5th Companies, or by their commander's name. The 2nd Company and the 3rd Company were also known as the Major's and the Lieutenant Colonel's Companies when the regiment departed from Korbach. The musket companies were organized with:

1 - Captain or Captain Lt	1 - Servant
1 - 1st Lieutenant	1 - Servant
1 - Ensign	1 - Servant
3 - Sergeants	1 - QM Sergeant
1 - Captain-at-arms	1 - Surgeon's Mate
1 - Free Corporal	6 - Corporals
1 - Fifer	1 - Solicitor
3 - Drummers	107 Privates
	131 - TOTAL

Personnel assigned to the various companies upon their departure from Korbach with the acquisitions and losses *en route* to America were as follows:

2nd Company

Captain Christoph Alberti (W!00004), 39 yrs old, Wildungen
1st Lieutenant Wilhelm Keppel (W100010), 21 yrs old, Gelnhausen, Hanau
Ensign Henrich Fried. Noelting (W100011), 26 yrs old, Pyrmont
Sgt. Jakob Todt (W200012), 48 yrs old, Helsen
Sgt. Christoph Embde (W200130), 32 yrs old, Goldhausen
Sgt. Dietrich Schotte (W200131), 25 yrs old, Karlshaven, Hesse
QM Sgt. Henrich Eisenberg (W200133), 35 yrs old, Vasbeck
Capt.-at-arms Konrad Trost (W200132), 32 yrs old, Landau
Surg. Mate Karl Fried. Pfister (W200134), 29 yrs old, Schwerin, Meckl.
Free Cpl. Schoenberg v. Spiegel (W200629), 17 yrs old, Pickelsheim, Pad.
Cpl. Henrich Beste (W200137), 29 yrs old, Korbach
Cpl. Karl Bruehne (W200135), 20 yrs old, Helsen
Cpl. Ernst Kobert (W200140), 23 yrs old, Neersen, Pyr.
Cpl. Henrich Gockel (W200136), 28 yrs old, Lelbach

The 3rd English-Waldeck Regiment

Cpl. Johannes Lutz (W200139), 30 yrs. old, Langenscheid, A.Z.
Cpl. Otto Wiedlaacke (W200138), 23 yrs old, Polle, Hanover
Fifer Friedrich Berckenhauser (W200141), 22 yrs old, Korbach
Fifer Martin Tanner (W200014), 15 yrs old, Strasbourg
Drummer Christian Diste (W200144), 16 yrs old, Volckenmissen
Drummer Johannes Unger (W200143), 16 yrs old, Strothe
Drummer Jeremias Warlich (W200142), 24 yrs old, Wildungen
Servant Henrich Zurmuehlen (W200631), 29 yrs old, Barssen, Pyr., and

Privates

Johannes Becker (W200145), 21 yrs old, Luetersheim
Matthias Becker (W200146), 20 yrs old, Rhenegge
Daniel Beisenhertz (W200147), 21 yrs old, Sachsenberg
Henrich Berges (W200148), 42 yrs old, Mengeringhausen
Bernhard Beyer (W200149), 20 yrs old, Armsfeld
Franz Biggs (W200150), 25 yrs old, Beringhausen
Jakob Blaufus (W200151), 24 yrs old, Ernsthausen
Philipp Boettger (W200152), 19 yrs old, Bremen
Otto Bruehne (W200153), 21 yrs old, Adorf
Friedrich Budde (W200154), 23 yrs old, Hoerle
Leonhard Koberl (W200155), 18 yrs old, Koenig Gr. Erbach
Balthasar Kaltwasser (W200156), 17 yrs old, Wetzlar
Henrich Klaaus (W200157), 17 yrs old, Schmillinghausen
Christian Dan. Knipp (W200158), 17 yrs old, Goddelsheim
Barthold Knoechel (W200159), 22 yrs old, Mandern
Adam Kreutzer (W200160), 21 yrs old, Haddamar, Hesse
Gottfried Jak. Kuester (W200161), 18 yrs old, Wildungen
Ludwig Kuester (W200162), 18 yrs old, Helsen
Henrich Kuethe (W200263), 20 yrs old, Bassdorf, Darm.
Joh. Jost Dantz (W200164), 20 yrs old, Bergfreiheit
Josef Dillinger (W200165), 28 yrs old, Braunschweig
Christian Dietz (W200621), 38 yrs old, Wildungen
Daniel Dietz (W200166), 19 yrs old, Braunau
Stefan Dietz (W200167), 40 yrs old, Kleinern
Joh. Jost Drewes (W200168), 19 yrs old, Bringhausen
Henrich Duckenberg (W200169), 20 yrs old, Oberurff, Hesse
Christian Eisenberg (W200170), 20 yrs old, Vasbeck
Henrich Eisenberg (W200171), 17 yrs old, Vasbeck
Joh. Christian Eisenberg (W200172), 20 yrs old, Vasbeck
Henrich Figge (W200173), 36 yrs old, Ober-Waroldern
Friedrich Fingerhut (W200174), 18 yrs old, Gembeck
Henrich Fischer (W200175), 18 yrs old, Ammenhausen

The 3rd English-Waldeck Regiment

Dietrich Theo. Frede (W200176), 18 yrs old, Grossenberg, Pyr.
Georg Friedeborn (W200177), 20 yrs old, Usseln
Henrich Genuit (W200178), 26 yrs old, Twiste
Henrich Gerhard (W200179), 17 yrs old, Willingen
Johannes Gockel (W200180), 26 yrs old, Kleinern
Henrich Goebel (W200181), 24 yrs old, Willingen
Philipp Gosmann (W200182), 24 yrs old, Wetterburg
Philipp Grimm (W200183), 19 yrs old, Zweibruecken
Ernst Hahne (W200184), 25 yrs old, Adorf
Johannes Hammersdorf (W200185), 30 yrs old, Heidelberg
Matthias Hauschild (W200186), 17 yrs old, Waldeck
Philipp Hen. Hentze (W200187), 19 yrs old, Wrexen
Andreas Herbert (W200188), 18 yrs old, Sebecksen, Han.
Georg Hoehle (W200189), 19 yrs old, Bringhausen
Adam Hohmann (W200190), 23 yrs old, Hueddingen
Konrad Hohmann (W200191), 33 yrs old, Giflitz
Peter Hugen (W200192), 31 yrs old, Elberfeld
Franz Humbracht (W200193), 23 yrs old, Anraff
Friedrich Jaeger (W200194), 18 yrs old, Oesdorf, Pyr.
Friedrich Lacour (W200195), 24 yrs old, Copenhagen, Den.
Philipp Henr. Lange (W200196), 19 yrs old, Wirmighausen
Wilhelm Littlet (W200197), 19 yrs old, Libstotd, Prussia
Henrich Lueckel (W200198), 25 yrs old, Bergfreiheit
Jost Menckel (W200199), 18 yrs old, Altenlotheim
Johannes Meybaum (W200200), 20 yrs old, Volkmarsen
Henrich Meyer (W200201), 28 yrs old, Netze
Friedrich Molle (W200202), 18 yrs old, Mengeringhausen
Daniel Mueller (W200203), 20 yrs old, Schorbach, Hesse
Henrich Mueller (W200204), 20 yrs old, Sachsenhausen
Johannes Mueller (W200205), 23 yrs old, Schlitz, Goertz
Nikolaus Mueller (W200206), 32 yrs old, Koenig, Erbach
Bernhard Mundhenck (W200207), 20 yrs old, Hagen, Pyr.
Barthold Nasemann (W200208), 20 yrs old, Wildungen
Henrich Pfeil (W200209) 17 yrs old, Hamburg
Philipp Rabensprock (W200210), 20 yrs old, Bergheim
Henrich Rauch (W200211), 50 yrs old, Albertshausen
                        (Arolsen Saegemuehle)
Henrich Reinhard (W200212), 18 yrs old, Braunsen (Rhena)
Christoph Roelcke (W200213), 27 yrs old, Boehne
Justus Runte (W200214), 24 yrs old, Lelbach
Karl Sander (W200215), 18 yrs old, Bevern, Braunsch.

The 3rd English-Waldeck Regiment

Bernhard Schaper (W200216), 21 yrs old, Holtzhausen, Pyr.
Jakob Josef Schepp (W200217), 22 yrs old, Homburg, Darm.
Jost Schimmel (W200218), 26 yrs old, Meineringhausen
Georg Schmeck (W200219), 19 yrs old, Helsen
Jakob Schmeck (W200220), 26 yrs old, Mandern
Johannes Schmeck (W200221), 17 yrs old, Mandern
Karl Schnabel (W200222), 18 yrs old, Zweibruecken
Henrich Schneider (W200223), 18 yrs old, Ober-Waroldern
Ludwig Schnitzius (W200224), 20 yrs old, Hogheim
Josef Schrantz (W200225), 17 yrs old, Canstein, Koeln
Christoph Schultze (W200226), 22 yrs old, Holtzhausen, Pyr
Friedrich Schwencke (W200227), 19 yrs old, Helsen
Georg Six (W200228), 19 yrs old, Erdenbrick, Witg.
Friedrich Sonnenschein (W200229), 19 yrs old, Sachsenhausen
Georg Sperling (W200230), 21 yrs old, Ellingrothe
Philipp Steinmeyer (W200231), 22 yrs old, Oesdorf, Pyr.
Henrich Stiesing (W200232), 18 yrs old, Dehausen
Johannes Stoecker (W200233), 18 yrs old, Wrexen
Stefan Struebe (W200234), 20 yrs old, Benkhausen
Ludwig Stuckenbrock (W200235), 16 yrs old, Holtzhausenh, Pyr.
Friedrich Stuhldreher (W200236), 20 yrs old, Muehlhausen
Wilhelm Sude (W200237), 21 yrs old, Muehlhausen
Friedrich Teigtmeyer (W200238), 45 yrs old, Goettingen
Christian Tente (W200239), 17 yrs old, Sachsenhausen
Geo. Henrich Ursprung (W200240), 22 yrs old, Reinhardshausen
Christoph Voepel (W200241), 17 yrs old, Neudorf
Wilhelm Voepel (W200242), 20 yrs old, Sachsenhausen
Johannes Wagener (W200243), 24 yrs old, Inzig, Holo.
Christoph Weitenkamp (W200244), 18 yrs old, Goettingen
Johannes Werke (W200245), 24 yrs old, Bendorf, Ansbach
Johannes Wetterhacke (W200246), 26 yrs old, Goddelsheim, Car.
Johannes Winterberg (W200247), 20 yrs old, Gembeck
Anton Wolff (W200248), 36 yrs old, Brincksen, Pad.
Friedrich Zoellner (W200249), 22 yrs old, Hafen, Pyr.

One man who marched from Korbach on May 20, 1776, deserted the next day at Berentrik. This was Private Adam Aschauer, 18 yrs old, Wethen.

The 3rd English-Waldeck Regiment

A new recruit who apparently was enlisted during the first day's march was: Drummer Christian Kriegsmann (W200105), Mengeringhausen, Fifer Tanner (W200014) transferred to 1 Company on May 29, 1776.

One hundred twenty-nine men of 2 Company appear to have marched from Korbach on May 20, 1776. One man deserted *en route* to the port, one man joined the company, and one man transferred out, so that 128 men sailed from Bremerlehe. Friedrich Teigtmeyer (W200238) died *en route* to America on October 5, 1776. Therefore 127 men of 2 Company have been identified as having arrived in America.

3 Company

Capt. Lt. Alexander von. Baumbach (W100007), Amenau, Ob. Hesse
1st Lieutenant Friedrich von.Wilmowsky (W100012), Korbach
Ensign Henrich Jakob Knipschild,(W100013S), Korbach
Sgt. Wilhelm Ursall (W200250C), 23 yrs old, Holtzhausen, Pyr.
Sgt. Jakob Graebe (W200251), 34 yrs old, Rhoden
Sgt. Henrich Schumacher (W200252), 28 yrs old, Mengeringhausen
QM Sgt. Georg Ulner (W200254), 19 yrs old, Marburg
Capt.-at-arms Anton Pohlmann (W200253), 35 yrs old, Giebringhausen
Surg. Mate Henrich Dan. Beck (W200255), 22 yrs old, Arolsen
Free Cpl. Christian Lud. Schmidt (W200626), 18 yrs old, Arolsen
Cpl. Christoph Budde (W200260), 34 yrs old, Fuerstenberg
Cpl. Johannes Knoechel (W200256), 27 yrs old, Albertshausen
Cpl. Georg Muus (W200259), 23 yrs old, Wildungen
Cpl. Henrich Muus (W200261), 40 yrs old, Wethen
Cpl Johannes Rudelbach (W200258), 36 yrs old, Wildungen
Cpl. Christian Wienand (W2000257), 27 yrs old, Rhenegge
Fifer Christian Reute,(W200262), 46 yrs old, Rhena
Drummer Christian Haase (W200265), 16 yrs old, Mengeringhausen
Drummer Christian Rohde (W200263), 29 yrs old, Ober-Werbe
Drummer Konrad Trand (W200264), 16 yrs old, Wildungen
Cadet Wilhelm v. Hanxleden (W200371), 30 yrs old, Girshausen, and

Privates

Friedrich Albracht (W200266), 26 yrs old, Wethen
Johannes Albracht (W200267), 24 yrs old, Wega

The 3rd English-Waldeck Regiment

Christian Amelung (W200268), 21 yrs old, Wetterburg
Christoph Arend (W200269), 17 yrs old, Bringhausen
Friedrich Bauer (W200270), 24 yrs old, Wehrtheim
Jakob Becker (W200271), 20 yrs old, Adorf
Christian Bergmann (W200272), 16 yrs old, Fuerstenberg
Johannes Birckmann (W200273), 18 yrs old, Reiningen
Wilhelm Brand (W200274), 21 yrs old, Rhoden
Friedrich Buntrock (W200275), 18 yrs old, Elleringhausen
Georg Kaesemeyer (W200276), 44 yrs old, Holtzhausen, Pyr.
Peter Kaus (W200277), 44 yrs old, Beckerswill
Henrich Kinold (W200278), 52 yrs old, Trentelburg, Hesse
Kaspar Klahold (W200280), 27 yrs old, Reisebeck, Koeln
Joh. Henrich Klapp (W200281), 20 yrs old, Sachsenhausen
Phil. Peter Klaus (W200281), 23 yrs old, Schmillinghausen
Karl Kleine (W200283), 19 yrs old, Bringhausen
Christian Knoechel (W200279), 19 yrs old, Albertshausen
Johannes Koch (W200284), 21 yrs old, Mehlen
Phil. David Kremer (W200285), 48 yrs old, Wildungen
Peter Kremer (W200286), 23 yrs old, Hemfurth
Johannes Kunckel (W200287), 24 yrs old, Massborn, Hanau
Leonhard Diamor (W200288), 18 yrs old, Werzlar
Henrich Dicke (W200289), 23 yrs old, Anraff
Christian Dullmann (W200290), 17 yrs old, Helmighausen
Christian Figge (W200291), 20 yrs old, Elleringhausen
Wilhelm Figge (W200292), 28 yrs old, Mengeringhausen
Matthias Flamme (W200293), 22 yrs old, Rhenegge
Christian Francke (W200295), 20 yrs old, Mengeringhausen
Johannes Frantz (W200296), 17 yrs old, Wellen
Adam Geitz (W200297), 18 yrs old, Hemfurth
Georg Gerhard (W200298), 17 yrs old, Willingen
Moritz Gerlach (W200299), 40 yrs old, Gellershausen
Johannes Goebel (W200300), 17 yrs old, Willingen
Friedrich Graebe (W200301), 23 yrs old, Mengeringhausen
Joh. Henrich Graebing (W200302), 20 yrs old, Freienhagen
Andreas Guergel (W200303), 22 yrs old, Fulda
Philipp Heinemann (W200304), 18 yrs old, Boehne
Balthasar Heinschel (W200305), 35 yrs old, Lippersdorf
Philipp Henrich (W200306), 21 yrs old, Giflitz
Henrich Hering (W200307), 23 yrs old, Frebershausen
Stefan Hertzog (W200308), 33 yrs old, Wellen
Johannes Hesse (W200309), 18 yrs old, Luetersheim

The 3rd English-Waldeck Regiment

Henrich Hoelscher (W200310), 18 yrs old, Holtzhausen, Pyr.
Johannes Holtzappel (W200311), 26 yrs old, Bergfreiheit
Stefan Christoph Horn (W200312), 17 yrs old, Neudorf
Johann Geo. Jost (W200313), 21 yrs old, Ulrichstein, Darm.
Henrich Lange (W200314), 20 yrs old, Wirmighausen
Johannes Leeser (W200315), 16 yrs old, Fuerstenberg
Henrich Lemmering (W200559), 35 yrs old, Wals Roden, Han.
Ludwig Wilhelm Lincker (W200316), 24 yrs old, Affersleben
Wilhelm Lindner (W200317), 19 yrs old, Nordenbeck
Konrad Lock (W200318), 20 yrs old, Heimershausen
David Lohrmann (W200436), 17 yrs old, Homburg
Valentin Malches (W200319), 20 yrs old, Fritzlar
Daniel Martin (W200320), 18 yrs old, Namur
Peter Martin (W200321), 19 yrs old, Wega
Valentin Maurer (W200322), 28 yrs old, Maeckelbach, Kurpf.
Henrich May (W200323), 49 yrs old, Marburg
Daniel Mechel (W200324), 19 yrs old, Buehle
Christoph Meier (W200325), 20 yrs old, Ober-Waroldern
Philipp Meister (W200326), 18 yrs old, Helsen
Wilhelm Phil. Melcher (W200327), 18 yrs old, Arolsen
Bartholomaeus Joh. Mauser (W200328), 18 yrs old, Anraff
Adam Meuske (W200329), 46 yrs old, Landau
Johannes Meuske (W200330), 22 yrs old, Wildungen
Konrad Meyer (W2200331), 36 yrs old, Wildungen
Johannes Mieting (W200569), 24 yrs old, Wildungen
Johannes Mitze (W200332), 18 yrs old, Sachsenhausen
Christoph Mueller (W200333), 17 yrs old, Helsen
Daniel Mueller (W200334), 16 yrs old, Armsfeld
Kaspar Mueller (W200335), 21 yrs old, Haarfach, Darm.
Konrad Osterhold (W200336), 32 yrs old, Gellershausen
Friedrich Otto (W200337), 30 yrs old, Pyrmont
Kaspar Pickel (W200583), 16 yrs old, Weilar
Reinhard Pletz (W200338), 19 yrs old, Muenden
Christoph Raabe (W200339), 18 yrs old, Sachsenberg
Friedrich Raabe (W200340), 19 yrs old, Bringhausen
Henrich Raabe (W200341), 17 yrs old, Bringhausen
Johannes Rode (W200342), 49 yrs old, Strothe
Johannes Roegel (W200343), 26 yrs old, Krimma, Sachsen
Friedrich Roemer (W200344), 19 yrs old, Hesperinghausen
Daniel Rohde (W200345), 19 yrs old, Meineringhausen
Franz Schirr (W200346), 25 yrs old, Wildungen

The 3rd English-Waldeck Regiment

Henrich Schleiermacher (W200347), 36 yrs old, Wildungen
Adam Schmid (W200348), 24 yrs old, Bringhausen
Georg Schmidt (W200349), 18 yrs old, Caltholrtzhausen
Johannes Schmidt (W200350), 30 yrs old, Caltholtzhausen
Konrad Schmidt (W200603), 40 yrs old, Affoldern
Friedrich Schroeder (W200351), 30 yrs old, Bergheim
Hermann Seil (W200352), 18 yrs old, Schweinsburg
Dietrich Siebel (W200353), 18 yrs old, Buehle
Henr. Hermann Sievers (W200354), 18 yrs old, Holtzhausen, Pyr.
Friedrich Soeltzer (W200355), 19 yrs old, Goddelsheim
Henrich Stallmann (W200356), 18 yrs old, Elleringhausen
Konrad Steineck (W200357), 24 yrs old, Heimershausen
Wilhelm Stoltz (W200358), 30 yrs old, Elsoff
Jost Stremme (W200259), 17 yrs old, Usseln
Johannes Suiss (W200360), 30 yrs old, Nieder-Buehl
Johannes Tewes (W200361), 18 yrs old, Sachsenberg
Peter Thumerich (W200362), 39 yrs old, Bergheim
Johannes Ulrich (W200363), 17 yrs old, Gellershausen
Lorenz Ulricxh (W200364), 21 yrs old, Gelleershausen
Franz Weber (W200365), 20 yrs old, Lowesen, Pyr.
Anton Weinhold (W200366), 19 yrs old, Troppau
Adam Weirauch (W200367), 19 yrs old, Waldbolau
Jakob Wilhelm (W200368), 22 yrs old, Ober-Werbe
Karl Winckelmann (W200369), 15 yrs old, Hamburg
Michael Zentler (W200370), 22 yrs old, Tiefensaal.

Two men who marched from Korbach with the regiment and who were sent back on May 22 and 23, 1776, were Privates Konrad Galle, 20 yrs old, Oesdorf, Pyrmont, and Henrich Stuckenbrock, 31 yrs old, Holtzhausen, Pyr.

Two who deserted on the march from Korbach on May 21 and 22, 1776, were Privates Friedrich Schelp, 25 yrs old, Hagen, Pyrmont, and Georg Schemming, 35 yrs old, Kirchhain.

Two men, who marched to Bremerlehe with 3 Company, sailed to England with 1 Company, and were finally sent to America with 5 Company. They were Privates Henrich Lemmering (W200559), 35, Wals Roden, Han., and Johannes

The 3rd English-Waldeck Regiment

Mieting (W200569), 32, Wildungen,.

One man, who transferred to 4 Company at Bremerlehe on May 30, was Private David Lohrmann (W200436), 17 yrs old, Hamburg,.

Two men, who transferred to 5 Company at Bremerlehe on May 30, 1776, were Privates Kaspar Pickel (W200583), 15 yrs old, Weilar, and Konrad Schmidt (W200603), 40 yrs old, Affoldern,.

One man, who enlisted in 3 Company during the march, on May 22, 1776, was Private Wilhelm Fleischhut (W200294), 23 yrs old, Friedewald, Hesse,.

One hundred thirty-four men appear to have marched from Korbach with 3 Company on May 20, 1776. One man joined *en route*, but two were sent back after the march began, two deserted, and five men were transferred to other companies prior to the unit sailing for America. Therefore, 126 men have been identified as having arrived in America.

The 3rd English-Waldeck Regiment
4 Company

Captain Christian Fried. Pentzel (W100005), Arolsen
1st Lt. Gerhard Henr. Heldring (W100014), Rinteln
Ensign Karl Christian Hohmann (W100015), Bergheim
Sgt. Henrich Todt (W200372), 53 yrs old, Gembeck
Sgt. Konrad Schmidtmann (W200373), 46 yrs old, Adorf
Sgt. Joh. Henrich Heckmann (W200374), 34 yrs old, Bringhausen
QM Sgt. Franz Phil. Wirths (W200376C), 19 yrs old, Thalitter
Capt.-at-arms August Greiser (W200375), 19 yrs old, Unna, Prussia
Surg. Mate Joh. Henrich Hoffmeister (W200377), 24 yrs old, Blankenburg
Free Cpl. Karl Mueller (W200378), 15 yrs old, Thalitter
Cpl. Henrich Berthold (W200384), 28 yrs old, Korbach
Cpl. Ludwig Goette (W200382), 25 yrs old, Korbach
Cpl. Christian Nelle (W200381), 27 yrs old, Wetterburg
Cpl. Bernhard Saure (W200383), 25 yrs old, Rhadern.
Cpl. Philipp Schaeffer (W200379), 23 yrs old, Landau
Cpl. Karl Philipp Steuernagel (W200380), 20 yrs old, Helaen
Fifer Johannes Flamme (W200385), 15 yrs old, Sudeck
Drummer Jakob Clemens (W200388), 17 yrs old, Helsen
Drummer Christeian Francke (W200386), 19 yrs old, Helsen
Drummer Jakob Heinemann (W200387), 17 yrs old, Boehne
Servant Joh. Henr. Kleinenhagen (W201121), Ober-Waroldern
Servant Joh. Henrich Saenger (W200625), 19 yrs old, Boehne, and
                  Privates
Dietmar Banse (W200390), 23 yrs old, Bessa, Hesse
Joh. Henrich Batister (W200391), 21 yrs old, Emmern, Han.
Dietrich Henr. Beckmann (W200392), 24 yrs old, Roehne, Pad.
Ludwig Berger (W200393), 17 yrs old, Spangenberg
Joh. Wilhelm Bette (W200394), 22 yrs old, Usseln
Henrich Bock (W200395), 46 yrs old, Netze
Wilhelm Buecking (W200396), 36 yrs old, Liggerechtrode
Konrad Bunse (W200397), 18 yrs old, Stormbruch
Jakob Butterweck (W200398), 19 yrs old, Elleringhausen
Joh. Georg Cantzler (W200399), 16 yrs old, Wetzlar
Joh. Henrich Keitel (W200400), 19 yrs old, Nieder-Werbe
Joh. Friedrich Kelter (W200401), 22 yrs old, Rhenegge
Moritz Kestings.(W200402), 20 yrs old, Helsen
Daniel Klapp (W200403), 16 yrs old, Meineringhausen
Joh. Jakob Knipschild (W200404), 19 yrs old, Nieder-Waroldern
Johannes Knueppel (W200405), 17 yrs old, Buehle

The 3rd English-Waldeck Regiment

Peter Knueppel (W200406), 21 yrs old, Odershausen
Nikolaus Kohl (W200407), 20 yrs old, Frankfurt
Franz Henr. Kuester (W200408), 16 yrs old, Grossenbergen
Joh. Hermann Demmer (W200409), 20 yrs old, Berndorf
Franz Eisen (W200411), 21 yrs old, Koenigshagen
Joh. Georg Engelhard (W200412), 44 yrs old, Immighausen
Bernhard Figge (W200413), 20 yrs old, Adorf
Christian Frese (W200414), 18 yrs old, Wetterburg
Franz Henr. Genuit (W200415), 18 yrs old, Usseln
David Daniel Giede (W200416), 20 yrs old, Boehne
Georg Giesenschlager (W200417), 30 yrs old, Berleburg
Franz Gleicher (W200418), 30 yrs old, Neusaal, Hungary
Johannes Goebel (W200419), 20 yrs old, Landau
Johannes Goebel (W200420), 24 yrs old, Rattlar
Friedrich Goette (W200421), 18 yrs old, Rhoden
Johannes Graebe (W200422), 20 yrs old, Berndorf (Adorf)
Joh. Friedrich Gunstmann (W200423), 20 yrs old, Kohlgrund
Joh. Erdmann Guttermilch (W200424), 24 yrs old, Danzig
Ludwig Hancke (W200425), 23 yrs old, Steghenhagen
Daniel Heller (W200426), 20 yrs old, Anraff
Henrich Henckelmann (W200427), 20 yrs old, Wethen
Henrich Hoffmann (W200428), 20 yrs old, Gellershausen
Joh. Henr. Bern. Hunecke (W200429), 45 yrs old, Hagen, Pyr.
Johannes Jaeger (W200430), 21 yrs old, Usseln
Joh. Adam Jakob (W200431), 43 yrs old, Lispenhausen
Bernhard Leimbach (W200432), 19 yrs old, Ober-Niess
Joh. Henrich Lindig (W200433), 27 yrs old, Raamss
Konrad Lindner (W200434), 28 yrs old, Usseln
Wilhelm Lindner (W200435), 30 yrs old, Usseln
Joh. Henrich Meyer (W200437), 45 yrs old, Marck Altendorf
Daniel Michael (W200438), 16 yrs old, Reinhardshaausen
Philipp Moehlen (W200439), 18 yrs old, Wirmighausen
Christoph Moer (W200440), 25 yrs old, Bringhausen, Hesse
Joh. Wilhelm Moering (W200441), 20 yrs old, Barssen, Pyr.
Henrich Mueller (W200442), 23 yrs old, Katzenfort
Joh. Peter Mueller (W200443), 21 yrs old, Ober-Urff, Hesse
Gottfried Joh. Neuendorf (W200444), 23 yrs old, Herborn
Johannes Nolte (W200445), 21 yrs old, Buehle
Emanuel Paer (W200446), 24 yrs old, Mandern
Rudolph Pape (W200092), 26 yrs old, Oesdorf, Pyr.
Samuel Peter (W200448), 24 yrs old, Magdeburg

The 3rd English-Waldeck Regiment

Peter Peuster (W200447), 20 yrs old, Nieder-Werbe
Konrad Pilger (W200449), 23 yrs old, Bergfreiheit
Joh. Henrich Piphard (W200450), 24 yrs old, Roerda b/Eschwege
Joh. Wilhelm Rencke (W200451), 21 yrs old, Schwerin
Jakob Rennert (W200452), 18 yrs old, Buehle
Jakob Reuter (W200453), 28 yrs old, Wirmighausen
Johannes Ritter (W200454), 16 yrs old, Goddelsheim
Philipp Roehling (W200455), 26 yrs old, Udorf, Koeln
Joh. Philipp Roll (W200456), 18 yrs old, Nieder-Hill
Joh. Peter Rosenburg (W200457), 16 yrs old, Zierenberg
Johannes Runte (W200458), 22 yrs old, Lelbach
Peter Schade (W200459), 18 yrs old, Elberberg, Hesse
Andreas Schaeffer (W200460), 18 yrs old, Mehlen
Joh. Henr. Schlossmueller (W200462), 48 yrs old, Holtzhausen, Pyr.
Franz Schmidt (W200463), 39 yrs old, Oberdufenbach
Jakob Schmidt (W200464), 27 yrs old, Ristein
Franz Fried. Schreyer (W200465), 19 yrs old, Stirtzenhart
Andreas Schultze (W200628), 19 yrs old, Boemighausen
Joh. Stefan Schultze (W200466), 19 yrs old, Netze
Joh. Henrich Schwerd (W200467), 24 yrs old, Neersen, Pyr.
Geo. Wm. Joh.Seltsam (W200468), 28 yrs old, Nieder-Wildungen
Franz Adolf Siebel (W200469), 18 yrs old, Korbach
Joh. Jakob Siebert (W200470), 15 yrs old, Eberberg
Stefan Stempel (W200471), 20 yrs old, Goddelsheim
Joh. Henrich Stiehl (W200472), 19 yrs old, Wildungen
Johannes Stremme (W200473), 20 yrs old, Usseln
Marcus Trainer (W200474), 36 yrs old, Somenhart
Christian Traitling (W200475), 17 yrs old, Memmigen
Joh. Philipp Troll (W200476), 22 yrs old, Mengeringhausen
Joh. Peter Ulrich (W200477), 22 yrs old, Frebershausen
Johannes Valand (W200478), 16 yrs old, Berndorf
Joh. Jost Valentin (W200479), 22 yrs old, Sintz
Joh. Konrad Verglass (W200480), 21 yrs old, Hanover
Philipp Henr. Volcke (W200481), 24 yrs old, Kuhlgrund
Johannes Wagener (W200482), 18 yrs old, Mehlen
Kaspar Wagener (W200483), 27 yrs old, Mehlen
Werner Wagener (W200484), Luetersheim
Karl Wahl (W200485), 23 yrs old, Wildungen
Hermann Weineck (W200487), 18 yrs old, Falckenburg
Henrich Werner (W200489), 21 yrs old, Odershausen
Henrich Wasserfeld (W200486), 20 yrs old, Helsen

The 3rd English-Waldeck Regiment

Henrich Wibbecke (W200490), 30 yrs old, Netze
Henrich Wilke (W200491), 18 yrs old, Anraff
Johannes Wollenhaupt (W200492), 26 yrs old, Zueschen
Konrad Zimmermann (W200493), 26 yrs old, Landau

Four men, who marched from Korbach on May 20, 1776, with 4 Company, deserted *en route* to the Bremerlehe; but one, Konrad Zimmermann (W200493), returned to duty on the same day. The others were Privates Franz Kohlbrei, 19 yrs old, Holtzhausen, Pyrmont; Philipp Mueller, 20 yrs old, Lelbach, Hesse; and Justus Schutler, 20 yrs old, Boemighausen.

One man, who deserted prior to the company's departure from Korbach, was returned to duty on May 31, 1776. He was Private Franz Christian Alberti (W200389), 20 yrs old, Helsen.

One man, who was transferred to 4 Company from 3 Company, on May 30, 1776, was Private David Lohrmann (W200436), 17 yrs old, Hamburg.

One man, who began the march from Korbach with 4 Company, was transferred to 1 Company. He was Private Rudolph Pape (W200092), 29 yrs old, Pyrmont..

Two men were enlisted into 4 Company after the regiment departed Korbach. They were Privates Friedrich Doetike (W200410), 23 yrs old, Hameln, and Johannes Wellner (W200488), 22 yrs old, Braunau..

Of the 129 men who marched from Korbach on May 20, 1776, three did not arrive at Bremerlehe, one man transferred from the company, and four men joined the company prior to the unit sailing to America. Two men, Sergeant Schmidtmann (W200373) and Private Johann Henrich Meyer (W200437), died *en route*, so that 127 men of 4 Company have been identified as having arrived in America.

The 3rd English-Waldeck Regiment

5 Company

Captain Georg von Haacke (W100006), Laas, Witgen.
1st Lieutenant Joh. Wilhelm Leonhardi (W100016), Mengeringhausen
Ensign Andreas Geo. Brumhard (W100017), Nieder-Wildungen
Sgt. Christoph Frese (W200494), 54 yrs old, Holtzhausen, Pyr.
Sgt. Gustav Renno (W200495), 26 yrs old, Schwartzenau
Sgt. Theodor Wilstach (W200496), 23 yrs old, Korbach
QM Sgt. Philipp Frese (W200498), 22 yrs old, Sudeck
Capt.-at-arms Franz Henkeler (W200497), 28 yrs old, Korbach
Surg.-Mate Eberhard Meyer (W200499), 31 yrs old, Ulm
Free Cpl. August Hohmann (W200500C), 16 yrs old, Bergheim
Cpl. Bernhard Berges (W200501), 22 yrs old, Mengeringhausen
Cpl. Hermann Bruckhauser (W200505), 20 yrs old, Todtenhausen
Cpl. Philipp Reismann (W200503), 30 yrs old, Kleinern
Cpl. Wilhelm Schaeffer (W200595), 19 yrs old, Kloster Marxhausen
Cpl. Wilhelm Schwalbach (W200504), 19 yrs old, Elmershausen
Cpl. Julius Simshauser (W200502), 24 yrs old, Sachsenhausen
Fifer Henrich Koch (W200506), 16 yrs old, Carlshaven, Hesse
Drummer, Christian Huthmann (W200507), 18 yrs old, Mengeringhausen
Drummer Johannes Vahle (W200509), 16 yrs old, Welda, Pad.
Drummer Philipp Wiegand (W200508), 17 yrs old, Helmighausen
Servant Anton Raab (W200623), 21 yrs old, Neuroth
(Raab may not have marched from Korbach with 5 Company, but was certainly with the regiment when it set out from that place on May 20, 1776.) And

Privates

Karl Altvater (W200510), 16 yrs old, Friedburg
Johannes Assmann (W200511), 16 yrs old, Hildesheim
Georg Bauer (W200512), 28 yrs old, Bergzabern
Andreas Baumueller (W200513), 19 yrs old, Kleinern
Johannes Becker (W200514), 23 yrs old, Bergheim
Johannes Berges (W200515), 20 yrs old, Mengeringhausen
Christian Bickmann (W200516), 25 yrs old, Gembeck
Otto Bigge (W200517), 22 yrs old, Sudeck
Joh. Georg Bock (W200518), 20 yrs old, Wenzigerode
Christian Brand (W200519), 21 yrs old, Hamburg
Dan. Christian Brandenstein (W200520), 33 yrs old, Koenigshagen
Bernhard Henr. Buddecker (W200521), 17 yrs old, Wrexen
Johannes Burghard (W200522), 23 yrs old, Heringen

The 3rd English-Waldeck Regiment

Joh. Henrich Knocke (W200523), 17 yrs old, Dorf Itter
Joh. Henrich Koehler (W200524), 23 yrs old, Boehne
Christian Kroll (W200525), 27 yrs old, Bergheim
Konrad Kruse (W200526), 17 yrs old, Wrexen
Valentin Demuth (W200527), 24 yrs old, Homburg
Philipp Duesse (W200528), 17 yrs old, Boehne
Johannes Durst (W200529), 24 yrs old, Oranienburg
Jakob Christoph Engelhard (W200530), 23 yrs old, Wirmighausen
Peter Erhard (W200531), 20 yrs old, Odewald
Joh. Adam Ferst (W200532), 18 yrs old, Bringhausen
Fried. Anton Fischer (W200533), 19 yrs old, Holtzhausen, Pyr.
Paul Fleck (W200534), 26 yrs old, Neukirchen
Henrich Francke (W200535), 37 yrs old, Hanover
Friedrich Frese (W200536), 18 yrs old, Vasbeck
Philipp Gans (W200537), 25 yrs old, Wrexen
Georg Geitz (W200538), 18 yrs old, Bringhausen
Georg Ludwig Gier (W200539), 40 yrs old, Eutin, Holstein
Johaannes Goebel (W200540), 22, Rattlar
Christian Goedecke (W200541), 15 yrs old, Vasbeck
Jakob Haase (W200542), 37 yrs old, Sachsenhausen
Kaspar Hagemeyer (W200543), 20 yrs old, Alraft
Christian Hansmann (W200544), 18 yrs old, Ziegenhain, Hesse
Adam Hartmann (W200545), 19 yrs old, Reinhartshausen
Johannes Hartmann (W200546), 18 yrs old, Welda, Pad.
Henrich Heinecke (W200547), 19 yrs old, Stewels
Konrad Hendel (W200548), 30 yrs old, Sudeck
Jost Herdes (W200549), 18 yrs old, Buehle
Michael Hoehle (W200550), 17 yrs old, Koenigshagen
Wilhelm Hoehne (W200551), 39 yrs old, Anraff
Henrich Hornsberger (W200552), 18 yrs old, Rhoden
Karl Wilhelm Itzmann (W200554), 29 yrs old, Langensaltz
Barthold Jaeger (W200555), 30 yrs old, Rattlar
Karl Junckermann (W200556), 26 yrs old, Mengeringhausen
Nikolaus Lahr (W200558), 40 yrs old, Grebenstein
Henrich Limpert (W200560), 23 yrs old, Korbach
Philipp Luenart (W200561), 19 yrs old, Waldeck
Franz Mangel (W200562), 21 yrs old, Anraff
Georg Meckel (W200563), 23 yrs old, Muenster
Zacharias Meier (W200564), 18 yrs old, Sachsenhausen
Bernhard Mengeringhausen (W200565), 18 yrs old, Padberg, Koeln
Henrich Meyer (W200566), 19 yrs old, Holtzhausen, Pyr.

The 3rd English-Waldeck Regiment

Jakob Meyer (W200567), 28 yrs old, Kleinern
Johannes Michael (W200568), 27 yrs old, Dehausen
Henrich Mincke (W200570), 21 yrs old, Kirchberg, Hesse
Christian Mueller (W200571), 23 yrs old, Muehlhausen
Franz Mueller (W200572), 15 yrs old, Reitzenhagen
Friedrich Mueller (W200573), 28 yrs old, Buedingen
Henrich Mundhencke (W200574), 19 yrs old, Dahle, Pyr.
Jakob Muus (W200575), 24 yrs old, Wethen
Daniel v. Nehm (W200576), 24 yrs old, Helmighausen
Wilhelm Neumeyer (W200577), 18 yrs old, Fuerstenberg
Jokob Wilhelm Nolt (W200578), 17 yrs old, Wetzlar
Friedrich Nolte (W200579), 16 yrs old, Herbsen
Matthias Ochse (W200580), 18 yrs old, Mandern
Konrad Oschmann (W200581), 20 yrs old, Albertshausen
Wilhelm Packe (W200582), 17 yrs old, Braunau
Henrich Pieper (W200584), 21 yrs old, Muehlhausen
Claude Prieur (W200585), 47 yrs old, Sugee, France
Johannes Rabanaus (W200586), 24 yrs old, Mehlen
Wilhelm Range (W200587), 36 yrs old, Korbach
Josef Rischer (W200588), 22 yrs old, Prausnitz
August Rittmeyer (W200589), 16 yrs old, Hildesheim
Friedrich Rodewald (W200590), 17 yrs old, Pyrmont
Johannes Salzmann (W200591), 30 yrs old, Luetersheim
Johannes Schaeffer (W200592), 21 yrs old, Dehausen
Joh. Georg Schaeffer (W200593), 24 yrs old, Fetzigerode
Thomas Schaeffer (W200594), 18 yrs old, Sachsenhausen
Jakob Scharschmid (W200596), 17 yrs old, Nieder-Werbe
Friedrich Schele (W200597), 16 yrs old, Hanover
Joh. Georg Schimmel (W200598), 17 yrs old, Heuchelheim
Friedrich Schmidt (Sr.) (W200600), 25 yrs old, Holtzhausen, Pyr.
Konrad Schmidt (W200599), 20 yrs old, Frankenau, Hesse
Philipp Schmidt (W200602), 24 yrs old, Muehlhausen
Geo. David Schuetler (W200604), 28 yrs old, Helmighausen
Wilhelm Schuetz (W200605), 22 yrs old, Volkhardinghausen
Georg Tent (W200606), 18 yrs old, Mengeringhausen
Johannes Thor (W200607), 26 yrs old, Bringhausen
Philipp Uhle (W200608), 25 yrs old, Stadtberg, Koeln
Henrich Voepel (W200609), 18 yrs old, Dehausen
Johannes Vollmar (W200610), 39 yrs old, Wehr, Hesse
Johannes Weidenhagen (W200611), 22 yrs old, Mandern
Ludwig Welcker (W200612), 17 yrs old, Eickelsachsen

The 3rd English-Waldeck Regiment

Gottfried Wiegand (W200613), 19 yrs old, Mengeringhausen
Thomas Wieser (W200614), 49 yrs old, Weissenheim
Gottlieb Zange (W200615), 16 yrs old, Bautzen
Kaspar Zeiger (W200616), 24 yrs old, Altenlothheim
Franz Ziegler (W200617), 42 yrs old, Untersterode
Henrich Zimmermann (W200618), 20 yrs old, Pyrmont.

Four men, who marched from Korbach on May 20, 1776, with 5 Company, but who deserted *en route* to Bremerlehe, were Privates Friedrich Kleinhorst, 20 yrs old, Rhoden; Christoph Emde, 20, Strothe; Bernhard Tuschof, 17 yrs old, Rhoden; and Johannes Volke, 25 yrs old, Heddinghausen, Koeln.

Another man, who joined 5 Company after it departed Korbach, deserted before the unit arrived at Bremerlehe. He was Private Georg Koch, Kleinenberg, Paderborn.

One man joined 5 Company as a new recruit after the march began. He was Private Hermann Huth (W200553), 17 yrs old, Bremen..

Three men, who marched from Korbach with other companies joined 5 Company prior to the unit sailing from Bremerlehe. These men were Privates:

Johannes Lahme (W200557), 17 yrs old, Korbach
Kaspar Pickel (W200583), 16 yrs old, Weiler and,
Konrad Schmidt, (W200603), 40 yrs old, Affoldern.

Two men, who marched from Korbach to Bremerlehe with 3 Company, and then sailed to England with 1 Company, joined 5 Company for the voyage to America. They were Henrich Lemmering (W200559), 35 yrs old, Wals Roden, Han., and Johannes Mieting(W200569), 32 yrs old, Wildungen..

One hundred twenty-six men of 5 Company marched from Korbach on May 20, 1776. Two men joined the company *en route* to Bremerlehe and five men deserted before reaching the port. Three men joined the company at Bremerlehe, so 126 men

The 3rd English-Waldeck Regiment

sailed for England. Two men were transferred to 5 Company prior to the unit's sailing from England. One man, Hoehne (W200551), died aboard ship on the crossing, so 127 men of 5 Company have been identified as having arrived in America.

Artillery

Only eleven men of the Artillery detachment, which had a strength of two bombardiers and twelve cannoneers, with two three-pound cannons, have been identified.

Bombardier Martin Heidorn (W300009), Pyrmont
Bombardier Wilhelm Schultze (W300014), Pyrmont

And cannoneers:
Friedrich Bever (W300001), Hameln
Karl Brauns (W300002), Pyrmont
Henrich Goecke (W300005), Pyrmont
Friedrich Haacke (W300007), Hoya
Simon Haacke (W300008), Griessem
Gottfried Hentze (W300010), Hameln
Wilhelm Huebsch (W300011), Hameln
Henrich Litzau (W300012), Hameln
Christian Wenthe (W300016), Hameln

Summary

The number of men identified by name, who arrived in America with the original contingent from Waldeck in October 1776, were assigned as follows:

Staff - 11	4 Company - 127
1 Company - 132	5 Company - 127
2 Company - 127	Artillery - 11
3 Company - 126	**Total** - 661

The 3rd English-Waldeck Regiment

In addition to the 661 officers and men identified as having arrived in America, and those who marched from Korbach but never reached America, the following men were recruited into the regiment but remained in Europe as indicated, according to information extracted from *HETRINA:*

1 Company

Fifer Karl Fiesler, 14 yrs old, Heringhausen, On pass
Fifer Friedrich Siebert, 14 yrs old, Gruenau, On pass
And privates
Andreas Birckenfeld, 20 yrs old, Sachsenhausen, On pass
Peter Kramer, 22 yrs old, Zueschen, On leave
Christian Eberhard, Transferred
Daniel Figge, 31 yrs old, Wilgen, On leave
Franz Kuethe, 21 yrs old, Landau, Discharged
Valentin Roester, 46 yrs old, Bergfreiheit, Discharged
Friedrich Schultze, 25 yrs old, Volkhardinghausen, Discharged

2 Company - Privates

Konrad Braun, 19 yrs old, Ebhausen, Discharged
Friedrich Horschler, 52 yrs old, Landau, On leave
Konrad Niemeyer, 19 yrs old, Oesdorf, Pyr., Died
Henrich Ohm, 21 yrs old, Neersen, Pyr., Discharged
Henrich Ramspoth, 20 yrs old, Wrexen, On pass
Friedrich Vogel, 26 yrs old, Twiste, On leave

3 Company - Privates

Wilhelm Becker, 28 yrs old, Berndorf, Discharged
Henrich Bornemann, 42 yrs old, Dehausen, Discharged
Christian Bruemann, 17 yrs old, Immighausen, Discharged
Konrad Galle, 20 yrs old, Oesdorf, Pyr., Released
Christian Hüllebrand, 21 yrs old, Buchenberg, Discharged
Jakob Mauske, 23 yrs old, Wildungen, Discharged
Anton Ostwald, 20 yrs old, Beringhausen, On leave
Hermann Senff, 34 yrs old, Neersen, Pyr., Released
Henrich Stukenbruk, 31 yrs old, Holtzhausen, Pyr., Released

4 Company - Privates

Andreas Bernighausen, 20 yrs old, Willingen, Discharged
Christoph Kamm, 29 yrs old, Rhadern, Medical discharge
Dietrich Kempfert, 22 yrs old, Dahle, Pyr., Medical discharge
Joh. Henrich Keiser, 25 yrs old, Numburg, Medical discharge
Joh. Franz Hagemeyer, 16 yrs old, Elleringhausen, Medical discharge
Daniel Mann, 24 yrs old, Wrexen, Medical discharge

The 3rd English-Waldeck Regiment

Joh. Arendt Nolte, 24 yrs old, Kuelte, Discharged
Kaspar Pape, 26 yrs old, Patberg, On leave
Joh. Georg Rhode, 17 yrs old, Mengeringhausen, Discharged
Philipp Treier, 45 yrs old, Mestinghausen, On leave
Christoph Zimmermann, 46 yrs old, Mengeringhausen, Discharged

5 Company - Privates
Henrich Koppenrath, 17 yrs old, Westheim, Pyr., Died
Gottfried Egerding, 20 yrs old, Boemighausen, Released
Georg Fax, 20 yrs old, Giflitz, Released
Georg Gottmann, 36 yrs old, Elleringhausen, Released
Peter Markolt, 26 yrs old, Albertshausen, Incompetent
Henrich Schaeffer, 23 yrs old, Pyrmont, Dismissed

Others recruited into the regiment, but who remained in Europe, include the following men who deserted on dates listed, before the regiment departed from Korbach, according to *HETRINA*. All were privates.

1 Company
Wilhelm Becker, 20 yrs old, Muenden, April 29
Johannes Kespar, 22 yrs old, Wilgen, April 28
Jakob Herbert, 34 yrs old, Battenberg, May 14
Konrad Schroeder, 20 yrs old, Goddelsheim, April 30
Ludwig Unger, 23 yrs old, Rhoden, April 24
Jakob Wolff, 24 yrs old, Artberg, May 14

2 Company
Henrich Embde, 25 yrs old, Ober-Waroldern, May 18
Henrich Embde, 21 yrs old, Willingen, May 2
Andreas Engelbrecht, 20 yrs old, Usseln, May 2
Anton Hemmerling, 16 yrs old, Raubach, March 31
Georg Prick, 18 yrs old, Immighausen, May 2
Henrich Schneider, 17 yrs old, Wetzlar, April 19

3 Company
Wilhelm Bremer, 20 yrs old, Benkhausen, May 6
Henrich Kann, 19 yrs old, Immighausen, April 30
Ulrich Gothard, 17 yrs old, Adorf, April 30
Konrad Prentzel, 23 yrs old, Zueschen, May 3
Georg Henrich Schmid, 22 yrs old, Rhena, April 20

The 3rd English-Waldeck Regiment
4 Company
Franz Konrad Buckert, 33 yrs old, Fuerstenberg, May 6
Johann Stefan Ditmar, 22 yrs old, Nieder-Waroldern, April 28
Johannes Gude, 17 yrs old, Stadtberg, April 9
Christoph Propper, 21 yrs old, Wrexen, April 28
Otto Schnettler, 21 yrs old, Bergfreiheit, April 28
Johann Adam Wagener, 26 yrs old, Bergfreiheit, April 28
5 Company
Theodor Kesthans, 26 yrs old, Mengeringhausen, April 30
Georg Kramer, 23 yrs old, Willingen, April 29
Franz Euler, 20 yrs old, Goddelsheim, April 29
Johannes Leveringhausen, 27 yrs old, Kuelte, April 22
Jost Henrich Linnekugel, 30 yrs old, Korbach, March 20
Henrich Meinberg, 23 yrs old, Neersen, Pyrmont, May 17
Christoph Schaeffer, 35 yrs old, Hoeringhausen, March 31
Franz Schneider, 23 yrs old, Ober-Waroldern, May 18
Georg Schnell, 20 yrs old, Muenden, April 29
Johannes Steinhard, 21 yrs old, Wrexen, April 29
Konrad Weineke, 20 yrs old, Hasten, Hanover, May 5

Prince Friedrich had been hard-pressed to provide the regiment for English service. A number of the men had to be taken from the two Waldeck regiments in Dutch service. This not only provided bodies for the new 3rd English-Waldeck Regiment, but in effect provided a solid cadre of experienced soldiers. Approximately 200 men were obtained in this manner. Others were recruited, or possibly drafted, in Waldeck so that native Waldeckers constituted about 400 of the men sent to America in 1776.[31]

Men for the Waldeck Regiment were recruited in neighboring states. also. The recruiters, states where they were active, and periods of recruiting, included the following: Ensign, later Lieutenant, Le Suire from 1776 to 1783, Sergeant Gerla from 1776 to 1783, and Captain Romrodt from 1776 to 1778 in Solms; Lieutenant Becker from 1776 to 1777 in Wetzlar, and Friedberg, and in 1777 in Wittgenstein and Erbach; Sergeant Goebel from 1777 to 1783 in Wetzlar, Friedberg, Wurms, and Speyer; Lieutenant Noezel from 1777 to 1778 and again in 1781

The 3rd English-Waldeck Regiment

in Franken; and Captain Osten from 1781 to 1782 in Wetzlar, Friedberg, and Sachsen. There were also recruiting activities in Bremen, Eichfeld, Frankfurt, Hamburg, Hesse-Homburg, Hildesheim, Muehlhausen, Nordhausen, and Pyrmont at various times during the war,[32] but it was considered a necessity to have a number of native Waldeckers in the ranks as a means of preventing desertions.[33]

Once recruited, the men donned the regimental uniform, described by James Flexner in the following portrayal of the "Hessians" in New York. "The slaves of Anspach and Waldeck were there - the first somber as night, the second gaudy as noon ... the immovable stiff German (Jaeger) could hardly be taken as part of the same army as the careless and half-savage Highlander" Scot.[34]

The 'gaudy' Waldeck uniform consisted of a blue coat with yellow collar, cuffs, and lapels. Gilt buttons fastened into plain button-holes and the coat was worn over a white vest and breeches. Hats or caps were edged with a wide yellow scallop. The whole uniform, made of cheap, coarse cloth, was completed with heavy, black cloth gaiters, secured with metal buttons.[35] A bearskin cap, after the Dutch fashion, but without a front-plate, and a yellow cloth bag trimmed with white lace and a white tassel, made the grenadier uniform even more distinguishable.[36]

The English Deputy Quartermaster General Briscoe wrote to John Smith, the secretary to the Commander-in-Chief, on May 1, 1779, that he found no waste of tents, but on the arrival of new ones, men cut up old tents for trousers. This practice was probably common among the German soldiers, also.[37]

The most complete description of the Waldeck uniform, however, is found in Haarmann's work, based on notes found in papers of Landgrave Ludwig IX of Hesse-Darmstadt, in the Hessen State Archives, Darmstadt, Germany.[38]

> The basic regimental uniform was a blue cloth coat with a yellow baize lining; yellow cloth collar, cuffs and lapels; with white metal

The 3rd English-Waldeck Regiment

buttons, arranged 1-2-3 on the lapels and 3 below the lapel; a slash cuff with two buttons on the cuff and two on the sleeve above the cuff. White cloth waistcoat and breeches. Black cocked hat trimmed with a white woolen edging. Non-commissioned Officers: Sergeants and certain other non-commissioned officers were issued uniforms of a better quality than those furnished corporals and privates. They were further distinguished by a wide silver lace edging on their cocked hats, silver epaulettes, and, hat cordons and sword-knot worked with silver. Corporals were denoted by a narrow silver lace edging on their hats.

Musicians: The drum-major, musicians, and drummers wore a uniform the reverse of those given above, that is, yellow coats with blue facings. The drum-majors coat was trimmed with 11 and 1/2 ells of wide silver lace and 9 and 1/2 ells of narrow silver lace; the manner of which this lace was worn on the coat is not known. The musicians' and drummers' coats were trimmed with a woolen lace, in the same quantities as that allowed for the drum-major.

Surgeon's Mates: It has not been definitely established, but it appears the five surgeon's mates had blue coats with yellow linings, but no yellow facings, and white small clothes.

Drivers: Blue suits, with yellow coat linings.

Artillerymen: Blue uniform with red facings and yellow buttons. Straw-coloured waistcoat and breeches. Bombardiers were distinguished by gold-coloured epaulettes. The artillery driver had a blue suit with red coat lining.

No description of the colours borne by the regiment have been found to date, although it is known that each battalion company carried one.

Supplying the regiment with uniforms, weapons, and equipment was the task of the court agents, Jakob Marc and Stieglitz. The regimental commissary, Philipp Marc, who served with the regiment in America, was a brother of Jakob Marc.[39]

Contractors who supplied the regiment during the war included the Kuelte Cloth Factory, which provided cloth between the years 1777 and 1783, and G. F. Besserling of Rotterdam, who supplied cloth during the years 1779 and 1780. Tents were obtained from Tapestry Dietrich of Kassel in 1777 and 1778. Weapons were obtained from Holland from 1777 to 1780; and from rifle-maker Thomas Wilhelm Pister of

The 3rd English-Waldeck Regiment

Schmalkalden from 1776 to 1782; from sword-maker Georg Konrad Schmoeckell of Kassel from 1776 to 1782; and from G.A Ampfurt of Hameln from 1777 to 1778.[40]

Before cost figures for the Waldeck Regiment can have any significance it is necessary to show the total number of men that Waldeck furnished to England. In addition to the 670-man unit which Prince Friedrich provided initially, the yearly shipments of replacements were 89 men in 1777, 140 men in 1778, 23 men in 1779, 144 men in 1781, and 159 men in 1782 for a total of 1,225 men. These are the figures given by von Eelking, who cited Venturini as his source, and they have been used by most writers since.[41]

While these figures are probably close enough for the purpose at hand, they are not accurate as may readily be seen when it is noted that even the original 670-man unit did not include the fourteen-man artillery detachment, for which the English War Office estimated the cost to be nineteen shillings, four pence, or nearly one pound sterling, per day.[42]

Joseph Rosengarten estimated that the average mercenary cost England thirty thalers, and that Waldeck received about 140,000 pounds sterling between 1776 and 1783.[43] Pierre Augustin Caron de Beaumarchais estimated the costs which England paid to Waldeck for 1776 at 15,4583 pounds, and he was apparently using the figures given in the Parliament.[44] Von Eelking also used a figure of 140,000 pounds as the expense money for Waldeck which the Parliament voted during the course of the war.[45] Other material indicates payments to Waldeck for the period 1776 through 1783 amounted to 131,746 pounds, 2 shillings, and 2 and 1/4 pence, and that Waldeck shared in another 120,369 pounds, 11 shillings, and 7 pence in 1784, which was divided among the German states which supplied England with auxiliary troop units.[46]

All the above estimates appear to be based on the following figures extracted from documents in the Hesse State Archives at Marburg. The cost for the 3rd English-Waldeck Regiment was

The 3rd English-Waldeck Regiment

figured from April 23 to December 24, 1776, being 247 days pay at 7,675 pounds, 15 shillings, 7 and 3/4 pence; subsidy for this period at a rate of 25,050 crowns banco per year was 4,078 pounds, 19 shillings, 9 and 1/2 pence and levy money for 655 men of the regiment at 30 crowns banco per man came to 4,728 pounds, 5 shillings, and 7 and 1/2 pence; or a total of 16,483 pounds, 1 shilling, and 3/4 pence.[47]

Faucitt later came to an agreement with the Office of the Secretary of State for Waldeck which allowed a 13-day pay deduction, which may have indicated that the regiment was not up to strength by an agreed date. The subsidy for the artillery detachment of 85 pounds, 18 shillings, and 5 pence was for 249 days commencing May 5.

While levy money was only figured in the costs for 1776, this plus pay and subsidy payments during the period which the regiment spent in English service came to the following amounts:

Adjusted	247 days in	1776	16,391.3. 8 and 1/2
	365	1777	17,849.3. 10 and 3/4
(Assuming same for)		1778	17,849.3.10 and 3/4
	365	1779	17,976.18. 10 and 3/4
			(extra pay to the colonel)
	366	1780	18,009.6. 9
	365	1781	17,976.18.10 and 3/4
	365	1782	17,976.18.10 and 3/4
(Assuming)	247 days	1783	16,391.3.8 and 1/2

Total = 140,420 pounds, 18 shillings, 7 and 3/4 pence

The organizational positions within the regiment and the individual pay and subsistence as of April 22, 1776, were established at the following rates:

1 Lieutenant Colonel & Captain - 17 shillings pay and 13 shillings subsistence

The 3rd English-Waldeck Regiment

1 Major & Captain - 15 shillings and 11 shillings, 6 pence
3 Captains more, each 10 shillings - 1 pound, 10 shillings, and 7 shillings, 6 pence
2 Captain Lieutenants, each 5 shillings, 8 and 1/2 pence - 11 shillings, 4 pence, and 4 shillings, 6 pence
5 1st Lieutenants, each 5 shillings, 8 and 1/2 pence - 1 pound, 3 shillings, 5 pence, and 3 shillings, 6 pence
5 2nd Lieutenants, each 3 shillings, 8 pence - 18 shillings, 4 pence, and 3 shillings
1 Adjutant - 4 shillings, and 3 shillings
1 Auditor (Commissary) - 4 shillings, and probably 3 shillings subsistence
1 Quartermaster - 4 shillings, 8 pence, and 3 shillings, 6 pence
1 Chaplain - 6 shillings, 8 pence, and 5 shillings
1 Regimental Surgeon - 4 shillings, and 3 shillings
5 Surgeon's Mates, each 2 shillings, 6 pence - 12 shillings, 6 pence, and 2 shillings

The table then has a shilling/pence figure before the other positions within the regiment, which may indicate the daily subsistence rate for the various pay grades.

(1s) 15 Sergeants, each 1 shilling, 6 pence - 1 pound, 2 shillings, 6 pence, and 15 shillings
(1s) 5 QM Sergeants, each 1 shilling, 3 pence - 6 shilling, 3 pence, and 5 shillings
(1s) 5 Captains-at-arms, each 1 shilling, 3 pence - 6 shilling, 3 pence, and 5 shilling
(8p) 4 Free Corporals, each 1 shilling - 4 shilling, and 2 shilling, 8 pence
(8p) 30 Corporals, each 1 shilling - 1 pound, ten shilling, and -
(18p) 1 Drum-major - 1 shilling, 5 and 1/2 pence, and -
(8p) 15 Drummers, each 1 shilling - 15 shilling, and -
(8p) 6 Fifers - 7 shilling, 3 and 3/4 pence, and -
(8p) 5 Solicitors, each 10 and 1/2 pence - 4 shilling, 4 and 1/2 pence, and -
         538 Privates, each 8 pence - 17 pounds, 18 shilling, 8 pence, and 6 pence
(1s/6p) 2 Provost and Assistant - 2 shilling, 11 and 1/2 pence, and -
(6p) 15 Officers ' Servants, each 8 pence - 10 shilling, and -
(8p) 1 Servant, Military Chest - 11 and 1/2 pence, and -

The 3rd English-Waldeck Regiment

(8p)   1 Servant for Medicine - 11 and 1/2 pence, and -
670 Total Pay - 31 pounds, 1 shilling, 6 and 1/4 pence

The artillery detachment bombardiers were paid at the rate of 1 shilling, 8 pence per day, and cannoneers at the rate of 1 shilling, 4 pence per day.[48]

Von Eelking reported that when the troops of the Waldeck Regiment were inspected prior to marching off on their way to America, a fight broke out with some native workmen, but the troops were able to continue their march.[49] However, this writer has not found the source of this information, nor any confirmation. Concerning the march to the port, a letter from William Fraser to William Fox, of May 31, 1776, contains inclosures which indicate the Waldeckers were at Vegasack on May 29, and at Bremerlehe on May 31, 1776.[50]

The 3rd English-Waldeck Regiment

The regiment, with a strength of 690 men, left Korbach on May 20, 1776, moved down the Weser, through Bremen to Vegasack. The men were sworn into English service at Bremerlehe. According to Colonel von Hanxleden's report to his prince, the regiment sailed from Vegasack at 5 A.M. in sixteen boats. When they arrived in Bremerlehe, the tide was at the ebb, necessitating a one-hour wait before entering the canal to Lehe. Therefore, the regiment was put ashore with small boats. Colonel William Faucitt, the English officer who had drawn up the treaty by which the Waldeck soldiers were to enter English service, arrived at Lehe at noon and the troops were mustered at about 4 P.M. After a close inspection, completed about 7 P.M., the troops reentered the same boats. Everything was finished by 9 P.M.[51]

Three ships were assigned to carry the Waldeckers to Portsmouth, England, and on to America. They lay about a cannon shot off shore and had been waiting for the arrival of the troops for twelve days. The colonel and his primary staff officers, and 271 men were assigned on board the *Jacob Cornelius*, which appeared to be "a good ship". The second ship, *Benjamin*, was to carry 249 men, and the remaining 196 men were assigned on board *Abraham*. At the time of writing his report, the colonel had not yet inspected the last two ship, but they appeared adequate. The captains were all Hollanders, but on each ship an English naval officer was responsible for over-seeing the feeding of the troops. During calm weather, fifteen men could exercise on deck at a time, and these exercises were planned to combat boredom.

Colonel Faucitt pushed so hard for the sailing on June 1, that some provisions had to be left behind. The troops were very crowded aboard ship and, as the food did not appear half-enough, Colonel von Hanxleden had ten thousand pounds of bread loaded aboard ship. The bread, made from cognac and rise, was to be sold to the troops to repay the cost of baking and would supplement the ships' rations.

The 3rd English-Waldeck Regiment

On May 31, 1776, the regiment embarked on board the three waiting ships. According to victualling reports, the *Jacob Cornelius*, Master John Waterson, victualled 144 men of the Colonel's Company and 115 men of the Major's Company on the crossing to America. The *Jan Abraham*, Master Martin Digby, victualled 190 men from the companies of Captain von Horn, and *Benjamin*, Master George Knight, victualled 35 men of 2 Company, 78 men of 4 Company, and 131 men of 5 Company.[52]

Contrary winds delayed the departure from Bremerlehe until June 3, and contrary winds *en route* to Portsmouth delayed arrival at that destination until June 20. Colonel von Hanxleden immediately went ashore to report the Waldeckers' arrival and to receive further orders. The impression which he received ashore, according to his report to Prince Friedrich, was that the regiment would sail with the Brunswick troops for service in Canada.[53]

Getting ships enough to transport the large reinforcements and their equipment to America was a gigantic undertaking. Contracting for ships and having them in the right place at the right time posed many problems as there was a shortage of shipping throughout the war, and within the English government, different departments competed for ships. The War Office worked out the transport requirements. Then the American Secretary was notified, and, in turn, he would notify the Admiralty, which was responsible for transporting troops and clothing. However, the Treasury was responsible for victualling the troops and securing supply ships.[54] Nevertheless, on May 23, 1776, having contracted for many Dutch ships, Lord Sandwich reported to King George that the work of getting enough ships for the spring convoys had been brought to a conclusion with less delay and difficulty than expected.[55]

Two months before the formal treaty was signed between England and Waldeck, Germain had written to General Guy Carleton, commanding the King's troops in Canada, that reinforcements were to be sent to Canada, including the foreign

The 3rd English-Waldeck Regiment

contingents of Brunswick and Waldeck,[56] and in the notes to Thomas Jones' *History of New York*, there is a reference cited, a "List of Forces sent to Canada in Spring 1776", which included an entry concerning the 670-man Waldeck unit.[57]

As March drew to a close, Germain included copies of the recent treaties concluded with the various German states and informed General [William] Howe that, among others, the Waldeckers were to go to Canada. There were still some problems in obtaining transports, and Germain was uncertain when the 2nd Division of Hessians would sail.[58]

Captain Georg Pausch, commander of the Hesse-Hanau Artillery detachment, scheduled to sail to Canada with the Hanau, Brunswick, and Waldeck units, made inquiries at Spithead on June 4, 1776, as to the arrival times of the other units, but could learn nothing of their whereabouts. On June 16, he learned that the Brunswickers and Waldeckers were nearing Spithead and the next day he received information that the Brunswickers, Waldeckers, and the Artillery, plus some other units, were to sail directly to Canada.[59]

By June 20, at least some of the Brunswickers and Waldeckers were in Portsmouth harbor, as a Brunswick officer recorded in his diary on that date that at eleven o'clock, Colonel von Hanxleden, commanding officer of the Waldeck Regiment, went on board the *Friesland*, and there reported that he had arrived that morning with his regiment, in three ships.[60]

A later diary entry for the same date, recorded the arrival at Portsmouth of fifteen ships of the 2nd Division of Hessians.[61]

The next day, June 21, 1776, saw a flurry of letter writing as the English authorities had decided to leave the English 47th Regiment, which the Waldeckers were to have replaced, in Canada, and send the Waldeck Regiment to General Howe. The corps of Waldeckers, according to Germain, "in excellent Condition, very well Appointed and express(ing) the greatest willingness for the Service", was to sail with the 2nd Division of Hessians.[62]

The 3rd English-Waldeck Regiment

Germain also wrote to General Carleton, in Canada, that the King was sending the Waldeck Regiment and its Artillery to General Howe. Carleton was to keep the 47th Regiment in Canada, and this, regardless of what Howe might say.[63]

Lieutenant General Wilhelm von Knyphausen, commanding the 2nd Division of Hessians, was directed to take his Hessians, the Waldeckers, and the other units and men destined for New York under his command. Lieutenant Colonel von Hanxleden was informed of the change, and that he was to sail under the orders of General von Knyphausen. Both commanders acknowledged the change in letters to Germain, two days later.[64]

Finally, Captain Maximilian Jacobs of HMS *Amazon* received orders from the Admiralty that the Waldeckers he was to have had in his convoy to Canada would be going to New York under escort of Captain Charles Fielding of HMS *Diamond*.[65]

On June 22, 1776, Captain Pausch reported the remaining Hessian troops had arrived in Holland ships during the preceding night. He also noted that the Waldeckers were reportedly to join with the Hessians for the crossing to America.[66]

The original plan to send the Waldeckers to Canada continued to stick in some peoples' minds, however. On July 29, 1776, on the basis of a rumor that the 2nd Division of Brunswickers, with whom the Waldeckers were to have sailed, had arrived at Quebec, although only one ship carrying Hesse-Hanau Artillery had actually arrived, the Brunswick commanding general, Friedrich von Riedesel, wrote to his prince, "Our second division together with a battalion of Waldeck have at last arrived at Lundy, after passing Quebec." He continued on to explain that he would command nine battalions in three brigades, with brigade commanders from Brunswick, Hesse-Hanau, and Waldeck, unless the Waldeck commander were only a lieutenant colonel, in which case, a Brunswick colonel would command that brigade.[67]

The 3rd English-Waldeck Regiment

Still later, on September 25, 1776, the Pennsylvania *Journal* carried an extract of a letter from Ticonderoga, to the effect that Carleton's force on Lake Champlain, including Waldeckers, would suffer from the strength of the American fleet.[68]

On June 15, 1776, official correspondence indicated that the *Diamond*, 32 guns, Captain Richard Fielding; the *Lark*, 32 guns, Rodney Smith, commander; the *Ambuscade*, 32 guns, John Macartney, commander; and the *Unicorn*, 20 guns, John Ford, commander, were to convoy the 2nd Division of Hessians to the army with General Howe.[69]

The London *Chronicle* on March 26, 1776, had reported the *Ambuscade* as fitting out at Chatham, and a few days previous, that the *Unicorn*, a new warship, had been placed in commission and the command given to Captain John Ford. On May 16, the frigates *Ambuscade* and *Diamond* arrived at Spithead from The Downs to convoy the rest of the Hessians to America.[70]

As the ships of the convoy and the escort vessels continued to assemble, instructions and counter-instructions flowed between London and Portsmouth. Captain Pausch recorded that all the transports at Spithead were being supplied with water and provisions for a quarter of a year.[71]

Captain Fielding received orders from the Admiralty, dated June 22, 1776, to take command of an escort consisting of *Diamond, Ambuscade, Unicorn,* and *Lark,* and to convoy transports carrying the 2nd Division of Hessians, the Waldeck Regiment, and some English units. Other escort vessels may have been *Garland,* Captain Richard Pearson,. and *Matty.* He was also to convoy transports carrying 402 German recruits and two officers, replacements for English units serving in America. These last recruits were on board *Minerva, Neptune, Jane & Isabella,* and *Elliot.* Other ships to be taken in the convoy were *John, Chambri,* and *Susannah,* carrying British recruits from Chatham and Dover to America; the victuallers *Triton, Generous Friend, Tuscany Frigate, John, Nancy, Sally,* and

The 3rd English-Waldeck Regiment

Wolf. The *Jane*, at Portsmouth laden with wagons and stores, was to join at Spithead. Three additional victuallers, *Northam*, *Edward*, and *Adventure*, were to proceed with the *Diamond* convoy, if they arrived in time. And, one hundred "landsmen" were to be distributed aboard the outbound escort vessels, including the *Garland*, to be further assigned to naval vessels on the American station.[72]

Records indicate that on June 28, 1776, eighty men of 2 Company and 35 men of 4 Company of the Waldeck Regiment were transferred aboard the transport *Adamant*, Master Josias Walker, at Spithead. The records show that the 35 men of 2 Company were transferred off *Benjamin* on June 24, so 45 men of 2 Company must have been transferred off *Jacob Cornelius*, probably at the same time. The number of men of 4 Company taken from *Benjamin* or from *Jan Abraham* is not shown. As all three Dutch transports had been over-crowded, it seems safe to assume some men were taken from each ship. Of note also, is the fact that records show that the men of the Waldeck Regiment on all four ships debarked at New York on October 23, 1776.[73]

On June 29, 1776, according to reports in the London *Chronicle*, the *Diamond*, *Unicorn*, and *Lark*, with a convoy of 22 ships, sailed from St. Helen's without waiting for some ships that were to have been in the convoy and carrying horses to General Howe's army. A later edition of the paper cited a letter of July 7, which reported the fleet had entered Plymouth harbor "this day" from Portsmouth, and would sail for America as soon as the winds permitted. Meantime, French intelligence sources reported to Paris on July 12, that the fleet had been forced by adverse winds to enter Plymouth harbor on July 6.[74]

Two weeks later, on July 20, Captain Fielding's convoy, which had been delayed for such a long time by contrary winds, sailed for America.[75]

By letter of July 23, 1776, Philipp Stevens of the Admiralty notified Vice-Admiral Richard Lord Howe that the convoy with

The 3rd English-Waldeck Regiment

the Hessians and Waldeckers had put to sea from Spithead on June 28, but that the *Adventure, John, Chambri,* and *Susannah* had not been able to join, and HMS *Lark* had been dispatched to Cork, Ireland.[76]

The *Dinah*, Master Alexander Brown, was a victualler in the fleet under escort of HMS *Perseus*, which departed from St. Helen's on July 30, 1776. *En route* to America, *Dinah* and another victualler, *Burstwick*, became separated from the convoy. *Dinah* was captured by an American privateer, but the crew was put on board the *Burstwick*, which was allowed to continue on its way. On September 22, *Burstwick* joined *Diamond's* convoy and entered New York with that group of ships.[77]

Discipline and routine aboard ships in *Diamond's* convoy must have been similar to the King's instructions of February 1777, for the Ansbach troops. All men were required to be on deck every morning, berths were to be cleaned, and bedding aired. Smoking between decks was forbidden, as was gambling and the selling of liquor. No one was allowed ashore without permission of the officer commanding the troops, and even then, a non-commissioned officer had to accompany any private soldiers. Finally, three pence per day was taken from the pay of soldiers, officers, non-commissioned officers, and privates, for rations consumed aboard ship.[78]

The *Unicorn*, one of the fastest ships in the English navy, parted company from the fleet off Nantucket Shoals, to pursue an American ship, but the *Diamond* arrived off Sandy Hook on October 18, 1776, not a single ship having been lost from the convoy. The New York *Gazette* reported the arrival of 65 sail of vessels under the convoy of *Diamond* and *Ambuscade*, and that the troops included the 2nd Division of Hessians, 1,000 Waldeckers, and a number of English recruits, or about 8,000 men in total.[79]

The fleet also delivered 2,000 draft horses to General Howe's command.[80]

The 3rd English-Waldeck Regiment

In recording the arrival of the *Diamond's* convoy, Ambrose Serle noted that the fleet had arrived just ahead of a violent wind switch, from southeast to northwest. This change of wind direction would have scattered the fleet, or might even have kept the ships out of New York harbor until the following spring.[81] This would have been disastrous. As it was, the Hessians and Waldeckers had been five months on the crossing. Fifty Hessians of the 2nd Division had died *en route* to America, and 600 men were sick when the convoy at last reached its destination. The Waldeckers lost five men on the crossing and eighty men were sick on arrival.[82]

The five men of the Waldeck Regiment, who died on the crossing, were:

Christoph Kurtze (W200052), 1 Company
Friedrich Teigtmeyer (W200238), 2 Company
Sergeant Schmidtmann (W200373), and
Johannes Meyer (W200437), both of 4 Company, and
Wilhelm Hoehne (W200551), 5 Company.[83]

Ambrose Serle recorded that the Hessians and other troops debarked on October 22, and then went up the East River and through Hellgate in flatboats, toward the grand army. They were rowed to a drum beat with trumpets and fifes sounding, and colors flying.[84]

Next day the last of the Germans were landed at Myers Neck, a peninsula near New Rochelle.[85]

General Howe's report of November 30, 1776, to Lord George Germain gives the date of arrival of the 2nd Division of Hessians and the Regiment of Waldeck as October 22, probably indicating the date the first troops arrived in the New Rochelle area. It continues with the information that these troops were ordered to remain there to cover the disembarkation of the stores and provisions.[86] But it was only the original regiment and artillery of the Waldeck contingent, probably about 675 men, which arrived at New Rochelle on October 22 and 23,

The 3rd English-Waldeck Regiment

although Mollo gives the figure 1,225 men, which was the total manpower commitment by Waldeck for the entire war.[87]

Undoubtedly one of the first activities after the Waldeck transports arrived at New York was the transfer of the sick to hospitals on land. The first man to die in America from the Waldeck Regiment was Corporal Johann Friedrich Hanstein (W200007) of the Grenadier Company, who died in a hospital on October 21, 1776. Others who died of illness in the hospital prior to the end of the year, were:

Michael Zentler (W200370), 3 Company. on November 2
Johannes Koch (W200284), 3 Company, on November 2, although he may have died of wounds received in an action on October 27
Philipp Puettmann (W200094), 1 Company, on November 15
Peter Happe (W200069), 1 Company, on December 5
Henrich Steinbach (W200111), 1 Company, on December 7
Wagon-servant Christian Ruesel (W400007), of the Staff, on December 8, and
Henrich Bock (W200395), 4 Company, on December 22.

The hospital may have been in Harlem, as Happe is listed as having died at Harlem.[88]

The 3rd English-Waldeck Regiment

The newly arrived troops joined a large, victorious army. General Howe's command, including numerous British and Hessian units, during the summer, had beaten the Americans on Long Island and then driven them from New York. Now the two opposing armies were facing one another near White Plains. After the engagement at that location, and the capture of Forts Washington and Lee, Howe would pursue Washington across New Jersey and then go into winter quarters. General Washington, with his steadily decreasing force, could not accept the European practice or he would have no army by spring. Instead, on Christmas 1776, he launched a surprise attack on the Hessian brigade quartered at Trenton. His victory revitalized the army and, as noted in the pages that follow, forced Howe's command, including the Waldeck Regiment, to withdraw from most areas of New Jersey.

Shortly after the Waldeckers arrived in America, the unit began taking casualties. During 1776 and early 1777 the men of Hesse-Cassel and Waldeck were the only Hessian contingents in Howe's command, and these troops suffered thirteen killed, 63 wounded, and 23 missing from October 9 to October 28.[89] A portion, or all thirteen Waldeckers reported as missing during the period from September 17 to November 16, according to a return of losses from Howe's army, were among the 23 men noted as missing by von Eelking.[90]

Some, possibly all, of the men missing in action were among the men involved in a minor action in late October. Although Baurmeister's text seems to indicate the following occurrence happened on October 29, it probably refers to an incident which took place two days earlier. Eighteen men of the Waldeck Regiment were "Marauding" near Maroroneck. They were attacked by forty rebels who disarmed them and took a subaltern and twelve men captive. Two men, who were seriously wounded, were left on the field.[91] Those two men were apparently Philipp Steinmeyer (W200231), 2 Company, who died of his wounds on November 1, 1776, and thus was the first

47

The 3rd English-Waldeck Regiment

battle casualty, and Friedrich Zoellner (W200249), of either 2 Company or 4 Company, who was invalided home on February 21, 1777.[92]

Others who may have been involved in the incident include:

Captain -at-arms Anton Pohlmann (W2000253) 3 Company, who died in the hospital, probably of wounds, on November 9.
Johannes Koch (W200284) 3 Company, who died on November 2
Johann Philipp Roll (W200456) 4 Company reported wounded in October
Johann Peter Ulrich (W200477) and
Jaspar Wagener (W200483) 5 Company, both of whom were listed as prisoners of war in October
Wilhelm Kann (W200032) 1 Company, and
Johann Adam Ferst (W200532), and
Wilhelm Neumeyer (W200577), the last two of 5 Company, listed as prisoners of war in December.[93]

General William Heath's *Memoirs*, under the date of October 27, 1776, indicate a heavy cannonade could be heard in the morning toward Fort Washington, and that later in the day, thirteen Hessians (Waldeckers ?) and two or three British prisoners were brought in.[94]

Lieutenant James McMichael of the Pennsylvania Line, the same day, recorded the event in a bit more detail. He wrote, "Our scouting party" brought in thirteen Waldeck and three regulars as prisoners of war.[95] Another account of the incident, written by Tench Tilghman, is to the effect that twelve Waldeckers were taken prisoner on October 27. The prisoners were amazed at the kind treatment they were given, and were willing to remain with their captors. The Waldeckers told of being torn from their country, and, if their comrades knew how good everything was with the Americans, all would lay down their arms and join the Americans.[96]

Finally, Trevelyan cites the Baurmeister report of the incident and then continues on to the effect that in expressing the willingness of the Waldeckers to surrender, the men "did not claim to express the sentiments of the Hessians or Brunswickers;

The 3rd English-Waldeck Regiment

but the event proved that they had every title to speak for the Waldeck regiment. That regiment, during the next five years, neither did nor suffered much.[97]

On October 28, 1776, General von Knyphausen and the 2nd Division of Hessians moved out, but the Waldeck Regiment remained at New Rochelle.[98] Sir George Osborn, or one of his aides, wrote that General von Heister, commanding general of all the Hessian contingent in America, wanted 15,000 pounds so the Hessian troops could be paid, and added that the Hessians were to be mustered every two months. The Waldeck Regiment was not under General von Heister, however, as they were an independent command under the regimental commander, Lieutenant Colonel von Hanxleden, and, being only recently arrived, would be mustered soon.[99]

Knyphausen's move, with his six regiments of Hessians, was apparently to Kingsbridge, while the Waldeckers remained in New Rochelle.[100] However, the Waldeck guard left at New Rochelle[101] may have been only a small part of the regiment, as Baurmeister wrote that the Knyphausen corps was encamped behind Fort Independence, where General Martin Schmidt had also sent the Hessian Wissenbach Regiment, and the Waldeck Regiment, except for fifty men of the Waldeck Regiment who remained at New Rochelle.[102]

Knyphausen's force had moved from New Rochelle to Mile Square, Valentine's Hill, Kingsbridge, crossed Dykemann's Bridge, and encamped at the north end of Manhattan. The Waldeckers followed, also by way of Mile Square and Valentine's Hill, and settled in the ruins at Fort Independence on November 4.[103]

When the Americans had abandoned the fort, they left a large amount of shot and shell behind.[104] Other reports indicate the regiment took post at a bridge over the Bronx River, three miles above the bridge in West Chester near Delancey's Mill.[105] The bridge over the Bronx River, where the Waldeckers were posted, appears to have been Williams Bridge,[106] and it would

The 3rd English-Waldeck Regiment

seem at least a possibility that only a detachment - maybe fifty men left at Rochelle earlier - of the regiment was assigned to guard the bridge, while the bulk of the regiment was at Fort Independence.

After some minor delays, General Howe launched his attack on Fort Washington on November 16, 1776,[107] with the Hessians and Waldeckers under General von Knyphausen making the main attack. These men were trained in the tactics of Frederick the Great of Prussia and, while all officers were not members of the nobility, most were, and the regiments certainly contained some excellent officers and men.[108]

Indicative of the practice of European military officers to serve in various armies as a means of gaining knowledge, recognition, and advancement, is the case of Chretien Louis Philipps De Sundahl (or Sunnahl), who was born in 1734. He entered the service of the Prince of Waldeck in 1754 and in 1779 was appointed captain-commander of the Royal Deux Ponts, a unit employed by the French in America during the Revolution, in effect fighting against the Waldeckers.[109]

However, the Waldeckers of Knyphausen's command were not "Yagers, that is riflemen," as set forth in John Adlun's *Memoirs*,[110]. This error would also tend to discredit his comment that in the attack on Fort Washington, 1,500 British with fixed bayonets were behind the Germans. The British twice charged the Germans after they failed to carry the positions held by Colonel Moses Rawlings. Thus encouraged, however, the Germans marched briskly up to the defenses and charged with bayonets.[111]

An account from the diary of Ensign Joseph Wiedeshalat (possibly the name should be Wiederhold) is that at 5:30A.M. "we went over Kingsbridge to York Island, namely the following regiments: Knyphausen, Huyn, Buenau, Rall, Lossberg, and Waldeck, were joined by Wutginau and the grenadier battalion, and formed two columns; the column on the right consisted of the Lossberg, Rall, the grenadier battalion, Koehler and

The 3rd English-Waldeck Regiment

Waldeck, was led by Col. (Johann) Rall and was stationed in a wood until the appointed time. The column on the left consisted of the regiments - Wutginau, Knyphausen, Huyn, and Buenau and was led by Maj.-Gen. Schmid. His Excellency Lieut.-Gen. von Knyphausen commanded the whole attack." The avant-garde on the left, included a Captain Mandern von Wutginau, Lieutenant Georg Wilhelm von Loewenfels and the diarist. The lieutenant died on the field, the captain died of his wounds the next day, but the writer survived unscathed.[112]

There is also a version of the battle in the *Pennsylvania Magazine of History and Biography* which mentions that Lieutenant von Loewenfels fell during the battle, according to a diary entry by Captain Andreas Wiederhold.[113]

Richard Ketchum, who gives a disproportionately large share of the credit for the capture of Fort Washington to the Waldeckers, writes that the Hessians on the attack were angry because the Americans, on November 9, had striped the bodies of thirteen German soldiers, including an officer, who was killed in a skirmish below Kingsbridge.[114]

The capture of Fort Washington resulted in large losses for the regiments under General von Knyphausen's command. The Waldeckers had six killed and sixteen wounded of a total 77 killed and 381 wounded within the command.[115] Force gives the casualty count for the Waldeckers but a much lower total count of only 58 killed within the entire command.[116]

The Waldeckers killed in the action were:

Georg Backhaus (W200022), 1 Company
Wilhelm Brand (W200274), 3 Company
Johann Philipp Roll (W200456), 4 Company and
Bernhard Bueddecker (W200521)
Johann Henrich Knocke (W200523), and
Paul Fleck (W200534), 5 Company.[117]

Seventeen Waldeckers are listed in the *HETRINA* as having been wounded during November 1776, but possibly all were not

The 3rd English-Waldeck Regiment wounded at Fort Washington. Four of the men wounded in the attack, died in the hospital later. They were:

Johannes Werle (W200245), 2 Company, who died November 17
Daniel Scheideler (W200100), 5 Company, who died November 23
Henrich Giesing (W200062), 5 Company, who died December 5; and
Konrad Lock (W200318), 3 Company, who died December 7.[118]

Others wounded in November 1776, were:

Christoph Andre (W200019) and
Johannes Kesthans (W200034), 1 Company
Dietrich Frede (W200176) and
Corporal Otto Wiedlaake (W200138), 2 Company
Adam Schmidt (W200348) and
Adam Weirauch (W200367), 3 Company
Ludwig Berger (W200393)
Johann Henrich Keitel (W200400)
Henrich Mueller (W200442), and
Adolf Siebel (W200469), 4 Company and
Henrich Pieper (W200584)
David Schuettler (W200604), and
Johannes Weidenhagen (W200611), 5 Company.[119]

Following the assault on Fort Washington, orders were issued at British Army Headquarters at Delancey's Mill, that "Every assistance (was) to be given toward carrying the Hessian wounded to Morrisania."[120] Even before the reports of heavy Hessian losses at Fort Washington reached England, the king directed the "Regimental Surgeons belonging to the several Corps of Foreign Troops serving under your (General Howe's) Command, should be supplied from the General Hospital with the necessary medicines in the same manner as those of the British Forces."[121]

Despite the heavy losses, the Hessians and Waldeckers had conducted themselves well in the attack on the fort, and even Trevelyan wrote that when the report of the successful attack reached Waldeck and Hesse-Cassel, the sovereigns felt a thrill of

The 3rd English-Waldeck Regiment

conscious honesty that the English King had received some value from their troops.[122]

On November 18, 1776, Private Wilhelm Fleischhuth (W200294), 3 Company, was released from the regiment for an unknown reason and Volunteer Christian Karl Mueller (W200080), who had apparently been transferred from 2 Company after the regiment left Germany, was released from the Hesse-Cassel forces December 2.[123] The *HETRINA* indicates Mueller was taken into 3 Company of the Donop Regiment in March 1777 as a free corporal, was transferred to 2 Company of the same regiment in May 1778, and separated in America in February 1779.[124]

On November 2, 1776, the Waldeck Regiment was ordered to take post at Jones', "and extend away toward Delancey's." A November 30 order was for the regiment to hold ready to move to Amboy on the shortest notice.[125]

At the beginning of December, General Howe ordered the Waldeck Regiment to embark at King's Wharf and sail to Amboy,[126] and on December 2, John Morgan of Ramapongh wrote to General Charles Lee of having received a report that there were not more than 1,000 Hessians and Waldeckers at Hackensack, and no British.[127] However, Ambrose Serle wrote that the Waldeckers embarked for Amboy on Thursday, December 5, 1776.[128]

The movement of the Waldeck Regiment was part of General Howe's general advance through New Jersey, and as Colonel Rall's brigade moved on toward Maidenhead on December 7, he left the Hessian Lossberg Regiment in Elizabethtown until such time as it would be relieved by the Waldeck Regiment. On December 12, the Waldeckers arrived at Elizabethtown. This was four days after Howe arrived at Trenton.[129] Nevertheless, the English historian Belcher wrote that Washington escaped across the Delaware River as the British arrived at Trenton, and "a German band came marching

The 3rd English-Waldeck Regiment

in pompously at the head of Waldeckers and Hessians some thousand strong."[130]

Colonel Rall had continued his advance toward Trenton in mid-December, and the Lossberg Regiment once again had been left behind, this time at Brunswick, until relieved by the Waldeck Regiment.[131] However, the Waldeck Regiment seems never to have arrived at Brunswick, although the Lossberg Regiment did rejoin Rall prior to the affair at Trenton at Christmas time. Instead, on December 20, General Alexander McDougall made a report to Washington that only Waldeckers were at Elizabethtown, where they had already been for two weeks. "The drums had beat" on this morning, and the Waldeckers were to have marched, but did not do so due to bad weather. McDougall did not know where the regiment was to have gone, but Brunswick seems a probability.[132]

A New Jersey militia colonel reported to General Washington on December 27, 1776, that the enemy still had 500 or 600 Highlanders at Newark and as many Waldeckers at Elizabethtown, but as a result of the defeat at Trenton, the English outposts had been withdrawn to Brunswick.[133]

When Colonel Rall's brigade, including the Lossberg Regiment, went into winter quarters at Trenton, and the Waldeck Regiment had gone into winter quarters at Elizabethtown, General Howe had written to Germain setting forth the need of foreign troops for the next year's campaign. In addition to new clothing, tents, and camp equipment, Howe estimated the Hessians would need 200 men and the Waldeckers thirty men to replace losses suffered in the campaign of 1776.[134]

General Howe never would have believed when writing his estimate that battle casualties during the winter would render his estimate of replacement needs completely inadequate. On December 29, General William Maxwell, at Morristown, New Jersey, wrote Washington to request guidance in disposing of the Highlanders and Hessians (including Waldeckers?) who were being captured daily.[135]

The 3rd English-Waldeck Regiment

Washington, who had captured nearly 900 Hessians of Rall's brigade at the Trenton outpost on the day after Christmas, now, on December 30, ordered his subordinate, General McDougall, and his command to profit from the enemy's disposition. The instructions were simple, "Get as many men as you can and strike at Elizabethtown. Intelligence indicates that among the forces in that area are 500 Waldeckers at Elizabethtown."[136]

As the year 1776 drew to a close, neither General Howe nor the men of the Waldeck Regiment realized that Howe's estimate of manpower requirements for the Waldeck Regiment for the next campaign were as badly underestimated as the defeat of the Hessians at Trenton had made that estimate. But the death of one man, Georg Schmidt (W200349), 3 Company, killed in action by the Americans on December 27, and the wounding of two others, Christian Brand (W200519), 5 Company and Johannes Schmidt (W200350), 3 Company, during December was indicative of things to come in the new year.[137]

During 1776, 666 men have been identified as having sailed for America with the Waldeck Regiment. Of this number, five men died *en route*, so that 661 men arrived in America. Eight men died of illness before the end of the year and thirteen died as a result of combat, for a total of 21 deaths within the regiment after it reached America. Probably thirteen men were made prisoners of war following the October 27 action and two men were released from the regiment. Based on these figures, the number of men serving in the Waldeck regiment as the year 1776 drew to a close would appear to be 625, plus thirteen men in prisoner of war status.

The 3rd English-Waldeck Regiment
1777

As the Americans became more daring after the affair at Trenton, many minor skirmishes occurred between the Americans and the King's men, including the Waldeckers. In one such action on January 4, 1777, a Major Richard Crewe, 17th Light Dragoons, leading a combined English-Waldeck command, attempted to cut-off a detachment of Americans, but because the Waldeckers did not behave well, only four or five Americans were captured, and the major was himself nearly cut-off and captured.[1]

This incident may have been one mentioned by the American general, George Clinton, writing to Colonel Sparhawk from Pyramus, about a clash between the American militia and some German troops on January 4, in which seven Germans were killed and three made prisoners. The Americans lost three men.[2]

Clinton, in the same letter, reported another engagement during which the militia killed ten and captured forty Hessians (Waldeckers ?) near Morristown, New Jersey, on January 5, 1777. The Kemble *Journals* contain a clearer account of the action. According to the British adjutant, a Lieutenant Mesnard (Cornet Friederich Metzer) of the 17th Light Dragoons went out (from Elizabethtown) with twelve light horse and fifty Waldeckers. After a march of four miles the force halted in a hollow. Just then a body of Americans appeared. The Waldeckers, unable to retreat uphill, entered a house, but after an exchange of gun-fire, all were captured. Lieutenant Mesnard escaped through Springfield.[3]

On January 6, 1777, Archibald Robertson, of the British army, recorded that a patrol of fifty Waldeckers from Elizabethtown had been taken.[4]

Both Robert M. Ketchum and Albert H. Bill take note of the capture of fifty Waldeck soldiers in Monmouth County, New Jersey, opposite Staten Island, by local militia, in the early days

The 3rd English-Waldeck Regiment of 1777, with the surrender taking place after the Waldeckers had suffered the loss of eight to ten men.[5]

The Pennsylvania Evening Post of January 16 and 23 provided far more details. According to the reports in the newspaper, General Maxwell had marched on Elizabethtown and in the process of capturing the town, had made fifty Waldeckers and forty Scots prisoners of war The paper reported that the British at Elizabethtown would not let the Waldeckers stand sentry at the outposts because some had deserted to the Americans.

The later edition of the paper put the date of the action as Sunday morning, January 5, and the location as "near Springfield". The Waldeckers suffered eight to ten killed and wounded, with 39 or 40 being captured, including two officers, by a force of like size, without loss.[6] It appears that the newspaper account may have been based on General Washington's letter to the President of Congress, dated January 7, 1777, at Morristown.[7]

The *New Jersey Archives*, Second Series, Vol. 1, page 270, is cited in a *History of Union County, New Jersey* as the source of information that General Maxwell attacked Springfield on January 5, captured ninety prisoners, and then moved on to Newark, forcing the British to fall back to Perth Amboy and Brunswick.[8]

General Henry Knox wrote his wife to explain the January 5 battle as one with sixty Waldeckers, all of whom were killed or captured, in Monmouth County, in the lower part of the Jerseys.[9]

Freeman's Journal for January 28 printed a letter of January 9, 1777, to the effect that the British had abandoned Elizabethtown following an attack by the Americans which resulted in the capture of thirty Waldeckers, fifty Highlanders, and about thirty fully-loaded baggage wagons. The British had withdrawn to Amboy and Brunswick and, as there was an eclipse of the sun expected on January 9, the Americans planned

The 3rd English-Waldeck Regiment

another attack on the Germans to "take advantage of their ignorant superstition".[10]

In his *Memoirs*, General Heath, who failed to take notice of the capture of fifty Waldeck soldiers on January 5, 1777, did record the capture of thirty Waldeckers near Elizabethtown on January 8, by General Maxwell and a force of New Jersey militia and Continentals.[11]

Many other writers have taken note of the capture of men of the Waldeck Regiment during the early days of January 1777. General John Cadwalader, wrote from Morristown to the Pennsylvania Council of Safety that some Jersey militia had captured fifty Waldeckers near Elizabethtown on January 8.[12] Adjutant Muenchhausen recorded that since Trenton, Washington's constant harassment of the King's troops had forced the abandonment of Elizabethtown and that eighty Waldeckers had been captured.[13] A war journal by an unidentified writer set forth a sequence of events in which General Vaughan assembled some royal troops at Elizabethtown, but abandoned that place on January 7 after some Waldeck soldiers, some Highlanders, and some baggage wagons fell into the hands of the Continentals.[14] Even Trevelyan wrote that Howe's chain of outposts fell, including Hackensack and Elizabethtown in the heart of the district Howe had undertaken to protect. A band of militiamen killed or captured a detachment of fifty Waldeckers and an amount of baggage.[15]

No wonder that an American veteran of the war, Major John Clark, wrote in later years that while assigned to the flying camp, he participated in a raid on Staten Island which resulted in the capture of sixty Waldeck soldiers.[16] His story seems to be based on two separate events, the fighting near Springfield in January 1777 and an attack on Staten Island later in the same month. The general confusion of events following the Hessian defeat at Trenton, the inaccurate reporting and recording of these events, and the loss of memory by participants during later

The 3rd English-Waldeck Regiment

years have befuddled the minds of both participants and historians.

It appears that two separate engagements occurred on January 5 and January 8, that the Americans captured a large number of Waldeck soldiers, and that, as Kemble wrote, General Vaughan marched back to Amboy with the British 71st Regiment and the Waldeck Regiment on January 7.[17]

Another source of confusion for students of the period is Kemble's entry for January 8, 1777, in regard to troop strength. Kemble listed 1,043 men of Ansbach as part of the force with the commander-in-chief. However, the Ansbach-Bayreuth contingent did not arrive in New York until June 2-4, 1777. He also gives the Waldeck strength on Staten Island as 330 men with no explanation of where the rest of the regiment was to be found.[18] Assuming the regiment had lost eighty men, killed, captured, deserted, dead of illness, or in the hospital, 200 men are still unaccounted for.

Of the men made prisoner during the January fighting in New Jersey, 36 men were reported on the road from Pennington and Wellston to Morristown on January 12, 1777, and four days later, a party of Tories and one Hessian (Waldecker ?) were reported in the jail at Morristown.[19]

The Pennsylvania Evening Post of January 14, 1777, reported that on the previous night, a party of Waldeckers arrived in Philadelphia, having been captured in the East Jersies.[20]

Among the men killed during the fighting in the Springfield area, were:

Kaspar Hagemeyer (W200543), 5 Company, on January 4
Philipp Knust (W200039) and
Philipp Schneider (W200106) 1 Company; and
Karl Altvater (W200510) and,
Gottlieb Zange (W200615), 5 Company, all on January 5 and
Henrich Limpert (W200560), 5 Company, on January.[21]

The 3rd English-Waldeck Regiment

Four men are listed in the *HETRINA* as having been wounded in January, 1777. There were:

Henrich Koch (W200042), 1 Company; who was also reported as missing in action in January and who died in a Philadelphia hospital, possibly of his wounds, in November 1777
Karl Mueller (W200082), 1 Company,
Daniel Mechel (W200324), 3 Company; and
Henrich Piphard (W200450), 4 Company.[22]

No definitive list of men of the Waldeck Regiment captured in the Springfield area in early1777 has been found. However, based on *HETRINA* entries, prisoner of war exchange lists, and Sir George Osborn's report to Germain in May 1777 that there were 101 men of the Waldeck Regiment being held prisoners at Lancaster, Pennsylvania, the following men probably were among those captured. An asterisk indicates men exchanged from prisoner status in July 1778.[23]

Captain Georg von Haacke (W100006), 5 Company*
Lieutenant Gerhard Henrich Heldring (W100014), 4 Company*

From 1 Company

Christian Albrecht (W200018)
Ludwig Bauerschmidt (W200024)
Friedrich Breuninger (W200028)
Henrich Kauffmann (W200033)
Friedrich Koch (W200041)
Christian Koppe (W200047)*
Franz Cramer (W200048)
Georg Kruhm (W200050)*
Adam Drube (W200054)
Christian Goebel (W200063)*
Georg Grubert (W200066)

Corp. Joh. Meisner (W200008)*
Johannes Mertz (W200076)*
Georg Meyer (W200128)*
Capt/Arms v. Nehm (W200004)*
Anton Noll (W200088)
Fried. Joh. Phil. Pleuger (W200095)
Ulrich Schreiber (W200108)
Wilhelm Taubert (W200114)*
Georg Thielemann (W200117)
Georg Wissemann (W200125)

From 2 Company

Johannes Becker (W200145)*
Bernhard Beyer (W200149)*
Franz Bigge (W200150)
Cpl. Karl Bruehne (W200135)
Henrich Klaus (W200157)

Phil. Henr. Lange (W200196)
Johannes Meybaum (W200200)
Daniel Mueller (W200203)*
Karl Sander (W200215)
Georg Schmeck (W200219)

The 3rd English-Waldeck Regiment

Johannes Dantz (W200164)
Henrich Gerhard (W200179)
Philipp Hentze (W200187)*
Josef Schrantz (W200225)*
Friedrich Schwencke (W200227)
Johannes Wagener (W200243)*

From 3 Company

Henrich Kinold (W200278)*
Johannes Klapp (W200281)
Christian Knoechel (W200279)*
Cpl;. Joh. Knoechel (W200256)
Johannes Kunckel (W200287)
Henrich Dicke (W200289)
Matthias Flamme (W200293)*
Henrich Graebing (W200302)
Joh. Georg Just (W200313)*
Henrich May (W200323)
Joh. Barth. Meuser (W200328)
Konrad Meyer (W200331)*
Cpl. Georg Muus (W200259)
Cpl. Henrich Muus (W200261)*
Friedrich Roemer (W200344)*
Wilhelm Stoltz (W200358)*
Anton Weinhold (W200366)

From 4 Company

Dietmar Banse (W200390)
Joh. Henr. Batister (W200391)
Ludwig Berger (W200393)*
Wilhelm Buecking (W200396)
Konrad Bunse (W200397)
Daniel Klapp (W200403)
Christoph Moer (W200440)
Wilhelm Rencke (W200451)
Peter Rosenberg (W200457)
Jakob Siebert (W200470)
Peter Knueppel (W200406)
Nikolaus Kohl (W200407)
Geo. Giessenschlaeger (W200417)*
Johannes Graebe (W200422)
Drum. Jak. Heinemann (W200385)*
Henrich Henckelmann (W200427)
Christian Treitling (W200475)
Johann Valentin (W200479)
Karl Wahl (W200485)
Henrich Wilke (W200491)*

From 5 Company

Georg Bock (W22518)
Peter Erhard (W200531)
Friedrich Frese (W200536)
Georg Geitz (W200538)*
Geo. Ludwig Gier (W200539)
Drummer Chrn. Huthmann (W200507)
Franz Mangel (W200562)
Georg Meckel (W200563)*
Henrich Meyer (W200566)
Henrich Wincke (W200570)*
Cpl. Philipp Weismann (W200503)*
Friedrich Rodewald (W200590)*
Johannes Salzmann (W2200591)*
Thomas Schaefer (W200594)
Friedrich Schmidt (W200600)*
Henrich Voepel (W200609)*
Thomas Wieser (W200614)
Henrich Zimmermann (W200618)*

During March 1777, Sergeant Friedrich von Axleben (W200010C), 1 Company, was promoted to ensign and assigned duty with 5 Company.[24]

The 3rd English-Waldeck Regiment

In March 1777, the then Lieutenant Colonel, Ludwig von Dalwigk (W100002S) was separated in America; and on February 21, 1777, Friedrich Zoellner (W200249), who had been wounded in October of the previous year, was invalided to Europe.[25]

Probably Zoellner was the Waldeck soldier who sailed from New York on February 17, 1777, aboard the transport *Ann*, Master Joseph Rudd. One individual was noted on the victualling report as receiving 38 rations on the trip to Deptford, where the ship arrived March 23, 1777.[26]

In addition to the men lost as a result of combat during the early days of 1777, the Waldeck Regiment lost 24 men between January and the end of June, 1777, due to illness.[27] They were:

Johannes Stremme (W200473), 4 Company, on January 6
Henrich Goebel (W200181), 2 Company, on January 19
Fifer Martin Tanner (W200014), 1 Company, on February 21
Georg Gerhard (W200298), 3 Company, on February 26
Peter Thumerich (W200362), 3 Company, on March 8
Andreas Schaeffer (W200461), 4 Company, on March 11
Christian Amelung (W200268), 3 Company, on March 18
Franz Schmidt (W200463), 4 Company, on March 18
Cpl. Ernst Jung (W200011), 1 Company ,on March 27
Konrad Koch (W200043), 1 Company, on March 27
Henrich Schlossmueller (W200462), 4 Company, on April 4
Joh. Henrich Piphard (W200450), 4 Company, on April 5, possibly of wounds
Henrich Wasserfeld (W200486), 4 Company, on April 8
Matthias Ochse (W200580), 5 Company, on April 25
Henrich Schmidt (W200103), 1 Company, on April 30
Johannes Grob (W200065), 1 Company, on May 14
Henrich Lemmering (W200559), 5 Company, on May 16
Friedrich Haacke (W200007), Artillery, on May 20
Cpl. Karl Zwick (W200127), 1 Company, on May 20
Paulus Nolle (W200089), 1 Company, on June 2
Johannes Winterberg (W200247), 3 Company, on June 16
Konrad Osterhold (W200336), 3 Company, on June 20
Christoph Raabe (W200339), 3 Company, on June 20, and
Konrad Schmidt (W200603), 5 Company, on June 30.

The 3rd English-Waldeck Regiment

Desertion became a major problem for the Waldeck Regiment during 1777, also.[28] Among those who deserted were:

Johannes Kuhlmann (W201195), 1 Company, on January 6
Georg Grubert (W200066), 1 Company, on January 6
Rudolph Pape (W200o92), 1 Company, on January 6
Leonhard Walter (W200119), 1 Company, on January 6
Barthold Frede (W200061), 1 Company, on January 13
Andreas Herter (W200072), 1 Company, on January 13
Andreas Reineck (W200096), 1 Company, on January 13
Johannes Wetterhacke (W200246), 2 Company, on April 2
Johannes Birckmann (W200273), 3 Company, on April 3
Andreas Guergel (W200303), 3 Company, on April 3
Cpl. Henrich Baste (W200137), 2 Company, on April 5
Henrich Lange (W200314), 3 Company, on April 5. (He returned to duty on January 7, 1778.)
Cpl. Bernhard Saure (W200383), 4 Company, on April 5
Servant Joh. Henr. Kleimenhagen (W201121), 4 Company, on April 5
Henrich Mueller (W200442), 4 Company, on April 6
Friedrich Lacour (W200195), 2 Company, on April 7
Joh. Konrad Verglass (W200480), 4 Company, on April 7
Joh. Adam Jakob (W200431) 4 Company, on April 17
Henrich Schneider (W200223), 2 Company, on April 19
Servant Peter Winter (W201158), 4 Company, on June 17, and
Vol. Valentin Demuth (W200527), 5 Company, on August 99, 1777.

Concerning these deserters, only limited information is available. James Reed of Reading, Pennsylvania, wrote on January 28, 1777, that he had only seen one copy of a resolve by Congress to treat the Hessian prisoners well, and he felt because of the general irritation against the Hessians, that some who would desert, as four Waldeckers had in the previous week, might be maltreated if they proceeded toward Reading.[29] Also the *Philadelphia Evening Post* of April 23, 1777, carried an extract of a letter from Morristown with information that three Waldeck soldiers, who had deserted, had just come from Amboy.[30]

The 3rd English-Waldeck Regiment

Muster Master Osborn wrote to Germain on May 15, 1777, that the Waldeck contingent had fifteen deserters during the previous winter. Also, of the fifty men who were believed to have enlisted with the Americans, from among the Waldeck prisoners of war at Lancaster, fourteen had deserted back to their own regiment.[31]

The Waldeck Regiment's activities during the early months of 1777 are obscure. The Hessians (and Waldeckers ?) still in New Jersey were dying of scurvy at this time, which may explain some of the deaths among the Waldeck soldiers.[32]

Strength of the Waldeck Regiment, according to a table in "An Historical Journal", for the date of May 8, 1777, was 13 officers, 5 staff, 45 non-commissioned officers, 14 drummers, and 330 privates. This same table also lists the Ansbach-Bayreuth forces as 1,043 privates of a total strength of 1,236 men, "with the commander-in-chief".[33]

A comparable report from German sources provides the following strength figures for the Waldeck Regiment as of May 4, 1777:[34]

1 - Commandant	4 - 1st Lieutenants
1 - Major	1 - Sub-Lieutenant
2 - Captains	4 - Ensigns
2 - Captain Lieutenants	
24 - Non-Commissioned Officers	24 - Corporals
4 - Free Corporals	17 - Musicians
5 - Medics	491 - Privates
9 - Staff	2 - Wagon Servants
15 - Servants (Batmen)	5 - Soliccitors

611 - TOTAL (These figures include the prisoners of war held by the Americans, with the exception of the two officers.)

As the 1777 season for active campaigning began, General Lee, on June 4, was taken aboard the *Centurion*, for security reasons,[35] and on June 11, Howe left for Brunswick, leaving two

The 3rd English-Waldeck Regiment

battalions of Ansbach-Bayreuth, the Waldeck Regiment, and the British 55th Regiment at Amboy.[36]

Next day, General von Heister and most of the main British force left Amboy for Brunswick, leaving the previously mentioned troops at Amboy under the command of the Ansbach Colonel Friedrich Ludwig Albrecht von Eyb.[37]

On June 22, the regiments at Amboy were ordered to strike their tents, and some British troops, Koehler's Hessian Grenadier Battalion, and the Waldeck Regiment were ordered to cross to Staten Island at Billop's Ferry at six o'clock in the morning.[38] They were to encamp near the redoubts on Staten Island. The redoubts were at St. George, near present day Fort Hill. They were earthen fortifications known as Fort Knyphausen and commanded the harbor in the area of The Watering Place.[39]

Apparently the orders of June 22 were cancelled, as British Headquarters' *After Orders* of 10:30 P.M., June 28, 1777, directed the 35th and 52nd English Regiments, Koehler's Grenadiers, and Loos' Hessian Regiment, the Ansbach and Waldeck Regiments to cross at the ferry to Staten Island at daybreak the next day.[40]

On June 29, Captain Muenchhausen noted the movement to Staten Island in his diary, and made the following entry concerning the men of Ansbach-Bayreuth. "The Anspachers are exceedingly tall and handsome fellows. Without doubt these Anspach regiments are the tallest and best looking regiments of all those here."[41]

Archibald Robertson also commented on the movement to Staten Island and wrote that the Hessians marched to The Narrows and that the Ansbach regiments, the Waldeckers, Koehler's Grenadiers, and some British went to The Watering Place on July 21.[42]

On July 9, 1777, The British left the defense of Staten Island to the 52nd Regiment, the Bayreuth Regiment, and the Waldeck Regiment, encamped to the rear of the redoubt, which had six iron 6-pound cannons and an artillery detachment. A

The 3rd English-Waldeck Regiment

subaltern and forty men from each regiment with a captain from one of the regiments were to mount guard and maintain communications on Staten Island, where Colonel August Valentin von Voit von Salzburg was to command until Brigadier John Campbell arrived. Provincials defended the west side of the island, where Major General Skinner held the command.[43]

On July 14, 1777, Baurmeister noted that, of the Germans, one Bayreuth Regiment and the Waldeck Regiment, were on Staten Island under Brigadier General Campbell.[44]

While the regimental strength in America was steadily declining during 1776-1777, recruiting of replacements for the Waldeck Regiment continued in Europe. On March 24, 1777, Colonel Faucitt, at Bremerlehe, wrote to the Earl of Suffolk that the Waldeck recruits and a force of Hessian chasseurs would be embarked as soon as they arrived at the port.[45]

Two days later Faucitt reported that the Waldeck troops, "who are in general in a good state," were aboard ship.[46]

An Admiralty letter of early April stated that the captain of the *St. Albans* would have orders to take under his command the convoy carrying the rest of the Hessian chaussers and the Waldeck recruits, expected daily at Spithead.[47]

Apparently there was a change of plans. Captain George Ourry of HMS *Somerset* was ordered on April 3 to take the convoy with Hessian chaussers and Ansbach troops, and the recruits to New York, with the utmost haste. An enclosure to this letter, which was from the Admiralty to Richard, Lord Howe, listed the following ships for the Ansbach-Bayreuth troops: *Stag*, Master James Saunders; *Friendship*, Master William Coldstream; *Symmetry*, Master William Foxen; *Durand*, Master William Maab; *Myrtle*, Master William Walker; *Hopewell*, Master William Hepden; *Diana*, Master Thomas Brown; *Providence* (2nd), Master Richard Ware; *Juno*, Master Robert Smith; and *Polly*, no master listed.

The 3rd English-Waldeck Regiment

For the Hessian chaussers and recruits the ships listed were: *Lively*, Master Robert Wetherden; *Apollo*, Master James Adamson; and *Providence* (1st), Master James Watson.[48]

Viscount Weymouth, writing from Whitehall on April 3, 1777, notified the Admiralty that the Hessian chaussers and the Waldeck recruits were to go with the convoy, if they arrived in time. The same date, the officer commanding the Hessian chaussers and the recruits, was notified to proceed at once to New York under the officer commanding the Ansbach-Bayreuth troops.[49]

Two months later, on Tuesday, June 3, 1777, Ambrose Serle made an entry in his journal that the *Somerset* and seventeen transports and ships arrived at New York with 1,200 Waldeckers, etc.,[50] And Lieutenant Colonel Sir George Osborn wrote to Germain on July 4 that the Ansbachers, Hessians, and Waldeck recruits had arrived at New York. He added that Generals von Heister and von Mirbach and Colonel Block were returning to Germany on the next ship.[51]

An enclosure to the above letter gave foreign troops strength in North America on June 28, 1777, as 12,777 Hessians; 1,293 Ansbachers; and 679 Waldeckers, for a total of 14,749, including sick, prisoners, etc.[52]

Reports of June 3 and 24, 1777, give the same 679 figure for the total Waldeck force, but only give the location for the 333 men on Staten Island,[53] and Captain Muenchhausen, reporting the distribution of the King's forces in America as of June 6, 1777, did not even list the men of the Waldeck Regiment.[54]

However, Waldeckers were on Staten Island and the *Somerset's* convoy did bring another 87 men from Waldeck for service with the regiment. According to a victualling report, *Gala*, Master Henry Jackson, victualled 90 men of the Waldeck military on a voyage from Bremerlehe to Amboy during the period March 25 to June 15, 1777.[55]

The 3rd English-Waldeck Regiment

The following men have been identified in the 1777 recruit shipment for the Waldeck Regiment. Although the shipment appears to have sailed with 89 men plus the escort officer, Lieutenant Becker, two men supposedly died *en route*[56] Of those who arrived in America, the following have been identified:

Sergeant Wilhelm Goedeling, (W200702), Sachsenhausen
Drummer Karl Pfennig, (W201146), Goddelsheim

Privates

Karl Ammenhaeuser, (W200632), Rittersheim
Christian Becker, (W200637), Kronweissenburg
Georg Bender, (W201109), Malchen
Johannes Besselbach, (W200642), Mannheim
Philipp Beusch, (W201193), Neidelheim
Ignatius Bieber, (W201110), Wien
Jakob Bieg, (W200644),
Philipp Boehmer, (W200650), Odenbach
Adam Buecher, (W200654), Engishausen
Peter Buseck, (W200658), Braunfels
Josef Carnish, (W200660), Wien
Georg Kirschner, (W200662), Obernett, Mein.
Johannes Kirschner, (W200663), Oberellen
Ludwig Kohlboersch, (W201126), Braunfels
Johannes Conet, (W200669), Stuttgart
Johannes Krafft, (W200670), Gnadenthal
Henrich Kuempel, (W200676), Lauterbach
Christoph Kuntzmann, (W201128), Harburg
Christoph Kussenbauer, (W200678), born 1761/62, Unterriexingen
Johannes Decker, (W201129), born 1727/28, Helminghausen, Hesse
Philipp Decker, (W200581), Giessen
Georg Dehm, (W200682), Buschberg, Bamb.
Friedrich Deierlein, (W200683), Roet/Rets
Georg Eckhard, (W200686), Braunfels
Andreas Eichenger, (W200687)
Michael Erle, (W200688), Sibrechthausen
Peter Ernst, (W200689)
Jakob Fauser, (W200691)
Johannes Fischer, (W201131), Braendel, Mainz
Georg Fuehrer, (W200699)

The 3rd English-Waldeck Regiment

Konrad Guthmann, (W201134), Schoenberg, Pfalz
Jakob Hagener, (W200708), Oberbiel
Georg Hermann, (W200713), Philippstein
Dietrich Hinterthuer, (W200716), Goettingen
Nickolaus Holtzmann, (W201136), Kentheim
Ludwig Juncker, (W201191), Holtzhausen, Darm.
Johannes Loeffler, (W200727), Wallersdorf
Friedrich Mercker, (W200732), Berlin
Wilhelm Mielig, (W200734), Giessen
Andreas Muenster, (W200735), Idstein
Gottfried Nikolaus, (W200738), Altenburg
Peter Oppenhaeuser, (W200743), Arzbach
Jost Pfennig, (W201145), Goddelsheim
Johannes Risch, (W200751), Ulm
Friedrich Roehrig, (W200753)
Andreas Salmeyer, (W201160), Gunzenhausen
Jakob Schade, (W201167), Weinfeld, Switz.
Michael Schlauderbach, (W200766), Nuernberg
Felix Schmidt, (W200768)
Friedrich Schmidt (Jr.), (W200769), Holzhausen
Peter Schumann, (W200783), Frankfurt
Daniel Sondermann, (W200789), Oberinse
Valentin Stein, (W201149), Kassel
Eberhard Stoessel, (W200793), Altenkirchen
Philipp Tewes, (W200794)
Lorenz Thaler, (W200795), Ammendorf
Gottlob Weiss, (W200804), Waldenburg
Wilhelm Wersinger, (W200809)
Martin Wetterwald, (W200810), Vilisan, Switz.
Georg Weybrenner, (W200811), Loehnberg
Christoph Wiegmann, (W200812), Koenigsberg
Peter Winter, (W201158), Einhausen
Johannes Wuertz, (W200813), Gruenewik, Berg.
Peter Ziegenhainer, (W200815), Altenkirchen
Peter Zipp, (W200816), Dillhausen

Another 38 men, listed below, have been identified as having served in America and are either members of the Waldeck Regiment, who 1) arrived in America with the original contingent in 1776, 2) were in the initial 1777 recruit transport,

The 3rd English-Waldeck Regiment

3) were enlisted in America, or 4) were possibly in a second recruit shipment in 1777.[57] A running strength summary for the Waldeck Regiment seems to indicate that during the period August 25 through October 24, 1777, the regiment received an additional 38 recruits. These new arrivals, plus the 661 men assigned, gave the regiment a strength of 30 men above the treaty requirements.[58] However, it is possible that these recruits were still in Waldeck being assembled for the next year's shipment.

Sgt. Amandus Hemmerling, (W200712)
Cpl. Joh. Henr. Daniel Brey, (W201116), Immighausen
Cpl. Johannes Budelbach, (W200653)
Cpl. Wilhelm Scriba, (W200785)
Drummer Justinus Berger, (W200639), Mannheim
Drummer Wilhelm Boehne, (W200651), Twiste
Servant Joh. Wilhelm Pelzhaenger, (W201164)
                    Privates
Andreas Baus, (W200635), Enzweihingen
Christoph Beck, (W201108) born 1756/57, Arolsen
Franz Karl Beck, (W200636), Pressbach, Bamb.
Ludwig Bornemann, (W200652), Bovenden
Christoph Cleemann, (W200666), Sachsen
Joachim Joh. Gose, (W200704), born 1749/50, Wehrstedt
Christoph Hofmann, (W201192), Sindringen
Henrich Landesberger, (W200724), Loeh
Christoph Lende, (W201138), Dilchen, Schwaben
Peter Licht, (W200725), Felsen
Christian Mueller, (W200645)
Johannes Mueller, (W200674), Gemingen
Ludwig Mueller, (W200679)
Philipp Friedrich Muench, (W201143), Ottlar
Andreas Nassler, (W200736), born 1749/50, Katzenstein
Matthias Ohlhaber, (W200741)
Josef Perle, (W200744), Hallstadt
Johannes Pflantzer, (W200748), Linz
Friedrich Schmidt (Sr.), (W201194), Leipzig
Johannes Schoenberger, (W200776), Hess, Salzburg
Martin Schultze, (W200601), Hassenberg

The 3rd English-Waldeck Regiment

Kaspar Stempler, (W200792)
Johannes Strehle, (W201150), Hohenhard
Henr. Fried. Thiemann, (W200796), Minden
Konrad Vercken, (W201153), Hameln
Georg Vollmueller, (W201156), Lauterbach

Cannoneers

Henrich Depmeier, (W300003), born 1753/54, Hameln
Kaspar Effe, (W300004)
Jakob Graebe, (W300006), born 1744/45, Kassel
Gottfried Stabroth, (W300013), born 1753/54, Berlin
Erdmann Zenecke, (W300017), Goeritz, France

Another new-comer to America in 1777 was Johann Christoph Wagner, Chaplain of the Bayreuth Regiment of the Ansbach-Bayreuth force. After the war, he remained in America, having been discharged at his own request. He had been promised work in Frederick, Maryland, but soon went to Nova Scotia. He received 400 acres of land in Clements Township, Annapolis Royal. A dispute as to who should be the preacher among the settlers in that area led to his return to Germany.[59]

On the night of August 22-23, 1777, Generals John Sullivan, William Smallwood, and Prudhomme DeBorre led an attack on the west side of Staten Island with 2,000 men. Initially the attack was successful and a number of Loyalist defenders were captured. One report was to the effect that four colonels, six major, many officers, and 350 men were captured, before the rebels began to withdraw. Then Brigadier Campbell with the 52nd Regiment and the 3rd Waldeck Regiment marched to the assistance of the provincials, leaving a regiment of Ansbach-Bayreuth to guard the camp.

Campbell's reinforcements successfully drove the Americans from Staten Island, cannonading the boats loaded with the retreating soldiers and inflicting heavy casualties. Reports vary widely as to the American losses. Captain von Muenchhausen recorded American prisoners taken, as one colonel, two majors, several other officers, and 123 men of the American rear guard.

The 3rd English-Waldeck Regiment

A much higher figure is given by Mackenzie, who reported 120 Americans killed and 340 taken prisoner. His record of British losses consisted of five killed, seven wounded, and eighty taken prisoner, most of whom were probably provincials.[60]

The heat of the day, the heat of the battle, or the heavy load which the eighteenth century soldier carried, took a greater toll of the Waldeck Regiment than the battle with Sullivan's men. Three Waldeck soldiers died of fatigue while on the march on August 23. They were:

Jakob Butterweck (W200398), 4 Company
Stefan Dietz (W200167), 2 Company and
Jakob Muus (W200575), 5 Company.[61]

The British in turn sent an expedition into New Jersey the next month, when the Waldeck, Ansbach, and English grenadiers landed at Elizabeth Point on September 11, 1777, and marched on Newark. General Clinton reported to General Howe, now off on his Philadelphia venture, that landings had been made in four places. In addition to the force including the Waldeckers, General Vaughan led a force which crossed the North River at Fort Lee and across Hackensack and New Bridge. On September 18, 1777, the British forces withdrew from New Jersey.[62]

A summary of troop strength of the forces under General Clinton in the New York area on October 1, 1777, signed by J. Paterson, Adjutant General, North America, and taken from the *Parliamentary Register*, provided the following information on the Waldeck Regiment, while ignoring the artillery:[63]

Commissioned officers and staff: 1 colonel, 1 major, 4 captains, 9 lieutenants, 1 chaplain, 1 adjutant, 1 quartermaster, 1 surgeon, 5 surgeon's mates

Present and fit for duty: 24 sergeants, 17 drummers, and 378 rank and file

The 3rd English-Waldeck Regiment

On command: 1 sergeant and 32 rank and file; no one on leave or on recruiting duty.
Prisoners of war: 1 sergeant, 2 drummers, and 101 rank and file (No mention of Captain Haacke and Lieutenant Heldring, who were also prisoners of war.)
Sick: 3 sergeants and 46 rank and file - no wounded
Total effectives: 29 sergeants, 19 drummers, and 557 rank and file
Wanting to complete: 3 drummers and 14 rank and file.

After having captured Forts Clinton and Montgomery on the Hudson River, in early October 1777, General Clinton once again embarked a force on the Hudson on October 13, 1777, which included the Waldeck soldiers and the Ansbachers. On October 18, the Waldeckers and the 45th Regiment returned back down the river and landed at Spitting Devil. Later the Waldeck Regiment returned to Staten Island.[64]

The Waldeck soldiers captured in January 1777, were a problem for their captors, not because they were unruly prisoners, but because they were prisoners and required safe-keeping. It appears however, that they may have been preferred to British prisoners. As early as January 19, 1777, William Atlee wrote to the Council of Safety of Pennsylvania that when the British prisoners were sent to Lancaster, they had been sick. Now they were recovered and could march, and as room was needed for the Hessians and Waldeckers, the British were being sent to the Council. The same day, the Hessians and Waldeckers arrived at Lancaster under escort of Lieutenants Jordan and Miller, and the prisoners were put in the barracks.[65]

There are numerous entries in diaries, journals, and official documents concerning the Waldeck prisoners. On February 6, 1777, a Mr. Robert Jewel was directed to deliver the Hessians and Waldeckers, who were prisoners in his custody, to Colonel Isaac Melcher.[66]

Governor George Clinton recorded a diary entry on February 20, 1777, that four Waldeckers and two British privates had been brought into Windsor, New York, as

The 3rd English-Waldeck Regiment

prisoners, and the next day, that 25 prisoners previously captured were sent from Morristown to Pennsylvania.[67]

The 25 prisoners sent from Morristown, possibly including the four Waldeck privates captured on February 20, may have been the 25 prisoners sent to Philadelphia under the care of Robert Mullin, February 27, 1777. The list of prisoners contains the names of four Waldeckers

Charles Briant - possibly Christian Brand (W200519), 5 Company
Henry Chinman - possibly Henrich Kinhold, (W200278), 3 Company
Cunrod King - possibly Konrad Koenig, (W200045), 1 Company and
Peter Grimes, none of whom can be positively identfied.[68]

On March 8, 1777, Christopher Ludwig wrote Congress that many Hessian and Waldeck prisoners, especially single men, wanted to stay in America. They should be allowed to work to support themselves outside prisoner of war status.[69]

Sir George Osborn wrote Germain on March 15, 1777, that the Hessian prisoners had not entered the service with the enemy, but that thirteen Waldeckers had done so. However, nine had later quit the American service.[70]

Two months later, on May 15, Osborn reported to Germain that he had inspected and mustered the Waldeck Regiment "last week". They needed 54 men to complete the regiment, 55 were sick, and 101 were prisoners of war. The men's clothing was exceedingly bad, but Colonel von Hanxleden expected new uniforms by the first ships. The regiment's weapons were new and in perfect order, but in general the men themselves were very uncleanly and unhealthy for the want of care. They had little practice in exercise and maneuver, and appeared more in want of these skills than the other foreign troops. Fifteen men had deserted from the regiment during the winter, and of fifty men who were believed to have joined the American army from the 101 prisoners of war at Lancaster, fourteen had deserted back to their own service.[71]

The 3rd English-Waldeck Regiment

Finally, one English, one Scot, and two Waldeck officers (Captain von Haacke and Lieutenant Heldring) visited Bethlehem, Pennsylvania, on April 3, 1777. They were prisoners of war on parole, *en route* to Maryland.[72]

On August 24, 1777, The Congressional Board of War, fearing an attack on Lancaster by the forces under General Howe, ordered the prisoners moved from that place to Reading, Pennsylvania. As it was believed many of the prisoners would try to stay with the Mennonites in the Lancaster area, the militia was to use particular care in collecting men who might try to hide.[73]

An entry in the diary of a Moravian pastor of the Hebron Church at Lebanon, Pennsylvania, on August 25, 1777, was to the effect that because General Howe was rumored to be in Maryland, all the prisoners of war at Lancaster and Reading were to be moved to Lebanon. Houses in the community had already been chosen and prepared for the arrival of the prisoners.[74]

Next day the prisoners arrived and were to be put up in churches and schools. The pastor noted that hostile people wanted to put the prisoners in the Moravian's parsonage, also. The prisoners, numbering about 340, arrived in Lebanon toward evening and Colonel Curtis Grubb, Sub-lieutenant of Lancaster County, sent word to the pastor to vacate the parsonage so as to provide quarters for the soldiers. The pastor protested because the parsonage was not a public building. He was supported by his church officials, but to no avail.[75]

By 9 A.M. on August 29, 1777, 400 men had arrived in Lebanon and only the four lower rooms of the Moravian parsonage were left to church use. Two hundred men were billeted in the meeting and private rooms of the parsonage. By late afternoon the next day, 208 prisoners of the Hessian von Knyphausen Regiment, but not the entire regiment, arrived. Mixed with these were other Hessian and Waldeck prisoners, so

The 3rd English-Waldeck Regiment

that no real discipline was to be expected. Therefore, men of the guard force were hurried into town.[76]

At 10 A.M. on October 29, 1777, the Barracks Master Dave Krause went to the parsonage and informed the prisoners that they were to be ready to leave for Lebanon in half an hour, as they were being moved to the Lutheran Church. Shortly thereafter, Captain David Oldenbruck (the diary entry is Oldenburg) arrived with a detachment of militia and the prisoners were taken away. Three weeks later, the pastor noted that the Lutheran Church in Lebanon was to be used as a powder magazine.[77]

Four members of the Waldeck Regiment died of wounds during the last half of 1777, although the dates do not correspond with any significant battle. The men who died were:

Daniel Meckel (W200324), 3 Company, on August 1
Johannes Roegel, (W200343), 3 Company, on August 7
Johannes Goebel, (W200420), 4 Company, and
August Rittmeyer, (W200589), 5 Company, both on October 4.[78]
Henrich Koch's (W200042), death was noted earlier.

Another 42 men died of illness in the period from July through December 1777. Those with an asterisk having arrived in America with the 1777 recruit transport in June.[79]

Johannes Suiss, (W200360), 3 Company, on July 7
Valentin Maurer, (W200322), 3 Company, on July 11
Emanuel Paer, (W200446), 4 Company, on July 13
Drummer Karl Pfennig, (W201146)*, 2 Company, on July 19
Fifer Christian Reuter, (W200262), 3 Company, on July 19
Konrad Guthmann, (W201134)*, 1 Company, on July 25
Jakob Schmidt, (W200464), 4 Company, on July 25
Cpl. Christian Wienand, (W200257), 3 Company, on July 27
Drummer Adam Knueppel, (W200017), 1 Company, on August 1
Ludwig Juncker, (W201191), 1 Company, on August 5
Cannoneer Simon Haacke, (W300008), Artillery,. on August 5

The 3rd English-Waldeck Regiment

Can. Gottfried Hentze, (W300010), Artillery,. on August 5
George Cantzler, (W200399), 4 Company, on August 7
Wilhelm Sude, (W200237), 2 Company, on August 9
Johannes Fischer, (W201131)*, 3 Company, on August 11
Cpl. Schoenberg von Spiegel, (W200629), 2 Company, on August 12
Christoph Weitenkamp, (W200244), 2 Company, on August 12
Jakob Schade, (W201167)*, 1 Company, on August 14
Cpl. Joh. Henr. Brey, (W201116)*, 4 Company, on August 14
Ludwig Kohlboersch, (W201126)* 1 Company, on August 16
Jost Schimmel, (W200218), 2 Company, on August 17
Philipp Beusch, (W201193), 5 Company, on August 20
Henrich Stallmann, (W200356), 3 Company, on August 27
Christoph Mueller, (W200333), 3 Company, on September 2
Can. Henrich Goecke, (W300005), Artillery, on September 3
Friedrich Stuhldreher, (W200236), 2 Company, on September 3
Konrad Vercken, (W201153)*, 1 Company, on September 5
Matthias Hauschild, (W200186), 2 Company, on September 6
Konrad Kunstmann, (W201128)*, 2 Company, on September 7
Nikolaus Lahr, (W200558), 5 Company, on September 8
Karl von Rhena, (W200115), 1 Company, on September 13
Martin Schultze, (W200601)* 3 Company, on September 14
Georg Vollmueller, (W201156)*, 3 Company, on September 23
Moritz Kesting, (W200402), 4 Company, on September 26
Jakob Mette, (W200077), 1 Company, on September 29
Peter Mauer, (W200075), 1 Company, on October 2
Adam Mueske, (W200329), 3 Company, on October 2
Friedrich Goette, (W200421), 4 Company, on October 11
Georg Bender, (W201109)*, 4 Company, on October 15
Johannes Schmeck, (W200221), 2 Company, on October 21
Daniel Knipp, (W200158), 2 Company, on October 27, and
Johannes Rode, (W200342), 3 Company, on December 30.

Two sergeants were released to return to Europe in 1777, Sergeant Henrich Schumacher (W200252), 3 Company on July 15 and Quartermaster Sergeant Arnold Franz Riemenschneider (W200005) 1 Company on July 16.[80]

During 1777, a recruit shipment which sailed with 89 men plus one escort officer, delivered 87 men to the Waldeck Regiment in America, although only 67 have been identified. Another 38 men, acquired in an as yet undetermined manner,

The 3rd English-Waldeck Regiment

have also been identified in America, making the total new men identified in America during 1777, 105 men. Losses were four men released, of whom three returned to Europe, twenty deserters, 69 non-combat deaths, and eleven combat deaths, plus 94 men made prisoners of war. At the end of the year, the estimated strength of the Waldeck Regiment was 550 men, plus 106 prisoners of war.

The 3rd English-Waldeck Regiment
1778

The early months of 1778 were a relatively quiet period for the Waldeck Regiment., and personnel changes seem to have created most of the activity in the unit.

As of April 23, 1778, the regiment consisted of:

1 Colonel	1 Major
2 Captains	2 Captain Lieutenants
4 1st Lieutenants	5 Sub-Lieutenants
1 Adjutant	1 Regimental Quartermaster
1 Chaplain	1 Regimental Surgeon
1 Commissary (Auditor)	5 Surgeon's Mates
1 Provost	1 Regimental Drummer
2 Wagon Servants	28 Non-Commissioned Officers
31 Corporals	19 Musicians
509 Privates	20 Servants and Solicitors

TOTAL - 636, or 34 men short of treaty strength.[1]

A month later the strength report indicated only 24 men short and provided the further information that 1 surgeon and 5 soldiers were absent with permission; 2 drummers and 92 men, plus 2 officers, were prisoners of war; and 2 sergeants, 1 drummer, and 27 soldiers were sick.[2]

Henrich Lange, (W200314), 3 Company, who had deserted on April 5, 1777, returned to duty on January 7, 1778. Andreas Sahlmeyer, (W201166), 5 Company, was listed as missing in August 1778, and then as a deserter on August 18. Two months later, on October 25, he returned to duty, but is not listed again in the *HETRINA* as being with the regiment.[3]

The other deserters from the regiment in 1778, deserted from prisoner of war status.[4] Men of the 3rd Company who deserted on May 4, 1778, were:

Dietmar Banse (W200390)   Joh. Wilhelm Rencke (W200451)
Henrich Batister (W200391)   Joh. Peter Rosenberg (W200457)

The 3rd English-Waldeck Regiment

Nikolaus Kohl (W200407)   Jakob Siebert (W200470)
Christoph Moer (W200440)

Four men deserted from prisoner of war status at Lancaster on June 6, 1778. They were members of 1 Company:

Friedrich Breuninger (W200029)   Adam Drube (W200054)
Friedrich Koch (W200041)   Philipp Pleuger (W200095)

Two men of 3 Company, apparently about to be exchanged, deserted from prisoner of war status on July 24 at York Point. They were:

Johannes Kunckel (W200287)   Henrich May (W200323)

May returned to duty in May 1783.

Two others of 5 Company deserted from York Point on August 5. They were:

Peter Erhard (W200531)   Ludwig Gier (W200539)

Gier returned to duty in December 1782.

Three men of 2 Company deserted from prisoner of war status on August 1, 1778. They were:

Franz Bigge (W200150)   Johannes Mueller (W200205)
Wilhelm Littlet (W200197)

Littlet returned to duty by November 1780, according to the *HETRINA*, but as the regiment was in Florida at that time, it must be assumed that he served with another contingent of troops, or journeyed to Florida on a supply ship, or returned prior to November 1778.

In January 1778, Johannes Braun (W200028), 1 Company, was reported as having died, although the *HETRINA* entry seems in error as Braun is listed as an invalid, also, who returned

The 3rd English-Waldeck Regiment

home in either January or February of 1778.[5] (The date of regimental release from duty of unit members is not clear.)

Six other men of the Waldeck Regiment were released from service in 1778, and while all were reported as separated in America, that does not necessarily mean that they remained in America. The six were:

Christoph Beck (W201108), 3 Company, separated on September 6, after being declared an invalid

Ludwig Berger (W200393), 4 Company, wounded at Fort Washington in 1776, apparently captured in New Jersey in January 1777, and returned from prisoner of war status in July 1778. He was then declared an invalid and separated on October 24.

Corporal Henrich Brueckhauser (W200505), 5 Company, separated on September 6 after being declared an invalid.

Johannes Decker (W201129), 4 Company, declared an invalid and separated on June 10.

Franz Geicher (W200418), 4 Company, declared an invalid and separated on June 30.

Christian Wilhelm (W200124), 1 Company, declared an invalid and separated on October 24.

Other men of the Waldeck Regiment who were declared to be invalids in 1778, were:[6]

Henrich Kinhold (W200278), 3 Company
Peter Gabelaender (W201133), 4 Company
Peter Hugen (W200199), 2 Company
Hermann Huth (W200553), 5 Company
Wilhelm Itzmann (W200554), 5 Company
Andreas Schultze (W200628), 4 Company
Christoph Thomas (W201151), 2 Company, and
Kaspar Anton Vogel (W201155), 5 Company.

The original commander of 5 Company, Konrad von Horn, was a major when he returned to Waldeck in October 1778. As the *Echo*, Master J. Menenir, sailed from New York on October 8, 1778, and arrived at Portsmouth, England, on January 1, 1779, with eleven Waldeckers, it seems safe to assume those

The 3rd English-Waldeck Regiment

men were Major von Horn and a group of invalids being returned to Waldeck.[7]

On September 8, 1778, Fifer Christian Kroll (W200525), 1 Company, and Corporal Otto Wiedlaake (W200138), 2 Company, were released from the Waldeck Regiment so that they could join the English 55th Regiment. Apparently this transfer was worked out by the men involved, and two men from the English army, Georg Andreas (W201106), born 1757/58 in Harthausen, and Henrich Brabender (W201113), born 1750/51 in Twiste entered the Waldeck Regiment in their stead.[8]

There were apparently no combat deaths in the Waldeck Regiment during 1778, but while the regiment was still on duty on Staten Island, fourteen men died of accident or illness.[9] These men were:

Nikolaus Holtzmann (W201136), 1 Company, on January 14
Anton Wolff (W200248), 2 Company, on January 21
Friedrich Buntrock (W200275), 3 Company, on January 30
Cannoneer Friedrich Bever (W300001), Arty., on March 28
Henrich Rauch (W200211), 2 Company on April 3
Adam Kreutzer (W200160), 2 Company, on April 12
Georg Kaesemeyer (W200276), 3 Company, on May 6
Christian Treitling (W200475), 4 Company, who died in a prisoner of war camp on May 24
Henrich Weineck (W200487), 4 Company, who died in prisoner of war camp on July 8
Johannes Knueppel (W200405), 4 Company, who drowned while bathing on August 21
Valentin Stein (W201149), 3 Company, who died of fatigue during a march on August 25
Wilhelm Buecking (W200396), 4 Company, who died in a Philadelphia hospital on September 19
Kaspar Anton Vogel (W201155), 5 Company, on September 19, and
Sebastian Reinhard (W201165), 2 Company, on October 13.

When the Hessian and Waldeck prisoners of war were moved from the Moravian parsonage into the Lutheran Church in Lebanon, some prisoners might have been left in the

The 3rd English-Waldeck Regiment

parsonage or more prisoners may have moved into the parsonage later. At any rate, the pastor made a diary entry on March 11, 1778, that everything was in an uproar. Amidst the terrible confusion, the Hessians (and Waldeckers ?) were getting ready to leave. The preparations took all morning, but at last, about noon, the prisoners marched off, having done terrible destruction. The meeting room was a "pig sty".[10]

On April 21, 1778, forty Hessian (and Waldeck ?) exchanged prisoners, entered Philadelphia,[11] but while a few prisoners were being exchanged, others were being encouraged to enter American service. Enlisting prisoners and deserters was forbidden, but the Board of War wrote to William Augustus Atlee, deputy commissary of prisoners at Lancaster on May 27, 1778, to encourage the prisoners to enlist in Pulaski's Corps, if they were not shoemakers or tailors, and if they were not married in Europe or with wives under English control. A week later, the instructions were reversed, and Atlee was ordered to stop all recruiting, including recruiting for Pulaski's Corp.[12]

Although the negotiations for the exchange of prisoners had been an on and off activity for some time, it was not until June 9, 1778, when the English Commissary Joshua Lorring and the American Commissary General for Prisoners, Elias Boudinot, reached an agreement for a large scale exchange. By the terms of this pact, 2,200 prisoners held by the Americans were to be exchanged for a cartel account from the Americans, including many of the men captured at Fort Washington, but none of the Convention prisoners of General Burgoyne's army were to be included.[13]

The exchange began at once. On June 13, pastor Henry Melchior Muhlenberg wrote in his journal that during the morning, militiamen from Reading had marched past his home at New Providence, Pennsylvania, escorting English and Hessian (and Waldeck ?) prisoners being taken for exchange.[14]

A summary of prisoner exchange lists and work lists indicate that members of the Waldeck Regiment at Lancaster at

The 3rd English-Waldeck Regiment

the time of this prisoner exchange were in the following numbers:[15]

1 Company - 9	5 Company - 10
2 Company - 9	Unknown - 5
3 Company - 6	
4 Company - 6	TOTAL - 45

Extracts from a separate list of prisoners at Lancaster in 1777 and 1778, show the following Waldeck soldiers among the 372 men sent to Philadelphia for exchange on June 17, 1778, under escort of Captain Michale Opp. The men were exchanged in July, with the exceptions as noted here:[16]

Johannes Becker (W200145), 2 Company
Ludwig Berger (W200393), 4 Company (Ludwig Becker in reference)
Bernhard Beyer (W200149), 2 Company
Franz Bigge (W200150), 2 Company (deserted prior to exchange)
Henrich Kinold (W299278), 3 Company
Henrich Klaus (W200157), 2 Company
Peter Knueppel (W200406), 4 Company
Christian Koppe (W2000047), 1 Company
Georg Kruhm (W200050), 1 Company
Matthias Flamme (W200293), 3 Company
Georg Geitz (W200538), 5 Company
Christian Goebel (W200061), 1 Company
Henrich Henckelmann (W200427), 4 Company
Philipp Hentze (W200187), 2 Company
Georg Meckel (W200563), 5 Company
Corporal Johannes Meisner (W200008), 1 Company
Johannes Mertz (W200076), 1 Company
Konrad Meyer (W200331), 3 Company
Joh. Georg Meyer (W200128), 1 Company
Georg Henrich Mincke (W200570), 5 Company
Wilhelm Neumeyer (W200577), 5 Company (not exchanged in 1778)
Corporal Philipp Reismann (W200503), 5 Company
Friedrich Rodewald (W200590), 5 Company
Friedrich Roemer (W200344), 3 Company
Josef Schrantz (W200225), 2 Company

The 3rd English-Waldeck Regiment

Wilhelm Stoltz (W200358), 3 Company
Wilhelm Taubert (W200116), 1 Company
Henrich Voepel (W200609), 5 Company, and
Henrich Zimmermann (W200618), 5 Company.

A second list of prisoners sent for exchange on June 21, 1778, contained 171 names, including the following Waldeck soldiers, who were exchanged in July:[17]

Georg Giesenschlager (W200417), 4 Company
Georg Jost (W200313), 3 Company, (Gost in reference)
Drummer Jakob Heinemann (W200387), 4 Company
Corporal Henrich Muus (W200261), 3 Company
Daniel Mueller (W200203), 2 Company
Johannes Salzmann (W200591), 5 Company
Friedrich Schmidt, Sr. (W200600), 5 Company
Johannes Valentin (W200479), 4 Company
Johannes Wagener (W200243), 2 Company
Henrich Wilke (W200491), 4 Company

In addition, the following Waldeck soldiers' names were on the list, but had been scratched off:

Christian Albrecht (W200018), 1 Company, who was not exchanged in 1778
Peter Erhard (W200531), 5 Company, who deserted on August 5, 1778, from York Point, and
Henrich Meyer (W200566), 5 Company, who was not exchanged in 1778.

The lists of deserters during 1778 and the men exchanged from prisoner of war status reveal that there were probably other Waldeck soldiers released from captivity during this period. Three men listed in the *HETRINA* as exchanged are Captain von Haacke, Lieutenant Heldring, and Christoph Knoeckel (W200279), all of whom returned to the regiment in July 1778.[18]

On June 22, 1778, the Americans sent a flag of truce from the Pennsylvania shore to HMS *Eagle*, lying off Reedy Island

The 3rd English-Waldeck Regiment

near New Castle, Delaware, to inform the admiral that 500 Hessians had arrived at Philadelphia, to be exchanged.[19]

The progress of the prisoners to be exchanged was reported again in early July in the *New Jersey Gazette*. Six hundred and fifty prisoners, chiefly Hessians, had passed through Trenton from the westward, on their way to Elizabethtown and exchange.[20] Montresor's journal entry for July 15 noted that 800 Hessians had arrived at Staten Island after being exchanged.[21]

A July list of Hessian and Waldeck prisoners of war, in which Atlee notified an unspecified party of some prisoners being sent forward for exchange, contained the names of three men of Colonel von Hanxleden's Company. Possibly they represent replacements for three men whose names were scratched off the June exchange lists. The three Waldeckers in the new list appear to be Jakob Koch, Martin Tisch, and Ciriacus Wagener, none of whom can be identified by this writer.[22]

Another copy of a Lancaster prisoner of war exchange list contains the names of the following Waldeck soldiers.[23] There are no dates, but it appears to be names used to make the composite list.

Christoph Knoechel (W200279), 3 Company
Matthias Flamme (W200293), 3 Company
Henrich Henckelmann (W200427), 4 Company
Henrich Voepel (W200609), 5 Company, and
Georg Henrich Mincke (W200570), 5 Company.

On July 19, 1778, a number of prisoners of war were exchanged in New York. A Baurmeister letter states that 500 of the prisoners had returned by way of Elizabethtown and that all looked well.[24] Another 399 exchanged prisoners arrived at New York from Connecticut on July 22 and 23.[25] This would seem to be the same 800 men reported in the *New York Gazette and Weekly Mercury* of July 27, as having arrived from New Jersey and Connecticut.[26]

The 3rd English-Waldeck Regiment

On July 29, 1778, a third list of prisoners, to be sent from Lancaster to Philadelphia for exchange, contained the names of three Waldeck soldiers. The escort officers for this move were Lieutenant William Vanlier and Stephen Stephanson of the 9th Pennsylvania Regiment.[27] The Waldeckers were:

Corporal Karl Friedrich Bruehne (W200135), 2 Company
Konrad Bunse (W200397), 4 Company, and
Josef Thomas Wieser (W200614), 5 Company.

These three men are among the following individuals listed in the *HETRINA* as having returned to the regiment from prisoner of war status in August 1778.[28]

Ludwig Bauerschmidt (W200024), 1 Company
Corporal Karl Bruehne (W200135), 2 Company
Konrad Bunse (W200397), 4 Company
Henrich Kauffmann (W200033), 1 Company
Daniel Klapp (W200403), 4 Company
Franz Cramer (W200048), 1 Company
Johannes Graebe (W200422), 4 Company
Joh. Bartholameus Meuser (W200328), 3 Company
Anton Noll (W200088), 1 Company
Karl Wahl (W200215), 4 Company, and
Josef Thomas Wieser (W200614), 5 Company.

Other groups of prisoners which arrived at New York during the remainder of the year included prisoners of war previously held in Virginia, Maryland, and Pennsylvania, but no indication has been found that any of the exchanged prisoners were members of the Waldeck Regiment. Lists of prisoners absent from jail at Lancaster on November 6, 1779, and November 20, 1780, contain the name of a Waldeck private, Johannes Mueller, who can not be identified by this writer.[29]

- - - - - - -

On March 10, 1778, Colonel Faucitt wrote to the Earl of Suffolk from Hannover that the Ansbach, Hanau, and Waldeck recruits

The 3rd English-Waldeck Regiment

were at the port awaiting the arrival of transports,[30] and two months later, on May 7, Germain wrote the Admiralty that those same recruits, intended for New York, were at Portsmouth and again in need of transports.[31]

One fleet, commanded by Admiral Marriot Arbuthnot arrived at New York on August 25, 1778, without a hospital ship, and over 100 men of the 6,600 men on board had died *en route*. The illness and disease brought ashore soon had 6,000 men of the garrison down sick.[32]

In the first week of September 1778, more ships arrived bringing provisions, 500 Hessians, 200 Ansbachers, and 100 Waldeck soldiers. Nineteen men had died *en route* and many others had to be hospitalized.[33]

The Waldeckers among the new arrivals were 137 recruits for the Waldeck Regiment. These men had made the crossing on the *Two Brothers*, Master Joseph Patton. Originally there were 142 men in the shipment, counting the escort officers, but three men had died *en route*. According to the victualling report they had departed from Spithead on April 6, 1778, and arrived at New York on September 13, 1778.[34]

On April 5, 1778, Colonel Faucitt mustered the Waldeckers at Bremerlehe, and reported their strength and organization, as:[35]

1 - Captain	1 - 1st Lieutenant
1 - Sergeant	1 - Free Corporal
1 - Surgeon's Mate	1 - Cannoneer
2 - Fifers	2 - Drummers
4 - Corporals	128 - Privates

142 - TOTAL

Next day, Faucitt still gave the same strength figures for the recruits, but on April 29, 1778, Major Sebisch signed a return on board the *Zwei Brueder (Two Brothers)*, using the same figures but with one exception. Instead of 128 privates, Sebisch reported only 126, and

The 3rd English-Waldeck Regiment

noted that Adam Bauer (W201160) had died on April 19 and Henrich Hofmeister (W201161) on April 27, 1778.[36]

Finally, a September report by Major Sebisch listed only 125 privates aboard the *Zwei Brueder* as a third man, Friedrich Alex (W200051), had died *en route* to America, on June 26, 1779. Sebisch also noted that 39 men were sick and that eight wives and three children accompanied the recruits.[37]

The lieutenant with the recruits was probably Lieutenant Becker, who also served as an escort officer, and together with Captain/Major Sebisch, returned to Europe after delivering the recruits to Colonel von Hanxleden.

The muster roll of recruits of the 3rd English-Waldeck Regiment taken into English service at Bremerlehe on April 5, 1778, and reviewed on Staten Island on September 21, 1778, included the following names, with the men assigned to companies as indicated, and birth dates and places, when known:[38]

Artillery
Cannoneer Christian Thietke, (W300015), from Lueder

1 Company
Corporal Christian Berlin (W200641)
Fifer Christian Klee (W200664)
Drummer Christian Bauer (W200634), born at Gotha

Privates
Johannes Behr (W200638), born 1745/46 in Landau
Paul Bless (W200648), Erbach
Johannes Braun (W201114), Brey
Gottlieb Fichtner (W200692), Waltersdorf
Friedrich Fischer (W200695), Nuernberg
Johannes Francke (W201132), Malsfeld
Christoph Freese (W200697), Collstadt
Christoph Graebes (W200705), Doellnitz
Konrad Herold (W200714), Nuernberg
Henrich Hufeisen (W200720), Ober-Werbe
David Huthmann (W200722), Mengeringhausen
Nikolaus Mueller (W200694), Eckenrad, Fulda
Paul Oberlaender (W200739), Boemersheim
Friedrich Oppendahl (W200742), Nienburg
Friedrich Ritter (W200752), Leipzig

The 3rd English-Waldeck Regiment

August Saltzmann (W200758), Halberstadt
Wilhelm Schaeffer (W200763), born 1740/41 in Witzenhausen
Henrich Schmidt (W200633), Roemersberg
Henrich Stallmann (W200791), Kohlgrund
Joh,. Henrich Weber (W200802), Wahlen
Johannes Weitner (W200806), from Homberg (sick)

2 Company

Sgt. Friedrich Schum (W200782), born 1746/47 in Schmalkalden
Free Cpl. Bernhard Schreiber (W200779C), Mengeringhausen
Cpl. Christian Coette (W200703), Korbach
Drummer Jakob Peter (W200746)

Privates

Johannes Bless (W200647), Erbach (sick)
Philipp Block (W200642), Aalen
Michael Burghard (W200656), (sick)
Henrich Kabel (W201118), Klingelbach, Darmstadt, (sick)
Henrich Kaspar (W201119), Gross-Gerau (sick)
Friedrich Kluecks (W200667), Troeglitz, (sick)
Henrich Knies (W200668), Buedingen
Georg Koral (W201127), Duensbach, (sick)
Valentin Kreutzer (W200673), Schlitz
Adam Fischer (W200693), Fuerstenau, (sick)
Henr. Konrad Hoffmann (W200717), Nuernberg
Gottfried Maetsch (W201139), Freudenstadt (sick)
Kaspar Matthias (W200729), Ober-werbe
Georg Peter (W200745)
Sebastian Reinhard (W201165), born 1760/61 in Bentheim, (sick)
Adolf Schaacke (W200759), born 1761/62 in Kohlgrund
Henrich Schmidt (W200770)
Konrad Schmidt (W200771), Stadtbergen
Christoph Schuessler (W200781), (sick)
Friedrich Josef Seck (W200786), Hildburghausen
Christoph Thomas (W201151), Boxberg (sick)
Adam Weinkauff (W200803)
Leonhard Weitner (W200807), Untereffach

3 Company

Surg. Mate Friedrich Schrage (W200778), Oerzen
Cpl. Georg Rupp (W200755), Grossteichbach

Privates

Peter Braun (W201115), Stade
Theodor Geo. Bunse (W200655), Korbach

The 3rd English-Waldeck Regiment

Henrich Klee (W200665)
Balthasar Henr. Kreutzer (W200672), Langenfeld, (sick)
Ludwig Enslin (W201130)
Alisius Fass (W200690), Dannhausen
Sebastian Friedinger (W200698), Grunershofen
Michael Goebel (W200701), Gellershausen
Georg Griesheim (W200706), Meisdorf
Alexander Hartel (W200710), Unteroewisheim, (sick)
Johannes Heilig (W200711), Clausthal
Kaspar Hesse (W200715), born 1749/50 in Saalbach, (sick)
Kaspar Hohmann (W200718), born 1754/55 in Starfeld, Hesse, (sick)
Andreas Homberger (W200719), born 1760/61 in Frankfurt, (sick)
Johannes Lichtner (W200726), (sick)
Friedrich Marckert (W200728), Barchfeld
Michael Pfitzer (W200747), Goepingen
Anton Andreas Puoll (W200749), Samiza, Italy
Willibald Schade (W200761), Herrenden, (sick)
Peter Schmidt (W200767), born 1751/52 in Hohenfeld, Fulda
David Schneider, SR. (W200774), Wetzlar
Christian Schoenefeld (W200777), Crimitzchen
Andreas Sorg (W200790), Unterreichenbach
Friedrich Uhlmann (W200799), (sick)
Johannes Weissenborn (W200805), Muehlhausen

4 Company - Privates

Joh. Nikolaus Alt (W201105), Dickersbach, (sick)
Philipp Bauer (W201107), (sick)
Adam Birck (W201111), Mergenthal, (sick)
Georg Bless (W200646)
Andreas Kesting (W201120), Sachsenhausen, (sick)
Philipp Klopfer (W201123), Buedingen
Josef Crollpath (W200675), Eichstaett
Salomon Dender (W200684), Niemandshausen, (sick)
Georg Dettendaler, (W200685), Duerrwangen
Peter Gabelaender (W201133), Hassfurth, (sick)
Ernst Chrn. Guenther (W200707), born 1751/52 in Clausthal
Karl Fried. Hahne (W200709), born 1742/43 in Bosenfeld, Hann. (sick)
Andreas Heckenroth (W201135), Blankenberg, Hesse
Christoph Hohmann (W201199), (sick)
Hermann Hundertmarck (W200721), born 1742/43 in Tallensen, (sick)
Johannes Meidt (W200730)
Georg Meyer (W201142), Lehmingen, (sick)

The 3rd English-Waldeck Regiment

Henrich Nolte (W200700)
Philipp Quands (W200750), Mainz
Michael Sachs (W200757), Weissenbach, (sick)
Christian Schaeffer (W200762)
Michael Schart (W200764), born 1750/51 in Kaltenthal
Anton Jost Schimmel (W200765)
Ludwig Schmidt (W200772), Erfurt
Leonard Schreyer (W200780), born 1760/61 in Hagen
Adam Semper (W200787), Reichenbach
Friedrich Siebert (W200788), born 1763/64 in Gronau, (sick)
Henrich Toenges (W200797)
Jakob Wendolph (W200808), Giebelhausen
Anton Wolff (W200624), Neuburg
Johannes Zahner (W200814)

5 Company

Corporal Jean Tuitel (W201152), Laasphe

Privates

Henrich Bergmann (W200649), Baccum
Michael Betz (W200643), Reineck
Johannes Born (W200620)
Johannes Burr (W200657), Zensenberg, (sick)
Jakob Kahler (W200659), born 1757/58 in Altenlotheim
Bernhard Kern (W200661), Schwaebisch Hall, (sick)
Josef Kleineisen (W201122)
Siegfried Kramer (W200671), Strasbourg
Friedrich Cummero (W200677), Koenigsberg
Martin Wilhelm Daentzer (W200680), (sick)
Georg Frantz (W200696), born 1751/52 in Geislingen
Kaspar Leidner (W201137), Freiburg, (sick)
Jean (Johannes) de Lior (W200723)
Kaspar Meckel (W201141), Goettingen
Ludwig Meltzer (W200731), Hannover-Muenden
Franz Meyer (W200733)
Wilhelm Neubauer (W200737), Halberstadt
Henrich Oehl (W200740), born 1753/54 in Berndorf
Johannes Rose (W200754), Welda
Ludwig Ruppert (W200756), Pyrmont
Johannes Schaacke (W200760), Kohlgrund
Franz Schneider (W200775), Billigheim, (sick)
Leonhard Truebenddoerfer (W200798), born 1760/61 in Morsbach (sick)
Christian Ulrich (W200800), born 1759/60 in Gemmingen, (sick)

The 3rd English-Waldeck Regiment

Kaspar Anton Vogel (W201155), born 1756/57 in Mehringhof, Koeln
Friedrich Volmer (W200801)

Died *en route* to America - Privates
Friedrich Alex (W200051), on June 26, 1778
Adam Bauer (W201160), on April 19, 1778
Henrich Hoffmeister (W201161), on April 27, 1778

Of the 140 men who sailed for America as recruits for the Waldeck Regiment in 1778, 137 arrived in America. Of this number, two men, Johann Ludwig Enslin (W201130) and Kaspar Anton Vogel (W201155), died on September 17 and 19, respectively, before the date of the muster and the 38 men so indicated were sick and probably in the hospital.

In summary, the muster signed by Colonel von Hanxleden and the Deputy Commissary General W. Porter listed total effectives as:

1 - Sergeant	1 - Free Corporal
1 - Surgeon's Mate	124 - Privates
4 - Corporals	3 - Died at sea
1 - Fifer	2 - Drummers
2 - Died at New York	139 - **Total**

A number of events reported by Steuernagel and Chaplain Waldeck, which occurred in 1778, received confirmation from other sources. Among events recorded in the Montresor *Journal* are the following[39]

1) A July 6 entry of the stationing on Staten Island of two brigades of British and the provincials returned from Philadelphia.

2) A report of the arrival of the French fleet under the command of Jean Baptiste, Comte D'Estaing and its taking station off Sandy Hook. Montresor recorded the fleet as eleven sail of the line and three frigates.

La Languedoc (D'Estaing)	94 guns	1160 men
Le Tonnant (Bouganville)	80	1100
Le Cesar (Le Brave)	74	900

The 3rd English-Waldeck Regiment

Le Hector (Moliere)	74	900
Le Cuerrier	74	900
Le Protecteur	74	900
Le Marseilleis	74	900
Le Zele	74	900
Le Vaillant (Du Lubin)	64	700
La Provence	64	700
La Fantasque	64	700
La Sagittaire	54	500
L'Engageant	26	300
Le Chimere	26	300
Le Clement	26	300

3) An August 28 entry that two private victuallers arrived from Glasgow, after a thirteen week passage, "much wanted".

4) The same date, six 74-gun ships of Byron's squadron arrived.

5) An account of September 28 of Colonel Baylor's Light Horse being cut to pieces near Tappan.

Baurmeister also recorded that six men of war of Byron's fleet were at anchor off Sandy Hook in late August, and that 2,000 sick from the fleet had been landed on Staten Island. Other events during 1778, about which Baurmeister commented, were:

1) The assignment of a number of British units on Staten Island after their return from Philadelphia.

2) The capture of a number of British ships at New York by the French.

3) Lord Howe's departure for Rhode Island.

4) Another fire in New York on August 3, and

5) A powder ship which blew up on August 4, having been struck by lightning.[40]

The journal of Henry Melchior Muhlenberg confirms other entries in the Waldeck diary. An entry for October 4, 1777, noted that the church at Lebanon was a prison for Hessian prisoners of war. On January 22, 1778, Muhlenberg wrote that he was glad Hessian army chaplains were ministering to the

The 3rd English-Waldeck Regiment

German congregations in New York, and on January 30, 1779, Muhlenberg received a letter from David Grimm of New York, asking Muhlenberg to provide good treatment to one of the Brunswick officer prisoners, Major Meibon, who was obviously a good friend of Grimm's.[41]

In March 1778, at least in part because of Burgoyne's defeat and the French treaty of alliance with the Americans, the King of England and his government decided on a number of drastic changes in the execution of the war in America. Not only was General Howe relieved of his command, but the new commander, Henry Clinton, was authorized to evacuate Philadelphia and even New York, if he deemed this step advisable. The reason for considering the evacuation was the government's planned dispersal of large forces from the American colonies to other parts of the British Empire in the Western Hemisphere. Reinforcements from New York were to be sent to Canada, 5,000 men were to be sent to St. Lucia, in the West Indies, and 3,000 men were to be sent to Florida, with ordnance stores and artillery. The men going to Florida included one division to go to St. Augustine, and one division to Pensacola, which was also to be assigned a general officer.[42]

General Clinton acknowledged receipt of his instructions on March 21, 1778, but reported that putting them into effect required that the admiral first assemble a fleet, as the ships were much dispersed. The new commander-in-chief later wrote that it was also necessary that he move to consolidate his forces at New York, where it would be easier to embark the troops for the West Indies and Pensacola.[43]

But after his arrival in New York, Clinton was in no hurry to reduce his command. On July 11, he wrote to Germain that because the French admiral, D'Estaing, was on the coast, the English admiral advised against dispatching fleets of transports to the West Indies and Florida.[44]

At the same time, July 20, the French admiral was planning, after attacking Rhode Island, to undertake "an as yet very

The 3rd English-Waldeck Regiment

secret" joint American-French attack on West Florida.[45] Possibly the English government had learned of this attack while it was still in the planning stage in Europe and had made the decision to sent troops to Florida based on this information.

The procrastination for which he became so well-known enabled Clinton to retain other men in his command, also. The 2,000 soldiers he intended to send to Canada, before the season became too far advanced, according to a letter to Germain on August 15, 1778, were not sent. One month later, on September 15, another letter to Germain explained that the season was too far along and the troops would not be sent to Canada in 1778.[46]

On October 8, 1778, Clinton wrote a letter to Germain which indicated his loss of confidence in an English victory in America. After stating that the admiral had assembled the ships for a convoy, Clinton wrote that he would send the troops to the West Indies and Florida, in a few days. The troops being sent to Florida were foreigners and provincials, so the "loss to the Army will not so much be felt" and the treaties by which the foreigners were engaged,, precluded their use in the West Indies. On the other hand, the loss of 5,000 British effectives for the West Indies "will be severely felt here". These transfers, plus the loss of another 700 to be sent to Halifax and 300 more to Bermuda, meant Clinton could not successfully attack Washington's army. Facing this dismal future, Clinton asked to be relieved of his command.[47]

Eighteenth century communications between New York and London were slow and drawn out. While he awaited a reply to his request to resign, Clinton still had to carry out his orders to the best of his ability, and so the embarkation of troops destined for the south began. America intelligence reported twelve ships at Sandy Hook on October 16, and next day, the count was 100 ships at that anchorage. By October 20, 250 ships were reported in the New York area, ready to embark troops, and some soldiers were already on board.[48]

The 3rd English-Waldeck Regiment

Even while ships were being collected at New York to transport troops to other parts of the Western Hemisphere, ships still sailed to England. Lord Sterling reported to Washington on October 25, 1778, that the fleet which had sailed from New York on the previous Monday and Tuesday, was bound, mostly for Europe. There were, however, few troops on board, other than invalids, transfers to other regiments, and some families.[49] Sterling also reported in the same letter that some Waldeckers and other troops had actually gone aboard the transports which appeared to be preparing to sail to the West Indies. He added that the escorts for the transports, seven or eight smaller ships of the line and at least twelve frigates, were also at Sandy Hook.[50]

Another report was that the troops on Staten Island were ready to embark, probably for the West Indies, and that they were destroying their fortifications.[51]

Mackenzie's diary contains a very detailed breakdown of the forces constituting General Clinton's command as of October 25, 1778. Under the heading of Embarked for Florida, he listed 551 rank and file of the Waldeck Regiment fit for duty and 660 effectives. The provincials of Allen's and Chalmer's units totaled 390 fit for duty and 442 effectives. Other units designated for transfer to East Florida brought the total force over 4,750 effectives.[52]

Not counted among the effectives, but also making the voyage to Pensacola, were most of the wives of the soldiers. On one transport, *Crawford*, there were four wives and their children.[53]

An October 16, 1778, embarkation list of members of the Waldeck Regiment embarked at Staten Island was signed by Ensign Stierlein. This list is of double importance, as it shows the regiment to be considerably over strength, but also gives the number of women and children sailing with each company. The breakdown by companies was as follows[54].

The 3rd English-Waldeck Regiment

Staff: 5 officers, 2 non-commissioned officers, 2 corporals and privates, and 2 servants - Total -11 persons.

----

1 Company (Grenadiers) - 3 officers, 6 non-commissioned officers, 5 musicians, 126 corporals and privates, 3 servants, 11 wives, and 5 children - Total - 159 persons

----

2 Company (Captain Alberti): 3 officers, 8 non-commissioned officers, 4 musicians, 123 corporals and privates, 2 servants, 7 wives, and 1 child - Total - 148 persons.

----

3 Company (Colonel von Hanxleden): 4 officers, 8 non-commissioned officers, 4 musicians, 124 corporals and privates, 4 servants, 8 wives, and 5 children - Total - 157 persons.

----

4 Company (Captain Pentzel): 3 officers, 7 non-commissioned officers, 4 musicians, 121 corporals and privates, 2 servants, 4 wives, and 4 children - Total - 145 persons.

----

5 Company (Major von Horn): 3 officers, 6 non-commissioned officers, 3 musicians, 123 corporals and privates, 2 servants, and 5 wives - Total - 145 persons.

Artillery: 2 non-commissioned officers, and 10 corporals and privates.

Total: 21 officers, 39 non-commissioned officers, 20 musicians, 629 corporals and privates, 15 servants, 35 wives, and 15 children - Total - 774 persons.

(Major von Horn had gone to Europe on leave and Quartermaster Sergeant Johann Philipp Frese (W200498) had been ordered back to Waldeck, probably on recruiting duty,)

Lieutenant Colonel Francis Downman of the Royal Artillery recorded the weather on November 1, 1778, as windy, cold, and rainy, as the convoy in which he sailed for the West Indies moved south from New York. That fleet apparently halted at Sandy Hook where next morning a north wind and clear skies made a very cold day. Finally, on November 3, the fleet went underway very early in the morning.[55]

The 3rd English-Waldeck Regiment

Kemble recorded that the Waldeckers and some provincials sailed under Brigadier General Campbell, and Clinton reported to Germain that Campbell's reinforcements, including the Waldeckers, had sailed with General Grant's forces on November 3, 1778.[56]

One fleet, which sailed from Sandy Hook on November 3, had grown to at least 108 ships, and with a favorable wind, after weighing anchor at seven o'clock in the morning, was out of sight of Amboy, within an hour.[57]

Because a variety of troop movements were taking place at this time, there is considerable confusion concerning fleets and sailing dates. On November 6 another convoy of troops sailed for Georgia under a Lieutenant Colonel [Archibald] Campbell. As Clinton had not been seen in New York for several days, the Americans speculated that he might have sailed with one of the fleets. If this were the case, New York would soon be in American hands again. But Clinton had not sailed, and if he had, it would have made little difference in the situation, as both a fleet, which sailed on November 3 and the one which sailed on November 6, returned from Sandy Hook to The Watering Place at Staten Island on November 12.[58]

On November 18, Clinton reported to Germain that the ships of the southern expedition still could not sail because of gale winds, and that several had been driven ashore and ten others had been driven out to sea from the Sandy Hook anchorage.[59]

One week later, on November 24, Clinton wrote that the fleet was again in condition to sail and he hoped the ships would sail that day. However, it was not until November 27 that the fleet once again sailed south.[60]

Lord Sterling reported to Washington on November 28, 1778, from Elizabethtown, that a "Second Embarkation of Troops from New York, is at length put to sea." The fleet had dropped down to Sandy Hook the day before, and sailed during the afternoon. Sterling was of the opinion that the 45-ship fleet

The 3rd English-Waldeck Regiment

was bound for the Floridas. Later that evening he supplied the additional information that the fleet consisted of 33 ships, [2 ships-of-the-line one of 40 and one of 60 guns, and 2 frigates, 1 snow, 9 brigs, and 10 schooners and sloops.[61]

The ships carrying the reinforcements to Pensacola in West Florida, and which had sailed on November 3, had not turned back to New York. Instead they continued on their course while the wind increased and the seas grew mountainous. On November 9, the *Solebay* frigate and nine transports broke off from the main fleet and continued southwest with the Waldeckers and provincials.[62]

The *Solebay*, Captain Thomas Symonds, was a sixth rated ship with 28 guns and a crew of 200 men. One of the transports, *Springfield*, may have been the same ship reported on April 3, 1777, as carrying ordnance stores and Indian presents to St. Augustine.[63]

It seems doubtful that the *Britannia*, on which the Waldeckers sailed to Pensacola, was the same *Britannia* used by General Howe during his stay in America. The general's ship was a big, luxurious ship owned by the East India Company, which had been sent over in 1776 for use by the general and his suite. There were two decks on the ship, each of which contained a hall and four staterooms, plus smaller rooms.[64]

On February 14, 1779, Baurmeister wrote that reports had reached New York from Kingston, Jamaica, that Brigadier General Campbell had arrived there with eight transports on December 5, 1778, and would proceed to Pensacola after a short rest.[65]

The number of deaths among members of the Waldeck Regiment while aboard ship on the voyage from New York to Jamaica, indicate the dangers of putting the new recruits, recently arrived from Europe, on board transport ships after only a brief period for recovery ashore.[66] Those who died during the closing days of 1778, were:

The 3rd English-Waldeck Regiment

Gottlieb Maetsch (W201139), a 1778 recruit for 2 Company, who died on *Britannia* at Staten Island on October 29
Philipp Klopfer (W201123), a 1778 recruit for 4 Company, who died on *Crawford*, at sea, on October 31.
Georg Meyer (W201142), a 1778 recruit for 4 Company, who died on *Crawford*, at sea, on November 5
Peter Braun (W201115), a 1778 recruit for 3 Company, who died on *Springfield* on November 10
Philipp Bauer (W201107), a 1778 recruit for 4 Company, who died on *Crawford*, at sea, on November 27
Christoph Hofmann (W201192), 4 Company, who died on *Crawford*, at sea, on November 28
Kaspar Leidner (W201137), a 1778 recruit for 5 Company, who died on *Britannia* in Port Royal on December 4
Daniel Klapp (W200403), 4 Company, who died on *Crawford* in Port Royal on December 5
Georg Koral (W201127), a 1778 recruit for 4 Company, who died on *Crawford at* Port Royal on December 9
Andreas Kesting (W201120), a 1778 recruit for 4 Company, who died on *Crawford* in Port Royal on December 10
Adam Birck (W201111), a 1778 recruit for 4 Company, who died in the hospital (in New York ??) on December 17
Joh. Philipp Troll (W200476), 4 Company, who died in the hospital (in New York ??) on December 19
Josef Kleineisen (W201122) a 1778 recruit for 5 Company, who died (in the hospital ??) on December 24, and
Philipp Schmidt (W200602), 5 Company, who died in the hospital (in New York ??) on December 24.

Running strength figures for the year 1778, indicate that during most of the year 1778, the Waldeck Regiment was on Staten Island and until the 1778 recruit shipment arrived, the regiment was between 26 and 33 men under strength. After the new men arrived, strength of the regiment increased to nearly 100 men more than the treaty requirement. Losses *en route* to Pensacola took a heavy toll, however, and by December 14, 1778, while lying at Kingston, Jamaica, the regiment was only 48 men over strength.[67]

The 3rd English-Waldeck Regiment

During 1778, 140 new Waldeck recruits sailed for America. Three men died *en route*, however, so that 137 men have been identified as having arrived in New York. Two members of the Waldeck Regiment transferred to the English army and in return, two members of the English 55th Regiment joined the Waldeck Regiment. Therefore, 894 men of the Waldeck Regiment are known to have sailed for America, ten men died *en route*, and 905 men have been identified as having served with the regiment in America, by the end of the year 1778.

There were no battle casualties in 1778, but illness and accident claimed the lives of another thirty men, two of whom were prisoners of war, raising the total non-combat deaths to 107. Seven men have been identified as having been released during the year as invalids, including one known to have returned to Europe. Reports indicate eleven men of the regiment returned to Europe in 1778. One of those was Major von Horn, who returned on leave, and another might have been Quartermaster Sergeant Philipp Frese (W200498), 5 Company, who apparently returned to Waldeck on recruiting duty. Two others who returned according to the victualling report may have been the escort officers, Sebisch and Becker. As they have not been counted as "sailed to" nor "arrived in" America, only nine men can be considered to have returned to Europe during 1778.

No new names were added to the prisoners of war, but 52 men did return to the Waldeck Regiment from prisoner status. One man, previously listed as a deserter, returned to the unit. Another man deserted during 1778, but returned to duty later in the year. An additional eighteen men deserted from prisoner of war status with no intent to return to the regiment. Thus, the number of deserters in 1778 was 19, with two of the men having returned to duty.

In summary, the Waldeck Regiment began the year with an estimated strength of 550 men, plus 106 prisoners of war. The arrival of the new recruits and men from prisoner status, which

The 3rd English-Waldeck Regiment

increased the strength considerably, was partially off-set by non-combat deaths and desertion from prisoner status. As a result, at the end of 1778, the Waldeck Regiment had an estimated strength of 700 men, plus those still prisoners of war.

The 3rd English-Waldeck Regiment
1779

On January 6, 1779, Brigadier General Campbell, having been assigned command in West Florida, superseding Lieutenant Colonel William Stiel of the 60th Regiment, sailed from Port Royal. Possibly part of his command of two provincial battalions and the Waldeck Regiment had sailed earlier.[1]

The Pensacola which General Campbell and the Waldeck troops entered was a small settlement. In 1763 it had contained about 100 huts, and although this number had doubled by 1779, the sight must have been depressing to the men.[2]

A hurricane on the previous October 9, had made the scene even more desolate, having destroyed most of the man-made improvements to the area and driven a number of ships ashore.[3]

Even before the general departed from Port Royal, the governor of Jamaica, John Dalling, had requested the return of a company of his (Dalling's) Regiment, which was in West Florida, and shortly after Campbell's arrival in West Florida, John Lorimer, M.D., was seeking appointment as chief surgeon and purveyor of hospitals in West Florida, at fifteen shillings per day.[4]

Other personnel in the area with whom the general and the Waldeckers seem to have had frequent contact, were: Arthur Niel and a Mr. Moore, both of whom had land holdings in the area between Pensacola and The Cliffs,[5] and Captain Rainsford, the fort adjutant and barracks master at Pensacola.[6]

The governor of West Florida when the Waldeckers arrived was Peter Chester and the lieutenant governor was Captain Elias Durnford, the local engineering officer and technically not within the chain of command for combat troops. Another military officer with important civil duties was John Stuart. He had left Cape Fear River, North Carolina, as a captain in June 1776, and arrived at Pensacola on the 24th of the following month. By 1779, Stuart was a colonel and the Indian Commissioner for the

The 3rd English-Waldeck Regiment

Southern District, just as Guy Johnson was for the Northern District.[7]

After Stuart's death on March 21, 1779, the position became splintered with Alexander Cameron becoming superintendent of the Mississippi District - Chickasaws and Choctaws - and Lieutenant Colonel Thomas Brown became superintendent of the Atlantic Division - Cherokees and Creeks. Stuart's son, Charles, also shared in the confused Indian Affairs Department.[8]

In addition to the troops which accompanied General Campbell, the English 16th Regiment and a portion of the 60th Regiment, the Royal Americans, whose ranks were filled mostly by Germans and criminals, as will be noted below, did not please Campbell.[9]

The miserable conditions which existed in Pensacola and West Florida were set forth in detail by Campbell in a letter to General Clinton, written at Pensacola during the period February 10 to March 21, 1779. There was even a shortage of shipping, which made it impossible for the new commander to send the Waldeck Regiment to the Mississippi as had been planned.[10]

One favorable aspect of the situation facing General Campbell was the fact that the Waldeck Regiment was overstrength and, even allowing for the sick and men still held prisoners of war by the Americans, could provide companies at full strength. On March 19, 1779, the regiment mustered:[11]

1 - Colonel	1 - Major (on leave)
3 - Captains	2 - Capain Lieutenants
5 - 1st Lieutenants	5 - Sub Lieutenants
1 - Adjutant	1 - Regimental Quartermaster
1 - Chaplain	1 - Regimental Surgeon
1 - Commissary	6 - Surgeon's Mates
1 - Regimental Drummer	2 - Provost and Assistant
2 - Wagon Servants	32 - Corporals, (2 sick)
30 - Non-commissioned officers (1 Sergeant recruiting)	
21 - Musicians (3 sick, 1 PW)	
15 - Servants	5 - Solicitors

The 3rd English-Waldeck Regiment

571 - Privates (27 sick, 11 PW)
Total - 707 men (1 sergeant, 2 corporals, 1 surgeon's mate, and 33 privates over treaty strength.)

While Campbell was wondering how to move the Waldeck Regiment even farther from its European homeland, the Prince of Waldeck realized he did not know where his subjects were. In March 1778, he had written to the English court to ask what had become of his regiment of soldiers.[12]

If he had known what his soldiers had been experiencing, and what was in their future, he would surely have called them home. Fourteen more of his men had apparently been left behind to die in the hospital at New York, many more were to die in West Florida, and still others were to die as prisoners of war in New Orleans, Vera Cruz, and Havana.

Those who were to die in New York in 1779, were:[13]

Johannes Francke (W201132), 1 Company, on January 2
Philipp Moehlen (W200439), 4 Company, on January 4
Christoph Thomas (W201151), 2 Company, on January 7
Henrich Kabel (W201118), 2 Company, on January 11
Andreas Heckenroth (W201135), 4 Company, on January 16
Henrich Caspar (W201119), 2 Company, on January 25
Cpl. Wilhelm Schwalbach (W200504), 5 Company, on February 3
Christoph Lende (W201138), 4 Company, on February 7
Michael Betz (W200643), 5 Company, on April 5
Hermann Ohms (W200091), 1 Company, on April 27
Johannes Hammersdorf (W200185), 2 Company, on May 2
Johannes Pflantzer (W200748), 5 Company, on May 6
Christoph Freese (W200697), 1 Company, on May 20, and
Georg Andreas (W201106), 1 Company, on May 27.

The long sea voyage, the change of climate, and the increasing deterioration of the health of the soldiers of the Waldeck Regiment was reflected in a high death rate among the men who arrived in Pensacola and remained there during 1779. The following individuals died at Pensacola during the year.[14]

The 3rd English-Waldeck Regiment

Provost Konrad Glaentzer (W400002), of the staff, on April 17
Michael Schart (W200764), 4 Company, on May 11
Hermann Hundertmarck (W200721), 4 Company, on May 21
Kaspar Hohmann (W200718), 3 Company, on May 28
Leonhard Truebendorfer (W200798), 5 Company, on June 3
Andreas Homburger (W200719), 3 Company, on June 8
Johannes Behr (W200638), 1 Company, on June 29
Christian Nolte (W200090), 1 Company, on July 7
Eberhard Leydenberg (W200073), 1 Company, on July 10
Franz Schneider (W200775), 5 Company, on July 14
Johannes Schmidt (W200350), 3 Company, on August 11
Michael Sachs (W200757), 4 Company, on August 14
Wilhelm Range (W200587), 5 Company, on August 17
Wilhelm Schade (W200761), 3 Company, on August 29
Friedrich Marckert (W200728), 3 Company, on September 29
Capt/arms Philipp Schaeffer (W200379), 4 Company, on October 17
Cpl. Christian Goette (W200703), 2 Company, on October 19
Sgt. Henrich Todt (W200372), 4 Company, on October 22
Johann Georg Meyer (W200128), 1 Company, on October 26
Friedrich Albracht (W200266), 3 Company, on November 5
Christoph Meyer (W200078), 4 Company, on December 4
Leonhard Weitner (W200807), 2 Company, on December 4
Friedrich Bauer (W200270), 3 Company, on December 8, and
Henrich Kuempel (W200676), 4 Company, on December 20.

General Campbell arrived in West Florida with orders not only to defend Pensacola and Mobile, but to establish a post near the Mississippi River and to defend English settlers in the area. He had insufficient shipping to move the needed troops in a body and the Waldeck Regiment, which he had "no objections to on account of military subordination and their commanding officer I both esteem and respect," were "unfit for active duty, their appointments, their dress, their discipline, nay their very make and form of body, disable them from acting with that rapidity and spirit ... necessary to repel an invader... They are improper troops for the woods and wilds of America," but probably good garrison soldiers. Still the limits of his command decreed that he send them to the Mississippi post, then located at Manchac.[15]

The 3rd English-Waldeck Regiment

A monthly return of the Waldeck Regiment signed by General Campbell, as of April 1, 1779, provides the following information.[16]

Officers and staff present - 1 colonel, 3 captains, 2 captain lieutenants, 1 1st lieutenant, 1 2nd lieutenant, 4 ensigns, 1 lieutenant and quartermaster, 1 ensign and adjutant, 1 chaplain, 1 judge advocate (auditor), 1 surgeon, 6 surgeon's mates, 1 drum major, 1 provost, and 1 assistant to the provost, and two wagon servants.

    Present for Duty: 28 sergeants, 17 drummers and fifers, 559 rank and file, 2 artillery sergeants, and 12 artillery rank and file
        Absent on Command and Recruiting: 1 sergeant
        Prisoners of the Rebels: 1 drummer and 11 rank and file
        Sick: 1 sergeant, 3 drummers and fifers, 20 rank and file
Total effectives: 30 sergeants, 21 drummers and fifers, 599 rank and file, 2 artillery sergeants, and 12 artillery rank and file.
    Wanting to Complete: None
    Above authorization: 1 sergeant and 31 rank and file.
    Since last report: 2 dead.
    Absent Officers: Major von Horn, since October 19, 1778, by leave of the commander-in-chief.
    N.B.: Lieutenant Heldring doing duty as assistant engineer. Ensign von Axleben under arrest by Colonel von Hanxleden for behavior unbecoming the character of a gentleman and an officer.

The situation at Pensacola seemed to be one of ever-new difficulties and misfortunes. In March 1779, The Indian Commissioner, Colonel Stuart, had died. In April, Campbell reported the annual fleet had apparently lost two ships during the Atlantic crossing and the *Lord Townsend* and its cargo had been totally destroyed in Port Royal harbor in Jamaica. Therefore, instead of twelve months supply of flour, Pensacola only had enough for fourteen weeks and there was only a little Indian corn as a substitute. The meat supply was adequate.[17]

Campbell also wrote to Admiral John Byron on May 1, 1779, that a naval force was much wanted at Pensacola,[18] and in England efforts to get sixty tons of shipping to carry Indian presents were in vain.[19]

The 3rd English-Waldeck Regiment

Meanwhile, the West Florida residents wanted to recall Governor Peter Chester, described as a weak-minded, avaricious tyrant, who had committed improper acts, and the new Indian Commissioner Cameron was pleading that "if properly supported", he could manage the Indians.[20]

Campbell's soon-to-be antagonist, Bernardo de Galvez, at New Orleans, was having problems, also, and feeling that his forces were inadequate to defend the Spanish territories from the superior English forces under General Campbell. On July 3, 1779, Galvez reported to the Governor of Havana that the English had reinforced Pensacola and that there were 400 men at Manchac and 300 Waldeck soldiers expected as an addition. While the British said the increased forces were being sent out in anticipation of an American attack down the Mississippi, Galvez was sure the build-up was directed against the Spaniards. But, instead of complaining about his situation as Campbell did under like circumstances, Galvez wrote that although he had only 400 men, many recruits unfamiliar with arms, he would see what he could do with what he had.[21]

And, while Galvez told his superiors the English were saying the Americans were coming down the Mississippi as an excuse to strengthen British defenses in the Mississippi region, Lieutenant Colonel Alexander Dickson at Manchac was reporting to General Campbell that the Spaniards were his source of information concerning the same movement against West Florida.[22]

In an attempt to carry out his orders to strengthen the post at Manchac, General Campbell sent a force of 300 men from the 16th and Waldeck Regiments, under Lieutenant Colonel Dickson, to the Mississippi area in the spring of 1779,[23] and von Eelking wrote that the grenadiers of the Waldeck Regiment were sent to Baton Rouge in 1779, and were followed by a company under Major von Horn, fifteen men of Colonel von Hanxleden's Company, and the Company of Captain Alberti.[24]

The 3rd English-Waldeck Regiment

As soon as the Waldeck Grenadiers arrived at Manchac, they began to suffer a disproportionately large number of deaths due to illness. Those who died at Manchac, all of 1 Company, except as noted, were:[25]

Jakob Bangert (W200023), on July 26
Sergeant Wilhelm Goedeling (W200702), on July 26
Karl Werbein (W200121), on July 26
Christoph Mueller (W200081), on July 28
Konrad Koenig (W200045), on August 1
Christian Scheuermann (W200101), on August 4
Georg Kluss (W200038), on August 5
Johannes Flamme (W200060), on August 5
Adam Schuettler (W200109), on August 7
Konrad Fischer (W200059), on August 8
Sergeant Konrad Thiele (W200003), on August 12
Christian Koppe (W200047), on August 13
Johannes Schleiermacher (W200102), on August 19
Daniel Sondermann (W200789), on August 17. His wife also died in 1779.
Henrich Neuschafer (W200087), on August 20
Johannes Weber (W200120), on August 23
Philipp Reismann (W200503), on August 24 (Transfer from 4 Company)
August Saltzmann (W200758), on August 27
Jost Pfennig (W201145), on August 27
Johannes Schaeffer (W200098), on August 28
Henrich Werner (W200489), on August 30
Johannes Frantz (W200296), on September 2
Johannes Stracke (W200111), on September 4, and
Michael Hoehle (W200550), 5 Company, on September 5.

On August 21, 1779, General Clinton wrote to Germain from New York, that unless Spain declared war, West Florida would be perfectly secure if only a frigate or two could be spared to protect Pensacola. The Pensacola defenses had been demolished by a hurricane the previous October.[26]

But Spain had already declared war on England. Senor Don Josef de Galvez, Governor of Havana, set forth the Spanish strategy for the war in America in a letter to one of his generals, Diego Josef Navarro, on August 29, 1778. The King of Spain

The 3rd English-Waldeck Regiment

had dictated the principal objective of Spanish arms in America during the war with England was to drive the English from the Gulf of Mexico and the banks of the Mississippi. The local forces were not to await assistance from Spain, but were to use available forces to attack Mobile and Pensacola. As Pensacola had probably received large reinforcements, Navarro was to mass 4,000 or 5,000 men, to prevent failure, and place everyone under the command of Bernardo de Galvez. This Galvez had won the support of the Choctaw Indians, also. A fleet was being assembled. The Americans were to launch a co-ordinated attack along the Mississippi at the same time, amd the French were to be asked to lend support.[27]

Even as the Governor of Havana was explaining the overall strategy, Bernardo de Galvez was carrying the war to the English, and on September 7, 1778, captured Fort Bute at Manchac. The 21-man garrison was made prisoners of war.[28]

The Spaniards at this period of the war also captured eight British vessels in the Mississippi-Manchac area, including one with a number of Waldeck troops on board. These troops were to have been a much needed reinforcement to Lieutenant Colonel Dickson's command.[29]

There is some variation in reporting the number of Waldeck soldiers captured at this time, on the Amite River, as Haynes puts the figure at 55, and Haarmann gives a figure of 56 men on the boat. However this may be only a variation in wording, as Ensign Noelting was killed fighting the attack by the Spaniards, leaving 55 men taken captive. Noelting had been wounded when the Spaniards ambushed the transport on the Amite River on September 4, 1779, and died of his wounds that night.[30]

According to Dickson's report the detachment of the Waldeck Regiment at the Amite River had 1 captain, 3 sergeants, 1 drummer, 1 servant, and 49 rank and file, all of whom were made prisoners of war. There were no Waldeck soldiers reported captured at Manchac, but at Thompson's Creek, the Spaniards made eight Waldeckers prisoners of war.[31]

The 3rd English-Waldeck Regiment

The following would seem to be a complete roster of the men of 2 Company captured with Captain Alberti on the Amite River on September 4, 1779.[32] Those with an asterisk died during their captivity:

Captain Christoph Alberti (W100004)
Servant Jakob Becker (W201169)*
Sergeant Dietrich Schotte (W200131)
Sergeant Friedrich Schum (W200782)*
Free Corporal Bernhard Schreiber (W200779C)
Drummer Johannes Unger (W200143)
Corporal Henrich Gockel (W200136)
Corporal Johannes Lutz (W200139)
Corporal Jeremias Warlich (W200142), (previously a drummer)
Daniel Beisenhertz (W200147)
Henrich Berges (W200148)
Jakob Blaufus (W200151)
Philipp Boettger (W200152)*
Otto Bruehne (W200153)*
Friedrich Budde (W200154)*
Leonhard Kabel (W200155)*
Balthasar Kaltwasser (W200156)
Josef Carnish (W200660)
Henrich Klaus (W200167)
Friedrich Kluecke (W200667)
Valentin Kreutzer (W200673)*
Ludwig Kuester (W200162)
Henrich Kuethe (W200163)
Philipp Decker (W200681)
Daniel Dietz (W200166)*
Christian Diste (W200144)
Jost Johann Drewes (W200158)
Henrich Fischer (W200175)
Georg Friedeborn (W200177)
Johannes Gockel (W200180)
Ernst Hahne (W200184)
Dietrich Hinterthuer (W200716)
Johannes Loefler (W200727)
Johannes Meybaum (W200200)
Bernhard Munthenck (W200207)

The 3rd English-Waldeck Regiment

Barthold Nasemann (W200208)*, died at Vera Cruz, August 6, 1780
Josef Perle (W200744)
Henrich Pfeil (W200209)
Philipp Rabensprock (W200210)
Henrich Reinhard (W200212), died on ship near Havana, February 12, 1781
Christian Roelcke (W200213)*
Adolf Schaake (W200759)*
Bernhard Schaper (W200216)
Ludwig Schnitzius (W200224)
Josef Schrantz (W200225)
Friedrich Sonnenschein (W200229)*
Henrich Stiesing (W200232)
Johannes Stoecker (W200233)
Eberhard Stoessel (W200793)
Stefan Struebe (W200234)
Ludwig Stuckenbruck (W200235)*, died on ship near Havana, September 4, 1780
Christian Tente (W200239)*
Konrad Trost (W200132)*, demoted from captain-at-arms, August 1779
Christoph Voepel (W200241)*
Johannes Wagener (W200243)

The Waldeck Regiment had lost a man on the Amite River previously when Henrich Flamme (W201176), 5 Company, servant for Lieutenant Leonhardi, drowned on August 12, 1779.[33] Other details of his accident are unknown, but the date indicates he left Pensacola early in the campaign.

The *Carteret* packet delivered notice of the Spanish declaration of war to General Campbell on September 9, 1779, after a quick passage, but the news arrived too late to help the British commander. Nothing seemed favorable for the defense of West Florida, but by detaining the *Carteret*, the general would at least have an armed vessel available for such use as might be necessary. Items of interest prior to receipt of the declaration of war were forwarded to England aboard the packet *Comet*.[34]

Upon receipt of the news of an expanded war, General Campbell began action to notify his field commanders that Spain had declared war and that the commanders were to prepare to launch attacks against the Spanish posts.[35] When the general requested a boat to carry his message to Manchac and other parts of West Florida, he was informed that no boat was available. He next requested the governor to declare martial law so as to force the local inhabitants to serve the military as need might arise, but the council of West Florida decided such action was illegal. The council did issue a proclamation commanding the inhabitants to enroll in the militia.[36]

So General Campbell wrote to his superior, General Clinton, in New York, that orders to attack the Spaniards could not be carried out. There was a lack of shipping, a shortage of artillery, and he, Campbell, had no confidence in his troops. Desertions were numerous, sickness was increasing, and Manchac was not safe. If Manchac were to fall, the security of the English Mississippi settlements would vanish.[37] Campbell did not know that it had already fallen and the situation was much worse than he imagined.

When Lieutenant Dickson decided to abandon the fortifications at Manchac, the Waldeckers at that post were sent to new defensive positions which had been selected at Baton Rouge. Later the rest of the command followed the men of Waldeck. On September 12, 1779, Galvez invested the new site, which properly could only be called a field redoubt, having been built in just six weeks. The garrison of 400 regulars under Lieutenant Colonel Dickson was drawn from the 16th and 60th Regiments, the Waldeck Regiment, a small independent company, and a Royal Artillery detachment, and was augmented by 150 settlers and armed negroes. A nine day siege ended when Galvez was able to set up his artillery. He opened fire on September 21 and after a three hour bombardment, the British at Baton Rouge surrendered.[38]

According to the articles of capitulation signed by Don Galvez and Lieutenant Colonel Dickson, the garrison was to march out with military honors and was to be taken back to

The 3rd English-Waldeck Regiment

Pensacola in Spanish vessels. Provisions used by the garrison *en route*, were to be paid for before the men could debark, however. The sick were to be provided for and those unable to move with the garrison were to be allowed to return when their condition permitted. But Galvez took exception to some of the provisions of the pact and insisted upon the garrison being made prisoners of war to be exchanged at the pleasure of the Spanish king. He also insisted that the fort at Manchac be surrendered by Dickson, but those troops would be allowed to return to Pensacola or Jamaica.[39]

No one from the garrison was to be maltreated in any way, and the civilian residents of the area were free to resettle, selling their property to the Spanish governor or remaining and becoming Spanish citizens, without being required to take up arms against England. Weapons, artillery, and provisions in general, were to become Spanish property.

Lieutenant Colonel Dickson felt compelled to write an apologia for surrendering his command, and the inhabitants of Baton Rouge and Natchez provided letters thanking him for his honorable resistance and for obtaining favorable terms regarding their future treatment by the Spaniards.[40]

The 3rd English-Waldeck Regiment

As to Waldeck losses at Baton Rouge, Lowell lists 25 Germans (Waldeckers) killed and eight wounded.[41] Von Eelking mentions two captains, three lieutenants, and three surgeon's mates of the Waldeck Regiment as being made prisoners at Baton Rouge, but seems to have put all the Waldeck losses in the Mississippi area together when he wrote that Waldeck lost Ensign Noelting, Lieutenant Leonhardi, and 22 others, plus a number wounded, and 200 officers and men made prisoners of war.[42]

Haarmann gives the losses at Baton Rouge as two officers and two enlisted men killed, and one officer and 29 other enlisted men, who later died of their wounds, among the 17 officers and 358 enlisted men of all English and German units who were made prisoners of war. He added that Captain Forster surrendered Fort Panmire at Natchez to the Spaniards on October 5, 1779, and that the Spaniards also had seized the small posts at Thompson's Creek and on the Amite River, making more than a score of men prisoners.[43]

An undated report of losses suffered by Lieutenant Colonel Dickson's West Florida command, in addition to those previously mentioned for Natchez and the Amite River, included: 2 captains, 3 lieutenants, 3 surgeon's mates, 8 sergeants, 6 drummers, 3 servants, and 176 rank and file made prisoners of war from the Waldeck Regiment. The Regiment also lost Ensign Noelting and one enlisted man killed, and 1 lieutenant, 1 surgeon's mate, 2 sergeants, and 19 rank and file dead since being made prisoners, including Lieutenant Leonhardi, who died *en route* to New Orleans.[44]

According to von Eelking, Lieutenant Leonhardi had distinguished himself at the storming of Fort Washington and again in this situation. Von Eelking also notes that the Waldeck soldiers had one officer, one non-commissioned officer, and six privates slightly wounded at Baton Rouge.[45]

Known Waldeck casualties at Baton Rouge, were:[46]

The 3rd English-Waldeck Regiment

Georg Hahne (W200067), 1 Company, killed on September 21
Surg. Mate Daniel Beck (W200255), 3 Company, slightly wounded
Christian Brand (W200519), 5 Company, slightly wounded
Christian Hausmann (W200544), 5 Company, slightly wounded
Valentin Linde (W200074), 1 Company, slightly wounded, and
Stefan Wichard (W200123), 1 Company, slightly wounded.

Another twelve men of the Waldeck Regiment died of illness at Baton Rouge prior to the capitulation, on dates indicated:[47]

Friedrich Schroeder (W200351), 3 Company, on September 6
Christoph Andre (W200019), 1 Company, on September 8
Friedrich Kober (W200040), 1 Company, on September 10
Henrich Dicke (W200289), 1 Company, on September 12 (transfer from 3 Company)
Johannes Faust (W200057), 1 Company, on September 12. His wife and child also died in 1779
Johann Georg Schaeffer (W200593), 5 Company, on September 13
Henrich Voepel (W200609), 5 Company, on September 13
Ludwig Meltzer (W200731), 5 Company, on September 14
Paul Oberlaender (W200739), 1 Company, on September 15
Henrich Mincke (W200570), 5 Company, on September 17
Jakob Haase (W200542), 5 Company, on September 18, and
Paul Bless (W200648), 1 Company, on September 19.

The following Waldeck personnel were made prisoners of war by Spain as a result of the capture of Baton Rouge and the outlying fortifications.[48] Those with an asterisk died during their captivity:

Captain Georg von Haacke (W100006)
1st Lieutenant Andreas Brumhard (W100017)
1st Lieutenant Karl Henrich Strubberg (W100009)
Sgt. Kaspar von Nehm (W200004)
Sgt. Henrich Schluckebier (W200002)*
QM Sgt. Alexander Siegler (W200110)*
Surg. Mate Ludwig Zick (W200006)*
Fifer Christoph Steinmeyer (W200013)
Drummer Jakob Matte (W200016)

The 3rd English-Waldeck Regiment

Drummer Theodor Repp (W200015)
Servant Lorenz Goebert (W200064)*
Cpl. Bernhard von Canstein (W200046)*
Cpl. Johannes Meisner (W200008)
Cpl. Philipp Mueller (W200084)
Cpl. Christoph Roemer (W200010)
Cpl. Christoph Weishaupt (W200012)
Cpl. Gottfried Wiegand (W200613) (transfer from 5 Company)
Ludwig Bauerschmidt (W200024)
Ludwig Berges (W200025)
Wilhelm Berghoever (W200026)
Georg Andreas Bock (W200027)
Johann Georg Bock (W200518)
Adam Kann (W200030)
Johannes Kann (W200031)
Henrich Kauffmann (W200033)
Johannes Kesthans (W200034)
Emanuel Kestings (W200035)*
Konrad Kleine (W200036)*
Jost Stefan Kluecker (W200037)
Barthold Knoechel (W200159)
Johannes Krafft (W200670)
Franz Cramer (W200048)
Johannes Kratz (W200049)*
Johann Jost Dantz (W200164)*
Thomas Dantz (W200053)
Henrich Ebersbach (W200055)
Andreas Eichinger (W200687)
Christoph Eisenberg (W200170)
Johannes Embde (W200056)
Peter Ernst (W200689)
Gottlieb Fichtner (W200692)
Jost Fischer (W200058)*
Philipp Hamel (W200068)
Daniel Hartmann (W200070)
Philipp Henrich (W200306) (transfer from 3 Company)
Henrich Herbold (W200071)
David Huthmann (W200722)
Henrich Landberger (W200724)*
Valentin Linde (W200074), wounded at Baton Rouge in September 1779
Johannes Michel (W200568)

The 3rd English-Waldeck Regiment

Johannes Moock (W200079)
Christian Mueller (W200645)
Karl Mueller (W200082)*
Kaspar Mueller (W200335), (transfer from 3 Company)
Konrad Mueller (W200083)
Nikolaus Mueller (W200694)*
Ferdinand Neumann (W200085)
Johannes Neumeyer (W200086)*
Anton Noll (W200088)
Friedrich Oppendahl (W200742)
Wilhelm Pique (W200093)
Henrich Riese (W200097)
Friedrich Rodewald (W200590)
Johannes Runte (W200458) (transfer from 4 Company)
Johannes Schaeffer (W200630)
Wilhelm Schaeffer (W200763)*
Johannes Schmidt (W200104)* (no record of capture, but died as prisoner)
Georg Schrauff (W200107)*, died on ship September 22, 1780
Konrad Schrauff (W200627)*
Ulrich Schreiber (W200108)
Friedrich Schwencke (W200227)
Henrich Wilhelm Stallmann (W200791)
Henrich Striepecke (W200114)
Jacob Walter (W200118)
Johann Henrich Weber (W200802)
Gottlob Weiss (W200804)
Johannes Weitner (W200806)*
Georg Weybrenner (W200811)*
Stefan Wichard (W200123), wounded at Baton Rouge in September 1779
Johannes Wuertz (W200813)*
Friedrich Zimmermann (W200126)

From 3 Company

Surg. Mate Daniel Beck (W200255), wounded at Baton Rouge in September 1779
Cpl. Johannes Holtzappel (W200311)* (previously a private)
Cpl. Georg Rupp (W200755)
Christoph Arend (W200269)
Karl Kleine (W200283)
Peter Kremer (W200286)
Balthasar Kreutzer (W200672)*
Christian Kriegsmann (W200105)* (transfer from 2 Company)

The 3rd English-Waldeck Regiment

Michael Erle (W200688)*
Christian Figge (W200291)
Matthies Flamme (W200293)
Johannes Goebel (W200300)
Henrich Hoelscher (W200310)
Stefan von Horn (W200312)*, died at Havana, December 16, 1780
Johannes Leeser (W200315)*
Christoph Meier (W200325)
Johannes Meuske (W200330)
Konrad Meyer (W200331)
Johannes Mitze (W200332)*
Daniel Mueller (W200334)
Franz Schirr (W200346)
Hermann Seil (W200352)*
Kaspar Stempfler (W200792)
Jost Stremme (W200359)*

From 4 Company

Four Company which had remained in Pensacola, suffered no losses due to combat in 1779.

From 5 Company

Capt. Lt. Augustin Alberti (W100008)
1st Lt. Wilhelm Leonhardi (W100016)*
Sgt. Christoph Frese (W200494)*
Sgt. Gustav Renno (W200495)*
Sgt. Theodor Wildstach (W200496)
Capt. at Arms Franz Henkeler (W200497)
Free Cpl. August Hohmann (W200500C)*, apparently his commission as an ensign had not yet reached him at the time of his capture
Surg. Mate Friedrich Schrage (W200778)* (transfer from 3 Company)
Fifer Johann Henrich Koch (W200506)
Drummer Johannes Vahle (W200509)
Drummer Philipp Wiegand (W200508)
Cpl. Bernhard Berges (W200501)
Cpl. Philipp Muus (W200009)* (transfer from 3 Company)
Cpl. Wilhelm Schaeffer (W200595)
Cpl. Wilhelm Scriba (W200785)
Cpl. August Simshaeuser (W200502)
Cpl. Jean Tuitel (W201152)
Servant Henrich Ulenbruch (W200099), possibly Captain Lieutenant August Alberti's servant

The 3rd English-Waldeck Regiment

Johannes Assmann (W200511)
Georg Bauer (W200512)
Andreas Baumueller (W200513)*
Johannes Becker (W200514)
Johannes Berges (W200515)
Henrich Bergmann (W200640)*
Christian Bickmann (W200516)
Otto Bigge (W200517)*
Ludwig Bornemann (W200652)*
Christian Brand (W200519), wounded at Baton Rouge in September 1779
Daniel Brandstein (W200520)
Johannes Burghard (W200522)
Johannes Burr (W200657)*
Jakob Kahler (W200659)*
Bernhard Kern (W200661)*
Wilhelm Koehler (W200044)* (transfer from 1 Company)
Johannes Conet (W200669)
Siegfried Kramer (W200671)
Konrad Kruse (W200526)*
Friedrich Deierlain (W200683)
Philipp Duesse (W200528)
Johannes Durst (W200529)
Jakob Engelhard (W200530)
Henrich Francke (W200535)
Georg Frantz (W200696)*
Friedrich Frese (W200536)*
Philipp Gans (W200537)*
Georg Geitz (W200538)
Johannes Goebel (W200540)
Christian Goedecke (W200541)
Joachim Gose (W200704)*
Christian Hansmann (W200544), wounded at Baton Rouge in September 1779
Adam Hartmann (W200545)*
Henrich Heinecke (W200547)
Konrad Hendel (W200548)
Jost Herdes (W200549)*
Hermann Huth (W200553)
Karl Wilhelm Itzmann (W200554)*, jumped overboard and drowned August 14, 1780
Barthold Jaeger (W200555)

The 3rd English-Waldeck Regiment

Karl Junckermann (W200556)
Johannes Lahme (W200557)
Jean de Lior (W200723)
Philipp Luenert (W200561)*, Died at Havana December 4, 1780
Georg Meckel (W200563)*
Kaspar Mechel (W201141)
Zacharias Meier (W200564)
Bernhard Mengeringhausen (W200565)
Jakob Meyer (W200567)
Johannes Mieting (W200569)
Christian Mueller (W200571)*
Franz Mueller (W200572)
Henrich Mundhencke (W200574)*
Andreas Nassler (W200736)*
Daniel von Nehm (W200576)
Wilhelm Neubauer (W200737)
Jakob Wilhelm Nolt (W200578)
Friedrich Nolte (W200579)
Henrich Oehl (W200740)*
Konrad Oschmann (W200581)*
Wilhelm Packe (W200582)*
Henrich Pieper (W200584)
Johannes Rabanus (W200586)*
Johannes Risch (W200751)
Josef Rischer (W200588)
Johannes Rose (W200754)
Ludwig Ruppert (W200756)
Johannes Salzmann (W200591)*
Johannes Schaake (W200 760)*
Jakob Scharschmid (W200596)
Johann Georg Schimmel (W200598)
Friedrich Schmidt, Sr; (W200600)*
Friedrich Schmidt (W201194)
Konrad Schmidt (W200599)
Georg David Schuetler (W200604)*
Wilhelm Schuetz (W200605)*
Michael Stiegler (W200112)*, (transfer from 1 Company)
Georg Tent (W200606)
Johannes Thor (W200607)
Philipp Uhle (W200608)
Christian Ulrich (W200800)*

The 3rd English-Waldeck Regiment

Johannes Vollmar (W200610)
Friedrich Volmar (W200801)*
Johannes Weidenhagen (W200611)
Ludwig Welcker (W200612)
Martin Wetterswald (W200810)
Kaspar Zeiger (W200616), and
Henrich Zimmermann (W200618)

The soldiers made prisoners of Spain in the fall of 1778 in the Mississippi region were held for a time in New Orleans, where the Waldeckers were allowed to enjoy a relative freedom of the city. After several months, the prisoners became a burden to the Spanish governor and on December 31, he wrote to Lieutenant Colonel Don Estaban Miro requesting that officer to propose some means of removing the English prisoners from New Orleans, leaving if need be, only the Germans. Galvez' letter also foresaw the need for extra large supplies of ammunition, should Pensacola be put under siege, and for a flag code to be used if Pensacola were captured before reinforcements for the Spaniards arrived.[49]

Possibly Miro solved the problem by removing all the prisoners. Some, if not all, of the Waldeck prisoners of war were sent to Vera Cruz, Mexico, in 1780, aboard the *Nuestra Senora del Carmen*, and in August 1780, from Vera Cruz to Havana on *El Cayman*.[50]

The death rate due to illness among the men sent to the Mississippi region continued high during their period as prisoners of war of Spain. Those who died, mostly at New Orleans, in the closing days of 1779, are listed here, beginning with Konrad Trost who died on September 5, indicating his capture prior to the fall of Baton Rouge.[51]

Konrad Trost (W200132), 2 Company, on September 5
Friedrich Budde (W200154), 2 Company, on September 9
Valentin Kreutzer (W200673), on September 9
Sgt. Friedrich Schum (W200782), 2 Company, on September 9
Wilhelm Schuetz (W200605), 5 Company, at Baton Rouge on September 22

The 3rd English-Waldeck Regiment

Justus Herdes (W200549), 5 Company, on September 25
1st Lt. Johann Wilhelm Leonhardi (W100016), 5 Company, on September 26 - A list in the Library of Congress gives a date of 1789 which is obviously in error.[52]
Georg Meckel (W200563), 5 Company, on October 6
Otto Bigge (W200517), 5 Company, on October 7
Adolf Schaake (W200759), 2 Company, on October 7
Henrich Mundhencke (W200574), 5 Company, on October 8
Hermann Bergmann (W200640), 5 Company, on October 9
Nikolaus Mueller (W200694), 1 Company, on October 9
Sgt. Christoph Frese (W200494), 5 Company, on October 19
Cpl. Johannes Holtzappel (W200311), 3 Company, on October 11
Friedrich Sonnenschein (W200229), 2 Company, on October 11
Philipp Boettger (W200152), 2 Company, on October 17
Wilhelm Schaeffer (W200763), 1 Company, on October 17
Hermann Seil (W200352), 3 Company, on October 17
Andreas Baummueller (W200513), 5 Company, on October 18
Jakob Becker (W201169), 2 Company, on October 20
Christoph Roelcke (W200213), 2 Company, on October 20
Friedrich Schmidt, Sr. (W200600), 5 Company, on October 21
Christoph Voepel (W200241), 2 Company, on October 22
Philipp Gans (W200537), 5 Company, on October 24
Bernhard Kern (W200661), 5 Company, on October 26
Johannes Weitner (W200806), 1 Company, on October 26
Johannes Leeser (W200315), 3 Company, on October 28
Jost Fischer (W200058), 1 Company, on October 31
Servant Lorenz Goebert (W200064), 1 Company, on October 31
Michael Erle (W200688), 3 Company, on November 3
Surg. Mate Friedrich Schrage (W200778), 5 Company, on November 3
Johannes Schmidt (W200104), 1 Company, on November 8
Christian Ulrich (W200800), 5 Company, on November 8
Konrad Kleine (W200036), 1 Company, on November 12
Johannes Hartmann (W200546), 5 Company, on November 14
Johannes Salzmann (W200591), 5 Company, on November 15
Andreas Nassler (W200736), 5 Company, on November 15
Balthasar Kreutzer (W200672), 3 Company, on November 18
Friedrich Frese (W200536), 5 Company, on November 18
Jakob Kahler (W200659), 5 Company, on November 22
Konrad Kruse (W200526), 5 Company, on November 24
Wilhelm Packe (W200582), 5 Company, on November 25
Georg David Schuetler (W200604), 5 Company, on November 27

The 3rd English-Waldeck Regiment

Konrad Oschmann (W200581), 5 Company, on November 28
Henrich Oehl (W200740), 5 Company, on December 2
Johannes Mitze (W200332), 3 Company, on December 5
Jost Stremme (W200359), 3 Company, on December 7
Jost Dantz (W200164), 1 Company, on December 8
Konrad Schrauff (W200627), 1 Company, on December 8
Cpl. Philipp Muus (W200009), 5 Company, on December 13
Johannes Kratz (W200049), 1 Company, on December 16
Sgt. Gustav Renno (W200495), 5 Company, on December 24, and
Johannes Rabanus (W200586), 5 Company, on December 26.

The 3rd English-Waldeck Regiment

On October 26, 1778, General Campbell, still at Pensacola, resumed his correspondence, writing to Vice Admiral Peter Parker, to request naval assistance. Parker wrote back, 100 days later, from the *Ruby*, at sea, to the effect that when he returned to Jamaica, he would sent what force he could spare to Pensacola.[53]

On October 27, 1779, the captain of the *Earl of Bathurst* wrote from Jamaica that the governor had put back on board part of the stores which he had unloaded. The ship had been held up at Jamaica due to having lost a mast, but would sail next day. It had been a slow crossing apparently, as William Knox wrote to John Boddington that "if the ordnance for St. Augustine goes by the same route as *Earl of Bathurst* took, it will arrive early in the next century."[54]

Campbell wrote to Lieutenant Colonel Fuser (at Savannah ?), on November 3, 1779, about the loss of the Mississippi settlements and expressed his concern that he had too few troops for the defense of Pensacola.[55]

Campbell then closed the year as he had opened it, with a lengthy letter to Germain, explaining all the reasons why he could not do what was expected of him. He had armed ships ready to take a force of 500 men as a reinforcement to the Mississippi region, and then heard of Dickson's capitulation, and had to change his plans to a defense of Pensacola. He even explained that he could have taken an even larger force, but by this time it was too late.[56]

Next the general explained the geography and topography of Pensacola and that he had his men at work fortifying Gage Hill with the hope of having guns mounted there in six weeks. His defensive plans had been weakened, however, when *Carteret* snuck out of port, just as *Earl Bathurst* arrived, and that the departed packet carried off an officer, two sergeants, and 25 men he had sent aboard as marines, plus his best harbor pilot.

Earl Bathurst had brought him none of the artillery, engineering and ordnance stores he had been led to expect, since

The 3rd English-Waldeck Regiment

Governor Dalling had taken all such supplies off the ship in Jamaica. Campbell was going to keep *Earl Bathurst* as a guard ship at Pensacola, mount a large number of guns on board, and anchor the ship within the bar.

The Indians were turning against the English, and Galvez, who captured Baton Rouge with a force containing 1,700 to 1,800 regulars had been reinforced by the Regiment of Spain.

Earl Bathurst, the *Union* sloop, and the victuallers *Earl of Denbigh* and *Brownhall*, just in from Cork, ensured a sufficient food supply, but the *Diligence* and *Comet*, packets, had been captured. The *Stork* was to be condemned and her men and guns put aboard *Earl Bathurst*.

Then to delay actions and put the decision for taking action on Germain, Campbell wrote, that if Germain wanted to go against New Orleans, he knew what was needed in the way of manpower. He must consider also the necessity for a naval force, shallow draft troop transports, and a train of artillery.

Four names appear in the *Hetrina* for the first time in 1779. Because of their assignments, it would appear that three of the men may have been young sons of members of the regiment taken into service not only to fill vacancies which existed, but as a means of providing relief for the families and full rations and pay for the individuals. The newly acquired men taken into the regiment, were[57]

Servant Jakob Becker (W201169), 2 Company, taken into service prior to October

Servant Henrich Flamme (W201176), 5 Company, born in Twiste. He drowned on the Amite River on August 12, 1779.

Fifer Friedrich Peter (W201144), born 1769/70 in Crailsheim, and taken into 4 Company in December 1779, and

David Schneider (W201200), born in Lauterbach, who may have been taken into 3 Company in April 1779, so that he could be tried for theft and then released from the regiment on April 12, 1779.

The 3rd English-Waldeck Regiment

Other personnel changes in the Waldeck Regiment in 1779 included the following:[58]

2nd Lt. Andreas Brumhard (W100017), 1 Company, was promoted to 1st lieutenant in April.
Ensign Henrich Jakob Knipschild (W100013), 3 Company, was promoted to 2nd lieutenant in April.
Ensign Karl von Horn (W100020), was commissioned in January and assigned to 5 Company.
Free Cpl. Karl Mueller (W200378C), 4 Company, was commissioned an ensign in April.
Captain Christian Friedrich Pentzel (W100005), 4 Company was promoted to major in April and went on leave in October.[59]
Free Cpl. Christian Schmidt (W200626C), 3 Company, was commissioned an ensign in April.
Johann Bernhard Hunecke (W200429), 4 Company, became a servant in February.
Daniel Rohde (W200345A), 3 Company was transferred to the Artillery by June.
Lorenz Ulrich (W200364A), 3 Company, was transferred to the Artillery by June.
Surg. Mate Friedrich Schrage (W200778), 3 Company, was transferred to 5 Company in April.
Cadet Bernhard von Canstein (W200046), 1 Company, was promoted to corporal in July.
Free Cpl. August Hohmann (W200500C), 5 Company, was commissioned an ensign in July.
Capt-at-arms Kaspar von Nehm (W200004), 1 Company, was promoted to sergeant in July
Capt-at-arms Konrad Trost (W200132), 2 Company, was demoted to private in August, and
1st Lt. Gerhard Henrich Heldring (W100014), 4 Company, went on leave in October.[60]

Three men were released from the Waldeck Regiment in 1779.[61]

Ensign Friedrich von Axleben (W200001C), 5 Company, was arrested in July for conduct unbecoming an officer, and separated on November 18.

The 3rd English-Waldeck Regiment

Surg. Mate Eberhard Meyer (W200499), 5 Company, was released on April 15, for unknown reasons, and David Schneider (W201200), 3 Company, was released for theft, as noted earlier.

During 1779, 21 men deserted from the Waldeck Regiment. All but one deserted at Manchac. The obvious conclusion to be drawn is that someone had planted a rumor among the soldiers that they would be welcomed into the settlement north of New Orleans, where an estimated 2,600 Germans had made their homes.[62]

The men who deserted, with three exceptions, were from 1 Company (the Grenadier Company). The deserters were:[63]

Konrad Harold (W200714), on July 9
Peter Oppenhaeuser (W200743), on July 9
Henrich Schmidt (W200633), on July 9
Drummer Christian Bauer (W200634), on July 10
Wilhelm Mielig (W200734), on July 17
Georg Wissemann (W200125), on July 17
Cpl. Christian Berlin (W200641), on July 19
Georg Kruhm (W200050), on July 19
Friedrich Mercker (W200732), on July 20
Johannes Braun (W201114), on August 2
Peter Buseck (W200658), on August 7
Peter Zipp (W200816), on August 7
Christoph Graebes (W200708), on August 8
Peter Licht (W200725), on August 8
Friedrich Fischeer (W200695), on August 12
Friedrich Ritter (W200752), on August 13
Franz Eisen (W200411), on August 18
Henrich Hufeisen (W200720), on August 19
Franz Karl Beck (W200636), 5 Company, on September 2 or 3
Franz Meyer (W200733), 5 Company, on September 2, and
Christian Schoenefeld (W200777), 3 Company, who deserted from Baton Rouge on September 12.

While the number of combat deaths suffered by the Waldeck Regiment was minimal during 1779, non-combat deaths took a

The 3rd English-Waldeck Regiment

heavy toll, desertions from the Grenadier Company had increased sharply, and nearly one-half of the regiment was in prisoner of war camp at New Orleans. As a result, personnel of 1 and 5 Company who were still at Pensacola were transferred to 3 Company. The personnel of 2 Company still at Pensacola were transferred to 4 Company, and the Waldeck prisoners of war from 3 Company were transferred, on paper, to 5 Company. The following transfers were reported in December 1779.[64]

Ignatius Bach Staedter (W200021), transferred from 1 Company to 3 Company
Fifer Christian Klee (W200664), transferred from 1 Company to 3 Company

Those transferred from 2 Company to 4 Company, included:

Johannes Becker (W200145)
Matthias Becker (W200146)
Bernhard Beyer (W200149)
Ignatius Bieber (W201110)
Johannes Bless (W200647)
Philipp Block (W200649)
Drummer Wilhelm Boehne (W200651)
Henrich Brabender (W201113)
Cpl. Karl Bruehne (W200135)
Michael Burghard (W200656)
1st Lt. Wilhelm Keppel (W100010)
Georg Kirschner (W200662)
Henrich Knies (W200668)
Cpl. Ernst Kobert (W200140)
Gottfried Kuester (W200161)
Christoph Kussenbauer (W200678)
Georg Dehm (W200682)
Josef Deilinger (W200165)
Christian Dietz (W200621)
Henrich Duckenberg (W200169)
QM Sgt. Henrich Eisenberg (W200133)
Henrich Eisenberg (W200171)

The 3rd English-Waldeck Regiment

Johann Christian Eisenberg (W200172)
Sgt. Christoph Embde (W200130)
Henrich Figge (W200173)
Friedrich Fingerhut (W200174)
Adam Fischer (W200693)
Dietrich Frede (W200176)
Henrich Genuit (W200178)
Henrich Gerhard (W200179)
Christian Goebel (W200063)
Philipp Gosmann (W200182)
Philipp Grimm (W200183)
Philipp Hentze (W200187)
Andreas Herbst (W200188)
George Hoehle (W200189)
Henrich Hoffmann (W200717)
Adam Hohmann (W200190)
Konrad Hohmann (W200191)
Peter Hugen (W200192)
Franz Humbracht (W200193)
Friedrich Jaeger (W200194)
Henrich Loeckel (W200198)
Kaspar Matthias (W200729)
Josef Menckel (W200199)
Henrich Meyer (W200201)
Friedrich Molle (W200202)
Daniel Mueller (W200203)
Henrich Mueller (W200204)
Nikolaus Mueller (W200206)
Georg Peter (W200745)
Drummer Jakob Peter (W200746)
Surg. Mate Karl Pfister (W200134)
Friedrich Roehrig (W200753)
Justus Runte (W200214)
Karl Sander (W200215)
Jakob Schepp (W200217)
Georg Schmeck (W200219)
Jakob Schmeck (W200220)
Konrad Schmidt (W200771)
Henrich Schmidt (W200770)
Ensign Ludwig Schmidt (W200676C)
Karl Schnabel (W200222)

The 3rd English-Waldeck Regiment

Christoph Schuessler (W200781)
Christoph Schultze (W200226)
Friedrich Seck (W200226)
Georg Six (W200228)
Georg Sperling (W200230)
Philipp Tewes (W200794)
Sgt. Jakob Todt (W200129)
Henrich Urspruch (W200240)
Wilhelm Voepel (W200242)
Adam Weinkauff (W200803), and
Jakob Werner (W200122).

Individuuals transferred from 3 Company to 5 Company during December 1779, were:

Christoph Arend (W200269)
Surg. Mate Daniel Henrich Beck (W200255)
Karl Kleine (W200283)
Fifer Johann Henrich Koch (W200506)
Peter Kremer (W200286)
Christian Figge (W200291)
Matthias Flamme (W200293)
Johannes Goebel (W200300)
Henrich Hoelscher (W200310)
Stefan von Horn (W200312)
Christoph Meier (W200325)
Johannes Meuske (W200330)
Konrad Meyer (W200331)
Daniel Mueller (W200334)
Cpl. Georg Rupp (W200755)
Franz Schirr (W200345), and
Kaspar Stempfler (W200792).

Soldiers of the Waldeck Regiment transferred from 5 Company to 3 Company during December 1779, were:

Johann Henrich Koehler (W200524)
Friedrich Cummero (W200677)
Martin Dantzer (W200680)
QM Sgt. Johann Philipp Frese (W200498) (in Europe)

The 3rd English-Waldeck Regiment

Lt. Col. Konrad Albert von Horn (W100003) (in Europe)
Ensign Karl von Horn (W100020) (in Europe)
Henrich Hornsberger (W200552)
Franz Mangel (W200562)
Kaspar Pickel (W200583)
Claude Prieur (W200585)
Johannes Schaeffer (W200592)
Friedrich Schele (W200597)
Thomas Wieser (W200614), and
Franz Ziegler (W200617).

These steps made for a more realistic organization and probably provided better discipline among the men at Pensacola, but the regiment desperately needed replacements from home. On October 14, 1778, Germain had sent returns showing the recruit shipments for the 1779 campaign for the Hessians to the Earl of Suffolk, but the returns for the Ansbach and Waldeck Regiments had not been received from America. Germain estimated ten percent of the establishments would be sufficient.[65]

Allowing for losses *en route* to America, this would have meant that the 1779 recruit shipment for the Waldeck Regiment should have been between 75 and 80 men. The number sent was much smaller, however, and an embarkation return of May 2, 1779, reported 21 Waldeckers of all ranks, including servants, to be the portion of a larger mercenary embarkation which also included 960 Hessians with the Waldeckers. The total aboard the transports, including women, numbered 1,044. There were many deserters from other armies among the recruits, and the others were "raw and clownish".[66] On May 27, 1779, Germain wrote the Lords of Admiraly of a need for a convoy to take recruits to New York, and the Waldeck recruits for West Florida were to wait at Portsmouth until there was transportation going to their destination.[67]

A June 4, 1779, strength report still carried the 1779 recruit shipment for the Waldeck Regiment as being *en route* with one lieutenant colonel plus 22 recruits.[68]

The 3rd English-Waldeck Regiment

In addition to Lieutenant Colonel von Horn, who was returning to America, the recruit shipment consisted of his son, Ensign Karl von Horn (W100020), and the following 21 men:

Friedrich Boehle (W200817), born 1762/63 in Ober-Waroldern, 4 Company

Wilhelm Henrich Boehle (W200818), born 1761/62 in Usseln, 3 Company

Henrich Boltze (W200819), born 1759/60 in Hameln, 3 Company

Adam Brauns (W200820), born 1739/40 in Landau, 3 Company

Henrich Kuethe (W200821), born 1761/62 in Waroldern, 3 Company

Henrich Flamme (W200822), born 1762/63 in Rhenegge, 3 Company

Henrich Flamme (W201124), born 1762/63 in Schmillighausen, 4 Company

Wilhelm Himmelmann (W200823), born 1760/61 in Schmillighausen, 4 Company

Franz Hinterberger (W200824), born 1763/64 in Ochsenffurt, 3 Company

Christian Meisner (W200825), born 1764/65 in Ernshausen, 3 Company

Johannes Misco (W200826), born 1761/62 in Willingen, 4 Company

Alexander Mueller (W200827), born 1749/50 in Holzhausen, 4 Company

Konrad Pape (W200828), born 1751/52 in Pyrmont, 4 Company

Henrich Schnepper (W200830), born 1762/63 in Landau, 3 Company

Anton Schuetz (W200831), born 1760/61 in Dehringhausen, 3 Company

Henrich Schuetz (W200832), born 1760/61 in Volkhardinghausen, 4 Company

Cadet Arnold Schumacher (W200833), born 1744/45 in Korbach, 4 Company

Cadet Friedrich Philipp Sude (W200834), born 1756/57 in Waldeck, 4 Company

Christian Todt (W200835), born 1762/63 in Dehringhausen, 4 Company

August (Justus) Westmeyer (W200836), born 1762/63 in Immighausen, 3 Company, and

Daniel Wiegold (W200837), born 1762/63 in Herzhausen, 2 Company.

The Waldeck Regiment had been over strength upon its arrival at Pensacola, but the unhealthy conditions in Florida had claimed the lives of over one-sixth of the regiment by the end of 1779. On December 22, of that year, the regiment was short of authorization by 5 non-commissioned officers, 1 Corporal, and 47 privates, even allowing for the recruits *en route* to West Florida and counting the men prisoners of war held by the

The 3rd English-Waldeck Regiment

Spaniards and the Americans. As December drew to a close, the regiment consisted of:[69]

1 - Colonel	1 - Lieutenant Colonel (with recruits)
1 - Major	2 - Captains
2 - Captain Lieutenants	5 - Lieutenants
5 - Sub-Lieutenants	23 - Non-coms
29 - Corporals	20 - Musicians
476 - Privates	1 - Quartermaster
1 - Adjutant	1 - Chaplain
1 - Commissary	1 - Surgeon Major
2 - Provost and Assistant	2 - Wagon Servants
15 - Servants	1 - Solicitors

Total: 600 Men

Nevertheless, in London, as late as June 4, 1780, officials still were using figures, including the recruits *en route* to Florida, which indicated the Waldeck Regiment was 72 men over treaty strength.[70]

- - - - - - - -

During 1779, 22 recruits sailed for America but did not arrive there in that year. Four names appear in the records for the first time and seem to represent persons taken into service in America. Therefore the total number of men who had sailed for America was 917, and 909 men have been identified as having served in America. There were two combat deaths and 128 non-combat deaths during the year, not including two wives and one child known to have died during 1779. Two hundred sixty seven men were made prisoners of war, of whom 54 died as prisoners. Three men were released from the regiment and 21 men deserted from posts at Manchac and Baton Rouge. As a result, the estimated strength of the Waldeck Regiment at the end of 1779 was 285 men, plus 221 others held as prisoners of war.

The 3rd English-Waldeck Regiment
1780

The year 1780 began with the Spaniard Don Galvez organizing an expedition against Mobile. In 1763, Mobile had 350 residents and was only slightly larger than Pensacola, but was, nevertheless, one of the more important sites in West Florida.[1]

While Galvez made plans to attack, Campbell, in Pensacola, made excuses. Even the Indians were becoming unfriendly. The Spaniards had gained many Choctaws over to their side, and Governor Chester was turning the Creek Indians against the English by making large land grants, grants of Indian lands, to himself and his friends. Further, the *Brownhall* victualler, carrying Indian presents, had been captured, and the Indians expected to be paid the equivalent of two shillings per day for their services.[2]

On February 12, 1780, the Spaniards were reported in force in Mobile Bay and the ultimate objective appeared to be Pensacola. Without naval assistance, Campbell expected the Spaniards would place his post under siege, as soon as they had captured Mobile.[3]

A gale in Mobile Bay on February 14, which dispersed Galvez' force of 750 men, provided temporary relief for Fort Charlotte, at Mobile,[4] and a storm at Havana on February 22-23, interfered with sending reinforcements to Galvez.[5] But the same hurricane, which destroyed the Spanish fleet at Havana, which was to be used to attack Pensacola, also wrecked a large part of the English squadron from Jamaica, so that Admiral Parker was unable to send assistance to General Campbell.[6]

The elements did not turn Galvez from his goal, however. His force was much stronger than Captain Elias Durnford's 300 men at Fort Charlotte, and on March 1, 1780, Galvez called on Durnford to surrender. This was refused initially, but on March 14, the British capitulated.[7]

The 3rd English-Waldeck Regiment

On March 5, 1780, General Campbell sent the remaining members of the 60th Regiment on the 72 mile march to Mobile. Haarmanns's account states that the Waldeckers set out the next day, and that General Campbell followed with the provincials and some artillery; a total force of 552 men. On March 10, the soldiers arrived at the Tensa River, about thirty miles above Mobile, and stopped to build rafts for moving down the river to Mobile.[8]

The trenches had been opened on the night of March 9, but bad weather had then caused a delay. The Spanish siege did not begin until March 12, when the first battery was put in position. Two days after the artillery commenced firing, Captain Durnford surrendered Fort Charlotte to the Spaniards. According to the Spaniards, 13 officers, 56 sailors, 113 soldiers, 70 militia, and 55 armed Negroes were captured, as well as 35 cannons and eight mortars. No Waldeck soldiers were assigned to the fort at Mobile. During the siege, the defenders also had one man killed and two of the eleven wounded men died later of their wounds.[9]

On March 17, Spanish scouts reported the relief column was in retreat toward Pensacola.[10]

Back at Pensacola, Campbell reported the loss to Germain and told of having marched to relieve the garrison at Mobile, only to arrive on the scene too late to accomplish the task. Of course, responsibility lay elsewhere, as even one frigate of naval aid would have prevented the disaster.[11]

On March 28, 1780, General Campbell reported the Spanish fleet had arrived at Pensacola and the next day gave the strength as 29 sail, including two ships-of-the-line. But in England things were viewed in a rosier light. Germain wrote Campbell on April 4, 1780, that it was too bad Manchac had been lost, but the forces at Jamaica should prevent attacks on Mobile or Pensacola. Germain even understood that the Choctaw would defect to Spain, but was sure the Chickasaws would join with the Cherokees and Creeks to control the Choctaws. And,

Alexander Cameron had reported a party of Indians near Mobile who would aid in protecting that place.[12]

Thomas Brown in Savannah, wrote to Clinton that he had received reports of Pensacola being cannonaded by the Spaniards on March 30, and also that the Creek Indians were helping Campbell, but the Choctaws were being rather backward.[13]

Galvez sent a flag of truce to Campbell on April 20, 1780, proposing the two commanders make an agreement to keep the Indians neutral, but Campbell refused the offer. The English had restrained the Indians. It was the Spaniards who had not done so. In addition, Campbell wrote, the flag of truce had acted like a spy and therefore was being detained.[14]

As if Indian problems were not enough disruption to defensive planning when they involved English-Spanish negotiations, the overall Indian policy of the English suffered due to the deaths of several Indian agents. Following Colonel John Stuart's death, Alexander Cameron, superintendent of the Chickasaws and Choctaws, died. His deputy, Charles Stuart, was captured at Mobile and died in prison, and John McIntosh, the Chickasaw agent, died in Indian country.[15]

Prior to April 5, 1780, the Spanish fleet departed from the Pensacola area, as Lieutenant James McNamara, in *Hound*, and Timothy Kelly, in *Port Royal*, arrived on that date with a convoy of four supply ships from Jamaica. They found the *Stork* condemned and sunk and *Earl Bathurst* disarmed. McNamara decided to stay at Pensacola, to rearm *Earl Bathurst*, and to keep *Port Royal* at Pensacola, also.[16]

Campbell wrote to Admiral Parker on May 13, 17680, that the arrival of sloops *Hound* and *Port Royal*, with their convoy, had deceived the enemy, but proper naval protection was still needed at Pensacola. Campbell also notified Germain that the Spaniards had mistakenly believed the small convoy was larger than it actually was, and that the fortifications had been

The 3rd English-Waldeck Regiment

improved and that there were 1,100 Indians at Pensacola. He also wrote that the Spaniards were afraid of the Indians.[17]

Lieutenant McNamara, captain of the *Hound*, however, wrote that the Spaniards had been blown from Pensacola just before his arrival on April 5 by a strong wind and the fleet had not returned. Captain Robert Dean of the copper-bottomed *Mentor*, which arrived at Pensacola on May 14, 1780, wrote that at that time Pensacola seemed safe from Spanish attack.[18]

England still faced problems of holding the allegiance of the Indians. A majority of the Chickasaws resisted the Spanish effort to turn them against England, but were in need of goods and ammunition. In England, however, the merchants were reluctant to send their ships to Pensacola, so it became necessary to send Indian presents and ordnance stores to Jamaica. The ship *Houghton* was to sail to both Jamaica and Pensacola during 1780, but as of July 1, was still at, or on its way to Portsmouth. As the English government feared Pensacola had already fallen, efforts to assist General Campbell in anyway seemed tentative, but continued.[19]

General Clinton, in the southern colonies, was aware of the deterioration of the situation in Pensacola, but in his opinion, he could do nothing to help. He did not have the necessary escort nor transport vessels to send a relief force, and felt the undertaking of such a voyage would be dangerous. Further, West Florida ought to be supported from Jamaica as he had nothing to spare in men or supplies. If Pensacola were to fall, St. Augustine would become the frontier. Cornwallis would then send Lieutenant Colonel Clark to take command at that place with a command including the Hessian Wissenbach Regiment and some provincials. The elements of the 60th Regiment at St. Augustine would be withdrawn and assigned to Savannah.[20]

The strength figures of General Campbell's command during the spring of 1780 showed nearly 550 Waldeckers in West Florida, plus nearly 600 British troops and provincials. These were the figures in use in New York and London. They certainly did not reflect the true conditions existing in Pensacola after the fall of Manchac, Baton Rouge, and Mobile.[21]

A State of the Regiment of Waldeck, dated Bury Street (London), June 4, 1780, indicates that, including the lieutenant colonel *en route* with one ensign and 21 recruits, the regiment had a total of 742 men and was 72 men over strength.[22]

The 1779 recruit transport of 22 men did arrive in the spring of 1780, but the activity of the *Mentor* and the many Indians at Pensacola probably were more important factors in at least partially offsetting the anxiety of awaiting the anticipated Spanish attack. During May, 1780, *Mentor* captured the Spanish vessels *Conception, St. Joseph,* and *El Santisco Sacremento,* a victualler. An English vessel lost during this period, reportedly taken by an American cruiser, was the packet *Carteret,* but Clinton informed Germain that the mail on board had been saved.[23]

Thomas Brown, whose interpreters received 50 pounds per annum - twenty pounds higher than allowed by the late Mr. Stuart - reported to Germain that a very large body of Creeks had marched to the assistance of General Campbell. Germain could only express the hope that they had arrived in time to cooperate with the King's forces before the Spanish invest Pensacola. Their presence may have had some value, as Charles Shaw, an Indian agent at Savannah, wrote to Germain later in the year that nothing saved Pensacola but a vast body of savages.[24]

In August 1780, *Mentor*, augmented by men from the *Stork*, captured the Spanish sloop *Baton Rouge*,[25] but this minor naval activity could have been nothing more than an annoyance to the Spaniards. Of the various possible causes for the Spanish fleet to leave Pensacola and to have allowed the port to remain open, the explanation of Lieutenant McNamara seems most plausible, and, while a certain fear of the Indians may have effected the Spaniards, the delay in moving on Pensacola once again was probably only due to the desire to mount an overwhelming assault.

Dealing with the Indians was a major consideration in the defense of Pensacola during the fall of 1780. Cameron wrote to Germain that the Chickasaws were reluctant of take part in the war, but one of the Indian agents, McIntosh, had had a party of them scouting in the Mississippi area. Another agent, Bethune, had gone to the Choctaws to try to influence their activities, but a major problem with the Indian attitudes was that Campbell did not know how to treat them, but Galvez did.[26]

On September 6, 1780, Germain wrote to Campbell that he should now have sufficient presents and provisions at Pensacola to retain the Indians, but the Admiralty, a month later, had the *Content* transport in England ready to load 150 tons of Indian presents and 45 tons of camp equipment for West Florida.[27]

Still, Cameron was dissatisfied with General Campbell, In a letter to Germain in late October, Cameron wrote that Campbell understood nothing of Indian affairs and would not support the Indians. Therefore, Cameron had exceeded his estimates in trying to hold the Indians' alligence. The Choctaws were united in the English interest and had harassed the Spaniards at Mobile, but Cameron felt the need to be able to furnish more goods to the Indians. As things stood, and being in poor health, he wished to resign - on half pay.[28]

Campbell also wrote that by the end of October 1780, the Choctaws appeared to have been gained to the English side. Nevertheless, he did not understand the Spaniard's failure to attack Pensacola, and had begun to fortify the Red Cliffs in anticipation of a Spanish assault. Also, rum was scarce and he had to buy clothing for the provincial troops of his command.[29]

At the same time, in England, Germain was writing to Campbell that he did not think Spain would attack Pensacola again, and he even hoped that Mobile could be recovered. Concerning Indian affairs, the local governor of West Florida was no longer to receive an allowance for entertaining the

Indians, and even if Cameron were to be placed over Creek Indian affairs, the various superintendents were to be subject to orders from the King's troop commanders. Additional supplies of Indian presents were to be sent to Pensacola during November 1780.[30]

On October 13, 1780, the ordnance office had requested William Knox to issue orders for victualling 183 Royal Artillery personnel aboard the *Dutton*, an armed storeship bound for Jamaica and Pensacola. Knox, at Whitehall, directed the necessary orders to the Admiralty and informed the ordnance officer that as no answer had been received after repeated inquiries for space on an ordnance ship, the Admiralty would take the Indian presents to Jamaica for forwarding to West Florida. Knox then informed the war office that the *Content* transport would take clothing and camp equipment to Jamaica.[31]

While Knox was concerned with moving supplies to West Florida, Galvez was moving his forces for an attack on Pensacola. In October 1780, Galvez sailed from Havana with a fleet of 64 warships and transports carrying 4,000 troops. Once again, however, Pensacola was saved by a hurricane which dispersed Galvez' fleet. He arrived back at Havana on November 17.[32]

Unaware of the Spanish fleet *en route* to Pensacola, Germain was sending secret information from London to Campbell that an attack was to be made on New Orleans from Jamaica, if possible.[33]

And the general in Pensacola was summarizing his activity, or inactivity, at Pensacola for the colonial secretary in London. Pensacola had escaped the hostile armament which appeared before the city on March 27, but a new Spanish fleet was on the way. A polacre captured by *Mentor* on October 30, seemed to be part of an offensive fleet as there were commissioners, carpenters, and smiths on board. The capture of a dismantled schooner laden with powder, by a trading sloop, provided the full plan of attack. The new Spanish fleet had departed Havana

The 3rd English-Waldeck Regiment

on October 10, but a storm also struck that fleet between October 20 and 26, and scattered the ships.[34]

Campbell had taken the five 32 pound cannons from Fort George and put them at the Red Cliffs under Captain Pentzel of the Waldeck Regiment.[35] He had fifty Waldeck rank and file, plus officers and non-commissioned officers. If the enemy were to appear, Campbell planned to reinforce the Cliffs with sailors and six more cannons.

Some Chickasaw chiefs had been to Pensacola to get ammunition and twenty of their warriors had promised to stay to help defend Pensacola. The general had purchased more presents for the Indians, as well as rum for the troops, but naval assistance which he could only request from Admiral Parker, and military assistance from Governor Dalling in Jamaica, was not forthcoming.

The Cliffs overlooked the sands of Aqueero, which the British called Tartar Point, and which is the present day site of the Naval Air Station. The garrison of the Cliffs during the closing days of English control of Pensacola numbered 139 men, serving eleven guns, including the five 32- pound cannons.[36]

On July 7, 1780, Germain sent a reply to the Prince of Waldeck's request for information regarding the location of his regiment.. Germain gave the prince the bad news that part of his regiment had been made prisoners of war in West Florida. To soften the blow, Germain continued that an exchange would be sought and the regiment would be given a better posting if possible. The same day, Germain wrote to Clinton that he wished the Waldeckers to be exchanged and that the regiment was then to be posted in a place more suited to their constitution.[37]

Possibly because it took until July 1780 to get an answer to his March 1779 letter, the Prince of Waldeck sent only one recruit to America in 1780. That recruit embarked on board the *Castor* at Bremerlehe on June 1, 1780. According to a note by Faucitt on a return of Hessian recruits, the Waldeck recruit was

The 3rd English-Waldeck Regiment

sent by the Prince of Waldeck and was destined for his regiment.[38]

On July 7, 1780, William Knox, at Whitehall, informed Captain Richard Bailey, that a Cadet Boehme was in charge of clothing for the Waldeck Regiment and was to have passage in a transport.[39] This was undoubtedly the same recruit who had sailed from Bremerlehe on the *Castor*. A Friedrich Boehme (W201112) appears in the *HETRINA* in June 1780 and is probably the individual mentioned by the two officials.[40]

Also, running strength figures which apparently were kept in Waldeck seem to indicate the regiment had a strength of 584 men on June 24, 1780. It was 107 men under strength by July 18, 1780, and the only recruit, Cadet Boehme, scheduled for America, still left the regiment 106 men below the treaty strength. By October 30, 1780, the regiment was 156 men under strength.[41]

A Matthias Weichsel (W201157), born 1744/1745 in Mainz, is listed initially in *HETRINA* as a member of the Waldeck Regiment in March 1780. He is then listed as being separated in America in August 1780, so that he could become an officer's servant.[42]

Friedrich Emde (W200773) also appears for the first time in the *HETRINA*, in 1780, as an officer's servant.[43]

The regiment acquired only limited reinforcements in 1780, but the losses continued to climb. Desertion from the regiment at Pensacola was held to only one individual in 1780. Peter Schmidt (W200767), 3 Company, who deserted on March 21,.[44] but there were numerous desertions from prisoner of war status, including the following men who joined the Spanish army, probably at New Orleans.[45]

Johannes Burghard (W200522), 5 Company, on July 1
Christian Hansmann (W200544), 5 Company, on July 1
Kaspar Meckel (W201141), 5 Company, on July 1
Johannes Rose (W200754), 5 Company, on July 1
Johannes Thor (W200607), 5 Company, on July 1

The 3rd English-Waldeck Regiment

Georg Bauer (W200512), 5 Company, on July 2
Jakob Blaufus (W200151), 2 Company, on July 2
Fifer Henrich Koch (W200506), 5 Company, on July 2
Johannes Krafft (W200670), 1 Company, on July 2
Hermann Huth (W200553), 5 Company, on July 2
Drummer Johannes Vahle (W200509), 5 Company, on July 2
David Huthmann (W200722), 1 Company, on July 3
Johannes Mieting (W200569), 5 Company, on July 3
Wilhelm Pique (W200093), 1 Company, on July 3
Kaspar Stempfler (W200792), 3 Company, on July 3
Jean de Lior (W200723), 5 Company, on July 4
Friedrich Nolte (W200579), 5 Company, on July 7
Josef Rischer (W200588), 5 Company, on July 7
Martin Wetterwald (W200810), 5 Company, on July 7
Philipp Uhle (W200608), 5 Company, on July 8
Philipp Decker (W200681), 2 Company, on July 9
Cpl. Wilhelm Schaeffer (W200595), 5 Company, on July 9
Friedrich Kluecke (W200667), 2 Company, on July 10
Franz Mueller (W200572), 5 Company, on July 11
Friedrich Schmidt (W201194), 5 Company, on July 11
Michael Stiegler (W200112), 5 Company, on July 11
Siegfried Kramer (W200671), 5 Company, on July 12
Dietrich Hinterthuer (W200716), 2 Company, on July 12
Cpl. Johannes Lutz (W200139), 2 Company, on July 12
Cpl. Georg Rupp (W200755), 3 Company, on July 12
Ludwig Schnitzius (W200224), 2 Company, on July 12
Drummer Philipp Wiegand (W200508), 5 Company, on July 12
Josef Carnisch (W200660), 2 Company, on July 13, and
Georg Bock (W200027), 1 Company, on July 13.

Other individuals who deserted from New Orleans during 1780, were:

Henrich Riese (W200097), 1 Company, on January 4
Friedrich Mueller (W200573), 5 Company, on June 24
Friedrich Deierlein (W200683), 5 Company, on June 14
Wilhelm Nolt (W200578), 5 Company, on July 14
Henrich Pfeil (W200209), 2 Company, on July 14
Ludwig Welcker (W200612), 5 Company, on July 14
Christian Bickmann (W200516), 5 Company, on July 15
Johannes Loeffler (W200727), 2 Company, on July 15

The 3rd English-Waldeck Regiment

Valentin Linde (W200074), 1 Company, on July 15
Kaspar Mueller (W200335), 1 Company, on July 15
Friedrich Oppendahl (W200742), 1 Company, on July 15
Gottlob Weiss (W200804), 1 Company, on July 15
Ferdinand Neumann (W200085), 1 Company, on July 16
Drummer Christian Diste (W200144), 2 Company, on July 18
Johannes Wagener (W200243), 2 Company, on July 18
Johannes Conet (W200669), 5 Company, on July 19
Eberhard Stoessel (W200793), 2 Company, on July 19
Balthasar Kaltwasser (W200156), 2 Company, on July 20
Johannes Durst (W200529), 5 Company, on July 20
Konrad Mueller (W200083), 1 Company, on July 20
Ludwig Ruppert (W200756), 5 Company, on July 20, and
Cpl. Gottfried Wiegand (W200613), 1 Company, on July 20.

After the prisoners were moved to Havana by the Spaniards, the following individuals deserted:

Servant Henrich Ulenbruck (W200099), 5 Company, on August 13
Cpl. Johannes Meisner (W200008), 1 Company, on October 3
Friedrich Schwencke (W200227), 1 Company, on October 4
Johannes Assmann (W200511), 5 Company, on October 5
Ludwig Kuester (W200162), 2 Company, on October 5
Henrich Kuethe (W200163), 2 Company, on October 5
Zacharias Meier (W200564), 5 Company, on October 5, and
Josef Schrantz (W200225), 2 Company, on October 5.

Deaths due to non-combat causes also took a toll among the prisoners held by Spain and among their comrades in Pensacola. Among those who died in Pensacola during 1780, were:[46]

Jakob Reuter (W200453), 4 Company, on February 7
Kaspar Hesse (W200715), 3 Company, on February 26
Leonhard Schreyer (W200780), 4 Company, on February 29
Georg Giessenschlager (W200417), 4 Company, on March 3
Karl Friedrich Hahne (W200709), 4 Company, on March 14
Friedrich Siebert (W200788), 4 Company, on April 6
Andreas Sorg (W200790), 3 Company, on June 28
Anton Andreas Puoll (W200749), 3 Company, on July 18
Cadet Arnold Schumacher (W200833), 4 Company, on July 29

The 3rd English-Waldeck Regiment

Henrich Gennit (W200178), 4 Company, on August 6
Henrich Figge (W200173), 4 Company, on August 7
Kaspar Matthias (W200729), 4 Company, on August 8
Servant Joh. Henr. Bern. Hunecke (W200429), 4 Company, on August 9
Leonhard Diamor (W200288), 3 Company, on August 9
Servant Joh. Wilh. Pelshaenger (W200164), 4 Company, on August 27
Adam Brauns (W200820), 4 Company, on November 3, and
Johann Georg Engelhard (W200412), 4 Company, on December 9.

Deaths among the prisoners of war held by Spain trace the movement of the prisoners during 1780 with the earliest deaths occurring in New Orleans, then at Vera Cruz, and finally in Havana. Among the prisoners who died in 1780, were:

At New Orleans

Daniel Dietz (W200166), 2 Company, on January 2
Johann Joachim Gose (W200704), 5 Company, on January 13
Adam Hartmann (W200545), 5 Company, on January 13
Christian Tente (W200239), 2 Company, on January 13
Johannes Lahme (W200557), 5 Company, on January 15
Otto Bruehne (W200153), 2 Company, on January 23
Ludwig Bornemann (W200652), 5 Company, on February 26
Johannes Burr (W200657), 5 Company, on February 26
Gottlieb Fichtner (W200692), 1 Company, on March 21
QM Sgt. Alexander Siegeler (W200110), 1 Company, on April 29
Henrich Landsberger (W200724), 1 Company, on June 16
Leonhard Kabel (W200155), 2 Company, on July 8
Karl Mueller (W200082), 1 Company, on July 9, and
Wilhelm Koehler (W200044), 5 Company, on July 16.

After Leaving New Orleans

Karl Wilhelm Itzmann (W200554), 5 Company, committed suicide by jumping overboard and drowning on August 4
Barthold Nassmann (W200208), 2 Company, died at Vera Cruz on August 6
Karl Junckermann (W200556), 5 Company, died at Vera Cruz on August 16

The 3rd English-Waldeck Regiment

Ludwig Stueckenbrock (W200235), 2 Company, died aboard ship near Havana on September 4
Georg Schrauff (W200107), 1 Company, died aboard ship on September 22
Cpl. Bernhard von Canstein (W200046), 1 Company, died at Havana on November 29, and
Philipp Luenert (W200561), 5 Company, died at Havana on December 16.

Others listed in *HETRINA* as dying in 1780, probably at Pensacola, were:[47]

Ernst Christian Guenther (W200707), 4 Company, in January
Ensign Karl von Horn (W100020), 3 Company, on July 19
Christian Frese (W200414), 4 Company, in November, and
Johannes Besselbach (W200642), 4 Company, in December.

Numerous promotions, for both officers and enlisted men, were made in 1780. As most of them occurred in April, it is possible that Lieutenant Colonel von Horn brought a new promotion authority for the Waldeck Regimental Commander. Among those promoted, were:[48]

Captain Christian Friedrich Pentzel (W100005), 4 Company, promoted to major in May. Pentzel may have been on leave during 1780, but it seems possible that while on leave, he may have been performing duty with the English army.
1st Lieutenant Gerhard Henrich Heldring (W1000014), 4 Company, promoted to captain lieutenant in April and possibly transferred to duty with the English army, as he was on leave during this period and, according to several sketches of fortifications, was serving as the assistant engineer at Pensacola.
Ensign Karl Christian Hohmann (W100015), was promoted to 2nd lieutenant in October
Ensign Christian Ludwig Schmidt (W200626C), 4 Company, was transferred to 3 Company in April, back to 4 Company the same month, and then to 2 Company in May.
Sgt. Wilhelm Theodor Ursall (W200250C), 3 Company, was promoted to ensign in April.
QM Sgt. Georg Ulner (W200354), 3 Company was promoted to sergeant in April.

The 3rd English-Waldeck Regiment

Cpl. Georg Muus (W200259), 3 Company, was promoted to QM sergeant in April.

Christian Francke (W200295) was promoted to corporal in April.

Philipp Meister (W200326) and Henrich Schleiermacher (W200347), both of 3 Company, were promoted to corporal in August.

Cpl. Henrich Muus (W200261), 3 Company, was demoted to private in May and promoted back to corporal in October. There are some indications that one form of punishment was to reduce a man's grade for a given period, at the end of that period, he resumed his former pay and position.

QM Sgt. August Greiser (W200375), 4 Company, was promoted to sergeant in April.

Cpl. Karl Bruehne (W200135) and Cpl. Christian Nelle (W200381), both of 4 Company, were promoted to captain-at-arms in April.

Bernhard Leimbach (W200432), Johann Henrich Lindig (W200433), and Karl Schnabel (W200212), all of 4 Company, were promoted to corporal in April.

Karl Sander (W200215), 4 Company, was promoted to corporal in August.

Drummer Jakob Heinemann (W200387), 4 Company, was promoted to private in May.

Franz Hinterberger (W200824), 3 Company, is listed in the *HETRINA* as a cadet promoted to free corporal in August.

Cpl. Christoph Budde (W200260S), 3 Company, was promoted to provost in April and transferred to the staff. The *HETRINA* lists a Konrad Glaentzer as provost with the regiment in 1776, and as having died in April 1779. A Konrad Glaentzer is then listed as provost until his death in April 1780. The 1779 date of death could be in error, or possibly the original provost had a son, who assumed the duties of provost in 1779.

Michael Goebel (W200701), and Johannes Heilig (W2000711), both of 3 Company, are listed as having deserted in March, but both are listed on duty later in the year, so the desertion entries may be in error.

Wilhelm Littlet (W200199), 2 Company, had deserted from prisoner of war status in August 1778, but was back on duty with 4 Company by November 1780.

Franz Mangel (W200562), 3 Company, was separated in America in December 1780 and assumed duty as a servant with the regiment.

Finally, Captain Lieutenant Augustin Alberti (W100008), 5 Company, is listed in *HETRINA* as a returned prisoner of war in June 1780. However, a

The 3rd English-Waldeck Regiment

list of officers of the Waldeck Regiment, signed by Lieutenant Colonel von Horn on January 1, 1782, lists Alberti as a prisoner of the Spaniards at Havana.

Twenty-three recruits joined the regiment from Waldeck in 1780, and two individuals were taken into service in America. Forty-three men died of non-combat causes (22 while prisoners of war) and 65 men deserted (all but one from prisoner status). Some of the deserters even joined the Spanish army. One man who had deserted in 1778 was back on duty by late 1780. At the end of the year, estimated strength of the Waldeck Regiment was 320 men, plus 130 men prisoners of war.

1781

In early January 1781, General Campbell decided to attack the Spaniards at Mobile and attempt to capture that former British outpost. But he made his move without considering all aspects of the task. As planned, a co-ordinated land and sea attack was to be made against a place known as French Village, or just The Village, held by 150 men. *Mentor, Hound,* and *Baton Rouge* were to supply the naval arm, while Colonel von Hanxleden led a mixed force of regulars, militia, and Indians overland. The ships sailed on January 4, but the shallow water in Mobile Bay made direct support of the land forces impossible.[1]

The size of the land forces seems difficult to establish as writers have used a widely varying group of figures. Lowell, possibly basing his figures on von Eelking, gives von Hanxleden's command a strength of 115 white men and 300 Choctaws. Haarmann puts the force at sixty Waldeckers, 100 men of the 60th Regiment, provincials, and cavalry, plus 300 Indians, and Marshall and Peckham say the command included 400 soldiers and 300 Indians.[2]

Haarmann seems to have taken his figures for the Waldeckers in the attack from von Eelking, also, as von Eelking gave the participation of the Waldeck Regiment as Captain Baumbach, Lieutenants Wilmowsky and Stierlein, Ensign Ursall, six non-commissioned officers, two musicians, and 47 rank and file, in addition to the colonel.[3]

On the morning of January 7, Colonel von Hanxleden led a bayonet attack against the Spanish defenders of The Village, but after some initial success, Hanxleden was killed and the attack failed. Haarmann attributes the failure to the Indians not supporting the regulars, but Cameron wrote Germain that the Indians did well but were repulsed. Cameron put the blame on Campbell's unwillingness to pay for the Indians service.

Cameron felt he could have gotten many more Indians to go on the mission, but was afraid of the cost. There were 744 Choctaws at Pensacola and 400 more on the Tombigbee River, but there were no provisions or presents for the Indians.[4]

Baurmeister recorded that the Spaniards were ready for the attack and therefore, it failed. He recorded the death of the Waldeck colonel and several Waldeck subalterns, and noted that only bad news was to be expected from Pensacola, as the Spaniards had strengthened their forces in that area. Marshall and Peckham were of the opinion that the failure of the attack was an encouragement to Galvez to attack Pensacola again, even though his October 1780 fleet had been scattered by a hurricane.[5]

Chester reported von Hanxleden's death and defeat to Germain in February 1781. Other casualties, as noted by Haarmann, were two officers and thirteen enlisted men killed, and three officers and nineteen enlisted men wounded.[6]

Farmar's *Journal* listed the officers killed as Colonel von Hanxleden and Lieutenant Stierlein of the Waldeck Regiment and Lieutenant Gordon of the 60th Regiment. He also reported thirteen privates killed and nineteen wounded.[7]

Waldeck soldiers killed in the attack on The Village, included:[8]

Wilhelm Stoltz (W200358), who died on January 7, and
Hermann Sievers (W200354), both of 3 Company, who died on January 9
Christoph Kussenbauer (W200678), 2 Company, who died on January 7

Wounded Waldeckers, were:

Michael Goebel (W200701) and
Georg Jost (W200313), both of 3 Company, who were seriously wounded.
Goebel was later listed as an invalid.
Sgt. Christoph Embde (W200130)
Fifer Friedrich Birckenhauer (W200141)
Georg Kirschner (W200662), and

The 3rd English-Waldeck Regiment

Henrich Eisenberg (W200171), all of 2 Company, all of whom were slightly wounded.

J.D. Holmes, in an article in the *Alabama Historical Quarterly* for Spring 1976, gives an interesting if not entirely accurate account of the battle of January 7, 1781. According to his account Hanxleden's son "attacked with such fury that he impaled himself on the Spanish bayonets." Holmes also recorded that "the Waldeck forces lost their colonel, all their officers, and the fifteen killed," and concludes his article by describing the Waldeck Regiment as one of Germany's bravest of the brave." He also had the Waldeck Regiment reaching Florida by marching overland from New York to Pensacola,[9]

Patrick Tonyn, Governor of East Florida, gave a summary of Spanish activity against West Florida to Germain for the period October 1780 to the end of January 1781. After noting the dispersal of the Spanish fleet in October, he informed Germain that some transports had been lost, three were decoyed into Pensacola and captured, and two, with ordnance stores, were captured by *Mentor*, and five had arrived safely at Mobile. Five hundred men had sailed from Havana for Mobile on December 7, followed by another 1,000 on December 13. Don Galvez, with two ships-of-the-line, was expected to sail on January 12, 1781, against Pensacola.[10]

The Cuban Council provided Galvez with 1,315 troops, which sailed aboard their transports in February 1781, accompanied by 1,348 men from New Orleans, and 905 men from Mobile.[11]

The packet *Diligence* arrived at Pensacola from Jamaica on February 14 with the news that Admiral Parker was assigning a 44-gun ship and a 32-gun frigate to Pensacola, but within a week, according to reports which a merchant in Augusta, Georgia, received via an express from Pensacola, the Spanish fleet had arrived at Pensacola and an army of 2,000 men had landed on Rose's Island. The ships then undertook the bombardment of the defensive works on Red Cliffs.[12]

A convoy of nine ships sailed from Pensacola on February 25, bound for England, under escort of *Hound*. On March 4, *Hound's* fleet sighted 38 sail about 270 miles out of Pensacola. This was the Spanish fleet which had sailed from Havana with Galvez' forces on February 28. This information was available in England by May 1, 1781.[13]

A Martin Navarro gave a report that the Spanish force, which he listed at 20 ships, had a total of 1,637 soldiers on board.[14]

The Spaniards arrived at Pensacola by sea on March 9 and at 6 in the evening, Captain Dean sent the brig *Childres* to notify Jamaica of the arrival of the Spanish fleet of 34 sail. Next day the *Mentor*'s launch captured a Spanish flag schooner, *Santo Servanto*, which had Galvez' personal effects on board.[15]

On March 11, the Spanish fleet's preparations to cross the bar at the harbor entrance were challenged by *Mentor*. However, after being hulled by 24-pound shot from Spanish guns at Santa Rosa Point, *Mentor* was forced to fall back to a position near Tartar Point.[16]

Don Galvez led the Spanish fleet into the harbor, despite the guns at The Cliffs, on March 18. At the time, the *Mentor's* captain was busy sending the ship's shot and powder up to Pensacola for use at Fort George. Two days later, rather than allow his ship to be captured, Captain Dean put most of his crew ashore and had a crew of twelve men sail *Mentor* up Middle River, where it soon capsized.[17]

While the Spaniards seemed to have complete naval supremacy at Pensacola, Governor Tonyn was writing to Germain that the Indians had brought word that warships and troops had arrived at Pensacola from Jamaica. In London, Germain was expressing his belief that Pensacola was still being held by General Campbell, and that Indian presents should be sent out, in the same amount as the previous year, but via Jamaica.[18]

There was no naval relief for Pensacola, however, and the only troop reinforcements were troops from Mobile, which reinforced Don Galvez on March 22, and more troops from New Orleans which arrived to support the Spanish at Pensacola on March 23.[19]

Lieutenant Miller and forty sailors from the *Mentor* were sent to the advanced redoubt on March 23 to bolster the defense of Pensacola, and the remaining members of the crew were quartered in tents near the city. The crew of *Port Royal* were put ashore, also.[20]

Campbell reported 21 ships off Pensacola on March 28, and 29 ships next day. Later he reported the arrival of a combined Spanish and French fleet, which landed 3,000 troops on April 21.[21]

On Saturday, April 21, Captain Dean recorded that an express from The Cliffs reported 22 sail; a combined Spanish and French fleet, had appeared off the bar.[22]

Other minor naval activities occurred on April 12, when an enemy galley had come down the Yamosa River with a schooner and a sloop, supposedly the *Poder de Dios* and the packet *Diligence*. A week later the Pensacola Major of Brigade, James Campbell, wrote to Donald McPherson and Henry Smith, captains or owners of the sloop *Christiana* and the galley *Ponchartrain*, to be sure that their vessels with munitions and provisions on board, did not fall into the hands of the Spaniards. Apparently those vessels had gone up the Escambia River with presents for the Indians.[23]

At the time of the Spanish siege of Pensacola, the defenses for the city, according to a sketch by Captain Lieutenant Heldring, consisted in part of the batteries located at The Cliffs guarding the harbor entrance and several strong points supporting one another, in a line from the city northward, designated Fort George, the Prince of Wales Battery, and the Queen's, or Advance, Redoubt.[24]

Actual combat activity increased sharply on April 24. Farmar reported an advance by 300 Spaniards in the morning, which was initially countered by the Indians. When the Indians were forced to retire, a force of provincials, supported by artillery, was able to drive the Spaniards away.[25]

The Spaniards had been a reconnaissance in force by the artillery and engineer chiefs of the Spanish army, who were planning an attack. They encountered an ambush and the resulting skirmish lasted until 9 A.M. During the clash, the original Spanish force was supported by five companies of light infantry. Spanish losses were two officers and fifteen men wounded.[26]

At twelve o'clock several Spanish naval officers joined a number of army officers in a test to determine the effectiveness of naval gunfire against the English fortifications. This test was conducted by an armed brigantine carrying two 24-pound cannons. They could not hit the fortifications from a point where the water still had a depth of fourteen feet, but the English counter-fire, which landed near their vessel, was reason for the Spaniards to consider the shore-based artillery with respect.[27]

According to Farmar's account, at 2 P.M., a brig approached land between the houses owned by Mr. Niel and Mr. Christie and opened fire on the fort. This bombardment was answered by fire from the Waldeck and provincial redoubts. At 3 P.M., Captain (William) Johnstone with a howitzer and a party of Waldeckers, went down to the beach and drove the brig away.[28]

Later that afternoon, Miranda wrote that there was another skirmish when the Spaniards at an advance post made contact with some English infantry, accompanied by Indians, at 4 P.M. Farmar noted this action at 5 o'clock and was of the opinion that the Spaniards were trying to gain an elevated area. However, the effort failed.[29]

The 3rd English-Waldeck Regiment

Both diarists reported the firing of a *feu de joie* during the evening. Farmar noted that a Mr. Dawes had arrived from Carolina with a report of the English success at Guilford Courthouse, and Miranda properly assumed Cornwallis had gained a victory over the American General Nathaniel Greene.[30]

The afternoon and evening activity of April 24 was also recorded by Captain Dean in the *Mentor's* log, with no notable difference in details, except that Dean's log entry is for the following day, April 25, probably due to his using Greenwich time instead of local time.[31]

As the Spaniards tightened their lines around Pensacola, it became necessary for the defenders to sally out in an effort to spike a few of the Spanish cannons. This was an accepted practice during siege operations during the eighteenth century and in some respects may have been a sign that Campbell had already decided to surrender his position. On May 4, Major John McDonald, of Chalmer's Maryland Loyalists, and 94 provincials, with a covering force of Waldeckers commanded by Lieutenant Colonel von Horn, stormed the enemy works, where 300 men were constructing new positions, and spiked six cannons. They also captured 1 captain, 2 lieutenants, and 4 privates, and inflicted 35 to 40 casualties. English losses were one man killed and one wounded.[32]

The sortie against the Spanish trenches on May 4 could not stop the ever-increasing pounding by the Spanish artillery, and at 9 A.M. on May 8, 1781, a Spanish shell exploded in a British powder magazine making the Queen's Redoubt untenable. The explosion killed 81 men and injured 24 others, but no Waldeckers were involved. The survivors fell back to the Prince of Wales Redoubt, while the Spaniards advanced at once and captured the heights above Fort George. General Campbell called a truce to discuss capitulation.[33]

Farquhar Bethune, one of the Indian agents, wrote to Lieutenant General Alexander Leslie, from Charleston on January 19, 1782, that after the chamade (call to parley between

The 3rd English-Waldeck Regiment

the English and Spaniards) had been beat, he marched out of the lines with the Choctaws and undertook a 250 mile journey on foot to the Choctaw nation.[34]

During the siege there were several instances of Indians gathering at Pensacola and of bringing captives into the garrison. A February 1, 1781, return of Indians at Pensacola, which was signed by Cameron, listed 744 Choctaws, 6 Chickasaws, 20 Alabama, and 18 Creeks. The *Mentor's* log recorded numerous instances of Indian activity. On April 9, 1781, sixty Creek entered Pensacola and on April 15, 100 Choctaws appeared. On April 19, the Creeks brought in a prisoner from Rosa Island and on April 30, the Indians brought in a Spanish prisoner.[35]

Farmar noted in his diary on April 12, that a party of Creeks who had accompanied a messenger from St. Augustine, brought in an enemy prisoner taken near Deer Point, and that they had killed three other enemies at that place. Regarding the prisoner captured by the Indians on April 30, Farmar added that the prisoner had been taken near the enemy's works, and the Indians gave up their prisoner reluctantly.[36]

Farmar's *Journal* is also the source for information that a half-breed son of a certain Colbert arrived at Pensacola on April 27 with 54 Chickasaws. This party was used to deliver ammunition to The Cliffs the next day at sunset.[37]

Previously, on Sunday, April 22, two Waldeck soldiers had been killed by some Indians while cutting branches for an abatis. The two men killed were: Christian Dietz (W200621) and Philipp Gosmann (W200182), both of 3 Company.[38]

It is of interest to note that William Knox, at Whitehall, wrote to Charles Shaw on June 6, 1781, a month after the fall of Pensacola, that the Creek Indians assistance to Pensacola would be welcome.[39]

The Spanish General Miranda recording events of May 7, noted that the humanity of General Campbell had saved a Spanish prisoner from the Indians by paying 200 pesos fuertes and a gift of rum. The prisoner had been taken to avenge the death of a relative of the Indians who had been killed at Mobile.[40]

Previously, Miranda had reported on May 6, that Indians sent by the Spaniards to check a report of The Cliffs having been abandoned, returned at 7 P.M. with two Waldeck prisoners. The Indians were paid triple for bringing the prisoners in alive. Describing the Indians' handling of prisoners, Miranda wrote, "It is a curious thing to see the manner in which these savages conduct their prisoners. In the midst of the procession they are led by the hands by an Indian who seizes them and controls them, and all with the greatest silence. They continue in order, manifesting their joy in their appearance and from time to time they repeat their shout of victory in a low, muffled voice.[41]

Although Germain had heard of no attack on Pensacola by May 1, 1781, after the magazine explosion and the loss of the Advance Redoubt, a white flag was raised at Fort George at 3 P.M. on May 8, and negotiations began. At 2 P.M. next day, negotiations were completed and at 3:30 in the afternoon, Galvez and two companies of Spanish grenadiers took possession of Pensacola city. On May 10, the garrison of Fort George formally laid down their arms.[42]

A description of the surrender ceremony, written by the Spanish commander Don Galvez, contains the following comments: "At 5:45 the ceremony took place as planned. General Campbell left Fort George at the head of his troops ... the political governor (of Pensacola) Pitre Chester (Peter Chester) with a town council then followed the Commander of Artillery, Mr. Thomson with all his troops: another two detachments followed, supplying a rear guard for the covered carts and the Regiment of Waldeck with its two flags and two artillery pieces."[43]

Galvez continued his account, noting that nine cannons were taken at The Cliffs and that there were 200 houses, with good furnishings and crystal, in Pensacola at that time. There were two good pavilions, for the officers and troops, with

The 3rd English-Waldeck Regiment

various warehouses. It also had four springs. He gave the strength of the English garrison as 1,700, plus 1,500 Negroes and Indians, and listed English casualties as 150 killed and 105 wounded. Spanish casualties were 119 killed and 133 wounded, of all ranks and including Galvez himself. He was of the opinion that most of the wounded would die. Another 46 individuals from the Spanish force had died of illness.[44]

English losses, according to Brigade Major James Campbell, were 90 killed and 46 wounded, including casualties resulting from the magazine explosion. Another 30 men of the Pensacola garrison had deserted during the siege.[45]

Surrender at The Cliffs took place on May 11. Galvez count of the captives in Pensacola totaled 1,113, not including Negroes nor the 56 men (English sources say 30) who had deserted to the Spanish. There were 224 women and children dependent upon the garrison. Three hundred Loyalists and British soldiers had fled toward Georgia while the negotiations were in progress, and as previously noted, the Indians had faded away when they saw the English were about to surrender.[46]

Baurmeister's record of the event used the same total figure of 1,113, including servants, women, children, and sailors. He noted that the Waldeck Regiment was much reduced and that one would expect a regimental strength of about 700 men, but Lieutenant Colonel von Horn reported a strength of only 356 men. Many of those missing were prisoners of Spain. Baurmeister also reported that a fort near New Orleans, Natchez, was still being defended by English forces when the troops left Pensacola.[47]

Count Frensdorf, in Arolsen, Waldeck, signed a "Present State of the Waldeck Regiment" on November 25, 1781, which appears to more fully represent the basis for the 356-man figure mentioned by Baurmeister, assuming a several month delay in Lieutenant Colonel von Horn's report reaching Waldeck. According to Frensdorf's report, there were:

The 3rd English-Waldeck Regiment

Present at Long Island: 15 non-commissioned officers, 12 corporals, 11 musicians, and 217 privates

Absent prisoners of war: 6 non-commissioned officers, 13 corporals, 5 musicians, and 139 privates

Total: 21 non-commissioned officers, 25 corporals, 16 musicians, and 356 privates.[48]

1776 treaty requirements: 29 non-commissioned officers, 30 corporals, 21 musicians, and 538 privates.

Vacancies: 8 non-commissioned officers, 5 corporals, 5 musicians, and 182 privates

The 129 recruits already raised for a planned shipment (in 1782) of 143 men, left a shortage of 71 men.

The Spanish-French force which Bernardo de Galvez commanded at Pensacola out-numbered the garrison by a wide margin. One assessment was that the combined forces included eleven Spanish and four French ships-of-the-line, two 38-gun frigates, three sloops of war, four galleys, and a number of other armed vessels. On land Galvez commanded 7,000 Spaniards, 3,000 French, some Americans, and Indians, and an immense artillery train. The source of this assessment was apparently a Mr. Gauld's Journal. Gauld, having been a volunteer and assistant in the engineering department at Pensacola, was a translator in both French and Spanish.[49]

Miranda had put the opposing forces at 3,701 Spaniards and French, including Negroes and militia, so that about 2,000 regulars were available for the attack. The consolidation of "our" detachment, plus 1,504 troops of "our" navy and 725 French increases the army to about 7,800 effectives. As to the number of General Campbell's defenders, they were an estimated 800 regulars, 200 seamen, and 1,000 Indians.[50]

The Cliffs, and the 139 officers and men serving there, were included in the surrender of Pensacola. Lieutenant William Hargood of the Royal Navy and 51 seamen who had served at Red Cliffs, awaited transfer to New York on cartel ships, along with the rest of *Mentor's* crew. The 210 seamen of the two

The 3rd English-Waldeck Regiment

naval vessels, who were among the force defending Pensacola, had served under army officers and expected to sail for New York with the soldiers on May 20. They actually sailed on June 4, 1781.[51]

Marshall and Peckham wrote that the Pensacola garrison sailed for Havana on June 1, and continued on to New York, arriving on July 12. Farmar recorded that after the surrender ceremony on May 10, the corps under General Campbell encamped the next day on the east side of Pensacola. On June 1 the men were embarked on Spanish transports and they sailed from Pensacola on June 4. The vessels carrying the men to be exchanged arrived at Havana on June 20, and after ten days of taking on water and provisions, the ships sailed for New York, arriving on July 12. The men were then cantoned at Newtown on Long Island.[52]

Information in Spanish archives indicates that two cartel ships were used to carry the Waldeck soldiers of the Pensacola garrison back to New York. These ships were the *San Pedro and San Pablo*, and the *Santa Rosalia*, captain Pedro Gatell. The Waldeck soldiers apparently boarded the ships on May 29. According to the list prepared by Lieutenant Colonel von Horn, the *San Pedro and San Pablo* carried 6 officers, 82 soldiers, 5 women and 7 children, for a total of 100 persons. However, he also listed himself and five other staff officers by name. As three of the positions were filled by civilians, it seems likely that part, if not all, of the staff personnel were on board but not included in the total.[53]

One hundred thirteen members of the Waldeck Regiment, including dependents, boarded the *Santa Rosalia* according to the list prepared by Major Pentzel. They were:[54]

1. Major Christian Friedrich Pentzel (W100005S)
2. His servant
3. Captain Lieutenant Augustin Christian Alberti (W100008)
4. His servant

The 3rd English-Waldeck Regiment

5. 2nd Lieutenant Karl Hohmann (W100015)
6. His servant.
7. Ensign Karl Mueller (W200378C)
8. Surg. Mate Johann Henrich Hoffmeister (W200377)
9. Sgt. Johann Henrich Heckmann (W200374)
10. Sgt. Franz Philipp Wirths (W200376)
11. QM Sgt. Karl Steuernagel (W200380)
12. Capt. at arms Christian Nelle (W200381)
13. Free Cpl. Friedrich Sude (W200834)
14. Cpl. Ludwig Goette (W200382)
15. Cpl. Henrich Berthold (W200384)
16. Cpl. Peter Mueller (W200443)
17. Cpl. Bernhard Leimbach (W200432)
18. Drummer Jakob Clemens (W200388)
19. Drummer Justinus Berger (W200639)

Privates and Dependents

20. Werner Wagener (W200484)
21. His wife (As the entry "la Femme"is listed, it appears to mean the wife of the preceding individual.)
22. Jakob Rennert (W200452)
23. Bernhard Figge (W200413)
24. Daniel Michael (W200438)
25. Johannes Knipschild (W200404)
26. Peter Schade (W200459)
27. Konrad Zimmermann (W200493)
28. Johannes Jaeger (W200430)
29. His wife
30. His child
31. Andreas Schultze (W200628)
32. Johann Friedrich Gunstmann (W2100423)
33. Franz Henrich Kuester (W200408)
34. Wilhelm Lindner (W200435)
35. Konrad Lindner (W200434)
36. Franz Genuit (W200415)
37. Philipp Roehling (W200455)
38. Johannes Wollenhaupt (W200492)
39. Dietrich Henrich Beckmann (W200392)
40. David Giede (W200416)
41. Johann Henrich Demmer (W200409)
42. Johann Wilhelm Bette (W200394)
43. Johannes Valand (W200478)

The 3rd English-Waldeck Regiment

44. Stefan Stempel (W200471)
45. Franz Adolf Siebel (W200469)
46. Johann Friedrich Kelter (W200401)
47. Johannes Goebel (W200419)
48. Daniel Heller (W200426)
49. Peter Peuster (W200447)
50. Johann Adam Schaeffer (W200460)
51. Henrich Hoffmann (W200428)
52. Johann Stefan Schultze (W200466)
53. Johann Henrich Stiehl (W200472)
54. Johann Henrich Keitel (W200400)
55. Johann Erdmann Guttermilch (W200424)
56. Johann Gottfried Neuendorf (W200444)
57. Franz Schreyer (W200465)
58. Johannes Wagener (W200482)
59. Johannes Ritter (W200454)
60. Marcus Trainer (W200474)
61. Johann Henrich Schwerd (W200467)
62. Johann Wilhelm Moering (W200441)
63. Franz Christian Alberti (W200389)
64. Friedrich Doedecke (W200410)
65. Henrich Friedrich Thiemann (W200796)
66. David Friedrich Lohrmann (W200436)
67. Wilhelm Wersinger (W200809)
68. Adam Buecker (W200654)
69. Georg Eckhard (W200686)
70. Ludwig Mueller (W200679)
71. Karl Ammenhaeuser (W200632)
72. Georg Hermann (W200713)
73. Andreas Muenster (W200735)
74. Felix Schmidt (W200768)
75. Johannes Graebe (W200422)
76. Peter Knueppel (W200406)
77. Konrad Bunse (W200397)
78. Johann Jost Valentin (W200479)
79. His child
80. Henrich Wilke (W200491)
81. Karl Wahl (W200485)
82. Henrich Henckelmann (W200427)
83. Johannes Mertz (W200076)
84. Christoph Cleemann (W200666)

The 3rd English-Waldeck Regiment

85. Christian Schaeffer (W200762)
86. Johannes Zahner (W200814)
87. Anton Schimmel (W200765)
88. Henrich Nolte (W200700)
89. Ludwig Schmidt (W200772)
90. His wife
91. Philip Quande (W200750)
92. Georg Dettendaler (W200685)
93. Adam Semper (W200787)
94. Josef Crollpath (W200675)
95. Georg Bless (W200646)
96. Johannes Meidt (W200730)
97. Henrich Toenges (W200797)
98. Christian Francke (W200386)
99. Johannes Flamme (W200385)
100. Johann Konrad Heinemann (W200387)
101. Christian Todt (W200835)
102. Konrad Pape (W200828)
103. Henrich Schuetz (W200832)
104. Friedrich Boehle (W200817)
105. Friedrich Knipschild (W201125)
106. Ignatius Bachstaedter (W200021)
107. His wife
108. Wilhelm Taubert (W200116)
109. Kaspar Zeiger (W200616)
110. Johann Georg Schmeck (W200219)
111. Bernhard Beyer (W200149)
112. Jost Josef Menckel (W200199), and
113. A free Negress.

Knowing nothing of the situation in Pensacola immediately after the surrender, but only wishing to have experienced officers with his regiment, the Prince of Waldeck wrote to Germain on May 14, 1781, that because of the death of Colonel von Hanxleden, Baron von Haacke, a prisoner of the Spaniards at New Orleans, should be exchanged.[55]

Letters more pertinent to the situation were those of General Campbell to Bernardo de Galvez on May 19, requesting the English aide, Lieutenant Gordon of the 16th Regiment be

The 3rd English-Waldeck Regiment

allowed to carry dispatches to Germain and Clinton. Captain Dean, commanding the British seamen, wanted to send dispatches to the Admiralty and to his admiral, and Lieutenant Colonel von Horn, of the Waldeck Regiment, desired his dispatches to the Prince of Waldeck be taken by Lieutenant Gordon, also.[56]

The 3rd English-Waldeck Regiment

One of the letters carried by Lieutenant Gordon was surely Campbell's letter of May 12, in which he informed Germain of the surrender of Pensacola. Campbell wrote that he planned to go to New York if he could get transportation, and that the men of his command had behaved well. Clinton gave his approval for Campbell's defense of Pensacola as gallant, and Germain wrote back in turn, that the King approved of the general's resistance. Campbell's exchange would be effected as soon as possible, there being no cartel with the Spaniards, and meantime Campbell appeared to be free to serve except against Spain or France. In fact, the entire garrison of Pensacola was only prevented from serving against Spain or France. The soldiers were to be returned to New York by the Spaniards in Spanish ships and could take up arms against the Americans.[57]

In his report of the surrender, Campbell gave the Waldeckers limited but specific praise. In addition to the English naval gun crews, the twelve artillerymen from Waldeck "were indefatigable in their exertions as they were incessantly on duty." Lieutenant Colonel von Horn and the provincial Major McDonald, were the only field officers in the garrison as Major Pentzel was on duty at The Cliffs, and both officers had carried heavy responsibilities. Finally, the Waldeck Lieutenant Heldring, "acting as sole engineer" did all that a young man with zeal and an ambition for honor could perform.[58]

Waldeck casualties during the siege were surprisingly few and included:[59]

Konrad Bunse (W200397), 4 Company, who was slightly wounded while serving at Red Cliffs on April 7
Cpl. Philipp Meister (W200326), 3 Company, who was lightly wounded at the Advance Redoubt on April 25, and
Christian Knoechel (W200279), who was killed, and
Sgt. Jakob Graebe (W200251), who was wounded, both of 3 Company, apparently by friendly fire from Fort George on April 12. Knoechel's death would seem to be the death referred to by Captain Dean of the *Mentor*, in his log entry for April 13, and Farmar's entry of April 12.

The 3rd English-Waldeck Regiment

On May 4, at the Advance Redoubt,

Ensign Theodor Ursall (W200250C), 3 Company, was killed by a cannon ball, and
Cpl. Konrad Pilger (W200449), 4 Company, was seriously wounded, later being declared an invalid.

Ursall's death was reported in the New York newspapers on July 7, 1781, and the *Mentor's* log entry of May 5, is that a lieutenant in the Waldeck Regiment was killed and a Waldeck sergeant wounded at the Advance Redoubt.

Robert Farmar recorded one Waldecker, one bombardier, and one sailor wounded by a shell on May 6, 1781. The next day he made a journal entry that a shell had landed where men were making fuses, resulting in one Waldecker killed and one wounded.[60]

These men were all at the Advance Redoubt and while the man wounded on May 6 has not been positively identified, three men were listed on a return of killed and wounded of the Waldeck Regiment under the date of May 7, They were:[61]

Cannoneer Henrich Litzau (W300012), killed
Cannoneer Christian Wenthe (W300016), seriously wounded, who died of his wounds on May 16, and
Cannoneer Christian Thietke (W300015), lightly wounded.

Non-combat deaths at Pensacola during 1781, included the following:

Cpl. Henrich Lindig (W200433), 4 Company, on January 26
Thomas Wieser (W200614), 3 Company, on April 15, and
Johannes Nolte (W200445), 4 Company on May 30.

Men who were captured in the Mississippi region and who died while in prisoner of war status during 1781, were:

The 3rd English-Waldeck Regiment

Henrich Reinhard (W200212), 2 Company, who died aboard ship near Havana on January 12
Johannes Wertz (W200913), 1 Company, who died at Havana on May 26
Georg Weybrenner (W200811), 1 Company, who died at New Orleans on July 19
Henrich Berges (W200148), 2 Company, who died aboard ship near Havana on August 27, and
Sgt. Henrich Schluckebier (W200002), 1 Company, who died at Kingston, Jamaica, on September 24, possibly after having been released from prisoner status.

Bernardo de Galvez does not specifically mention Waldeck soldiers deserting to the Spaniards during the siege of Pensacola in one version of his diary. In another version he does. In the Cuseck translation an entry of April 1, is to the effect that at 3 P.M. three Waldeck soldiers deserted to the Spaniards.

Dean noted in the *Mentor's* log that some Waldeckers and some provincials deserted Sunday, April 1. The three Waldeck soldiers were probably:[62]

Free Cpl. Franz Hinterberger (W200824)
Johannes Mueller (W200674), and
Lorenz Thaler (W200795), all of 3 Company.

The *Mentor's* log for April 6 contains information that a Waldeck soldier deserted to the enemy. This entry would seem to apply to:[63]

Alexander Hertel (W200710), who deserted on April 5.

Another entry for Monday, April 16, mentions another Waldeck deserter, probably:

Solomon Dender (W200684), 4 Company.

Miranda also reported a Waldeck soldier deserting to the Spaniards on Thursday, April 26. The man was probably:[64]

The 3rd English-Waldeck Regiment

Servant Matthias Weichsel (W201157S) of the staff.

Other entries by Miranda record a Waldeck deserter on Wednesday, May 2, and three German deserters on the next day. As there were Germans in the 60th Regiment, the distinction of Germans instead of Waldeckers may mean the last mentioned deserters were not from the Waldeck Regiment. The Waldeck deserter has not been further identified.[65]

On April 27, Miranda noted that two Germans of our foreign troops deserted in the afternoon, but as with reports of German deserters to the Spaniards, these may or may not have been Waldeckers.[66]

Other Waldeck soldiers who were reported as deserters, prior to the surrender of Pensacola, were:[67]

Friedrich Gummero (W200677), 3 Company, on April 2
Johannes Kirschner (W200663), 4 Company, on April 2
Jakob Hagener (W200708), 3 Company, on April 2
Johannes Heilig (W200711), 3 Company, on April 2
Peter Ziegenhainer (W200815), 3 Company, on April 2
Anton Wolff (W200624), 4 Company, on April 8, and
Wagoneer Johannes Wellner (W200488S), of the staff, on May 8.

On September 10, 1781, General Navarro wrote to Joseph de Galvez, Governor of Cuba, that on order of the Field Marshall, Commander General of this province (West Florida), and of the army of operations, dated July 15, a company of forty men, German deserters, had been recruited in the city of Pensacola, to serve in the province during the war, under the command of American Lieutenant Winter Lacount Canon. They were clothed and equipped and being paid like soldiers.[68]

Lowell makes no reference in *The Hessians* to Waldeckers joining the Spanish army after the capitulation of Pensacola, neither does von Eelking nor any other author that this writer has found. However, it seems likely that the men who deserted from the Waldeck Regiment during the siege and after the

The 3rd English-Waldeck Regiment

surrender of Pensacola, may have been persuaded to join the Spanish army by a number of arguments such as no more combat involvement, no more sea voyages, no prison camp, etc. Some of the Germans mentioned by Navarro may also have been from the English army. From the Waldeck Regiment, the following men may have joined the Spanish army. Four of the men were apparently recruited into the Waldeck Regiment in Pensacola, probably former members of the English army. They were:[69]

Johannes Netter (W200784), born in Ansbach, and
Melchior Obermann (W200619), born in Lauterbach. Both men are listed in the *HETRINA* as having joined 4 Company in April 1781, being separated the same month, and deserting on May 9. A notation beside their names on a list of deserters indicates that they may have been discharged from the Waldeck Regiment when it was discovered that they were deserters from the English army.
Lorenz Schappe (W200947), born in Nass, Saarbruecken, and
Friedrich Thiele (W200965), born in Hamburg, are listed in HETRINA as having joined 3 Company in April 1781, and deserting on May 9.

A Jakob Wieber is listed in HETRINA as deserting from 2 Company on May 17. As this is the only reference in HETRINA, and because Ignatius Bieber (W201110), 2 Company, is listed in HETRINA as deserting in May but not on the list of deserters, this writer assumes that the listing under the name Wieber to be in error. The correct entry probably should be Bieber.[70]

Other deserters during this period, who may have joined the Spanish army, were:[71]

Jakob Wendolph (W200808), 4 Company, on May 11
Johannes Schoeneberger (W200776), 4 Company, on May 12
Alexander Mueller (W200827), 2 Company, on May 13
Sebastian Friedinger (W200698), 3 Company, on May 15
Georg Griesheim (W200706), 3 Company, on May 15
Ludwig Lincker (W200316), 3 Company, on May 15
Samuel Peter (W200448), 4 Company, on May 15
Karl Winckelmann (W200369), 3 Company, on May 15

The 3rd English-Waldeck Regiment

Philipp Boehmer (W200650), 3 Company, on May 17
Georg Dehm (W200682), 4 Company, on May 17
Henrich Duckenberg (W200169), 4 Company, on May 17
Ludwig Hancker (W200425), 4 Company, on May 17
Henrich Hornsberger (W200552), 3 Company, on May 17
August (Justus) Runte (W200214), 4 Company, on May 17
Konrad Schmidt (W200771), 4 Company, on May 17
Adam Weirauch (W200367), 3 Company, on May 17
Jakob Werner (W200122), 4 Company, on May 17, and
Philipp Grimm (W200183), 2 Company, on May 29.

While the transports carrying the Waldeck Regiment to New York were taking on water and provisions at Havana, Philipp Block (W200649), 4 Company, deserted on July 24.[72] Peter Schumann (W200783), 4 Company, deserted at Havana on October 1, after possibly having been put ashore due to illness.

During 1781 the following men of the Waldeck Regiment deserted from prisoner of war status:

Christian Meier (W200325), 5 Company, deserted at New Orleans on July 15, and
Ernst Hahne (W200184), 2 Company, deserted at Havana on August 31.

An undated, unsigned report from the Hessen State Archives in Marburg gives the state of the 3rd Waldeck Regiment at the time of the surrender at Pensacola, as follows:[73]

11 - officers   14 - non-commissioned officers
13 - corporals   11 - musicians
215 - privates   10 - Cannoneers
11 - Servants   5 - Solicitors
10 - staff   50 - prisoners
Total - 350
Corps on separate service (which may mean prisoners of war)
3 - Officers   110 - non-commissioned officers and privates
125 - recruits for 1781   138 - recruits for 1782
Total - 376

172

The 3rd English-Waldeck Regiment

The 376 is then added to 350 for a total of 726, minus 684, which is the treaty strength of the Waldeck Regiment plus the Artillery detachment, and this gives a figure of 42 - the manpower overage for the regiment.

On June 4, 1781, the day the Pensacola garrison sailed on its return to New York, an official at Whitehall, in London, was writing to Governor Tonyn that no one in the government had yet heard of an attack on Pensacola.[74]

In the early days of July 1781, the Waldeckers and other members of the Pensacola garrison began arriving at New York. Lieutenant Johann Karl Philipp Krafft, of the Hesse Cassel troops, made an entry in his diary which seems to indicate that he thought the men had started for West Florida and then been captured, while *en route*, by Spanish ships. The Spaniards had then allowed the men to return to New York.[75]

Washington was notified by a letter of July 2, from Philadelphia, that there were reports of the Pensacola garrison returning to New York. The letter writer, Samuel Huntington, could not believe Galvez had done such a thing as allowing the garrison to return to fight against the Americans. William Sharpe expressed his surprise with Galvez' actions, also, and understood that the garrison from Pensacola could fight against the Americans and in effect represented a 1,000 man reinforcement for the English in the New York area. Edmond Randolph summed up the feeling in Congress. "But it is difficult to advise the Steps fit to be taken with respect to it."[76]

Richard Potts wrote that Spain was not worried about the consequences to Americans, and compared the Pensacola terms with the capitulation terms between General Pickens and Colonel Lee at Augusta (which prohibited captives fighting against Spain). In noting the feelings among the Americans, Mackenzie wrote in his diary only that the rebels were unhappy with Spain, but he then recorded the often overlooked factor that Spain had not even recognized the independence of the American colonies.[77]

The 3rd English-Waldeck Regiment

Baurmeister recorded the arrival of the first transport with British soldiers from Pensacola on July 4. His account is to the effect that Campbell was forced to surrender on May 12 (sic) to an army of 15,000 after a magazine exploded. The attacking force employed fifteen warships and eight frigates, one-third being from France, manned by 8,000 seamen and marines, along the coast and in the siege operations. While the garrison captives were at Havana, they had been made to agree not to serve against Spain or her allies, until exchanged, before being allowed to proceed on their way to New York.[78]

William Smith recorded in his diary, under date of Wednesday, July 11, 1781, that the Pensacola garrison had been arriving at New York for several days past. Two days later General Campbell arrived, according to Mackenzie's diary, and another cartel ship with troops from Pensacola arrived on July 14. Mackenzie reported that all the troops of the Pensacola garrison were cantoned at Newtown on Long Island.[79]

Later in the year, Mackenzie reported that the winter quarters for the Pensacola garrison were to be at Newtown, and that all officers belonging to that garrison were to be cantoned within the Newtown District, also.[80]

There are numerous references to the Pensacola garrison returning to New York. Baron Cromat de Bourg noted in his diary that an English deserter told the French on August 2, 1781, that troops recently arrived at New York were part of the garrison captured by Spain. Those troops were being cantoned on Long Island.[81]

Governor Clinton of New York also took note of the arrival of the Pensacola garrison at New York, and so did Baron von Closen of the French army.[82]

Surprisingly, the Pensacola Historical Society *Quarterly*, which is based on von Eelking's *Die Deutsche Huelfstruppen*, which in turn is based on the writings of Steuernagel and Waldeck for information on Florida, gives the strength of the Waldeck Regiment, upon its arrival in New York in 1781 as

The 3rd English-Waldeck Regiment

1,113 men. This figure is the number of men, excluding Negroes and Indians, which Galvez reported as the entire garrison of Pensacola. Furthermore, it represents more than the entire number of soldiers provided by Waldeck, up to that time, including the 1781 recruit shipment. The Society can not be censored for errors of this nature, however. Misinformation on the mercenaries is plentiful. The present volume being no exception, and Carrington and many other writers used the British official returns which listed 558 Waldeckers, 374 English, and 211 Provincials, or a total strength of 1,143 men in West Florida as of September 1, 1781.[83]

Not all of the men returning to New York from Pensacola had swift, uneventful trips. The Spanish cartel ship *St. Joseph and Joachim* with 160 men of the Pensacola garrison on board was captured by *The Fair American* and the *Holker*, American privateers, off the mouth of the Delaware River, while *en route* to New York. The privateers put thirty men ashore and sent the ship toward Philadelphia. The English flag privateer *General Arnold* soon recaptured the *St. Joseph and Joachim*, took 27 of the American "rebels" off, and sent the ship on its way to New York. Before reaching that destination, however, another American privateer captured the cartel ship. This privateer took five "rebels" out, but then allowed the ship to proceed to New York. Mackenzie was sure this violation of the flag of Spain would be resented by that nation.[84]

Baurmeister expressed his opinion that everyone was curious as to how this affair would be handled by the American Congress. He also provided the name of a privateer, *Surprise*, which assisted the *General Arnold* in retaking the *St. Joseph and Joachim*. Baurmeister further notes that all the Spanish cartel ships had departed from New York prior to August 19, 1781, "without misgivings", as they were escorted by two armed ships.[85]

The 3rd English-Waldeck Regiment

By 1781 the English had realized that their transports could avoid some risk of capture by the French if the ships sailed directly from Germany to New York, going north of the British Isles. In a secret letter to the Admiralty, Germain set out the number of men being furnished in 1781 by the German states. Hesse-Cassel was sending 850 recruits, Hanau was sending 60 chasseurs (jaegers) and a new corps of light infantry, numbering 850 men, and 500 Anhalt-Zerbsters, 250 Ansbach recruits, and 150 Waldeck recruits were expected, also.[86]

On April 12, 1781, Germain notified General Frederick Haldimand in Canada that recruits for Canada would sail directly from Germany to New York, passing north of Scotland, and would then proceed to Canada.[87]

When embarked on April 26, 1781, the German troop distribution, as forwarded by Faucitt, was:[88]

937 - Hesse-Cassel	903 - Hanauers
154 - Brunswickers	144 - Waldeckers
207 - Ansbachers	2,809 - total
441 - Anhalt-Zerbsters	23 - for the 60th Regiment

According to the assessment by Faucitt, sent to Viscount Stormont, and dated May 4, the men from Hesse-Cassel were better than in 1780. The Anhalt-Zerbst and Ansbach recruits were very fine, but the Waldeckers were of an inferior quality. The new corps provided by Hanau was better than Faucitt had expected, and even the recruits for the 60th Regiment appeared capable. The total transport of about 2,984 persons, included 171 women.[89]

Mackenzie's diary sums up the 1781 recruit shipment more thoroughly than the bits and pieces. After a thirteen week voyage from Bremerlehe, the fleet appeared in The Narrows at 11 A.M. on August 11. By 3 P.M. the fleet had anchored in the harbor. With an escort of the *Amphion*, 32-cannons, the *Ostrich*, and the *Britannia*, 23 transports had carried nearly 3,000 troops from Germany to New York. Along with other

The 3rd English-Waldeck Regiment

contingents, the Waldeck force which arrived in New York, included: 1 staff officer, 6 non-commissioned officers, 8 drummers, 128 rank and file, plus 8 women and 2 children, for a total of 153 persons.[90]

On the crossing, seven of the Waldeck recruits died, and one man died aboard ship in New York harbor. These men were: [91]

Peter Kremer (W200862), born in Barenstein, who died on July 16
Christian Kuehn (W200866), born in Tornow, who died on August 12
Johannes Hempelmann(W200897), born in Volkmarsen, who died on August 2
Jakob Michel (W200915), born in Erpfingen, who died on July 3
Johannes Roeder (W200941), born in Buehlertann, who died on August 6
Johannes Strosser (W200961), born in Geisenkirchen, Austria, who died on July 17
Gottlob Ulbricht (W200967), born in Sayda (Zeiden), who died on August 5, and
Wilhelm Weichselfelder (W200972), born in Schotten, who died on August 2.

The other Waldeck recruits, all of whom were apparently assigned to 3 Company, were:

Josef Aschenhauer (W200838), born in Hildesheim
Johannes Bangert (W200839)
Adam Barth (W200840)
Karl Bauer (W200841), born in Arolsen
Georg Baumgarten (W200842)
Lorenz Becker (W200843)
Michael Beringer (W200844)
Wilhelm Bestelmeier (W200845), born in Nuernberg
Fifer Franz Chrn Adam Bigge (W200846), born in Sudeck
Konrad Bock (W200847)
Ludwig (Lewis) Bremer (W200848)
Konrad Brock (W200849)
Ludwig Buchholtz (W200850)
Johannes Buehler (W200851), born in Reutlingen
Sebastian Buehler (W200852), born in Degerndorf

The 3rd English-Waldeck Regiment

Peter Burghann (W200853), born in Bovenden
Karl Kampf (W200854)
Bernhard Keipel (W200855)
Gottlieb Kessler (W200856)
Friedrich Christenau (W200857), born in Riga
Georg Knees (W200858), born in Reinershausen
Lorenz Kohl (W200859)
Fifer Nikolaus Collig (W200860)
Georg Krauss (W200861), born in Engolling
Karl Kreyeer (W200863)
Christian Kriegmann (W200864), born in Mengeringhausen
Drummer Friedrich Kriegsmann (W200865)
Johannes Kuhn (W200867), born in Holsdorf
Johannes Deege (W200868)
Jakob (Jean) de la Dior (W200869), born in Augsburg
Friedrich Dietrich (W200870), born in Oberelsungen
Henrich Engelhard (W200871), born 1765 in Nieder-Werbe
Christian Erb (W200872), born in Sondershausen
Jakob Fieberling (W200874)
Johannes Fieger (W200875), born in Eichstaett
Henrich Fischer (W200876), born in Ammenhausen
Ludwig Fischer (W200877)
Sebastian Francke (W200878), born in Nuernberg
August Freyse (W200879), born in Hannover
Drummer Anton Fricke (W200880)
Johannes Gerger (W200881)
Karl Gerhard (W200882), born in Dinkelsbuehl
Johannes Giebel (W200883), born 1766 in Barssen, Pyrmont
Christian Giessel (W200884), born in Datum, Ansbach
Cpl. Georg Goercke (W200885)
Johannes Grubert (W200886), born in Ederheim
Christoph Haag (W200887)
Henrich Haag (W200888), born in Zimmersrode
Jakob Hagel(n) (W200889), born in Prickingen
Peter Hamm (W200890), born in Aulenbach
Albrecht Hartig (W200891)
Anton Hartmann (W200892), born in Ronsberg
Ulrich Hartmann (W200893)
Drummer Philipp Hauschild (W201189), born 1765 in Waldeck
Peter Hauser (W200894)
Leonhard Heberlein (W200895), born 1763 in Obernzenn

The 3rd English-Waldeck Regiment

Jakob Heck (W200896), born in Endersbach
Friedrich Hertzog (W200898)
Johann Jost Hillebrand (W200899), born in Flechtdorf
Johannes Hoppe (W200900)
Peter Hunold (W200901), born in Medebach
Wilhelm Huthmann (W200902), born 1765 in Mengeringhausen
Martin Jonas (W21100903), born in Luxembourg
Philipp Laubach (W200904), born in Kleinern
Christian Laue (W200905), born in Oerzen
Adam Lentzer (W200906)
Friedrich Leutmann (W200907), born in Feuchtnau
Michael Lindauer (W200908)
Franz Lindemeyer (W200909), born in Buchendorf
Friedrich Joh. Meckler (W200910), born in Woltershausen
Ludwig Mertz (W200911)
Konrad Meyer (W200913), born in Wildungen
Georg Michael (W200914), born in Obershausen
Berthold Mueller (W200916)
Christian Mueller (W201162)
Surg. Mate Franz Mueller (W200918)
Georg Mueller (W200919)
Henrich Muenchmeyer (W200920), born 1741 in Mehlen
Ernst Neumeier (W200922)
Drummer Henrich Obermann (W200923)
Thomas Obkircher (W200925), born in Bobingen
Friedrich Patermann (W200926)
Christian Peters (W200927), born in Linden
Paul Samuel Peterson (W200928), born in Nagelsberg
Johannes Pfeiffer (W200929), born in Burgsolms
Adam Plado (W200930)
Michael Preiss (W200931), born in Vienna
Georg Joh. Probst (W200932)
Jost Rabensprock (W200933)
Georg Reese (W200935), born 1765 in Holtzhausen Pyrmont
Johannes Rehrohr (W200936)
Johannes Reichhard (W200937), born in Altenburg
Michael Reiss (W200938), born in Blaufelden
Cpl. Friedrich Renne (W200939), born in Hannover
Bernhard Reuter (W200940), born in 1732
Christian Rischebusch (W200942)
Konrad Roose (W200943)

The 3rd English-Waldeck Regiment

Karl Roquette (W200934)
Georg Rummel (W200944)
Johannes Sassmanshausen (W200945), born 1764 in Pente
Cpl. Georg Schaper (W200946)
Konrad Schenckel (W200948), born in Wiesenbach
Henrich Schmidt (W200949)
Christian Schmidtmann (W200950) born in Heselbrik
Thomas Schneider (W200951) born in Endebrueck
Joh. Zacharias Schramm (W200952)
Cpl. Johannes Schreier (W200921)
Michael Schultze (W200953) born in 1759 in Weissenbach
Philipp Schumacher (W200954) born in Lauterbach
Christian Siemon (W200829) born in Weissenfels
Chrn. Johannes Siemon (W201163) born in Augsburg
Christian Sinemus (W200955) born in Rhoden
Johannes Sinemus (W200956) born in Rhoden
Konrad Sinn (W200957) born in Wegenfeld
Sgt. Konrad Starcke (W200958)
Albrecht Steinmetz (W200959) born in Nuernberg
Ludwig Stremmel (W200960)
Karl Struck (W200962)
Wilhelm Tabroth (W200873) born in Neimen
Johannes Teichler (W200963) born in Stuhlweissenburg
Georg Teschel (W200964) born in Bavaria
Georg Tuchscheer (W200966) born in Westernau
Drummer Andreas Ulrich (W200968)
Josef Urbach (W200969)
Nikolaus Wagener (W200970) born in Zell
Johannes Wagenstahl (W200971)
Adam Weiss (W200973) born in Vienna
Johannes Weiss (W200974) born in Kupferzell
Nikolaus Weitzel (W200975) born in Echzell
August Wesserleim (W201190) born 1759 in Zittau
Henrich Weste (W200976) born in Reine
Samuel Wieth (W200977) born in Wittgenstein
Christian Wirth (W200978) born in Geschwind, and
Veit Wolff (W200979) born in Schwabia.

After the Waldeck Regiment returned to New York, there were no further desertions during the remainder of the year 1781, and apparently none of the 1781 recruits deserted, either.

The 3rd English-Waldeck Regiment

However, illness and accidents continued to take a serious toll within the ranks of the regiment. Among former members of the Pensacola garrison, the following Waldeck soldiers died at Newtown in 1781:[92]

Henrich Schwerd (W200467), 4 Company, on September 7
Friedrich Thiemann (W200796), 4 Company, on September 18
Peter Knueppel (W200406), 4 Company, on September 30
Henrich Knies (W200668), 2 Company, on October 10
Christian Cleemann (W200666), 4 Company, on October 16
Peter Hugen (W200192), 2 Company, on December 6
Servant Friedrich Emde (W200773) on December 10, and
Johannes Misco (W200826), 4 Company, on December 15.

Recruits, all of 3 Company, who had arrived in the 1781 recruit shipment, and who died in New York in 1781, were:

Philipp Schumacher (W200954), on August 13
Konrad Schenkel (W200948), on August 30, and
Paul Samuel Peterson (W200928), on September 9.

The recruits were then moved to Newtown, apparently, as those who died thereafter, all from 3 Company, were listed as having died at the hospital in Newtown. They were:

Nikolaus Weitzel (W200975), on September 19
Christian Peters (W200927), on September 20
Friedrich Leutmann (W200907), on September 21
Georg Knees (W200858), on September 24
Johann Jost Hillebrand (W200899), on October 1
August Freyse (W200879), on October 16
Georg Teschel (W200964), on October 19
Veit Wolff (W200979), on October 21
Christian Kriegsmann (W200864), on October 31
Johann Zacharias Schramm (W200952), on November 1
Christian Erb (W200872), on November 1
Jakob Hagel(n) (W200889), on November 22
Josef Aschenhauer (W200838), on November 23
Albrecht Steinmetz (W200959), on November 24

The 3rd English-Waldeck Regiment
Wilhelm Huthmann (W200902), on December 3
Drummer Philipp Hauschild (W201189), on December 11
Henrich Engelhard (W200871), on December 12, and
Fifer Franz Chrn. Adam Bigge (W200846), on December 23

Servant Lorenz Scheer (W201186) also died in New York on November 29. As his name appears in *HETRINA* for the first time in 1781, and his name is not on any recruit list, he may have been taken into the regiment in America.

Four men were released from the regiment in 1781, and all prior to the capitulation at Pensacola. All four men probably returned to Europe. Two had served throughout the war as servants for staff officers and one was Colonel von Hanxleden's son. Because their release meant they would probably not be prisoners of war, one can assume the reason for their release. Those released were:[93]

Sgt. Andreas Hemmeling (W200712), 3 Company, in April
Claude Prieur (W200585), who had been the servant to the regimental surgeon according to Chaplain Waldeck, released on April 25
Philipp Volcke (W200481), 4 Company, who had been the chaplain's servant, released on April 25, and
Cadet Wilhelm von Hanxleden (W200371), 3 Company, and the son of Colonel von Hanxleden, released on April 25.

Strength figures for the Waldeck Regiment at New York during the closing days of 1781 are of interest. On August 20, "victualled" figures for the regiment are: 385 men, 24 women, and 19 children. These figures would seem to indicate reference to Waldeckers of the Pensacola garrison and their dependents, and that they had not been sent to Long Island as of that date. The day previous, seven horses had been foraged, also, for members of the regiment.[94]

Mackenzie gives strength figures on a regular basis which leave the reader trying to understand what they mean. On September 1, 1781, he recorded 124 fit for duty, 127 sick, and 504 effectives for the Waldeck Regiment. This would seem to

The 3rd English-Waldeck Regiment

represent 124 recruits fit for duty, 127 sick of both the recruits and the Pensacola garrison, and a total of both detachments of 504 men.[95]

Although the terms of the capitulation would seem to have allowed the troops surrendered at Pensacola to fight against the Americans, it appears that Clinton kept these men separate from his other troops and assigned them no duties of a war-like nature until after some sort of exchange agreement was negotiated with Spain. The 1781 Waldeck recruits, however, were not affected by the surrender at Pensacola and so were assigned duties as if a separate command in no way connected with the Waldeckers at Newtown.

On September 15, Mackenzie listed only 131 Waldeck soldiers fit for duty, with no reference to those who were sick, nor to total effectives. It would seem therefore, that he was only reporting the men available from the 1781 recruit shipment. On October 1, his figures show 78 fit for duty, 43 sick, and a total of 121 effectives at Newtown, and again he seems to be reporting on the recruits only. Figures for October 15-23 are even more confusing as Mackenzie lists only 29 fit for duty and 83 sick, but arrives at a total of 113 effectives stationed at Paulus Hook with 373 men of Anhalt-Zerbst. Finally, for November 18, Mackenzie's figures are for the Pensacola garrison, in cantonments in Newtown. These figures show 173 men fit for duty, 122 sick, and a total of 947 effectives. The meaning of the number of men sick is uncertain, but the 947 effectives is obviously the total number of survivors from the Pensacola garrison, including the Waldeck Regiment, the 16th and 60th Regiments, and the provincial units.[96]

Meantime the war continued and General Clinton continued his vascilation as to how to conduct the war. He was firm, however, in his determination to keep the Waldeckers in the New York area. On August 26, when Clinton was contemplating an attack on Rhode Island, Mackenzie noted that

The 3rd English-Waldeck Regiment

the 1781 Waldeck recruit detachment would remain in the New York area of Hornshook. Then, a month later, after designating the troops best suited for use as a relief force for General Cornwallis, the 120 Waldeckers at Hallet's Cove were among the troops to be left at New York. When the relief force sailed on October 19, the Waldeckers did remain in the New York area.[97]

Eighty of the Waldeck recruits had been transferred from Long Island to Paulus Hook on October 7, and replaced 120 Brunswickers who were moved down to Denyce's Ferry. The garrison at Paulus Hook then consisted of the Waldeckers and the entire Anhalt-Zerbst contingent, which Mackenzie called a free corps, under the command of Lieutenant Colonel Andreas Emmerich. On October 13, a party of rebels attacked an advance post at Paulus Hook and captured one Waldeck soldier and one soldier from Anhalt-Zerbst.[98]

On November 15, Mackenzie recorded that the Waldeck and Anhalt-Zerbst soldiers at Paulus Hook, when relieved, were to move in sloops to Brooklyn. The Waldeckers would then march to Newtown. The Germans were to be relieved by English troops, who were to be at Denyce's Ferry at daybreak to take sloops to Paulus Hook. Next day, Mackenzie recorded the movement of the troops as planned.[98]

The most significant personnel changes in 1781 came about because of the death of the Waldeck commander and his adjutant at The Village, and the loss of Pensacola. Lieutenant Colonel von Horn assumed command of the regiment and appointed 1st Lieutenant Jakob Knipschild to be his adjutant, replacing the fallen Ensign Stierlein.[99]

Without guns to serve, the members of the Artillery detachment were transferred to 3 Company in June 1781. Those reassigned were:[100]

Bombardier Martin Heidorn (W300009)
Bombardier Wilhelm Schultze (W300014)
Cannoneer Karl Brauns (W300002)

The 3rd English-Waldeck Regiment

Cannoneer Henrich Depmeier (W300003)
Cannoneer Kaspar Effe (W300004)
Cannoneer Jakob Graebe (W300006)
Cannoneer Wilhelm Huebsch (W300011)
Cannoneer Daniel Rohde (W200345A)
Cannoneer Gottfried Stabroth (W300013)
Cannoneer Christian Thietke (W300015)
Cannoneer Lorenz Ulrich (W200364A), and
Cannoneer Erdmann Zencke (W300017).

One man, who may have previously served in an English unit at Pensacola, is listed in *HETRINA* as joining the Waldeck Regiment in April 1781.[101] That man was Johannes Meyer (W200912) of 4 Company. Others who joined the regiment in 1781, were:[102]

Servant Georg Bachmann (W201084), 2 Company.
Servant John Bop (W201170), 4 Company
Servant Johannes Budde (W201171), 3 Company
Servant Caesar (W291173), 4 Company. Apparently an American Negroe. Six other Negroes are listed in *HETRINA* as serving with the regiment, but no names are used to identify them.
Servant Wilhelm Kuehne (W201174), 4 Company
Servant Thomas Pinck (W201182), 3 Company
Servant Lorenz Scheer (W201186), company unknown
Servant Johannes Schmidt (W201187), 5 Company, and
Servant Johannes Way (W201188), 4 Company.

Other personnel changes within the Waldeck Regiment during 1781, were:[103]

Cpl. Johannes Schreier (W200921), one of the 1781 recruits, was demoted to private in September.
Cpl. Karl Schnabel (W200222), 4 Company, was demoted to private in June and returned to corporal in October, and
Friedrich Boehme (W201112), 3 Company, was promoted to corporal in December.
Lieutenants Brumhard and Strubberg are listed in *HETRINA* as returned to duty in 1781. As they were listed on a January 1782 return of Waldeck officers as being prisoners of Spain at Havana, the actual return to duty

The 3rd English-Waldeck Regiment

must have been between January 1 and March 20, 1782, when they were back on duty.

The annual strength report of March 20, 1782, also lists Sergeant Henrich Schluckebier (W200002), two privates, and one servant as having been released by the Spaniards between May 23 and December 31, 1781.[104]

Two additional letters written during 1781 should be noted. On June 5, Germain wrote to Clinton that Lieutenant Heldring of the 3rd Waldeck Regiment and acting engineer at Pensacola was to be given a captaincy in the English 60th Regiment. This would certainly seem to be a compliment of the highest order concerning Heldring's military knowledge and professionalism. As his own prince had promoted him to the rank of captain lieutenant the year before, and for other unknown reasons, Heldring seems not to have accepted the English commission.[105]

The second letter was written by Georg Hesse, at the Horse Guard, to a John Fischer, on September 22, stating that the Prince of Waldeck, who had just sent 140 recruits to his regiment in America, was willing to send more troops if the captive officers could be exchanged.[106]

The year 1781 was both the worst year, and in many ways, the best year that the Waldeck Regiment spent in America. The commander had been killed in an unsuccessful attack on The Village and the remnants of the regiment had been included in the surrender at Pensacola. But, the defense of Pensacola against a vastly superior force, was one of which the defenders could be proud. To the men of the Waldeck Regiment, the surrender terms meant an end to duty in the desolation of Florida and a return to the more hospitable New York.

During 1781, 142 recruits sailed for America, but eight died *en route*. Fourteen men were acquired from unknown sources so that the year saw another 148 men identified in America with the Waldeck Regiment. Eleven members of the regiment were killed in combat or died of their wounds; 38 men died of non-

The 3rd English-Waldeck Regiment

combat causes, including five members of the regiment who were prisoners of war. Four men were released from the regiment and probably returned to Europe and 42 men deserted, of whom two were prisoners of war. One man, unidentified, who had deserted from prisoner of war status, returned to the regiment.

As of the last day of 1781, the regiment had an estimated strength of 380 men, plus 105 men held as prisoners of war.

The 3rd English-Waldeck Regiment
1782

Lieutenant Colonel von Horn signed a roster of the officers of the Waldeck Regiment, at Newtown,, Long Island, on January 1782. The list contains the names of the officers and staff, as well as their date of rank, and if absent, where located. Names with asterisks were prisoners of the Spaniards at Havana:[1]

Lt. Col. Albrecht von Horn, date of rank April 14, 1779
Major Friedrich Pentzel, date of rank April 14, 1779
Capt. (Gren.) Georg von Haacke, date of rank April '19, 1776**
Capt. (Gren.) Christoph Alberti, date of rank September 20, 1777**
Capt. Lt. Alexander von Baumbach, date or rank March 16, 1776
Capt. Lt. August Alberti, date of rank March 5, 1777**
Capt. Lt. Gerhard Heldring, date of rank April 25, 1780
1st Lt. Wilhelm Keppel, date of rank March 7, 1776
1st Lt. Friedrich von Wilmowsky, date of rank March 8, 1776
1st Lt. (Gren.) Karl Strubberg, date of rank March 5, 1777**
1st Lt. (Gren.) Andreas Brumhard, date of rank April 14, 1779**
2nd Lt. Karl Hohmann, date of rank April 25, 1780
Ensign Ludwig Schmidt, date of rank April 14, 1779
Ensign Karl Mueller, date of rank April 15, 1779
Chaplain Philipp Waldeck, date of rank April 24, 1776
Adjutant Henr. Jakob Knipschild, date of rank April 25, 1780
Quartermaster Theodor Wiegand, date of rank March 2, 1776
Surgeon Ludwig Christian Mattern, date of rank April 20, 1776
Auditor Philipp Marc, date of rank March 2, 1776

The *HETRINA* indicates the following individuals were to have been exchanged by the Spaniards according to an agreement worked-out during January 1782. Those with an asterisk deserted at Havana prior to being exchanged.[2]

1 Company

Ludwig Bauerschmidt (W200024)
Ludwig Berges (W200025)
Wilhelm Berghoever (W200026)

The 3rd English-Waldeck Regiment

Joh. Georg Bock (W200518)
Adam Kann (W200030)**
Johannes Kann (W200031)
Henrich Kaufmann (W200033)
Johannes Kesthans (W200034)
Jost Stefan Kleucker (W200037)
Barthold Knoechel (W200159)**
Franz Cramer (W200048)**
Henrich Ebersbach (W200055)
Andreas Eichinger (W200687)
Christian Eisenberg (W200170)
Johannes Embde (W200056)
Peter Ernst (W200689)
Philipp Hamel (W200068)
Daniel Hartmann (W200070)
Philipp Henrich (W200306)
Henrich Herbold (W200071)
Drummer Jakob Matte (W200016)
Johannes Michael (W200568)**
Johannes Moock (W200079)
Christian Mueller (W200645)
Cpl. Philipp Mueller (W200084)
Sgt. Joh. Kaspar von Nehm (W200004)
Anton Noll (W200088)**
Drummer Theodor Repp (W200015)
Friedrich Rodewald (W200590)**
Cpl. Christoph Roemer (W200010)**
Johannes Runte (W200458)
Johannes Schaeffer (W200630)
Ulrich Schreiber (W200108)
Henr. Wilhelm Stallmann (W200791)**
Fifer Christoph Steinmeyer (W200013)
Henrich Striepecke (W200114)
Jakob Walter (W200118)**
Joh. Henrich Weber (W200802)**
Cpl. Christoph Weishaupt (W200012)
Stefan Wichard (W200123)

The 3rd English-Waldeck Regiment

2 Company

Daniel Beisenhertz (W200147)
Henrich Klaus (W200157)
Johann Jost Drewes (W2300168)**
Henrich Fischer (W200175)**
Georg Friedeborn (W200177)**
Cpl. Henrich Gockel (W200180)
Johannes Meybaum (W200200)
Bernhard Mundhenck (W200207)
Josef Perle (W200744)
Philipp Rabensprock (W200210)
Bernhard Schaper (W200216)
Sgt. Dietrich Schotte (W200131)
Free Cpl Bernhard Schreiber (W200779)
Henrich Stiesing (W200232)**
Johannes Stoecker (W200233)**
Drummer Johannes Unger (W200143)**
Cpl. Jeremias Warlich (W200142)**

5 Company

Christoph Arend (W200269)
Surg. Mate Daniel Beck (W200255)
Johannes Becker (W200514)
Cpl. Bernhard Berges (W200501)
Johannes Berges (W200515)
Christian Brand (W200519)
Chrn. Daniel Brandenstein (W200520)
Karl Kleine (W200283)**
Peter Kremer (W200286)
Philipp Duesse (W200528)**
Christian Jakob Engelhard (W200530)
Christian Figge (W200291)**
Matthias Flamme (W200293)
Henrich Francke (W200535)
Georg Geitz (W200538)
Johannes Goebel (W200300)**
Johannes Goebel (W200540)
Christian Goedecke (W200541)
Henrich Heinecke (W200547)

The 3rd English-Waldeck Regiment

Capt./Arms Franz Henckeler (W200497)
Konrad Handel (W200548)
Henrich Hoelscher (W200310)
Barthold Jaeger (W200555)
Bernhard Mengeringhausen (W200565)
Johannes Meuske (W200330)**
Jakob Meyer (W200567)
Konrad Meyer (W200331)
Daniel Mueller (W200334)
Daniel von Nehm (W200576)
Wilhelm Neubauer (W200737)
Henrich Pieper (W200584)
Johannes Risch (W200751)**
Jakob Scharschmid (W200596)
Joh. Georg Schimmel (W200598)**
Franz Schirr (W200346)
Konrad Schmidt (W200599)
Cpl. Wilhelm Scriba (W200785)
Cpl. Justus Simshaeuser (W200502)
Georg Tent (W200606)
Cpl. Jean Tuitel (W201152)**
Johannes Vollmar (W200610)
Johannes Weidenhagen (W200611)
Sgt. Franz Theo. Wildstach (W200496)
Kaspar Zeiger (W200616) and
Henrich Zimmermann (W200618)

On March 20, 1782, the 3rd Waldeck Regiment at Newtown, Long Island, reported the following manning for the regiment. Individual names added by this writer.[3]

Officers

1 Company - 2 1st lieutenants (Strubberg and Brumhard)
2 Company - 1 1st lieutenant (Keppel), 1 ensign (Schmidt)
3 Company - 1 captain lieutenant (Baumbach), 2 1st lieutenants (Wilmowsky and Knipschild, who was also adjutant)
4 Company - 1 major (Pentzel), 1 captain lieutenant (Heldring), 1 sub-lieutenant (Hohmann), 1 ensign (Mueller)
5 Company - 1 lieutenant colonel (Horn)

The 3rd English-Waldeck Regiment
Staff

1 regimental quartermaster (Wiegand)
1 adjutant - (Knipschild)
1 chaplain - (Waldeck)
1 regimental surgeon - (Mattern)
1 Commissary - (Marc)
2 Company surgeon's mates - (Pfister and Hoffmeister)
1 regimental drummer - (Glaentzer)
1 provost - (Budde)
1 equipment servant - (Reuter)
1 wagon servant - (Hufeisen), and
1 surgeon's mate with transport - (Schultze)

Captains von Haacke and Christoph Alberti and Surgeon's Mate Daniel Beck (W200255) were still prisoners of war.

Other than the officers listed above, the companies had a strength, as follows:

1 Company - 1 musician and 3 privates
2 Company - 4 non-commissioned officers, 3 corporals, 3 musicians, and 45 privates. One private was absent on command.
3 Company - 3 non-commissioned officers,, 6 corporals, 4 musicians, and 62 privates. One corporal and two privates were absent on command.
4 Company - 5 non-commissioned officers, 4 corporals, 3 musicians, and 73 privates. Three privates were absent on command.
5 Company - 12 privates
Artillery - 2 non-commissioned officers and 7 privates
Recruit transport - 1 non-commissioned officer, 3 corporals, 4 musicians, and 78 privates. (This would seem to be the 1781 recruit transport.) for a TOTAL of - 15 non-commissioned officers, 16 corporals, 15 musicians, and 273 privates, plus 7 artillery privates.

One corporal and six privates were on command in New York on baggage detail, and Cadet Boehme (W201112), who had been promoted to corporal in December 1781, was assigned to the recruit transport. One non-commissioned officer of 3 Company, Sergeant Amandus Hemmerling (W200712), was absent on recruiting duty.

The 3rd English-Waldeck Regiment

A very difficult to read note seems to the effect that two subalterns, one sergeant, one surgeon's mate, six musicians, four corporals, and 99 privates, and one staff servant of the above individuals, were or had been prisoners of war, but the words are so illegible that the translation may be in error.

The next breakdown appears to pertain to those individuals sick in quarters and those in hospital. Alberti, or 2 Company, had four privates sick, locally. The Vacant, or 3 Company, had one private sick, locally, and one private sick in Pensacola. The recruit transport had two musicians and fourteen privates sick, locally, and one private sick in New York.

A report of prisoners of war indicated 145 men still held prisoners by Spain and thirteen held by the Americans.

1 Company - 1 non-commissioned officer, 6 corporals, 3 musicians, and 43 privates held by Spain; 3 privates held by the Americans
2 Company - 2 non-commissioned officers, 2 corporals, 1 musician, and 28 privates held by Spain
3 Company - 13 privates held by Spain; 2 privates held by the Americans
4 Company - 2 privates held by the Americans
5 Company - 2 non-commissioned officers, 4 corporals, and 40 privates held by Spain, and
Recruit transport - 1 private held by the Americans.

All categories of troop dispositions added together gave the regiment the following effectives and shortages:

1 Company - 1 non-commissioned officer, 5 corporals, 4 musicians, and 49 privates; short - 4 non-commissioned officers, 1 musician, and 61 privates
2 Company - 6 non-commissioned officers, 5 corporals, 4 musicians, and 78 privates; short - 1 corporal and 29 privates
3 Company - 4 non-commissioned officers, 7 corporals, 4 musicians, and 81 privates; short - 26 privates
4 Company - 6 non-commissioned officers, 5 corporals, 3 musicians, and 83 privates; short - 1 c orporal, 1 musician, and 24 privates.
5 Company - 2 non-commissioned officers, 4 corporals, 1 musician, and 56 privates; short - 4 non-commissioned officers, 2 corporals, 3 musicians, and 51 privates

The 3rd English-Waldeck Regiment

Artillery - 2 non-commissioned officers and 8 privates, including one private sick; short - 4 privates

Recruit transport - 1 non-commissioned officer, 3 corporals, 6 musicians, and 94 privates

Losses during the period - 2 Company suffered two dead; 3 Company had 1 dead; 5 Company had one dead, and the recruit transport suffered eleven dead and one transferred, for a total of fifteen dead and one transferred. No combat casualties nor desertions were noted.

When the recruit transport figures are subtracted from the reported shortages, the regiment still was nine non-commissioned officers and 97 privates under strength and one musician was an overage.

Muster rolls in the Clements Library Manuscript Collection for all but the Grenadier Company of the Waldeck Regiment for the period December 25, 1781, to June 24, 1782, were signed by the company officers and/or Lieutenant Colonel von Horn for the Waldeckers and by William Potter, Commissary, for the English on June 12, 1782. The 1781 recruit shipment had been integrated into 3 Company by this time. Pentzel's Company was far over strength, while 2 and 5 Companies were companies in name only, being far under strength. At least part of the prisoners of war captured by Spain in West Florida had returned to duty. The following lists cover entries on the muster rolls, with an asterisk indicating men on detached duty and two asterisks indicate men reported as sick.[4]

2 Company - Captain Alberti's Company

Captain Christoph Alberti (W100004)
Servant Georg Bachmann (W201084)
Sgt. Dietrich Schotte (W200131)
Free Cpl. Bernhard Schreiber (W200779)
Cpl. Henrich Gockel (W200136), and privates
Bernhard Schaper (W200216)
Henrich Klaus (W200157)
Johannes Goebel (W200180)
Stefan Struebe (W200234)
Josef Perle (W200744)**

The 3rd English-Waldeck Regiment

Bernhard Munthenck (W200207)
Daniel Beisenhertz (W200147)*
Johannes Meybaum (W200200)*
Philipp Rabensprock (W200210)*, and
Solicitor.

Deserters from 2 Company in 1782, were:

Cpl. Jeremias Warlich (W200142), on March 21
Drummer Johannes Unger (W200143), on April 2,
Georg Stoesing (W200232), on March 28
Georg Friedeborn (W200177), on March 29
Henrich Fischer (W200175), on April 2
Jost Drewes (W200168), on April 14, and
Johannes Stoecker (W200233), on April 14.

Present - 1 captain, 1 servant, 1 sergeant, 1 free corporal, 1 corporal, and 5 privates
Absent - 4 privates and 1 solicitor
Effectives - 1 captain, 1 servant, 1 sergeant, 1 free corporal. 1 corporal, 9 privates, and 1 solicitor as of June 24, 1782
During this muster, deserted - 1 corporal, 1 drummer, and 5 privates

Signed at Newtown, Long Island, on July 12, 1782, by Captain von Haacke and William Potter, Commissary.

3 Company - Vacant Company

1st Lieutenant Friedrich von Wilmowsky (W100012)

Staff

Lt. Col. and Captain Albrecht von Horn (W100003S)
Major and Captain Friedrich Pentzel (W100005S)
Capt. Lieutenant Alexander von Baumbach (W100007)
Capt. Lieutenant Henrich Heldring (W100014)
Lt. and Quartermaster Karl Wiegand (W100022S)
Lt. and Adjutant Henrich Jakob Knipschild (W100013S)
Commissary Philipp Marc (W400003)
Chaplain Philipp Waldeck (W400005)

The 3rd English-Waldeck Regiment

Surgeon Major Christian Mattern (W400004)
Drum Major Christian Glaentzer (W400001)
Provost Christian Budde (W200260S)
Provost Asst. Bernhard Reuter (W200940S), transfer to staff on Feb. 24
Servant for the Chest Henrich Hufeisen (W201180S)
Fifer Christian Berckenhauser (W200141), and privates
Wilhelm Melcher (W200327)
Friedrich Peter (W201144)
Christian Klee (W200664)
Franz Christian Bigge (W200846) - died January 23, 1782 (previously reported as having died at Newtown on December 23, 1781), and Nikolaus Collig (W200860)

Men of 3 Company

Sgt. Jakob Graebe (W200251)
Sgt. Amandus Hemmerling (W200712), recruiting in Germany
Sgt. Georg Ulner (W200254)
Sgt. Konrad Starcke (W200958)
QM Sgt. Georg Muus (W200259)
Capt./Arms Johannes Knoechel (W200256), died March 17, 1782
Surg. Mate Franz Mueller (W200918)
Cpl. Johannes Rudelbach (W200256), baggage guard at NY
Cpl Stefan Hertzog (W200308)
Cpl. Christian Francke (W200295)**
Cpl. Henrich Schleiermacher (W200347)
Cpl. Philipp Meister (W200326)
Cpl. Henrich Muus (W200261)
Cpl. Georg Goercke (W200885)
Cpl. Georg Schaper (W200946)**
Cpl.. Friedrich Renne (W200939)
Corporal Friedrich Boehme (W201112)*, promoted from private December 25, 1781

Privates

Friedrich Otto (W200337)
Franz Weber (W200365)
Peter Kaus (W200277)
Johannes Albracht (W200267)
Henrich Kinold (W200278)
Joh. Georg Jost (W200313)
Philipp Klaus (W200282)

The 3rd English-Waldeck Regiment

Friedrich Graebe (W200301)
Jakob Wilhelm (W200368)
Konrad Steineck (W200357)
Wilhelm Figge (W200292)
Friedrich Soeltzer (W200355)
Moritz Gerlach (W200299)**
Philipp Kramer (W200285)**
Barthold Meuser (W200328)
Daniel Martin (W200320)
Johannes Ulrich (W200363)
Henrich Hering (W200307)
Jaspar Klahold (W200280), baggage guard at NY
Friedrich Roemer (W200344)
Friedrich Raabe (W200340)
Adam Schmid (W200348)
Henrich Raabe (W200341)
Johannes Tewes (W200361)
Jakob Becker (W200271)
Wilhelm Lindner (W200317)
Adam Geitz (W200297)
Valentin Malches (W200319)
Balthasar Heinschel (W200305)
Johannes Hesse (W200309)
Peter Martin (W200321)
Philipp Heinemann (W200304)
Reinhard Peltz (W200338)
Anton Weinhold (W200366)
Dietrich Siebel (W200353)*, at NY
Christian Bergmann (W200272)
Michael Schlauderbeck (W200766)
Christoph Wiegmann (W200812)
Gottfried Nikolaus (W200738)
Jakob Bieg (W200644)
Philipp Muench (W201143)
Georg Fuehrer (W200699)
David Schneider, Sr. (W200774)
Jakob Fauser (W200691)
Christian Becker (W200637)
Andreas Baus (W200635)
Henrich Lange (W200314)
Wilhelm Taubert (W200116)

The 3rd English-Waldeck Regiment

Henrich Arend (W200020)
Johannes Strehle (W201150)
Theodor Bunse (W200655)
Johannes Lichtner (W200726)
Henrich Klee (W200665)
Michael Pfitzer (W200747)
Alisius Fass (W200690)
Friedrich Uhlmann (W200799)
Johannes Weissenborn (W200805)
Ignatius Bachstaedter (W200021)
Johannes Schaeffer (W200592)
Franz Ziegler (W200617)
Henrich Koehler (W200524)
Friedrich Schele (W200597)
Kaspar Pickel (W200583)**
Martin Dantzer (W200680)
Henrich Kuethe (W200821)
Henrich Schnepper (W200830)
August Westmeier (W200836)
Henrich Boltze (W200819)
Henrich Flamme (W200822)
Anton Schuetz (W200831)
Christian Meisner (W200825)
Philipp Ebe (W200622)
Christian Dullmann (W200290)
Franz Mueller (W201172)
Daniel Rohde (W200345)**
Lorenz Ulrich (W200364)
Matthias Ohlhaber (W200741)
Michael Goebel (W200701)
Henrich Schmidt (W200949)*
Georg Mueller (W200919)*
Ludwig Bremer (W200848)**
Johannes Hoppe (W200900)*
Johannes Kuhn (W200867)*
Henrich Weste (W200976)*
Samuel Wieth (W200977)*
Wilhelm Tabroth (W200873)*
Johannes Michlaer (W200910)
Friedrich Petermann (W200926)**
Johannes Gerger (W200881)

The 3rd English-Waldeck Regiment

Wilhelm Bestelmeier (W200845)**
Karl Bauer (W200841)*
Johannes Reichhard (W200937)*
Gottlieb Kessler (W200937)*
Jakob Fieberling (W200874)
Sebastian Francke (W200878)
Christian Siemon (W200829)
Karl Gerhard (W200882)*
Peter Hauser (W200894)*
Christian Haag (W200887)
Johannes Grubert (W200886)*
Christian Giessel (W200884)**
Lorenz Kohl (W200859)*
Ludwig Stremmel (W200960)**
Thomas Schneider (W200951)
Johannes Pfeiffer (W2300929)**
Christian Laue (W200905)*
Bernhard Keipel (W200855)*
Henrich Fischer (W200876)**
Karl Kreyer (W200863)
Konrad Roose (W200943)*
Friedrich Christenau (W200857)
Konrad Meyer (W200913)
Ludwig Mertz (W200911)
Karl Kampf (W200854)*
Georg Rummel (W200944)**
Jean de la Dior (W200869)
Just Rabensprock (W200933)*
Konrad Bock (W200847)
Philipp Laubach (W200904)
Friedrich Hertzog (W200898)
Michael Reiss (W200938)**
Johannes Fieger (W200875)*
Johannes Rehrohr (W200936)*
Johannes Teichler (W200963)*
Albrecht Hartig (W200891)
Lorenz Becker (W200843)
Christian Schmidtmann (W200950)*
Ernst Neumeier (W200922)*
Christian Johann Siemon (W201163)
Peter Hunold (W200901)*

The 3rd English-Waldeck Regiment

Georg Michael (W200914)
Ulrich Hartmann (W200893)
Johannes Buehler (W200851)
Karl Roquette (W200934)*
Friedrich Lindemeier (W200909)
Peter Hamm (W200890)*
Georg Tuchscheer (W200966)*
Konrad Brock (W200849)
Adam Barth (W200840)
Georg Baumgarten (W200842)*
Johannes Deege (W200868)*
Christian Rischebusch (W200942)
Adam Lentzer (W200906)*
Adam Pflado (W200930)*
Ludwig Buchholtz (W200850)
Martin Jonas (W200903)*
Friedrich Diedrich (W200870)*
Peter Berghenn (W200853)*
Barthold Mueller (W200916)*
Nikolaus Wagener (W200970)*
Michael Lindauer (W200908)
Michael Beringer (W200844)*
Michael Preiss (W200931)
Josef Urbach (W200969)*
Georg Krauss (W200861)*
Jakob Heck (W200896)*
Johannes Weiss (W200974)
Thomas Obkircker (W200925)
Georg Probst (W200932)
Johannes Wagenstahl (W200971)*
Anton Hartmann (W200892)
Johannes Sinemus (W200956)*
Karl Struck (W200962)
Ludwig Fischer (W200877)**
Christian Sinemus (W200955)*
Johannes Schreier (W200921)*
Henrich Kleimenhagen (W201121)*, and
a solicitor

The 3rd English-Waldeck Regiment

(Henrich Kleimenhagen (W201121) had previously served as a servant with 4 Company but had deserted in 1777. He returned to duty on April 10, 1782.)

Servants

Franz Mangel (W200562)
Joh. Henrich Saenger (W200625)**
Johannes Budde (W201171)
Friedrich Neuschaefer (W201181)**
Thomas Pinck (W201182)

Artillery

Bombardier Wilhelm Schultze (W300014)
Bombardier Martin Heidorn (W300009)

Cannoneers

Henrich Depmeier (W300003)
Erdmann Zenecke (W300017)
Gottfried Stabroth (W300013)
Wilhelm Huebsch (W300011)
Christian Thietke (W300015), and
Kaspar Effe (W300004)**

(The two privates who had served with the Artillery, Daniel Rohde (W200345A) and Lorenz Ulrich (W200364A) are listed above with the privates, but as noted in the recapitulation below, were also considered as artillerymen.)

Personnel Changes

Friedrich Boehme (W201112), promoted to corporal on December 25, 171
Henrich Muenchmeier (W200920), died January 26, 1782
August Wesserlein (W201190), died January 28, 1782
Johannes Giebel (W200883), died January 30, 1782
Leonhad Heberlein (W200895), died January 31, 1782
Johannes Sassmannshausen (W200945), died February 19, 1782
Bernhard Reuter (W200940S), transferred to staff February 23, 1782
Michael Schultze (W200953), died March 3, 1782

The 3rd English-Waldeck Regiment

Georg Reese (W200935), died March 4, 11782
Christian Wirth (W200978), died April 11, 1782, and
Henrich Haag (W200888), died May 3, 1782

Recapitulation

Present - 1 1st lieutenant and 3 servants; Staff - 1 lieutenant colonel, 2 captain lieutenants, 1 quartermaster, 1 adjutant, 1 chaplain, 1 surgeon major, 1 drum major, 5 fifers, 1 provost, 1 provost assistant, 1 servant for the chest, 2 sergeants, 1 QM sergeant, 1 surgeon's mate, 6 corporals, 7 drummers, 106 privates; Artillery - 2 bombardiers and 7 cannoneers.

Absent - 2 servants; Staff - 1 major and 1 commissary; Artillery - 1 cannoneer.

Effectives - 1 1st lieutenant and 3 servants; Staff - 1 lieutenant colonel, 1 major, 2 captain lieutenants, 1 quartermaster, 1 adjutant, 1 commissary, 1 chaplain, 1 surgeon, 1 drum major, 5 fifers, 1 provost, 1 provost assistant, 1 servant for the chest, 4 sergeants, 1 QM sergeant, 1 surgeon's mate, 10 corporals, 8 drummers, 171 privates, 1 solicitor; Artillery - 2 bombardiers and 8 cannoneers, as of June 24, 1782.

During this muster - 1 fifer, 1 captain at arms, and 9 privates died; 1 private was promoted, 1 private was transferred, and 1 man was enlisted. (Franz Mueller may have been a new enlistee, or possibly the same man who deserted in 1777), and 1 provost assistant was received.

Signed at Newtown, Long Island, on July 12, 1782, by Lieutenant Colonel von Horn and William Potter, Commissary, for the period of 182 days from December 25, 1781, through June 24, 1782.

The 3rd English-Waldeck Regiment

4 Company - Major Pentzel's Company

1st Lieutenant Wilhelm Keppel (W100010)
2nd Lieutenant Karl Hohmann (W100015)
Ensign Christian Ludwig Schmidt (W200626C)
Ensign Karl Mueller (W200378C)
Sgt. Johann Henrich Heckmann (W200374)
Sgt. Franz Philipp Wirths (W200376)
Sgt. August Greiser (W200375)
Sgt. Jakob Todt (W200129)
Sgt. Christian Embde (W200130)
QM Sgt. Karl Steuernagel (W200380)
QM Sgt. Henrich Eisenberg (W200133)
Capt./Arms Christian Nelle (W200381)
Capt./Arms Karl Bruehne (W200135)
Surg. Mate Joh. Henrich Hoffmeister (W200377)
Surg. Mate Karl Pfister (W200134)
Free Cpl. Friedrich Sude (W200834)
Cpl. Ludwig Goette (W200382)
Cpl. Henrich Berthold (W200384)
Cpl. Joh. Peter Mueller (W200443)
Cpl. Konrad Pilger (W200449)
Cpl. Bernhard Leimbach (W200432)
Cpl. Ernst Kobert (W200140)
Cpl. Karl Sander (W200215)
Cpl. Karl Schnabel (W200222)
Drummer Jakob Clemens (W200388)
Drummer Justinus Berger (W200639)
Drummer Wilhelm Boehne (W200651), and
Drummer Jakob Peter (W200746)

Privates

Werner Wagener (W200484)
Jakob Rennert (W200452)
Bernhard Figge (W200413)
Daniel Michael (W200438)
Johannes Knipschild (W200404)
Peter Schade (W200459)
Henrich Wibbecke (W200490)
Konrad Zimmermann (W200493)
Johannes Jaeger (W200430)
Joh. Friedrich Gunstmann (W200423)

The 3rd English-Waldeck Regiment

Franz Henr. Kuester (W200408)
Wilhelm Lindner (W200435)
Konrad Lindner (W200434), baggage guard in NY
Franz Genuit (W200415)**
Philipp Roehring (W200455)**
Johannes Wollenhaupt (W200492)**
Dietrich Henr. Beckmann (W200392)
David Giede (W200416)
Joh. Hermann Demmer (W200409)
Joh. Wilhelm Bette (W200394)
Johannes Valand (W200478)
Stefan Stempel (W200471)
Franz Adolf Siebel (W200469)
Joh. Friedrich Kelter (W200401)
Johannes Goebel (W200419)
Daniel Heller (W200426)
Pewter Pauster (W200447)
Joh. Adam Schaeffer (W200450)
Henrich Hoffmann (W200428)
Joh. Stefan Schultze (W200466)**
Johannes Stiehl (W200472)
Joh. Henrich Keitel (W200400)**
Joh. Erdmann Guttermilch (W200424)
Joh. Gottfried Neuendorf (W200444)
Franz Schreyer (W200465)
Johannes Wagener (W200482)
Johannes Ritter (W200454)
Marcus Trainer (W200474)
Joh. Wilhelm Moering (W200441)
Georg Seltsam (W200468)**
Franz Chrn. Alberti (W200389)
Friedrich Doedecke (W200410)**
David Lohrmann (W200436)
Wilhelm Wersinger (W200809)
Georg Eckhard (W200686)
Adam Buecher (W200654)
Karl Ammenhaeuser (W200632)
Georg Hermann (W200713)
Andreas Muenster (W200735)
Felix Schmidt (W200768)
Johannes Graebe (W200422)

The 3rd English-Waldeck Regiment

Konrad Bunse (W200397)**
Joh. Jost Valentin (W200479)
Henrich Wilke (W200491)**
Karl Wahl (W200485)
Henrich Henckelmann (W200427)
Joh. Nikolaus Alt (W201105)
Christian Schaeffer (W200762)
Johannes Zahner (W200814)
Anton Schimmel (W200765)
Henrich Nolte (W200700)
Ludwig Schmidt (W200772)
Philipp Quands (W200750)
Georg Dettendaler (W200685)**
Adam Semper (W200787)
Josef Crollpath (W200675)
Georg Bless (W200646)
Johannes Meidt (W200730)
Henrich Toenges (W200797)
Christian Francke (W200386)
Joh. Konrad Heinemann (W200387)
Ludwig Mueller (W200679)
Christian Todt (W200835)
Konrad Pape (W200828)
Henrich Schuetz (W200832)
Friedrich Boehle (W200817)
Friedrich Knipschild (W201125)
Georg Schmeck (W200219)
Henrich Lueckel (W200198)
Georg Hoehle (W200189)
Georg Six (W200228)
Christoph Schultze (W200226)
Jakob Schepp (W200217)
Bernhard Beyer (W200149)
Henrich Meyer (W200201)
Johannes Becker (W200145)
Adam Hohmann (W200190)
Henrich Eisenberg (W200171)
Gottfried Kuester (W200161)
Franz Humbracht (W200193)
Philipp Henr. Hentze (W200187)
Henrich Mueller (W200204)

The 3rd English-Waldeck Regiment

Georg Sperling (W200230)
Nikolaus Mueller (W200206)
Dietrich Theo. Frede (W200176)
Johannes Schmeck (W200220)**
Matthias Becker (W200146)
Jost Josef Menckel (W200199)
Friedrich Molle (W200202)
Henrich Gerhard (W200179)
Friedrich Fingerhut (W200174)**
Georg Ursprund (W200240)
Joh. Chrn. Eisenberg (W200172)
Andreas Herbst (W200188)
Wilhelm Littlet (W200197)
Daniel Mueller (W200203)
Wilhelm Voepel (W200242)
Josef Deilinger (W200165)
Konrad Hohmann (W200191)
Philipp Tewes (W200794)
Georg Kirschner (W200662)
Christian Goebel (W200063), baggage guard at NY
Friedrich Roehrig (W200753)
Henrich Schmidt (W200770)
Christian Schuessler (W200781)
Georg Peter (W200745)
Adam Weinkauf (W200803)
Michael Burghard (W200656)
Henrich Hoffmann (W200717)
Friedrich Seck (W200786)
Adam Fischer (W200693)
Henrich Brabender (W201113)
Wilhelm Himmelmann (W200823)
Daniel Wiegold (W200837)
Henrich Flamme (W201124)
Johannes Meyer (W200912)*
Solicitor

(There were two men with the name Henrich Hoffmann in the company. One of these men was in New York with General Campbell.)

The 3rd English-Waldeck Regiment

Servants

Wilhelm Kuehne (W201174)**
Joh. Tom Way (W201188)
Joh. Bop (W201170)
Caesar (W201173)

Personnel Changes - All Privates

Andreas Schultze (W200628), died on April 22, 1782
Johannes Mertz (W200076), died on May 18, 1782
Friedrich Jaeger (W200194), died on May 21, 1782, and
Peter Schumann (W200783), deserted from the hospital ship in Havana on October 1, 1781.

Recapitulation

Present - 1 1st lieutenant, 1 2nd lieutenant, 2 ensigns, 4 sergeants, 2 QM sergeants, 2 captains-at-arms, 2 surgeon's mates, 1 free corporal, 8 corporals, 4 drummers, 111 privates, and 3 servants
Absent - 1 sergeant, 16 privates, 1 servant, and 1 solicitor
Effectives - 1 1st lieutenant, 1 2md lieutenant, 2 ensigns, 5 sergeants, 2 QM sergeants, 2 captain-at-arms, 2 surgeon's mates, 1 free corporal, 8 corporals, 4 drummers, 127 privates, 4 servants, and 1 solicitor
Deserted - 1 private
Died - 3 privates
Signed at Newtown, Long Island, on July 12, 1782, by Lieutenant Colonel von Horn and William Potter, Commissary, for the period of 182 days from December 15, 1781, to June 24, 1782, and by Keppel, Hohmann, Schmidt, and Mueller.

5 Company - Lieutenant Colonel von Horn's Company

Captain Lieutenant Augustin Alberti (W100008)
Sgt. Theodor Wildstach (W200496)
Captain-at-arms Franz Henckeler (W200497)
Surg. Mate Henrich Beck (W200255)
Cpl. Bernhard Berges (W200501)*
Cpl. Wilhelm Scriba (W200785)
Cpl. August Simshauser (W200502)
Cpl. Jean Tuitel (W201152), deserted March 31, 1782, and

The 3rd English-Waldeck Regiment

Servant Johannes Schmidt (W201187)

Privates

Daniel Brandenstein (W200520)
Johannes Vollmar (W200610)
Georg Geitz (W200538)
Konrad Fahnie (unknown)
Konrad Hendel (W200548)
Bathold Jaeger (W200555)
Georg Tent (W200606)
Kaspar Zeiger (W200616)
Johannes Weidenhagen (W200611)
Henrich Pieper (W200584)
Daniel von Nehm (W200576)
Bernhard Mengeringhausen (W200565)**
Johannes Becker (W200514)
Johannes Berges (W200515)
Jakob Engelhard (W200530)*
Henrich Heinecke (W200547)
Henrich Francke (W2300535)
Christian Brand (W200519)
Jakob Scharschmid (W200596)*
Jakob Meyer (W200567)*
Christian Goedecke (W200541)
Johannes Goebel, Sr. (W200540)
Wilhelm Neubauer (W200737)
Konrad Meyer (W200331)
Franz Schirr (W200346)
Henrich Hoelscher (W200310)
Daniel Mueller (W200334)
Matthias Flamme (W200293)
Peter Kremer (W200286)
Christoph Arend (W200269), and
Solicitor

(As the only name on the January 1782 list not accounted for is a Konrad Schmidt (W200599), it seems likely that the person preparing this list wrote a wrong last name, and Fahnie should be Schmidt.)

The 3rd English-Waldeck Regiment

Personnel Changes - All Privates, Deserters

Heinrich Zimmermann (W200618), on March 19, 1782
Johannes Risch (W200751), on March 19, 1782
Philipp Duesse (W200528), on March 24, 1782
Christian Figge (W200291), on March 24, 1782
Johannes Meuske (W200330), on March 24, 1782
Joh. Georg Schimmel (W200598), on March 25, 1782
Johannes Goebel, Jr. (W200300), on March 25, 1782, and
Karl Kleine (W200283), on March 31, 1782.

Recapitulation

Present - 1 captain, 1 servant, 1 captain-at-arms, 1 surgeon's mate, 2 corporals, and 24 privates
Absent - 1 sergeant, 1 corporal, 6 privates, and 1 solicitor
Effectives - 1 captain, 1 servant, 1 sergeant, 1 captain-at-arms, 1 surgeon's mate, 3 corporals, 30 privates, and 1 solicitor
During this muster, deserted - 1 corporal and 8 privates

Signed by Augustin Alberti, Haacke, and William Potter, Commissary, at Newtown, Long Island, on July 12, 1782, for the period of 182 days, from December 25, 1781, to June 24, 1782.

Steps were taken immediately after the muster to remedy the obvious disparity in the strength of the various companies and the shortage of non-commissioned officers and corporals. The following promotions and changes within the officer corps occurred in 1782.[5]

Sgt. Franz Philipp Wirths (W200376C), 4 Company, was promoted to ensign in 3 Company in March
Free Cpl. Bernhard Schreiber (W200779C), 2 Company, was promoted to ensign in April and transferred to 5 Company
Captain Lieutenant Alexander von Baumbach (W100007), 3 Company, was promoted to captain in April and made commander of 3 Company in August
Ensign Ludwig Schmidt (W200626C), 4 Company, was transferred to 2 Company in June, and

The 3rd English-Waldeck Regiment

Captain Georg von Haacke (W100006), 1 Company, was promoted to major in June.

The following promotions were made in June 1782:

Ludwig Bauerschmidt (W200024), 1 Company, to corporal
Capt/arms Karl Bruehne (W200135), 4 Company, to sergeant in 5 Company
Jost Kleucker (W200037), 1 Company to corporal
QM Sgt. Henrich Eisenberg (W200133), 2 Company to sergeant in 4 Company
Peter Ernst (W200497), 1 Company, to corporal
Capt/arms Franz Henckeler (W200497), 5 Company to sergeant
Konrad Hendel (W200548), 5 Company, to corporal
Cpl. Stefan Hertzog (W200308), 3 Company
Cpl. Philipp Mueller (W200084), 1 Company, and
Cpl. Wilhelm Scriba (W200785), 5 Company, to captain-at-arms
Cpl. August Simshaeuser (W200502), 5 Company, to QM sergeant
Georg Tent (W200606), 5 Company, to corporal
Cpl; Christoph Weishaupt (W200012), 1 Company, to sergeant, and
Kaspar Zeiger (W200616), 5 Company, to corporal.

Men transferred from 3 Company to 2 Company during 1782, included:

Wilhelm Bestelmeier (W200845)
Johannes Fieger (W200875)
Sebastian Francke (W200878)
Drummer Anton Fricke (W200880)
Jakob Heck (W200896)
Nikolaus Wagener (W200970)
Peter Hunold (W200901)
Johannes Rehrohr (W200936)
Johannes Reichhard (W200937)
Wilhelm Tabroth (W200873)
Georg Tuchscheer (W200966), and
Adam Weiss (W200973)

An even larger number of men were transferred at the same time from 4 Company to 2 Company, including:

The 3rd English-Waldeck Regiment

Johannes Becker (W200145)
Matthias Becker (W200146)
Benhard Beyer (W200149)
Servant John Bop (W201170)
Drummer Wilhelm Boehne (W200651)
Henrich Brabender (W201113)
Michael Burghard (W200656)
Georg Kirchner (W200662)
Cpl. Ernst Kobert (W200140)
Gottfried Kuester (W200161)
Josef Deilinger (W200165)
Sgt. Henrich Eisenberg (W200133)
Henrich Eisenberg (W200171)
Joh. Christian Eisenberg (W200172)
Friedrich Fingerhut (W200174)
Adam Fischer (W200693)
Henrich Flamme (W201124)
Dietrich Frede (W200176)
Henrich Gerhard (W200179)
Col. Henrich Gockel (W200136)
Christoph Goebel (W200063)
Philipp Henr. Hentze (W200187)
Andreas Herbst (W200188)
Wilhelm Himmelmann (W200823)
Georg Hoehle (W200189)
Henrich Hoffmann (W200717)
Adam Hohmann (W200190)
Konrad Hohmann (W200151)
Franz Humbracht (W200193)
Wilhelm Littlet (W200197)
Henrich Loeckel (W200198)
Jost Meckel (W200199)
Henrich Meyer (W200201)
Johannes Meyer (W200912)
Friedrich Molle (W200202)
Henrich Mueller (W200204)
Nikolaus Mueller (W200206)
Georg Peter (W200745)
Drummer Jakob Peter (W200746)
Surg. Mate Karl Pfister (W200134)

The 3rd English-Waldeck Regiment

Friedrich Roehrig (W200753)
Cpl. Karl Sander (W200215)
Jakob Schepp (W200217)
Georg Schmeck (W200219)
Jakob Schmeck (W200220)
Konrad Schmidt (W200771)
Cpl. Karl Schnabel (W200222)
Christian Schluessler (W200781)
Christoph Schultze (W200226)
Josef Friedrich Seck (W200786)
Georg Six (W200228)
Georg Sperling (W200230)
Philipp Tewes (W200794)
Sgt. Jakob Todt (W200129)
Georg Ursprung (W200240)
Wilhelm Voepel (W200242)
Adam Weinkauf (W200803), and
Daniel Wiegold (W200837)

Further assignment changes were made in July 1782, with the following men being transferred from 3 Company, to:

1 Company

Ignatius Bachstaedter (W200021)
Karl Bauer (W200841)
Lorenz Becker (W200843)
Konrad Bock (W200847)
Friedrich Christenau (W200857)
Fifer Christian Klee (W200664)
Johannes Deege (W200868)
Friedrich Diedrich (W200870)
Johannes Gerger (W200881)
Christoph Haag (W200887)
Albrecht Hartig (W200891)
Ulrich Hartmann (W200893)
Friedrich Hertzog (W200898)
Philipp Laubach (W200904)
Franz Lindemeyer (W200909)
Joh. Friedrich Meckeler (W200910)
Surg. Mate Franz Mueller (W200918)
Georg Probst (W200932)
Christian Rischebusch (W200942)

The 3rd English-Waldeck Regiment

Johannes Schreyer (W200921)
Joh. Christian Siemon (W201163)
Sgt. Konrad Starcke (W200958)
Ludwig Stremmel (W200960)
Karl Struck (W200962)
Drummer Andreas Urbach (W200968)
Josef Urbach, (W200969), and
Henrich Weste (W200976)

2 Company

Jakob de la Dior (W200869)
Cpl. Georg Schaper (W200946), and
Christian Schmidtmann (W200950)

4 Company

Peter Burghenn (W200853)
Karl Kreyer (W200863)
Drummer Friedrich Kriegsmann (W200865)
Christian Geissel (W200884)
Georg Michael (W200914)
Ernst Neumeier (W200922)
Friedrich Patermann (W200926)
Michael Reiss (W200938)
Karl Roquette (W200934)
Georg Rummel (W200944)
Konrad Sinn (W200957)
Johannes Teichler (W200963), and
Johannes Weiss (W200974)

5 Company

Johannes Beckes (W200982)
Drummer Johannes Bangert (W200839)
Adam Barth (W200840)
Michael Beringer (W200844)
Wilhelm Boehle (W200818)
Konrad Brock (W200849)
Ludwig Buchholtz (W200850)
Johannes Buehler (W200851)
Karl Kampf (W200854)
Bernhard Keipel (W200855)
Gottlieb Kessler (W200856)
Joh. Henrich Koehler (W200524)
Lorenz Kohl (W200859)
Georg Krauss (W200861)

The 3rd English-Waldeck Regiment

Johannes Kuhn (W200867)
Martin Dantzer (W200680)
Philipp Ebe (W200622)
Jakob Fieberling (W200874)
Henrich Fischer (W200876)
Ludwig Fischer (W200877)
Henrich Flammes (W200822)
Peter Hamm (W200890)
Johannes Hoppe (W200900)
Christian Laue (W200905)
Adam Lentzer (W200906)
Christian Meisner (W200825)
Ludwig Mertz (W200911)
Barthold Mueller (W200572)
Drummer Henrich Obermann (W200923)
Adam Pflado (W200930)
Kaspar Pickel (W200583)
Henrich Preiss (W200931)
Jost Rabensprock (W200933)
Cpl. Friedrich Renne (W200939)
Konrad Roose (W200943)
Johannes Schaeffer (W200592)
Friedrich Schele (W200597)
Henrich Schmidt (W200949)
Thomas Schneider (W200951)
Anton Schuetz (W200831)
Christian Siemon (W200829)
Christian Sinemus (W200955)
Johannes Sinemus (W200956)
Johannes Wagenstahl (W200971)
Samuel Wieth (W200977), and
Franz Ziegler (W200617)

In July 1782, Corporal Georg Goercke (W200885) was transferred from 5 Company to 1 Company, and the following men were transferred from 5 Company to 3 Company:

Christoph Arend (W200269)
Surg. Mate Daniel Beck (W200255)
Servant Johannes Budde (W201171)

The 3rd English-Waldeck Regiment

Peter Kremer (W200286)
Matthias Flamme (W200291)
Henrich Hoelscher (W200310)
Daniel Mueller (W200334), and
Franz Schirr (W200346).

Some minor realinement of individuals in August 1782 completed the reorganization of the regiment. Men transferred from 4 Company to 2 Company, were:

Phil. Henrich Hentze (W200187)
Henrich Hoffmann (W200428)
Konrad Hoffmann (W200717)
Friedrich Molle (W200202)
Daniel Mueller (W200203), and
Henrich Schmidt (W200770).

During August 1782, 1st Lieutenant Wilhelm Keppel and his servant, Tom Way (W201188), were transferred from 4 Company to 5 Company, and Captain Augustin Alberti and his servant, Johannes Schmidt (W201187), were transferred from 5 Company to 2 Company.

The 3rd English-Waldeck Regiment

When the fleet carrying the 1782 recruit shipment of Germans to America sailed on 31 May, the men of the Waldeck Regiment were on the *Enterprise*, along with the recruits for the Brunswick and Anhalt-Zerbst units. Personnel on the *Enterprise* were:[6]

for Waldeck - 1 officer, 134 men, and 13 women
for Brunswick - 1 officer and 23 men, and
for Anhalt-Zerbst - 1 officer and 21 men
for a Total - 194 persons, including 13 women.

The *Neptune* carried the equipment for the Waldeckers and Ansbachers.

Other ships in the convoy, which also carried recruits for Hesse-Cassel, Hesse-Hanau, and Ansbach-Bayreuth, were: *Rebecca, Ocean, Littledeale, Chudlugs, Hesperus, Berwick, Diane, Arab Mars, Sousinoun, Apollo*, and *Respite*. The escort frigates were the *Emerald*, 32 guns, *Cyclops*, 28 guns, and *Pettipoint*, 36 guns. The list of ships contains a breakdown by rank of the passengers aboard each ship, and the persons on the *Enterprise* were the officer, Ensign August Mueller (W100021), 5 non-commissioned officers, 1 surgeon's mate, 4 drummers, 124 recruits, and 16 women.[7]

The following personnel constituted the 1782 recruit draft for the Waldeck Regiment, according to a roster of names apparently recorded at Bremerlehe on May 31, 1782. The officer, Ensign Mueller was assigned to 5 Company, as were the men in the shipment, and probably stayed with the recruits until their return to Waldeck.[8]

Sergeant Moritz Stuckenbrock accompanied the shipment, probably as an experienced non-commissioned officer to assist Ensign Mueller, but as his name does not appear in the *HETRINA* at a later date, it can be assumed that he returned to Germany after the recruits were delivered in Halifax.

All men in the shipment have been identified and are listed below.

The 3rd English-Waldeck Regiment

Sgt. Jakob Loeblein (W201043)
Free Cpl. Friedrich Mueller (W201049)
Free Cpl. Daniel Pittius (W201060)
Surg. Mate Karl Schultze (W201079)
Cpl. Gottfried Brume (W200995)
Cpl. Daniel Hoffmann (W201030)
Drummer Alan Repp (W201147), or Christian Rohde (W201066)
Drummer Friedrich Siemon (W201148)
Drummer Johannes Vesper (W201154)
Drummer Johannes Wisseler (W201159)

Privates

Christoph Altner (W200980)
Ernst Andreas (W200981)
Johannes Backes (W200982)
Andreas (Adam) Bauer (W200984)
Matthias Bertram (W200985)
Henrich Bethe (W200986)
Christian Billerbeck (W200987)
Georg Boesam (W200988)
Ludwig Brandes (W200989)
Ludwig Brasser (W200990)
Georg Bressler (W200991)
Anton Breuninger (W200992)
Christoph Brey (W200993)
Friedrich Bubenleber (W200996)
Karl Bulle (W200997)
Ernst de la Kampf (W200998)
Jost Kaufmann (W200999)
Henrich Kelfs (W201000)
Anton Kiepe (W201001)
Valentin Kintzer (W201002)
Justus Klemen (W201004)
Anton Klucker (W201005)
Adam Klunck (W201006)
Daniel Kneile (W201007)
Adam (Kaspar) Koppenhoeffer (W201003)
Georg Kraemer (W201008)
Bernhard Krell (W201009)
Johannes Kuecher (W201010)
Georg Daudenberg (W201011)
Friedrich Dengel (W201012)

The 3rd English-Waldeck Regiment

Jakob Dicke (W201013)
Sebastian Dietrich (W201014)
Johannes Drechsler (W201015)
Johannes Fasshauer (W201016)
Jakob Flinschbach (W201017)
Georg Gottlieb (W201018)
Georg Graeber (W200924)
Henrich Greif (W201019)
Konrad Guenther (W201020)
Andreas Hahnefeld (W201021)
Wilhelm Hamel (W201022)
Henrich Hoppe (W201023)
Daniel Happel (W201024)
Thomas Hartmann (W201025)
Gottlieb Heinecke (W201026)
Christoph Heintz (W201027)
Peter Hertzig (W201028)
Andreas Heuster (W201029)
Georg Hoffmann (W201031)
Johannes Hoffmann (W201032)
Wolrath Hoffmann (W201033)
Jakob Indenkauff (W201034)
Josef Ingentron (W201035)
Josef Jutlein (W201036)
Gottfried (Georg) Lange (W201037)
Andreas Lengel (W201038)
Friedrich Lercher (W201039)
Bernhard Lesmann (W201040)
Friedrich Leugling (W201041)
Henrich Lindeborn (W201042)
Daniel Mann (W201044)
Wolrath Meinhard (W201045)
Adam Menger (W201046)
Thomas Meyer (W201047)
Andreas Mueller (W201048)
Johannes Muender (W201050)
Jost (Justus) Munterbach (W201051)
Friedrich Nahm (W201052)
Bernhard Naser (W201053)
Franz Neubauer (W201054)
Bernhard Neuschaeffer (W201168)

The 3rd English-Waldeck Regiment

Johannes Obacher (W201055)
Daniel Ohngefochten (W201056)
Nikolaus Oppenheimer (W201057)
Henrich Ostmeier (W201058)
Lorenz Pelz (W201059)
Friedrich Pittius (W201061)
Henrich Preiss (W201062)
Georg Reinhard (W201063)
Friedrich Repcke (W201064)
Friedrich Reuter (W201065)
Christian Rohde (W201066)
Georg Rohde (W201067)
Michael Rumpelhard (W201068)
Ludwig Saenger (W201069)
Henrich Schaeffer (W201070)
Konrad Schaeffer (W201071)
Johannes Schilling (W201072)
Gottfried Schimaneck (W201073)
Friedrich Schmidt (W201183)
Wilhelm Schmidtmann (W201074)
Philipp Schneider (W201075)
Friedrich Schnepper (W201076)
Henrich Schuette (W201077)
Andreas Schumacher (W201078)
Ludwig Schurck (W200917)
Jakob Schwartz (W201080)
Wilhelm Schwender (W201081)
Georg Senft (W201082)
Friedrich Siemon (W201083)
Josef Sommer (W201117)
Thomas Sommer (W201085)
Karl Staudinger (W201086)
Emanuel Steiger (W201087)
Friedrich Steinbach (W201088)
Henrich Sterner (W201089)
Jakob Stoltz (W201090)
Johannes Thiele (W201091)
Friedrich Troll (W201092)
Friedrich Trost (W201093)
Jakob Ulm (W201094)
Kaspar (Adam) Ulmer (W201094)

The 3rd English-Waldeck Regiment

Friedrich Voland (W201096)
Georg Wagener (W201097)
Andreas Wages (W201104)
Anton Walter (W201098)
Andreas Weber (W201100)
Jost Weil (W201101)
Wilhelm Weil (W201102)
Christian Weiss (W201103)

The following named individuals apparently started out from Waldeck with the 1782 recruits but their services were lost to the regiment for the reasons listed, prior to the recruits boarding ships for America.[9]

Sgt de Blanc - deserted
Cpl. Marionilke - deserted
Lueckel - deserted
Pals - deserted
Rausch - deserted
Blank - sent back
Fricke - sent back
Geldbach - sent back
Hermann - sent back
Rohde - sent back
Spudel - sent back
Drummel - sent back due to poor health
Schoper - sent back due to poor health
Schlund - sent back due to poor health
Thielemann - sent back due to poor health
Dannemann - discharged for bad conduct
Reichard - discharged for bad conduct
Basch - drowned in Weser, and
Peter - drowned in Weser.

Three names appear in the *HETRINA* for the first time during 1782.[10]

Servant Jakob Frantzer (W201178), 5 Company, apparently joined the regiment in August.
Henrich Materns (W201140), 1 Company, apparently joined in November.

220

The 3rd English-Waldeck Regiment

Servant Henrich Fockesen (W201177), 3 Company, apparently joined in December.

Three men previously listed as deserters, returned to the regiment. They were:[11]

Ludwig Georg Gier (W200539), 5 Company, deserted from prisoner of war status in 1778, but rejoined the regiment in December 1782.
Philipp Block (W200649), 4 Company, deserted in Havana in July 1781, but had rejoined the regiment by December 1782.
Konrad Schmidt (W200771), 4 Company, deserted at Pensacola in May 1781, but had rejoined the regiment by June 1782.

On July 29, 1782, all members of the Waldeck Regiment in the New York area, including the exchanged prisoners of war, finally broke winter quarters. Along with the second battalion of Anhalt-Zerbst, the "last" Ansbach recruits, and some picked men from the old corps, they camped at Brooklyn, under the Hesse-Hanau Colonel Johann Christoph Lentz. A mixed group, including escaped Brunswick Convention prisoners, some exchanged officers, Brunswick recruits under Captain von Walzogen, and some Hesse-Hanau jaeger recruits under Lieutenant Buenau, were also in Colonel Lentz' command. The troops, other than the Waldeckers, had come out of winter quarters on June 16.[12]

A Brigadier General John Campbell, at Halifax, wrote to the Earl of Shelburne, on August 17, 1782, that the German recruits had arrived on August 13. The victuallers, however, had not arrived. As Campbell thought a French fleet might be contemplating an attack on Penobscot, he planned to sent two hundred German recruits to that place. Baurmeister on November 1, 1782, recorded that Major Johannes Neumann of the Hesse-Cassel Seitz Regiment, had been detached from Halifax to Penobscot with the Zerbst, Ansbach, Waldeck, and Hanau recruits.[13]

The 3rd English-Waldeck Regiment

During the week of August 18-25, Baurmeister received word of the arrival of the German auxiliary and English recruits at Halifax. Judge Smith on September 1, also noted the report of 2,700 foreign troops arriving at Halifax, and Edmund Pendleton expressed his opinion in an October 14 letter to James Madison that 2,000 Germans lately arrived at Halifax would probably be sent to Canada.[14]

Jean Baptiste Donatien de Vimeaur, Comte de Rochambeau, however, when informed of the arrival of the Hessians at Halifax from Bremerlehe, after a two month crossing, was told the Germans were being transported to New York.[15]

Baurmeister noted that by September 12, 1782, the Waldeck Regiment had been transferred to Brooklyn, and by September 14, had been transferred to New York to perform garrison duty. Krafft also recorded in his diary that on Monday, September 23, the citizens, the Waldeck Regiment, and two battalions of Skinner's Provincials were doing service in the city. At 3 P.M. on Wednesday, October 23, according to Krafft, Lieutenant Hartmann was nicely buried by a Waldeck detail of two officers and fifty privates. The cold air that day disagreed with Krafft.[16]

As the war wound down with no significant fighting, the Waldeck Regiment suffered no combat deaths, but a number of men still died of illness in 1782, including:[17]

Fifer Franz Christian Bigge (W200846), 3 Company, who died at Newtown on January 26

Henrich Muenchmeyer (W200920), 3 Company, who died at Newtown on January 26

August Wesserlein (W201190), 3 Company, who died at Newtown on January 28

Johannes Giebel (W200883), 3 Company, who died at Newtown on January 30

Leonhard Heberlein (W200895), 3 Company, who died at Newtown on January 31

The 3rd English-Waldeck Regiment

Johannes Sassmannshausen (W200945), 3 Company, who died at Newtown on February 13
Michael Schultze (W200953), 3 Company, who died at Newtown on March 3
Georg Reese (W200935), 3 Company, who died at Newtown on March 4
Capt./Arms Johannes Knoechel (W200256), 3 Company, who died at Newtown on March 17
Christian Wirth (W200978), 3 Company, who died at Newtown on April 11
Andreas Schultze (W200628), 4 Company, who died at Newtown on April 22
Johannes Mertz (W200076), 4 Company, who died on Long Island on May 18
Friedrich Jaeger (W200194), 2 Company, who died on Long Island on May 21
Henrich Haag (W200888), 3 Company, who died at Newtown on May 30
Michael Reiss (W200938), 4 Company, who died on Long Island on July 12
Konrad Meyer (W200331), who died on Long Island on July 12
Josef Perle (W200744), 2 Company, who died at Newtown on July 12
Joh. Christian Siemon (W200829), 5 Company, who died at New York on October 2
Christian Schmidtmann (W200950), 2 Company, who died at New York on November 5, and
Sgt. Theodor Wildstach (W200496), 5 Company, who died at Flatbusch on November 10.

(As Newtown was on Long Island there may be no significance to listing some men as having died at Newtown and others on Long Island.)

The following listed men of the 1782 recruit shipment died of non-combat causes during 1782, also.

Johannes Backes (W200982), on November 9
Friedrich Lercher (W201039), on December 1
Henrich Ostmeier (W201058), on December 9
Anton Walter (W201098), on December 9, and
Henrich Preiss (W201062), on December 14.

Corporal Karl Schnabel (W200222), 2 Company, deserted on August 27, but apparently rejoined his company as a private in December 1782.[18]

The 3rd English-Waldeck Regiment

A much greater loss to the regiment and the Principality of Waldeck, however, was represented by the 26 men who deserted from prisoner of war status in Havana. Those men were:[19]

Johannes Risch (W200751), 5 Company, on March 19
Henrich Zimmermann (W200618), 5 Company, on March 19
Barthold Knoechel (W200159), 1 Company, on March 21
Friedrich Rodewald (W200590), 1 Company on March 21
Cpl. Jeremias Warlich (W200142), 2 Company, on March 21
Philipp Duesse (W200528), 5 Company, on March 24
Christian Figge (W200291), 3 Company, on March 24
Johannes Meuske (W200330), 3 Company, on March 24
Johannes Goeberl (W200300), 3 Company, on March 25
Joh. Georg Schimmel (W200598), 5 Company, on March 25
Franz Cramer (W200048), 1 Company, on March 28
Anton Noll (W200088), 1 Company, on March 28
Henr. Wilhelm Stallmann (W200791), 1 Company, on March 28
Henrich Stiesing (W200232), 2 Company, on March 28
Georg Friedeborn (W200177), 2 Company, on March 29
Johannes Michael (W200568), 1 Company, on March 29
Karl Kleine (W200283), 3 Company, on March 31
Cpl. Christoph Roemer (W200010), 1 Company, who deserted on March 31, but rejoined the regiment as a private by December 1782
Cpl. Johannes Tuitel (W201152), 5 Company, on March 31
Jakob Walter (W200118), 1 Company, on March 31
Joh. Henrich Weber (W200802), 1 Company, on March 31
Henrich Fischer (W200175), 2 Company, o9n April 2
Drummer Johannes Unger (W200143), 2 Company, on April 2
Adam Kann (W200030), 1 Company, on April 14
Joh. Jost Drewes (W200168), 2 Company, on April 14, and
Johannes Stoecker (W200233), 2 Company, on April 14.

The following six men of 5 Company, held prisoners by Spain, appear, according to the *HETRINA* to have deserted at Havana in March 1782, but all were back on duty with the regiment by June.[20]

Christian Brand (W200519)
Henrich Francke (W200535)
Johannes Goebel (W200540)

The 3rd English-Waldeck Regiment

Christian Goedecke (W200541)
Jakob Meyer (W200567), and
Jakob Scharschmid (W200596).

Additional reductions in strength resulted from the release from the regiment of the following individuals in 1782:[21]

Daniel Christian Mueller (W200203), 2 Company, reclaimed by the Hesse-Cassel von Knyphausen Regiment on December 5. According to *HETRINA*, he had deserted the Knyphausen Regiment in March 1776 (while that regiment was still in Germany ??), and
Bernhard Leimbach (W200432), 4 Company, released at Flatbusch as missing on December 16,

The following were released as invalids on December 19, and transferred back to Europe.

Henrich Kinold (W200278), 3 Company
Philipp Kramer (W200285), 3 Company
Friedrich Doedecke (W200410), 4 Company
Moritz Gerlach (W200299), 3 Company
Henrich Herbold (W200071), 1 Company
Cpl. Konrad Pilger (W200449), 4 Company
Georg Wilhelm Seltsam (W200468), 4 Company
Sgt. Jakob Todt (W200129), 2 Company
Johannes Vollmar (W200610), 5 Company, and
Konrad Zimmermann (W200493), 4 Company.

During 1782, 134 men sailed from Europe to join the Waldeck Regiment in America. Although they appear to have served only in Nova Scotia and Maine, and never to have actually served with the regiment, still they were part of the regiment. The regiment was further strengthened by 3 men, possibly recruited in America, and the return of 85 men from prisoner of war status. Unit losses were 25 deaths due to illness, 28 deserters, and eleven men released from the regiment. As of the last day of 1782, estimated strength of the regiment was 560 men, plus 15 men still carried as prisoners of war.

The 3rd English-Waldeck Regiment
1783

The signing of the preliminary peace treaty in 1783 resulted in both England and America releasing prisoners of war, and the large number of prisoners which had been held by the Americans meant the English would need a large number of ships to carry the men back to Europe. There was also the need to divert shipping to the use of moving Loyalists refugees from their provinces to Canada, Nova Scotia, and even to England.

Lord North wrote to Sir Guy Carleton, then commanding in New York, on April 18, that all foreign troops in New York and Nova Scotia were to be returned to Europe as soon as possible. If there were not enough transports available to embark all the troops, Carleton was to embark such number as he had transports for. At the same time, North wrote to Admiral Robert Digby to prepare transports for carrying all the foreign troops at New York. Again he mentioned that if only part of the troops could be transported, at least that number should be moved. The foreign troops at Halifax were to be returned to Europe, also. Further, such of the King's ships as were in the West Indies, would return home by way of New York to assist the evacuation.[1]

Apparently Carleton made the evacuation of Loyalists and former soldiers planning to settle in Nova Scotia his first priority, and he began sending numbers of those individuals to Nova Scotia at once. Many of the mercenaries who settled in Nova Scotia went to Clement Township in Halifax, where one settlement was for those from Hesse-Cassel and another for Waldeckers.[2]

On May 28, Carleton wrote Thomas Townshend that Congress had released the crown prisoners and that about 4,900 had arrived at New York. Previous correspondence with Washington had developed the fact that because of a lack of transports, the exchanged prisoners would be required to march overland from Maryland, Pennsylvania, and Virginia. Officers' expenses along the way were to be paid by the English and the

The 3rd English-Waldeck Regiment

Americans would provide provisions and an escort for the troops. The first division would reach Elizabethtown by May 9, marching from Lancaster the previous day. The second division would march on May 10, and the third division on May 11. The sick would be cared for and wagons would be furnished as needed.[3]

Although the report by Carleton mentioned 4,900 released prisoners, a return for the period May 8 to May 27, has 2,900 English, 96 Americans, and 1,322 German prisoners released for a total of only 4,318.[4]

Major John Clark, an American officer, recorded that a fleet of transports had arrived at New York on June 8, from the West Indies, to pick up the Hessians. A week later, to speed up the troops' embarkation, Lord North wrote Carleton that a general evacuation of New York was to take place immediately.[5] North also ordered Admiral Digby to begin the evacuation of New York. Three thousand tons of shipping had been sent from England and 5,000 tons more would follow. Six thousand tons, which had sailed previously for Halifax and Quebec, would then join Digby. Shipping was scarce in England, however, even though most of the West Indies fleet had already returned to England.[6]

The evacuation of New York was in full swing, even as Lord North sent his instructions. On June 15, the British guards and British and German Convention prisoners, to the number of 2,274, including women, had embarked for Nova Scotia with 1,654 destined for St. John's River, 205 for Annapolis Royal, 122 for Port Roseway, and 491 for Fort Cumberland.[7]

After the transports landed the refugees in Nova Scotia, they would collect the foreign troops in that province. There were many refugees in New York, over 7,000 had applied for passage, and once they were evacuated, the German troops were to be embarked.[8]

On July 8, an additional 1,335 Loyalists were embarked for Nova Scotia and 516 for Canada. Next day, three companies of

The 3rd English-Waldeck Regiment

the Hesse-Hanau Free Corps sailed down the East River in flatboats to embark at New York. The two remaining companies were to follow on July 15, in order to return to Germany. On July 15, the Waldeckers embarked, followed by the Anhalt-Zerbst contingent, and shortly thereafter, they sailed from New York.[9]

An embarkation return dated July 16, lists 269 officers, men, and women, plus 13 children of Hesse-Hanau; 418 men and women, plus 13 children from Waldeck; and 329 officers, man, and women, plus 11 children for Anhalt-Zerbst. There is no explanation of why no officers are mentioned among the Waldeckers.[10]

Although no members of the Waldeck Regiment died as a result of combat in 1783, many continued to die of illness, including the following men of the 1782 recruit shipment, who died on dates shown.[11]

Georg Graeber (W200924), on January 3
Christian Brey (W200993), on January 4
Cpl. Daniel Hoffmann (W201030), on January 10
Johannes Schilling (W201072), on January 10
Friedrich Steinbach (W201088), at Halifax on March 4
Ludwig Schurck (W200917), at Halifax on March 7
Wilhelm Weil (W201102), at Halifax on March 23
Matthias Bertram (W200985), at Halifax on March 25
Thomas Sommer (W201085), at Halifax on March 29
Sebastian Dietrich (W201014), at Halifax on April 11
Friedrich Nahm (W201052), at Halifax on May 3
Gottfried Schimaneck (W201073), at Halifax on May 7, and
Johannes Jutlein (W201036), at Halifax on July 16.

Others of the Waldeck Regiment who died during 1783, all from non-combat causes, were:

Johannes Weiss (W200974), 4 Company, who died at Flatbusch on February 16
Konrad Sinn (W200957), 4 Company, who died at Flatbusch on June 4, and

The 3rd English-Waldeck Regiment

Johannes Wollenhaupt (W200492), 3 Company, the last Waldeck soldier to die while in English service, died on the North Sea on his way back to Germany, on September 6

A note recording the death of Major Pentzel is not clear, but apparently he was accidently shot and killed while *en route* back to Waldeck on the Weser River on September 23, 1783.[12]

As prospects for peace and eventually news of the treaty ending the war presented the men of Waldeck with the realization that they would soon leave America and undertake another sea voyage, many of the soldiers decided to desert. It appears that all of the men who had been prisoners of the Americans since late 1776 or early 1777 deserted rather than return to Europe. The men in this category, all listed as deserting on July 15, 1783, were:[13]

Peter Ulrich (W200477) and
Kaspar Wagener (W200483), both of 4 Company, who deserted from West Chester,

and the following who were listed as deserting from Elizabethtown:

Christian Albrecht (W200018), 1 Company
Wilhelm Kann (W200032), 1 Company
Johannes Klapp (W200281), 3 Company
Henrich Graebing (W200302), 3 Company
Drummer Christian Huthmann (W200507), 5 Company
Henrich Meyer (W200566), 5 Company
Wilhelm Neumeyer (W200577), 5 Company
Thomas Schaeffer (W200594), 5 Company
Georg Thielemann (W200117), 1 Company, and
Adam Verst (W200532), 5 Company.

Others who deserted from the Waldeck Regiment prior to the unit returning to Europe in 1783, were the following who deserted from Flatbusch on dates shown:

The 3rd English-Waldeck Regiment

Johannes Albracht (W299267), 3 Company, on May 5
Johannes Knipschild (W200404), 4 Company, on May 5
Friedrich Dietrich (W200870), 1 Company, on May 5
Henrich Flamme (W200822), 5 Company, on May 5
Johannes Flamme (W200385), 4 Company, on May 5
Matthias Flamme (W200293), 3 Company, on May 5
Erdmann Guttermilch (W200424), 4 Company, on May 5
Joh. Georg Bock (W200518), and
Johannes Schaeffer (W200630), both of 1 Company, on May 8
Henrich Boltze (W200819), 3 Company, on June 4
Christian Francke (W200295), 3 Company, on June 14
Friedrich Graebe (W200301),
Philipp Muench (W201143)
Christian Roemer (W200010), and
August Westmeyer (W200836), all of 3 Company, on July 2, and
Dietrich Siebel (W200353), 3 Company, who deserted from New York on July 16.

Roemer, who had been a corporal at the time of his desertion in 1782, may have rejoined the regiment as a private later in the same year, and then again deserted.

Two members of the 1782 recruit shipment deserted at Halifax on August 6, 1783.

Georg Gottlieb (W201018) and
Henrich Sterner (W201089).

Prior to the regiment embarking at New York for the return to Europe, those men desiring to stay in America were apparently given their discharge from the regiment. As a result, the following men were released at Flatbusch on July 15, 1783.[14]

From 1 Company
Ignatius Bachstaedter (W200021) and
Johannes Gerger (W200881)

From 2 Company
Josef Deilinger (W200165)
Adam Fischer (W200693)
Andreas Herbst (W200188)

The 3rd English-Waldeck Regiment

Henrich Hoffmann (W200717) and
Georg Tuch(scheer) (W200966)

From 3 Company

Surg. Mate Henrich Beck (W200255)
Cpl. Friedrich Boehme (W201112)
Christian Becker (W200637)
Kaspar Klahold (W200280)
Alisius Fass (W200690)
Anton Hartmann (W200892)
Johannes Jost (W200313)
Walentin Malches (W200319)
Daniel Martin (W200320)
Michael Pfitzer (W200747)
Michael Schlauderbeck (W200766)
David Schneider (W200774)
Konrad Steineck (W200357)
Johannes Weissenborn (W200805), and
Christian Wiegmann (W200812)

From 4 Company

Sgt. August Greiser (W200375)
Cpl. Peter Mueller (W200443)
Nikolaus Alt (W201105)
Karl Ammenhaeuser (W200632)
Adam Buecher (W200654)
Georg Eckhard (W200686)
Christian Giesel (W200884)
Philipp Roehling (W200455), and
Johannes Valentin (W200479)

From 5 Company

Georg Kraus (W200861)
Johannes Kuhn (W200867)
Peter Hamm (W200890)
Kaspar Pickel (W200583)
Friedrich Schele (W200597)
Thomas Schneider (W200951), and
Franz Ziegler (W200617)

From the Artillery

Erdmann Zenecke (W300017), and
Kaspar Effe (W300004).

The 3rd English-Waldeck Regiment

On July 18, 1783, possibly just prior to the regiment sailing for Europe, three men of 2 Company were released:

Georg Kirschner (W200662)
Friedrich Seck (W200786), and
Nikolaus Wagener (W200970).

Once the regiment was back on German soil desertions became even more numerous and as many of the men were not natives of Waldeck, their desertion may even have been encouraged.[15]

Wilhelm Neubauer (W200737), 5 Company, deserted at Bremen on September 19.
Jakob Heck (W200896), 2 Company, deserted on the Weser on September 22, and
Michael Preiss (W200931), 5 Company, deserted on the Weser on September 23.

The following men of the 1782 recruit shipment deserted at Bremen on September 30:

Surg. Mate Karl Schultze (W201079)
Ludwig Brasser (W200990)
Anton Breuninger (W200992)
Anton Breyer (W200994)
Karl Bulle (W200997)
Jost Kaufmann (W200999)
Anton Klucker (W201005)
Jakob Indenkauf (W201034)
Andreas Lengel (W201038)
Adam Menger (W201046)
Georg Reinhardf (W201063)
Michael Rumpelhard (W201068)
Karl Staudinger (W201086)
Emanuel Steiger (W201087)
Jakob Stolts (W201090)
Friedrich Troll (W201092)
Kaspar (Adam) Ulmer (W201095)
Georg Wagener (W201097)

The 3rd English-Waldeck Regiment

Wilhelm Walter (W201099), and
Andreas Weber (W201100)

Finally, three men deserted from the regiment at Korbach, in Waldeck:

Georg Michael (W200914), 4 Company, on October 10, 1783
Henrich Nolte (W200700), 4 Company, and
Jakob Schepp (W200217), 2 Company, on October 18.

The desertions after the regiment was again in Europe seem all the more difficult to understand when it appears that the Prince of Waldeck was only too willing to cut the size of his army when there was no market for it in foreign lands. Men released at Bremen on September 19, included[16]

From 1 Company

Karl Bauer (W200841)
Franz Lindemeyer (W200909)
Johannes Meckler (W200910)
Johannes Schreier (W200921), and
Henrich Weste (W200976)

From 2 Company

Wilhelm Bestelmeier (W200845)
Philipp Block (W200649)
Johannes Fieger (W200875)
Sebastian Francke (W200878)
Peter Hunold (W200901)
Johannes Reichhard (W200937)
Wilhelm Tabroth (W200873), and
Adam Weiss (W200973)

From 3 Company

Adam Baus (W200635)
Sebastian Buehler (W200852)
Karl Gerhard (W200882)
Johannes Grubert (W200886)
Martin Jonas (W200903)
Konrad Meyer (W200913)
Gottfried Nikolaus (W200738)
Thomas Obkircker (W200925), and

The 3rd English-Waldeck Regiment

Johannes Pfeiffer (W200929)

From 4 Company

Josef Crollpath (W200675)
Georg Dettendaler (W200685)
Georg Hermann (W200713)
Michael Fried. Lohrmann (W200436)
Andreas Muenster (W200735)
Philipp Quands (W200750)
Ludwig Schmidt (W200772)
Adam Semper (W200787), and
Johannes Teichler (W200963)

From 5 Company

Cpl. Friedrich Renne (W200939)
Georg Bachmann (W201084)
Christian Brand (W200519)
Johannes Buehler (W200851)
Georg Ludwig Gier (W200539), and
Christian Laue (W200905).

Johannes Siemon (W201163), 1 Company, was released on the Weser on September 20, and

Peter Burghenn (W200853), 4 Company, was released on the Weser on September 25.

After the regiment arrived at Korbach another 117 men were released:

From the Staff

Henrich Hufeisen (W201180S), on October 16

From 1 Company

Albrecht Hartig (W200891), on October 16
Henrich Materns (W201140), on October 16
Georg Probst (W200932), on October 16
Christian Rischebusch (W200942), on October 16
Ludwig Stremmel (W200960), on October 16
Karl Struck (W200962), on October 16
Josef Urbach (W200969), on October 16
Lorenz Becker (W200843), on October 17
Ulrich Hartmann (W200893), on October 17
Wilhelm Berghuever (W200026), on October 19
Ulrich Schreiber (W200108), on October 21, and

The 3rd English-Waldeck Regiment

Drummer Andreas Urbach (W200968), on October 26.

From 2 Company

Drummer Jakob Peter (W200746), on October 16
Michael Burghard (W200656), on October 16
Johannes Meyer (W200912), on October 16
Georg Peter (W200745), on October 16
Johannes Rehrohr (W200936), on October 16
Christian Schuessler (W200781), on October 16
Daniel Wiegold (W200837), on October 16
Sgt. Dietrich Schotte (W200131), on October 17
Adam Hohmann (W200190), on October 19
Georg Six (W200228), on October 19
Christian Goebel (W200063), on October 21
Konrad Hohmann (W200191), on October 21
Nikolaus Mueller (W200206), on October 21
Friedrich Roehrig (W200753), on October 21
Cpl. Georg Schaper (W200946), on October 24
Henrich Brabender (W201113), on October 24
Joh. Christian Eisenberg (W200172), on October 24
Henrich Flamme (W201124), on October 24
Wilhelm Littlet (W200197), on October 24, and
Henrich Lueckel (W200198), on October 24.

From 3 Company

Jakob Fauser (W200691), on October 16
Georg Fuehrer (W200699), on October 16
Johannes Lichtner (W200726), on October 16
Johannes Strehle (W201150), on October 16
Henrich Arend (W200020), on October 17
Georg Baumgarten (W200842), on October 17
Jakob Bieg (W200644), on October 17
Balthasar Heinschel (W200305), on October 17
Matthias Ohlhaber (W200741), on October 17
Anton Weinhold (W20036), on October 17
Jakob Becker (W200271), on October 19
Henrich Kleimenhagen (W201121), on October 19
Friedrich Uhlmann (W200799), on October 19
Drummer Christian Rohde (W200261), on October 20
Theodor Bunse (W200655), on October 20
Henrich Klee (W200665), on October 20
Wilhelm Figge (W200292,) on October 20
Philipp Heinemann (W200304), on October 20

The 3rd English-Waldeck Regiment

Wilhelm Lindner (W200435), on October 20
Peter Martin (W200321), on October 20
Georg Mueller (W200919), on October 20
Wilhelm Taubert (W200116), on October 20
Michael Goebel (W200701), on October 23, and
Henrich May (W200323), on October 23.

Henrich Lange (W200314) was given some kind of dishonorable discharge at Korbach on October 18, 1783.

From 4 Company

Free Cpl. Friedrich Sude (W200834), on October 16
Fifer Friedrich Peter (W201144), on October 16
Dietrich Henr. Beckmann (W200392), on October 16
Ludwig Mueller (W200679), on October 16
Anton Jost Schimmel (W200765), on October 16
Franz Fried. Schreyer (W200465), on October 16
Wilhelm Wersinger (W200809), on October 16
Johannes Zahner (W200814), on October 16
Georg Joh. Bless (W200646), on October 17
Karl Kreyer (W200863), on October 17
Gottfried Joh. Fried. Neuendorf (W200444), on October 17
Karl Roquette (W200934), on October 17
Johannes Meidr (W200730), on October 18
Marcus Trainer (W200474), on October 18
Drummer Justinus Berger (W200639), on October 20
Friedrich Boehle (W200817), on October 20
Konrad Bunse (W200397), on October 20
Joh. Friedrich Gunstmann (W200423), on October 20
Henrich Henckelmann (W200427), on October 20
Henrich Hoffmann (W200428), on October 20
Konrad Pape (W200828), on October 20
Henrich Schuetz (W200832), on October 20
Joh. Stefan Schultze (W200466), on October 20
Joh. Henrich Stiehl (W200472), on October 20, and
Johannes Wagener (W200482), on October 20.

From 5 Company

Adam Barth (W200840), on October 16
Michael Beringer (W200844), on October 16
Ludwig Buchholz (W200850), on October 16
Bernhard Keipel (W200855), on October 16

The 3rd English-Waldeck Regiment

Martin Dantzer (W200680), on October 16
Peter Hauser (W200894), on October 16
Michael Lindauer (W200908), on October 16
Christian Meisner (W200825), on October 16
Karl Kampf (W200854), on October 18
Jakob Fieberling (W200874), on October 18
Henrich Fischer (W200876), on October 18
Ludwig Mertz (W200911), on October 18
Barthold Mueller (W200916), on October 18
Adam Pflado (W200930), on October 18
Johannes Wagenstahl (W200971), on October 18
Henrich Francke (W200535), on October 19
Adam Lentzer (W200906), on October 19
Bernhard Mengeringhausen (W200565), on October 19
Christoph Mueller (W201162), on October 19
Jost Rabensprock (W200933), on October 19
Konrad Roose (W200943), on October 19
Henrich Schmidt (W200949), on October 19
Anton Schuetz (W200831), on October 19
Konrad Brock (W200849), and
Samuel Wieth (W200977), both on October 23

From the Artillery on October 16

Bombardier Wilhelm Schultze (W300014)
Bombardier Martin Heidorn (W300009)

Cannoneers

Karl Brauns (W300002)
Henrich Depmeier (W300003)
Jakob Graebe (W300006)
Wilhelm Huebsch (W300011)
Gottfried Stabroth (W300013), and
Christian Thietke (W300015).

Five members of the 1782 recruit shipment were released at Korbach on October 14, 1783.

Andreas (Adam) Bauer (W200983)
Adam Kaspar Koppenhoeffer (W201003)
Wilhelm Hamel (W201022)
Bernhard Naser (W201053), and
Friedrich Leugling (W201041)

The 3rd English-Waldeck Regiment

The following men of the 1782 recruit shipment were released at Korbach on October 22:

Sgt. Jakob Loeblein (W201043)
Drummer Karl Bauer (W200984)
Drummer Adam Ripp (W201147)
Christoph Altner (W200980)
Ernst Andreas (W200981)
Ernst de la Kampf (W200998)
Friedrich Dengel (W201012)
Johannes Drechsler (W201015)
Johannes Fasshauer (W201016)
Jakob Flinschbach (W201017)
Konrad Guenther (W201020)
Christian Heintz (W201027)
Gottfried Georg Lange (W201037)
Bernhard Lesmann (W201040)
Thomas Meyer (W201049)
Nikolaus Oppenheimer (W201057)
Johannes Probst (W201175) (see below)
Friedrich Repcke (W201064)
Andreas Schumacher (W201078)
Johannes Theile (W201091)
Jakob Ulm (W201094)
Jost Weil (W201101) and
Johannes Wissler (W201159).

Johannes Probst (W201175) was not on the roster of men who sailed to Halifax from Germany in 1782. It must be assumed that he was recruited into the regiment in America (Halifax).

Another seventeen men of the 1782 recruit shipment were released at Korbach on October 23:

Georg Bressler (W200991)
Anton Kiepe (W201001)
Adam Klunck (W201006)
Daniel Kneile (W201007)

The 3rd English-Waldeck Regiment

Georg Kramer (W201008)
Johannes Kuecher (W201010)
Jakob Dicke (W201011)
Daniel Happel (W201024)
Georg Hoffmann (W201031)
Bernhard Neuschaeffer (W201168)
Daniel Ohngefochten (W201056)
Friedrich Reuter (W201065)
Wilhelm Schmidtmann (W201074)
Philipp Schneider (W201075)
Jakob Schwartz (W201080)
Georg Senft (W201082), and
Johannes Wissler (W201159).

While most, if not all, of the Waldeck Regiment was homeward bound, another group of Loyalists embarked at New York for Nova Scotia on August 5. Fifty-four Loyalists and four Negroes were destined for Halifax, 173 loyalist and 420 Negroes for Port Roseway, and 669 Loyalists and 295 Negroes for St. John's River and Annapolis Royal. Governor John Parr, at Halifax, wrote Lord North on November 20, 1783, that he believed there were more than 25,000 refugees at Nova Scotia, but despite the approaching winter season, he would do his best to help them.[17]

On August 13, Admiral Digby, aboard *Amphion*, wrote to Lord North, that even with the shipping mentioned in North's letter of June 15, there would not be enough shipping to complete the evacuation of New York. The troops already sent were allowed a minimum of one and one-half tons per man, and the men at New York would need another 26,000 tons, plus 16,000 tons of victuallers. At the time of Digby's letter, most of the available shipping was being used to remove Loyalists and Hessians.[18]

On August 13, Carleton outlined his proposed final evacuation plans and even designated which troops would be withdrawn last. There were no Waldeck soldiers to be retained in New York, and in his effort to move the surplus troops from New York, Carleton sent men of the various remaining contingents on whatever ships, including naval vessels, that were available. Some Waldeck soldiers may have been taken aboard those ships for their return home.[19]

In November, Carleton wrote to Lord North that the Hessian commanders had not been able to prevent desertions as the embarkation to return to Europe progressed, but after embarking some 3,750 men, women, and children under Lieutenant General von Lossberg on November 8, Carleton hoped to have enough transport available by the end of the month to complete the evacuation of New York. He also mentioned to Lord North that the Hessians had behaved well.[20]

With the concurrence of the American Governor George Clinton, Carleton hoped to have evacuated New York City by November 25, retaining Staten Island and a few other places as necessary until the final evacuation. On November 21, 1,261 English officers, men and women, plus 104 children had been evacuated. English troops still in New York numbered 1,930 officers, men and women, plus 219 children.[21]

As the final outcome of the war in America had become more evident, efforts to determine if misconduct were the cause of military short-comings, and if the conduct of a few individuals merited censure, were initiated. Three trials were held, whose outcome are not known to this writer. There are indications in Learned's *Guide to German Manuscripts* that a court martial sat, probably in Waldeck, in 1782 to determine if Captain Augustin Alberti's conduct was proper when he and his command were captured on the Amite river. Major Sebisch, who had been the escort officer of at least one recruit shipment, was tried for misconduct, probably concerning his handling of funds, and Vice-corporal Reichert (not further identified) was tried for inciting to desert.[22]

The last year of the war saw a few deserters return to the regiment as a means of returning home. On the other hand, some men deserted so that they would not have to return to Europe. There were no new recruits sent out to America in

The 3rd English-Waldeck Regiment

1783, so while the regiment started the year with an estimated 560 men, plus 15 prisoners of war held by the Americans, by the end of October at least seventeen had died of non-combat causes, 244 had been released, and 57 had deserted, leaving an estimated strength of 250 men. The regiment which had an authorized strength of 670 men, plus a fourteen-man artillery detachment, had shrunk to less than one-third that number, and, in effect, the 3rd English-Waldeck Regiment had ceased to exist. The regiment was designated the 5th Battalion in later years and served briefly in Holland and for several years in South Africa.

The 3rd English-Waldeck Regiment

Summary

Research by this writer indicates 1,194 men, not counting escort personnel, sailed from Europe as members of the 3rd English-Waldeck Regiment. Another 64 men either sailed from Europe or were recruited in America, so that 1,220 have been identified, of whom eighteen died *en route* to America. While these are running figures compiled as the work was in progress, it is probably a fairly accurate assessment of the number of men who served in the regiment.

Regimental losses during the war amounted to eighteen deaths aboard ship coming to America, and another 358 deaths due to illness or accidents. Only 37 men died as a result of combat. Thirty-four men were released during the war for various reasons, and another 244 men were released after the war. About fifty of the released men stayed in America, along with the 227 men who deserted in the colonies, Nova Scotia, or the Caribbean area.

From the figures presented here, it seems that Venturini's figures, as quoted by von Eelking, are reasonably accurate for the Waldeck Regiment, and this is an indication that in all probability, his figures for other mercenary units are accurate, also.

When the regiment marched out of Korbach, on the way to the port of Bremerlehe, Master of the Hunt de Silve told the soldiers that when they returned they would all be riding in coaches. His remark was prophetic. -- On their return the men rode from Beverungen to Korbach -- in farm wagons!

The 3rd English-Waldeck Regiment

Addendum

Although listed among the men made prisoner in 1777, the following individuals appear to have been captured in 1776:

Christian Albrecht (W200018), 1 Company
Johannes Klapp (W200281), 3 Company
Henrich Graebing (W200302), 3 Company
Drummer Christian Huthmann (W200507), 5 Company
Henrich Meyer (W200566), 5 Company
Thomas Schaeffer (W200594), 5 Company, and
Georg Thielemann (W200117), 1 Company.

The following men, who were prisoners of the Americans, were either exchanged or escaped from prisoner of war status in 1777 or 1778:

Joh. Georg Bock (W200518)
Joh. Jost Dantz (W200164)
Friedrich Frese (W200536)
Johannes Meybaum (W200200)
Kaspar von Nehm (W200004)
Ulrich Schreiber (W200108)
Friedrich Schwencke (W200227)
Anton Weinhold (W200366), and
Georg Wissemann (W200125)

Personnel changes in the Waldeck Regiment in 1778, included:

Captain Lieutenant Augustin Alberti transferred from 1 Company to 5 Company in August, although the actual transfer may never have taken place as he was captured in 1779..
Cadet Bernhard von Canstein (W200046), 1 Company, was inducted into the regiment as a corporal in August.
Captain Georg von Haacke transferred from 5 Company to 1 Company in August.
Captain Konrad von Horn transferred from 1 Company to 5 Company in August.

The 3rd English-Waldeck Regiment

Fifer Wilhelm Melcher (W200323), 3 Company, had been reported as a private previously.

Servant Anton Raab (W200623), 1 Company, died, probably at Pensacola, on September 28, 1779.

Friedrich Mueller (W200573), 1 Company, was apparently taken captive at Baton Rouge on September 21, 1779.

Franz Mueller (W200572), 5 Company, appears to be the soldier, who as a prisoner of war, had joined the Spanish army and then deserted from the Spanish army before Pensacola on April 10, 1781, in order to rejoin the Waldeck Regiment.

Two additional men joined 1 Company of the Waldeck Regiment as servants in December 1781. They were:

Georg Castner (W201172), and
Daniel Hartmann (W201179)

The soldier captured at Paulus Hook on October 13, 1781, was apparently Christian Mueller (W201162). He was released from prisoner of war status in August 1782, and after returning to Germany in 1783, was released from the regiment on October 19.

It appears that Bernhard Reuter (W200940) died on February 23, 1782, and that another Bernhard Reuter (W201184S) possibly a son, was taken into the regiment and assigned to the staff as a servant in February 1782. Later it appears that he became an assistant to the provost.

Generals Clinton and Knyphausen embarked aboard the *Pearl* to return to Europe on May 13, 1782, as General Carleton had arrived at New York on May 5, to assume the position of commander-in-chief, according to Baurmeister, page 500.

Finally, Anton Noll (W200088), 1 Company, who had deserted from prisoner of war status at Havana on March 28, 1782, rejoined his company in May 1783.

The 3rd English-Waldeck Regiment

Henrich May (W200323), 3 Company, who had deserted while an American prisoner in 1778, rejoined the regiment in May 1783, also.

According to the Library of Congress 2493/477 (985), 50, the English Adjutant-General Frederick Mackenzie, at New York, notified Lieutenant Colonel von Horn on October 14, 1781, that Major Sebisch, his servant, and a Waldeck sergeant would be given passage back to Europe.

Library of Congress 2490/474 (978) contains information on the postwar activities of Christoph Alberti (W100004), Henrich Knipschild (W100013S), Philipp Marc (W400003), and Karl Henrich Strubberg (W100009). According to that document, Alberti was separated in America on February 23, 1781, but this seems most unlikely due to the many other references of his continued service with the regiment. Knipschild and Marc are noted as having been released from the regiment on August 24, 1783, so they could remain in America. The notation for Strubberg is blurred but seems to indicate that he entered the English army as a captain in December 1783.

The 3rd English-Waldeck Regiment
Notes 1776

1) Extract of a letter in the British Museum (BM) *Additional Manuscripts, BM, 42269*, "Stevens Transcripts," vol. VIII, 7-8.

2) Johann Gottfried Seume. "Adventures of a Hessian Recruit," *Proceedings of the Massachusetts Historical Society*, (Boston, 1889), vol. 4, 2nd Series, 7-12.

3) Joseph G. Rosengarten. "A Defense of the Hessians", *Pemmsylvania Magazine of History and Biography*, (Philadelphia, July 1899), vol. XXIII, 178-179.

4) Inge Auerbach and Otto Froehlich (Eds.). *Waldeck Truppen im amerikanischen Unabhaengigkeits krieg*, vol. V; Kenneth Scott. "Rivington's New York Newspaper, Excerpts from a Loyalist Press, 1773-1783", *New York Historical Society (NYHS) Collections*, (New York, 1973), vol. 84, 309.

5) Freiherr von Dalwigk. *Geschichte der Waldeckischen und kurhessische Stammtruppen der Infantrie Regiment Wttisch*, (3rd Kurhessischen) (Oldenburg, Germany, 1909), Nr. 83, 1681-1866.

6) Friedrich Kapp. "The Hessians of the Revolution", *The Historical Magazine* (New York, Jan. 1866), Vol. X, Series 1, 7-10.

7) Karl B. Demandt. *Geschichte des Landes Hessen* (Cassel, Germany, 1972), 532.

8). Max von Eelking. *Die deutschen Huelfstruppen im Nordamerikanischen Befreiungskrieg, 1776 bis 1783*, reprint edition (Cassel, Germany, 1976), 63n.

9) Charles Rainsford. "Commissary Rainsford's Journal of Transactions, Etc., 1776-1778", *NYHS Collections*, vol. XII (New York, 1879), 321.

10). Georg Pausch. *Georg Pausch's Journal and Reports of the Campaign in America*, Trans. Bruce E Burgoyne (Bowie, MD, 1996), 10.

The 3rd English-Waldeck Regiment

11) Edward J. Lowell. *The Hessians and the other German Auxiliaries of Great Britain in the Revolutionary War* (New York, 1884), 12.

12) Justin Winsor ed. *Narrative and Critical History of America*, (Boston, 1888), vol. II, 23.

13) Max von Eelking. *German Allied Troops in the North American War of Independence, 1776-1783*, Trans. Joseph G. Rosengrten, reprint edition (Baltimore, 1969), 16.

14. Lowell. *The Hessians*, 15; Carl Leopold Baurmeister. *Revolution in America: Confidential Letters and Journals, 1776-1784, of Adjutant-General Major Baurmeister of the Hessian Forces*. Trans. & Anno Bernhard A. Uhlendorf (New Brunswick, NJ, 1957), 8-9.

15) *Ibid.*

16) John Mollo and Malcolm McGregor. *Uniforms of the American Revolution* (New York, 1975), 27.

17) Eelking. *German Allied Troops*, 47.

18. D.B. Horn ed. *British Diplomatic Representatives, 1689-1789*, Camden Third Series, vol..XLVI, (London, 1932), 67.

19) Baurmeister, *Revolution in Americae*, 9.

20) Albert W. Haarmann. "The 3rd Waldeck Regiment in British Service, 1776-1783," *Army Historical Research Journal* (Autumn, 1970), 182.

21) Sir George Otto Trevelyan. *The American Revolution*, 3 vols. (New York, 1905), II, 43-44.

22) Haarmann, "The 3rd Waldeck Regiment," 182.

23) Horn, *British Diplomatic Representatives*, 67.

24) Eelking, *German Allied Troops*, 47.

25) Haarmann, "The 3rd Waldeck Regiment", 182.

26) Library of Congress (LC) Manuscripts. Copies of Manuscripts from the Hessen State Archives, Marburg, Germany, pertaining to the 3rd Waldeck Regiment, (Call numbers: 2480/464 - 2495/479, 2484/468 (968), 1 and 3.

The 3rd English-Waldeck Regiment

27) Bruce E. Burgoyne comp. *Waldeck Soldiers of the American Revolutionary War*, (Bowie, MD, 1991. This document is the source of most information on individual members of the Waldeck Regiment..

28) Philipp Waldeck. *Eighteenth Century America, As Noted in the Diary of Chaplain Philipp Waldeck (1776-1780)*, Trans. Bruce E. Burgoyne (Bowie, M, 1995).

29) LC 2484/468 (968).

30) John Charles Philipp von Krafft. *Journal of Lieutenant John Charles Philipp von Krafft*, reprint edition (New York, 1968).

31) HETRINA, LC 2484/968.

32) Marion D. Learned. *Guide to the Manuscript Materials Relating to American History in the German State Archives* (Washington, D.C., 1912), 144-149.

33) Horst Dippel. *Germany and the American Revolution, 1770-1800; A Sociohistorical Investigation of late Eighteenth-Century Political Thinking* (Wiesbaden, Germany, 1978), Bernhard A. Uhlendorf (trans.), 119-121.

34) James T. Flexner. *States Tyckmann, American Loyalist* (Boston, 1980), 24.

35) Charles M. Lefferts. *Uniforms of the American, British, French, and German Armies in the War of the American Revolution, 1775-1783*. (Old Greenwich, Conn., 1971), 266.

36) Mollo, *Uniforms*, 87 and 179.

37) K.G. Davies ed.. *Documents of the American Revolution, 1770-1783*, 21 vols. (Dublin, Ireland, 1981), XVI.

38) Haarmann. "The 3rd Waldeck Regiment," 183-184.

39) Wolfgang Medding. "Waldecker Soldaten kaempten im amerikanischen Unabhaegigkeitskrieg", in "Mein Waldeck" No. 5, Supplement to the *Waldeckischen Landeszeitung* (Arolsen, Germany), March, 1964.

40) Learned, *Guide*, 147.

41) Eelking, *German Allied Troops*, 257

The 3rd English-Waldeck Regiment

42) Davies, *Documents*, XIII, 62.
43) Joseph G. Rosengarten. *The German Soldier in the Wars of the United States* (Philadelphia, 1890), 63.
44) Benjamin F. Stevens. *Facsimilies of Manuscripts in European Archives Relating to America*, 24 vols. (London, 1891), XX, 1892.
45) Eelking, *German Allied Troops*, 18
46) BM 29454, "Abstract of Supplies voted in Parliament, 1761-1795," ff. 16-30, vol. 38383, Liverpool Papers, "Speeches of the 1st Earl, 1778-1782."
47) LC 2483/467 (966).
48) *Ibid.*
49) Eelking, *The German Allied Troops*, 47.
50) Davies, *Documents*, X, 306.
51) Medding, *"Waldecker Soldaten"*.
52) LC 2494/478 (1003), II, 155v-156. It seems strange that the "victualled" figure of official returns are lower than the figures of Colonel von Hanxleden's report, and both figures are higher than the number of men reportedly in the Waldeck contingent. A possible explanation may be that the colonel's report of the strength when the unit marched, 680 men, and the "victualled" figure may include the women who accompanied the unit. The colonel's higher figure of 716 assigned aboard ship may include the men of the regiment and the accompanying women and children.
53) Medding, *"Waldecker Soldaten"*.
54) Davies, *Documents*, X, 13.
55) William B. Clark ed.. *Naval Documents of the American Revolution*, 8 vols., (Washington, D.C., 1969), IV, 1137.
56) Davies, *Documents*, XII, 57.
57) Thomas Jones. *History of New York during the Revolutionary War*, Ed. T. Delancey, 2 vols., reprint edition (New York, 1968), I, 677.

The 3rd English-Waldeck Regiment

58) Clark, *Naval Documents*, IV, 1001-1004; BM *Additional Manuscripts*, vol. 42269; XII,117.
59) Pausch, *Journal*, 39-40.
60) "Diary of a Voyage from Stade ... of Ducal Brunswick Mercenaries." New York Historical Society *Quarterly Journal* (New York), VIII, Nr. 4, (October, 1927), 334-335.
61) *Ibid*.
62) BM.42269, XIII, 50.
63) *Ibid.*, X, 324.
64) *Ibid*.
65) Clark, *Naval Documents*, V, 428-429.
66) Pausch, *Journal*, 43.
67) Max von Eelking. *Memoirs and Letters, and Journals of Major General Riedesel*, Trans. William L. Stone, 2 vols. reprint addition (New York, 1969), I, 61-62.
68) Clark, *Naval Documents*, V, 993.
69) *Ibid*, VI, 419-420.
70) *Ibid.* V, 998, 1000, and 1129.
71) Pausch, *Journal*, 47.
72) Clark, *Naval Documents*, VI, 431-440.
73) LC 2494/478 (1003), II, 155v-156.
74) Clark, *Naval Documents*, VI, 456-457, 469, and 473.
75) *Ibid.*, VI, 481; Peter Force ed.. *American Archives*, Fifth Series, July 4, 1776 - September 3, 1783, 3 vols. (Washington, D.C., 1848-1653), I, 517. Force apparently used the date of the London *Gazette*, which he was citing as the date the fleet sailed for America, July 23, 1776.
76) Clark, *Naval Documents*, VI, 492.
77) *Ibid.*, VI, 1352-1353.
78) Rainsford, *Journal*, 359.
79) Clark, *Naval Documents*, VI, 1319, 1351-1352; B.J. Lossing, *Field Book of the Revolution*, 2 vols. (New York, 1851), II, 614n. Lossing's notation that 6,000 Waldeckers arrived at New York on October 18, 1776, would seem to be a typographical error.

The 3rd English-Waldeck Regiment

80) Robert Sears. *The Pictorial History of the American Revolution, with a Sketch of the Early History of the Country* (New York, 1847), 201.

81) Ambrose Serle. *The American Journal of Ambrose Serle, Secretary of Lord Howe, 1776-1778*, Trans. Edward H. Tatum (San Marino, Cal., 1940), 125; BM 42269, XXIII, 2044.

82) Davies, *Documents*, XII, 242.

83) LC, 2490/474 (978).

84) Serle, Journal, 117.

85) Clark, *Naval Documents*, VI, 1382-1383.

86) Davies, *Documents, XII,*, 259.

87) Mollo, *Uniforms*, 27.

88) LC 2490/474 (978).

89) Eelking, *German Allied Troops*, 49.

90) Force, *American Archives*, Fifth Series, III, 1055-1058.

91) Baurmeister, *Revolution in America*, 65.

92) LC 2490/474 (478).

93) *HETRINA*

94) William Heath. *Heath's Memoirs of the American War* (New York, 1904).

95) James McMichael. "Diary of Lieutenant James McMichael, of the Pennsylvania Line, 1776-1778," *Pennsylvania Magazine of History and Biography* (Philadelphia, 1892), XVI, 137.

96) Force, *American Archives*, Fifth Series, II, 1264.

97) Trevelyan, *The American Revolution*, II, 322.

98) Davies, *Documents*, XII, 261.

99) BM, .42270, XIX, ff, 149-152.

100) John C. Schwab. *The Revolutionary History of Fort Number Eight on Morris Heights* (New Haven, Conn., 1897), 25.

101) "Mount Washington and its Capture," *Magazine of American History*, (New York), vol. 1, no. 2 (February, 1877).

102) Baurmeister, *Revolution in America*, 66.

The 3rd English-Waldeck Regiment

103) Schwab, *Fort Number Eight*, 25-26.

104) Robert B. Roberts. *New York Forts in the American Revolution* (Cronburg, N.J., 1980), 287.

105) Force, *American Archives*, Fifth Series, III, 922-9215; Davies, *Documents*, XII, 261; *The Magazine of American History*, vol. 1, No. 2, has a map showing the Waldeck and Hessian troop dispositions during this period, on pages 63 and 64.

106) Schwab, *Fort Number Eight*, contains a map of the Harlem River and vicinity.

107) Interesting and detailed accounts of the attack are to be found in "The Capture of Colonel Moses Rawlings," *Maryland Historical Magazine* (Baltimore, 1976), vol. 71; and "Mount Washington and its Capture," *Magazine of American History*.

108) *Ibid.*, 77.

109) Ludwig von Closen. *The Military Journal of Baron Ludwig von Closen, 1780-1783*, Evelyn M. Acomb (trans. & ed.), (Chapel Hill, N.C., 1958), 362.

110) John Adlun. *Memoirs of the Life of John Adlun in the Revolutionary War*, Ed. Howard H. Peckam (Chicago, 1968), 64. The word jaeger means hunter and members of the Jaeger Corps were generally men of this profession, accustomed to the woods, weapons, and the use of independent judgment. The Waldeck Regiment did not have a Jaeger Corps.

111) *Ibid.*

112) Henry P. Johnston. *The Battle of Harlem Heights, September 16, 1776*, reprint editio (New York, 1970), 232.

113) Andreas Wiederhold. "The Capture of Fort Washington, New York, Described by Captain Andreas Wiederhold, of the Hessian Regiment Knyphausen," *Pennsylvania Magazine of History and Biography* (Philadelphia, 1899), XXIII, 96.

114) Richard M. Ketchum. *The Winter Soldiers* (Garden City, N.J., 1973), 142 and 149.

The 3rd English-Waldeck Regiment

115) Frederick Mackenzie. *Mackenzie Diaries*, 2 vols. (Cambridge, 1930), I, 110.
116) Force, *American Archives*, Fifth Series, III, 1055-1058.
117) LC 2490/474 (978).
118) *Ibid.*
119) *HETRINA*
120) Stephen Kemble. "Order Books of Lieutenant-Col Stephen Kemble, Adjutant General and Deputy Adjutant General of the British Forces in America, 1775-1778," *NYHS Collections*, (New York, 1883), 2nd part of vol. XVI, 409.
121) BM *42270*, XIV, 206.
122) Trevelyan, *The American Revolution*, III, 8-9.
123) LC, 2490/474 (978).
124) *HETRINA*
125) Kemble, "Order Books," II, 414 and 418
126) Baurmeister, *Revolution in America*, 74.
127) "Lee Papers," *NYHS Collections*, (New York, 1872), II, 327.
128) Serle, *Journal*, 155.
129) Baurmeister, *Revolution in America*, 74.
130) Christopher L. Ward. *The Delaware Continentals, 1776-1783* (Wilmington, Del., 1941), 562; Leonard Lundin. *Cockpit of the Revolution, The War for Independence in New Jersey* (New York, 1972), 168. This latter book also contains a map which shows the Waldeck Regiment at Elizabethtown during this time period.
131) Eelking, *German Allied Troops*, 53.
132) Force, *American Archives*, Fifth Series, III, 1316.
133) *Ibid.*, III, 1449.
134) *Ibid.*, III, 1318; BM 42270, XIX, 308.
135) Force, *American Archives*, Fifth Series, III, 1475.
136) *Ibid.*, III, 1488-1490.
137) LC 2490/474 (978).

The 3rd English-Waldeck Regiment
1777 Notes

1) Kemble, "Journals," XVI, 105.
2) George Clinton. *Public Papers of George Clinton, First Governor of New York, 1777-1795 and 1801-1804*, 10 vols., reprint edition (New York, 1973), I, 537.
3) *Ibid.*; Kemble, "Journals," I, 537; Muenchhausen, *At General Howe's Side*, 9 and 59.
4) Archibald Robertson. *Archibald Robertson, His Diaries and Sketches in America, 1762-1780.* Ed. Harry W. Leydenberg (New York, 1930), 121.
5) Ketchum. *The Winter Soldiers*, 389. Albert H. Bill. *The Campaign of Princeton, 1776-1777* (Princeton, NJ, 1948), 129.
6) William S. Stryker, ed. *Documents Relating to the Revolutionary History of the State of New Jersey*, 2nd Series, vol. I "Extracts from American Newspapers," 1776-1777 (Trenton, N.J., 1901), vol. I, 258 and 270.
7) Jared Sparks, ed. *The Writings of George Washington*, 12 vols. (Boston, 1858), IV, 264.
8) A. Van Doren Honeyman, ed. *History of Union County, New Jersey, 1664-1923)*, 2 vols. (New York, 1923), I, 138.
9) William S. Stryker. *The Battles of Trenton and Princeton*, reprint edition (Spartansburg, S.C., 1967), 451.
10) Frank Moore, comp. *The Diary of the American Revolution*, (New York, 1967), 193.
11) Heath. *Memoirs*, 118.
12) Samuel Hazard, comp. *Pennsylvania Archives*, 1st Series, vol.5, 1776-1777 (Philadelphia, 1853), 178.
13) Muenchhausen, *At General Howe's Side*, 9.
14) "An Historical Journal of the American War," *Massachusetts Historical Society Collections*, vol. II (Boston, 1793), 90.
15) Trevelyan. *The American Revolution*, III, 140.

The 3rd English-Waldeck Regiment

16) John Clark. "Memoirs of Major John Clark of York County, Pennsyl-vania," *Pennsylvania Magazine of History and Biography*, Cont. E.M. Spangler (Philadelphia, PA., 1896), XX, 77.

17) Kemble, "Journals," 106.

18) *Ibid.*, 107 and 118.

19) William Young. "Journal of Sergeant William Young, Written During the Jersey Campaign in the Winter of 1776-7," *Pennsylvania Magazine of History and Biography* (Philadelphia, 1884), vol. VIII, 155-178.

20) Stryker, *Documents*, 256.

21) LC 2490/474 (978).

22) *HETRINA*

23) *Ibid.*; Davies, *Documents*, XIV, 82-83; Johannes Schwalm Historical Association, Inc., *(JSHA)*, *Johannes Schwalm the Hessian* (Millville, PA, 1976), 231-246.

24) *HETRINA*

25) *Ibid.*

26) LC 2490/474 (978); 2494/478 (1003), II, 155v-156.

27) LC 2490/474 (978).

28) *Ibid.*, .

29) Hazard, *Pennsylvania Archives*, 204-205.

30) Stryker, *Documents*, 344.

31) Davies, *Documents*, 82-83; If these figures are correct, most of the men made prisoner of war in 1777 and not exchanged in 1778, must have enlisted in the American army.

32) Ludlin. *Cockpit of the Revolution*, 225.

33) "An Historical Journal," *100-101*.

34) LC 2494/468 (968).

35) Muenchhausen, *At General Howe's Side*, 13.

36) John Montresor. "Journal of Capt. John Montresor," *NYHS Collections*, Ed. G,I, Scull (New York, 1881), XIV, 421.

37) Muenchhausen, *At General Howe's Side*, 16; John Andre. *Major Andre's Journal, Operations of the British Army*

The 3rd English-Waldeck Regiment *under Lieutenant Generals Sir William Howe and Sir Henry Clinton, June 1777 to November 1778*, reprint edition (New York, 1968), 27.

38) Kemble. "Order Books," XVI, 445.
39) Robert B. Roberts. *New York Forts in the Revolution* (Cronbury, N.J., 1980), 326.
40) Kemble, "Order Books," 453.
41). Muenchhausen, *At General Howe's Side*, 19-20.
42) Robertson, "His Diaries," 139-140.
43) Kemble, "Order Books," 427.
44) Bernhard Uhlendorf and Edna Wosper eds.. *Letters from Major Baurmeister to Colonel von Jungkenn, Written During the Philadelphia Campaign, 1777-1778* (Philadelphia, 1937), 1.
45) Davies, *Documents*, XIII, 67.
46) *Ibid.*, XIII, 74.
47) Clark, *Naval Documents*, VIII, 738-739.
48) *Ibid.*
49) Davies, *Documents*, XIII, 72-73.
50) Serle, "Journal," 228.
51) Davies, *Documents*, XIII, 134.
52) *Ibid.*
53) Sparks, *The Writings of George Washington*, V, 542; Henry B. Carrington. *Battles of the American Revolution* (New York, 1877), 321.
54) Muenchhausen, *At General Howe's Side*.
55) LC 2494/478 (1003), II, 155v-156.
56) *Ibid.*; LC 2484/468 (968).
57) *HETRINA*
58) LC 2484/468 (968).
59) Erhard Staedtler. *Die Ansbach-Bayreuther Truppen in Amerikanischen Unabhaengigkeirskrieg, 1773-1783* (Nurenberg, Germany, 1956), 73 and 151.
60) Stryker, *Documents*, 461; Muenchhausen, *At General Howe's Side*, 28; Mackenzie. *Mackenzie Diaries*, I, 174-175.

The 3rd English-Waldeck Regiment

61) LC 2490/474 (978).
62) Kemble, "Journals," 132; Francis B. Lee ed.. *Documents Relating to the Revolutionary History of the State of New Jersey*, 2nd Series (Trenton, N.J., 1903), II, 42.
63) Clinton, *Clinton Papers*, II, opp. 516.
64) Kemble, "Journals." 136-141.
65) Hazard, *Pennsylvania Archives*, 538.
66) Samuel Hazard comp.). *Pennsylvania Collected Records*, Colonial Records (Harrisburg, PA, 1852), II, 116.
67) Clinton, *Clinton Papers*, I, 622.
68) Hazard *Pennsylvania Archives*, 437-438.
69) William W. Condit. "Christopher Ludwig, Patriotic Gingerbread Baker", *Pennsylvania Magazine of History and Biography* (Philadelphia, PA, 1957), vol. 81, 377.
70) Davies, *Documents*, XIII, 58.
71) *Ibid.*, XIV, 82-83.
72) John H. Jordan. "Bethlehem During the Revolution, Extracts from the Diaries in the Moravian Archives at Bethlehem, Pennsylvania." *Pennsylvania Magazine of History and Biography* (Philadelphia, PA, 1888), XII, 399.
73) Hazard, *Pennsylvania Archives*, 480-481.
74) John H. Heisey trans. and ed.. "Extracts from the Diaries of the Moravian Pastors of the Hebron Church, Lebanon, 1755-1814", *Pennsylvania Historical Association Quarterly Journal* (Philadelphia, PA, January 1967), XXXIV, Nr1, 58.
75) *Ibid.*, 55-56.
76) *Ibid.*, 56.
77) *Ibid.*
78) LC 2490/474 (978).
79) *Ibid.*
80) *Ibid.*

The 3rd English-Waldeck Regiment
1778 NOTES

1) LC, 2484/468 (968).
2) *Ibid.*
3) *HETRINA*
4) *Ibid.*, LC 2490/4474 (978).
5) *Ibid.*
6) *Ibid.*
7) LC 2494/478 (1003), II, 155v-156.
8) LC 2490/474 (978).
9) *Ibid.*
10) Heisey, "Diares of the Moravian Pastors," XXIV, 55.
11) Montresor, "Journals," 486.
12) Edmund C. Burnett ed.. *Letters of Members of the Continental Congress*, 8 vols., reprint edition (Glouster, Mass., 1963), III, 267n-268n and 279.
13) Serle, "Journal," 308..
14) Henry M. Muhlenberg. *The Journals of Henry Melchior Muhlenberg*, Trans. Therodore G. Tappert and John W. Doberstein, 3 vols. (Philadelphia, 1942-1958), III, 308.
15) Johannes Schwalm Historical Association, Inc. (JSHA). *Johannes Schwalm the Hessian* (Millville, Pa., 1976), 242. A check of the names of the unit and assignments indicates that 2 Company and 3 Company of the referenced tables are reversed from the Waldeck usage and that the table refers to 2 Company as the Company of Colonel von Hanxleden and to 3 Company as the Company of Major/Lieutenant Colonel von Dalwyck. Also, names in general have been changed by this writer to reflect the most common spelling and thereby to reduce confusion caused by phonetic and illiterate spelling of many of the names.
16) *Ibid.*, 239 passim.
17) *Ibid.*, JSHA, *Johannes Schwalm*, 229 passim.
18) *HETRINA*
19) Montresor, "Journals", XIX, 500.

20) Francis R. Lee (Ed.). *Documents Relating to the Revolutionary History of the State of New Jersey*, 2nd Series, vol. II (Trenton, 1903), II, 296.
21) Montresor, "Journals." XIX, 505.
22) JSHA, *Johannes Schwalm*, 26.
23) *Ibid.*, 245.
24) Robert o. Slagle. *The von Lossberg Regiment; a Chronicle of Hessian Participation in the American Revolution*, an unpublished doctoral dissertation, The American University (Washington, D.C., 1965), 149.
25) Montresor, "Journals," XIV, 149.
26) Lee, *Documents*, II, 320.
27) JSHA, *Johannes Schwalm*, 229 passim.
28) *HETRINA*
29) JSHA, *Johannes Schwalm*, 39.
30) Davies, *Documents*, XIII, 252.
31) *Ibid.*, XIII, 286.
32) William B. Willcox. *Portrait of a General, Sir Henry Clinton, in the War of Independence* (New York, 1964), 283-284.
33) Eelking. *German Allied Troops*, 159.
34) LC 2494/478 (1003), II, 155v-156.
35) *Ibid.* (1003), II, 125-125v and 135.
36) *Ibid.*
37) *Ibid.*
38) *Ibid.*, (1003), II, 136-137; .
39) Montresor, "Journals", XIV, 503-512.
40) Muenchhausen, *Revolution in America*, 189-197.
41) Muhlenberg, *Journals*, III, 83, 123, 213.
42) BM 42267, XI, 1069
43) *Ibid.*, XI, 1082, 1089.
44) *Ibid.*, XI, 1118.
45) *Ibid.*, VIII, 839.
46) *Ibid.*, XI, 1127, 1153.
47) *Ibid.*, XI, 1175.

The 3rd English-Waldeck Regiment

48) Bernard C. Steiner ed;. *Archives of Maryland, Journal and Correspondence of the Council of Maryland* (Baltimore, 1921), XXI, 219.
49) "Revolutionary Letters," *The Historical Magazine* (New York, November 1858), II, No. 11, 21.
50) *Ibid.*
51) Steiner, *Archives of Maryland,* XXI, 225.
52) Mackenzie, *Mackenzie Diaries,* I, 412.
53) Eelking, *Die deutschen Huelfstruppen,* 137n. Rosengarten, *The German Soldier,* 84. Rosengarten apparently misunderstood von Eelking's remark of four wives on *Crawford* to mean that there were only four wives with the regiment.
54) LC 2494/478 (1003), II, 153.
55) Francis A. Whinyates. *The Services of Lieut. Colonel Francis Downman, R.A. in France, North America, and the West Indies, Between the Years 1758 and 1784* (Woolwich, England, 1808), 89.
56) Kemble, "Journal." XVI, 165.: BM 42268, XII, 1207.
57) Carson I.A. Ritchie ed. "A New York Diary of the Revolutionary War", *Narratives of the Revolution in New York, a Collection of Articles from the New York Historical Society Quarterly* (New York, 1975), vol. 85, 259; "Revolutionary Letters," *The Historical Magazine, II, 41 and 322.*
58) *Ibid.,* 322; Ritchie, "A New York Diary," 260.
59) BM 42268, XII, 1221.
60) *Ibid.,* 1224; Ritchie, "A New York Diary," 261.
61) "Revolutionary Letters," *The Historical Magazine*, II, 322-323.
62) Whinyates, *The Services of Lieut. Colonel Downman,* 89.
63) Clark, *Naval Documents,* IV, 1091; VIII, 740.
64) Muenchhausen, *At General Howe's Side,* 21.
65) Baurmeister, *Revolution in America,* 256.
66) LC 2490/474 (978).
67) LC 2484/468 (968), 20.

The 3rd English-Waldeck Regiment
1779 NOTES

1) Baurmeister, *Revolution in America*, 266. The traanslator, Uhlendorf, felt compelled to comment in a note that as the Waldeck unit had been referred to previously as a regiment, it may have been reduced to battalion size by the time of leaving Jamaica. The more likely explanation is that the terms regiment and battalion were often used interchangeably and there was no significance to Baurmeister calling the Waldeck unit a battalion. Davies, *Documents*, XIII, 11.

2) Robert V. Haynes. *The Natchez District and the American Revolution* (Jackson, Mississippi, 1976), 5: Eelking, *The German Allied Troops*, 219.

3) Davies, *Documents*, XIII, 364 and XVI, 54-65.

4) *Ibid.*, XVI, 60-61.

5) *Ibid.*

6) *Ibid.* It is possible that Campbell and Colonel Charles Rainsford, who was commissary of troops working with the German mercenaries shipped from Dutch ports, were old friends and that Andrew was related to the Colonel.

7) Davies, *Documents*, XVII, 14.

8) *Ibid.*

9) Haynes, *The Natchez District*, 107.

10) Davies, *Documents*, XVII, 54-65.

11) LC, 2484/468 (968).

12) Davies, *Documents*, XVI, 58.

13) LC 2490/474 (978).

14) *Ibid.*

15) Davies, *Documents*, XVII, 54-65; Jack P.L. Holmes. "German Troops in Alabama During the American Revolution, The Battle of January 7, 1781," *The Alabama Quarterly Review* (Montgomery, Ala., Spring 1974), XXXVI, Nr. 2, 5. Holmes would have us believe these same troops marched overland from New York to Florida.

16) University of Michigan. "Monthly Return of the 3rd Regiment of Waldeck, Commanded by Colonel von Hanxleden, Pensacola the 1st April 1779," a Clements Library Manuscript (Ann Arbor, Mich.)

17) George S. Osborn. "Major General John Campbell in British West Florida," *The Florida Historical Quarterly* (Gainesville, Fla., April 1924), vol. XXVII, No. 4, 324.

18) Davies, *Documents*, XVI.

19) *Ibid.*, XVI, 102.

20) *Ibid.*, XVI, 99.

21) Lawrence Kinnaird ed.. "Spain in the Mississippi Valley, 1765-1794", *Annual Report of the American Historical Association* (Washington, D.C., 1949), II, 345.

22) Davies, *Documents*, XVI, 176.

23) Haynes, *The Natchez District*, 117.

24) Eelking, *German Allied Troops*, 220. The grenadiers had gone to Manchac originally and Major von Horn was still in Europe when his company left Pensacola.

25) LC 2490/474 (978).

26) Davies, *Documents*, XVI.

27) Kinnaird, "Spain in the Mississippi Valley," II, 355-357.

28) J. Leitch Wright, Jr. *Florida in the American Revolution* (Gainesville, Fla., 1975), 77.

29) "West Florida, The Capture of Baton Rouge by Galvez, September 21st, 1779," *The Florida Historical Quarterly* (Gainesville, Fla., October 1960), XII, Nr. 2, 257.

30) Haynes. *The Natchez District*, 114; Albert H. Haarmann. "The Spanish Conquest of British West Florida, 1779-1781," *The Florida Historical Society* (Gainesville, Fla., October 1960), XXXIX, Nr. 1, 113; LC 2487/471 (972), II, 157.

31) "West Florida," 265.

32) *HETRINA*, V; LC 2490/474 (978).

The 3rd English-Waldeck Regiment

33) *Ibid.*
34) Davies, *Documents*, XVII, 216-218.
35) *Ibid.*, XVI, 176.
36) *Ibid.*
37) *Ibid*, XVI, 177.
38) Haarmann, "The Spanish Conquest," 112; A Society of Gentlemen, *The History of the British Empire, From the Year 1765, to the Year 1783*, 2 vols., reprint edition (Boston, 1972), I, 423; Haynes, *The Natchez District*, 119.
39) "West Florida," 258-262.
40) Davies, *Documents*, XVI, 236.
41) Lowell, *The Hessians*, 301.
42) Eelking, *German Allied Troops*, 221.
43) Haarmann, "The Spanish Conquest," 113.
44) "West Florida," 264-265; Eelking, *Die Deutsche Huelfstruppen*, 142-143.
45) *Ibid.*
46) LC 2487/471 (972), II, 167.
47) LC 2490/474 (978).
48) *Ibid., HETRINA*.
49) Haynes, *The Natchez District*, 126; Kinnaird, "Spain in the Mississippi Valley," II, 366-368.
50) Haynes, *The Natchez District*, 126.
51) LC 2490/474 (978).
52) *Ibid.*
53) *Ibid.*, Davies, *Documents, XVI, 52 - 55*.
54) *Ibid.*, XVI, 242.
55) *Ibid.*, XVII, 260-267.
56) *HETRINA*; LC 2490/474 (978).
57) *HETRINA*.
58) *Ibid.*; LC 2490/474 (978); University of Michigan, "Monthly Return ... April 1st 1779."
59) Haynes, *The Natchez District*, 24.
60) LC 2490/474 (978).
61) *HETRINA*.

The 3rd English-Waldeck Regiment

62) Davies, *Documents*, XIII, 362.
63) *Ibid.*, XVI, 92.
64) *Ibid.*, XVI, 106.
65) LC 2484/468 (968), 11.
66) *HETRINA*.
67) LC 2484/468 (968).
68) *Ibid.*
69) University of Michigan, Muster Rolls ...1 April 1779.
70) LC 2484/468 (968).

The 3rd English-Waldeck Regiment
1780 NOTES

1) Haynes, *The Natchez District*, 6.
2) Davies, *Documents*, XIII, 288 and 321.
3) *Ibid.*
4) *Ibid.*, XVI, 320; Wright, *Florida in the American Revolution*, 79.
5) Kinnaird, "Spain in the Mississippi Valley," II, 374-375.
6) George C. Osborn. "Major General John Campbell in British West Florida," *The Florida Historical Quarterly* (Gainsville, Fla., April 1949), XXVII, Nr. 4, 337.
7) Davies, *Documents*, XVI, 321; Haarmann, "The Spanish Conquest," XXXIX, No. 1, 115 and 118.
8) *Ibid.*
9) *Ibid.*, 118-119.
10) *Ibid.*
11) Davies, *Documents*, XVI, 321; Holmes, "German Troops in Alabama," XXXVI, Nr. 1, 7. Holmes states that the loss of Mobile was due to the Waldeckers arriving at Mobile too late.
12) Davies, *Documents*, XVI, 295 and XVIII, 73.
13) *Ibid.*, XVI, 321.
14) *Ibid.*, XVI, 326.
15) Wright, *Florida in the American Revolution*, 87.
16) James A. Servies ed.. *The Log of HMS Mentor, 1780-1781* (Pensacola, Fla., 1982), 3.
17) Davies, *Documents*, XVI, 326.
18) *Ibid.*, XVI, 462; Servies, *The Log of HMS Mentor*, 4.
19) Davies, *Documents*, XVI, 355-356.
20) *Ibid.*, XVIII, 118; Benjamin F. Stevens ed.. *Clinton Cornwallis Controversy*, (London, 1888), 231.
21) Carrington, *Battles of the American Revolution*, 502. Most writers use the strength figures given in the official returns from New York during this period, and these figures are not even close to the correct figures for Pensacola.

The 3rd English-Waldeck Regiment

22) LC 2484/468 (968), 11.
23) Servies, *The Log of HMS Mentor*, 11-12; Davies, *Documents*.
24) *Ibid.*, XVIII, 115-116.
25) Servies, *The Log of HMS Mentor*, 12-13.
26) Davies, *Documents*, XVI, 392.
27) *Ibid.*, XVI, 412.
28) *Ibid.*, XVI, 428.
29) *Ibid.*, XVI, 427.
30) *Ibid.*, XVI, 428-429.
31) *Ibid.*, XVI, 414.
32) Haarmann, "The Spanish Conquest," 121.
33) Davies, *Documents*, XVI, 428.
34) *Ibid.*, XVIII, 232-234.
35) Stanley Faye. *The Spanish and British Fortifications of Pensacola, 1698-1821* (Pensacola, Fla., 1977), 277. Faye's work also includes some plans and maps of Pensacola and its fortifications drawn by English engineer Elias Durnford and the Waldecker, Captain Lieutenant Henrich Heldring.
36) Davies, *Documents*, XVI, 361.
37) "Return of Hessian Recruits after their Embarkation at Bremerlehe 1st June 1789," Clements Library Manuscript, University of Michigan (Ann Arbor).
38) Davies, *Documents*, XVI, 362.
39) *HETRINA*, V.
40) LC 2484/468 (968), 19-20.
41) *HETRINA*.
42) *Ibid.*
43) LC 2490/474 (978).
44) *Ibid.*
45) *Ibid.*
46) *Ibid.*; *HETRINA*.
47) *Ibid.*; "List of Officers of the 3rd Regiment of Waldeck, Newtown, Long Island the 1st January 1782,"

The 3rd English-Waldeck Regiment
Clements Library Manuscript, University of Michigan, Ann Arbor.
48) *HETRINA*.

The 3rd English-Waldeck Regiment
1781 NOTES

1) Servies, *The Log of HMS Mentor*, 3; Haarmann, "The Spanish Conquest." Haarmann wrote that the land attack was to have been supported by two frigates.
2) *Ibid,.* 124 ; Lowell, *The Hessians*, 253.; Douglas W. Marshall and Howard H.. Peckham. *Campaigns of the American Revolution; and Atlas of Manuscript Maps* (Ann Arbor, Mich., 1976), 124n.
3) Eelking, *Die Deutsche Huelfstruppen,* 147n.
4) Haarmann, "The Spanish Conquest," 120.; Davies, *Documents*, XIX, 39.
5) Baurmeister, *Revolution in America*, 432.; Marshall and Peckham, *Campaigns*, 124.
6) Davies, *Documents*, XIX, 44.; Haarmann, "The Spanish Conquest, 120.
7) Robert Farmar. "Robert Farmar's Journal of the Siege of Pensacola", *The Historical Magazine*, (New York, 1860), IV, 171.
8) LC 2487/471 (972), 167 and 2490/474 (p78).
9) Holmes, "German Troops in Alabama," XXXVI, Nr. 1, 8-9. The writer of the present volume has found no indication that Colonel von Hanxleden's son was wounded, although he was separated from the unit and returned to Europe in April 1781. Certainly, not all of the Waldeck officers were killed or wounded.
10) Davies, *Documents*, XX, 46-47.
11) Marshall and Peckham, *Campaigns*, 124.
12) Davies, *Documents*, XIX, 97. The time of the Spanish fleet's arrival at Pensacola seems in error, and probably should be March 9, 1781.
13) *Ibid.*, XIX, 104 ; Servies, *The Log of HMS Mentor*, 21.
14) Kinnaird, "Spain in the Mississippi Valley "II, 421-423.

15) Davies, *Documents*, XIX, 101; Servies, *The Log of HMS Mentor*, 21-22.
16) *Ibid.*, 22-23.
17) *Ibid.*, 23.
18) Davies, *Documents*, XIX, 69.
19) *Ibid.*, XIX, 101.
20) Servies, *The Log of HMS Mentor*, 23-24.
21) Davies, *Documents*, XIX, 101.
22) Servies, *The Log of HMS Mentor*, 178.; Marshall and Peckham, *Campaigns*, 124, seem to combine the arrival of the joint French-Spanish fleet in April with the troop landings the previous month. Their book contains a map of the siege area at Pensacola on page 125.
23) Servies, *The Log of HMS Mentor*, 175.; Davies, *Documents*, XIX, 106.
24) Faye, *The Spanish and British Fortifications*, 180-181.
25) Farmar, "Journal," 169.
26) Miranda. "Miranda's Diary of the Siege of Pensacola, 1781", *The Florida Historical Quarterly*, Trans.Donald E. Worcester (Gainsville, Fla., January 1971), XXIX, Nr. 3, 177.
27) *Ibid.*, 178.
28) Farmar, "Journal," 169.
29) *Ibid.*, 169-179 ; Miranda, "Diary," 177.
30) *Ibid.*, 178 ; Farmar, "Journal," 169.
31) Servies, *The Log of HMS Mentor*, 180. The log dates run from noon to noon.
32) *Ibid.*, 184; Farmar, "Journal," 170; Miranda, "Diary," 185-188.
33) Haynes, *The Natchez District*, 133 ; Faye, *Spanish and British Fortifications*, 279 ; Servies, *The Log of HMS Mentor*, 186 ; Davies, *Documents*, XXI, 29.
34) *Ibid.*, XXI, 29.
35) *Ibid.*, XIX, 39; Servies, *The Log of HMS Mentor*, 174-182.
36) Farmar, "Journal," 166-170.

37) *Ibid.*, 169.
38) *Ibid.*; LC 2490/474 (978).
39) Davies, *Documents*, XIX, 120.
40) Miranda, "Diary," 190-191.
41) *Ibid.*, 189.
42) *Ibid.*, 192; Davies, *Documents*, XIX, 118 ; Servies, *The Log of HMS Mentor*,186-187. Captain Dean's entries in Mentor's log at this point are all one day later than the dates recorded for the same events by Miranda and Farmar possibly due to the use of Greenwich time.
43) Bernardo de Galvez. "Bernardo de Galvez's Combat Diary for the Battle of Pensacola, 1781," *The Florida Historical Quarterly*, Eds. Maury Baker and Margaret Bissler Haas (Gainsville, Fla., July 1977), LVI, Nr. 1, 195.
44) *Ibid.*, 196-197.
45) Davies, *Documents*, XIX, 105.
46) Haarmann, "*The Spanish Conquest*", 132-133 ; Gaspar Cusachs (Trans.). "Diary of Operations Against Pensacola", *The Louisiana Historical Quarterly*, (New Orleans, 1917-18), vol. 1, 75. Galvez reported that 103 women and 123 children were in the garrison.
47) Baurmeister, *Revolution in America*, 452.
48) LC 2484/468 (968), 21.
49) "Note from 'An Account of the Surveys of Florida', London, 1790, page, 3." *The Historical Magazine* (New York, 1860), IV, 171.
50) Miranda, "Diary," 176.
51) Servies, *The Log of HMS Mentor*, 24-25 ; Cusachs, "Diary of Operations", 75.
52) Marshall and Peckham, *Campaigns*, 124 ; Farmar, "Journal",171.
53) Davies, *Documents*, XIX, 107.
54) Kinnaird, "Spain in the Mississippi Valley", 427-428.
55) Davies, *Documents*, XIX, 105.
56) *Ibid.*, XX, 141.

The 3rd English-Waldeck Regiment

57) Farmar, "Journal," 168; Servies, *The Log of HMS Mentor*, 176; Kinnaird, "Spain in the Mississippi Valley", 170; Scott, "Rivington's New York Newspaper," vol.84, 264 ; LC 2490/474 (978).
58) Farmar, "Journal," 170-171.
59) LC 2487/471 (972), II, 167. and 2490/474 (978). Litzau is listed as having died on May 8.
60) *Ibid.*
61) Galvez, "Combat Diary," 61; Cusachs, "Diary of Operations," 61.
62) Servies, *The Log of HMS Mentor*, 172; LC 2490/474 (978).
63) *Ibid.*; Servies, *The Log of HMS Mentor*, 174-177.
64) Miranda, "Diary," 180-185; LC 2490/474 (978).
65) Servies, *The Log of HMS Mentor*, 175; Farmar, "Journal," 168.
66) Miranda, "Diary," 18.
67) LC 2490/474 (978).
68) Kinnaird, "Spain in the Mississippi Valley," II, 435.
69) *HETRINA*; LC 2490/474 (978).
70) *Ibid.*; *HETRINA*.
71) LC 2490/474 (978).
72) *Ibid.*; LC 2490/474 (978).
73) LC 2482/468 (968), 15.
74) Davies, *Documents*, XIX, 118.
75) John C.P. von Krafft. *Journal of Lieutenant John Charles Philip von Krafft, of the Regiment von Bose, 1776-1784*, reprint edition (New York, 1968), 142.
76) Edmund C. Burnett ed. *Letters of Members of the Continental Congress*, 8 vols. (Washington, D.C., 1921-1936), VI, 132, 150-151, and 154-156.
77) *Ibid.*, 154-156 ; Mackenzie, *Diaries*, II, 578.
78) Baurmeister, *Revolution in America*, 451.
79) Sabine, *Historical Memoirs*, 427; Mackenzie, *Diaries*, II, 566.

80) *Ibid.*, II, 694.
81) "Diary of a French Officer," *Magazine of American History* (New York, 1880), IV, 303.
82) Clinton, *Public Papers*, VII, 111; Closen, *The Revolutionary Journal*, 103.
83) Louis Krupp trans.. *German Mercenaries in Pensacola During the American Revolution, 1779-1781* (Pensacola, Fla., 1977), 32. Carrington, *Battles of the American Revolution*, 646.
84) Mackenzie *Diaries*, II, 578.
85) Baurmeister, *Revolution in America*, 450.
86) Davies, *Documents*, XIX, 68.
87) *Ibid.*, XX, 109.
88) *Ibid.*, XIX, 104.
89) *Ibid.*, XIX, 107-108.
90) *Ibid.*, XIX, 166; Sabine, *Historical Memoirs*, 429; Stevens, *Clinton-Cornwallis Controversy*, II, 123 and 226-229.
91) Mackenzie, *Diaries*, II, 589.
92) LC 2495/479 (1004) ; and 2490/474 (978).
93) *Ibid.*; *HETRINA*.
94) LC 2490/474 (978).
95) "Proceedings of a Board of General Officers of the British Army at New York, 1781," *NYHS Collections* (New York, 1916), vol. 49, 87-92.
96) Mackenzie, *Diaries*, II, 609).
97) *Ibid.*, II, 632, 654, 677, and 697.
98) *Ibid.*, II, 599 and 637. Hallet's Cove is now Astoria and constitutes the 4th and 5th wards of Brooklyn.
99) *Ibid.*, II, 657 and 661; Baurmeister, *Revolution in America*, 465.
100) Mackenzie, *Diaries*, II, 695-697.
101) *HETRINA*.
102) *Ibid.*
103) *Ibid.*
104) *Ibid.*

The 3rd English-Waldeck Regiment

105) *Ibid.*; "List of Officers of the 3rd Regiment of Waldeck, Newtown, Long Island the 1st January 1782," Clements Library Manuscript, University of Michigan, Ann Arbor; LC 2489/473 (975), II, 79-79v.

106) *Ibid.*

The 3rd English-Waldeck Regiment
1782 NOTES

1) "List of Officers".
2) *HETRINA*.
3) LC 2389/473 (975), I, 79.
4) "Muster Rolls," April 1, 1779, Clements Library Manuscript, Univer-sity of Michigan Ann Arbor.
5) *HETRINA*.
6) LC 2493/477 (1002), 112..
7) *Ibid.*, (1002), 100. The count of thirteen women seems to represent the latest information then available, and possibly the three women originally scheduled to sail with the regiment were left in Germany.
8) *Ibid.*, (1002), 113.; *HETRINA*.
9) *LC 2493/477* (1002), 112.
10) *Ibid.*
11) *Ibid.*
12) Baurmeister, *Revolution in America*, 511.
13) Davies, *Documents*, XIX, 324.; Baurmeister, *Revolution in America*,534-535.
14) *Ibid.*, 522 ; Sabine, *Historical Memoirs*, 548, "Letters of Edmund Pendleton ." *Massachusetts Historical Society Proceedings* (Boston, 1906), 2nd Series, XIX, 164.
15) Closen, *The Revolutionary Journal*, 234.
16) Baurmeister, Revolution in America, 522 and 524; Krafft, *Journal*,169-171.
17) LC 2490/474 (978).
18) *Ibid.*
19) *Ibid.*; LC 2490/474 (978).
20) *HETRINA*.
21) *Ibid., III and V ; LC 2490/474 (978).*

The 3rd English-Waldeck Regiment
1783 NOTES

1) Davies, *Documents*, XIX, 390.
2) Erhard Staedtler. *Die Ansbach-Bayreuther Truppen in Amerikanischen Unabhaengigkeitskrieg, 1773-1783*, (Nuernberg, Germany, 1956), 73.
3) Davies, *Documents*, XIX, 398-399.
4) *Ibid.*, 399,
5) Clark, Memoirs, 95-97; Davies, *Documents*, XIX, 408.
6) *Ibid*, XIX, 409.
7) *Ibid.*
8) *Ibid.*
9) *Ibid*, XIX, 414 ; Krafft, *Journal*, 186; Eelking, *The German Allied Troops*, 259.
10) Davies, *Documents*, XIX, 414.
11) LC 2490/474 (978).
12) *Ibid.*
13) *Ibid.*
14) *Ibid.*
15) *Ibid.*
16) *Ibid.*; *HETRINA*.
17) Davies *Documents*, XIX, 423 and 450.
18) *Ibid*, XIX,428.
19) *Ibid.*, XXI, 213 ; Eelking, *The German Allied Troops*, 261.
20) Davies, *Documents*, XIX, 449.
21) *Ibid.*, XIX, 451.
22) Max D. Learned. *Guide to the Manuscript Materials Relating to American History in the German State Archives* (Washington, D.C., 1919), 147.

The 3rd English-Waldeck Regiment
Bibliography

This is only a limited bibliography, listing sources which were used in preparing the present volume.

Manuscripts

British Museum, Additional Manuscripts (BM), with call numbers:

29454	42268
38383	42269
42267	42270

Library of Congress, (LC) copies of manuscripts in the Hessen State Archives in Marburg, Germany, with call numbers:

2480/464	2490/474
2483/467	2493/477
2484/468	2494/478
2487/471	2495/479
2489/473	

University of Michigan Clements Library at Ann Arbor, Michigan:

"List of Officers of the 3rd Regiment of Waldeck; Newtown, Long Island the 1st January 1782"
"Monthly Return of the 3rd Regiment of Waldeck, Commanded by Colonel von Hanxleden, Pensacola the 1st April 1779"
"Muster Rolls"
"Return of Hessian Recruits after their Embarkation at Bremerlehe, 1st June 1779".

The 3rd English-Waldeck Regiment
Diaries, Journals, and Memoirs

Adlun, John. *Memoirs of the Life of John Adlun in the Revolutionary War*. Trams. Howard H. Peckham (Chicago, Caxton Club, 1968).

Anon. "Diary of a French Officer", *Magazine of American History* (New York, 1880).

Anon. "Diary of a Voyage from Stade ... of Ducal Brunswick Mercenaries", New York Historical Society (NYHS) *Quarterly Journal* (New York, October 1921).

Anon. "An Historical Journal of the American War", *Massachusetts Historical Society Collections* (Boston, 1793).

Baurmeister, Carl Leopold. *Revolution in America: Confidential Letters and Journals, 1776-1784, of Adjutant-General Major Baurmeister of the Hessian Forces*. Trans. & Anno. Bernhard A. Uhlendorf (New Brunswick, NJ, Rutgers Univerrsity Press, 1957).

Clark, John. "Memoirs of Major John Clark of York County, Pennsylvania", *Pennsylvania Magazine of History and Biography*. Cont. E.M. Spangler (Philadelphia, 1896).

Closen, Ludwig von. *The Military Journal of Baron Ludwig von Closen, 1780-1783*, Trans. & Ed. Evelyn M. Acomb.(Chapel Hill, NC, 1958).

Cusacks, Gaspar, trans. "Diary of Operations Against Pensacola", *The Louisiana Historical Quarterly* (New Orleans, 1917-18)

Farmar, Robert. "Robert Farmar's Journal of the Siege of Pensacola", *The Historical Magazine* (New York, 1860).

Galvez, Bernardo de. "Bernardo de Galvez's Combat Diary of the Battle of Pensacola, 1781", *The Florida Historical Quarterly*. Eds. Maury Baker and Margaret Bissler Haas. (Gainesville, FL, July 1971).

Heath, William. *Heath's Memoirs of the American War* (New York, A. Wessels Co., 1904).

The 3rd English-Waldeck Regiment

Heisey, John H., trans. & ed. "Extracts from the Diaries of the Moravian Pastors of the Hebron Church, Lebanon, 1755-1814", *Pennsylvania Historical Association Quarterly* (Philadelphia, January 1967).

Johannes Schwalm Historical Association, Inc. (JSHA). *Johannes Schwalm the Hessian.* (Millville, PA, Precision Printers, Inc., 1976).

Jordan, John H., trans, and ed. Bethlehem During the Revolution; Extracts from the Diaries in the Moravian Archives at Bethlehem, Pennsylvania", *Pennsylvania Magazine of History and Biography* (Philadelphia, 1888).

Krafft, John Charles Philipp von. *Journal of Lieutenant John Charles Philipp von Krafft*, reprint edition (New York, The New York Times & Arno Press, 1968).

Mackenzie, Frederick. *Diary of Frederick Mackenzie, being a Daily Narrative of his Military Service as an Officer of the Royal Welsch Fusiliers during the years 1775-1781 in Massachusetts, Rhode Island, and New York* (Cambridge, Harvard University Press, 1930.

McMichael, James. "Diary of Lieutenant James McMichael, of the Pennsylvania Line, 1776-1778", *Pennsylvania Magazine of History and Biography* (Philadelphia, 1892).

Miranda, Francisco de. "Miranda's Diary of the Siege of Pensacola, 1781", *The Florida Historical Quarterl.*, Trans. Donald E. Worcester (Gainesville, FL, January 1971).

Montresor, John. Journal of Captain John Montreseor", *New York Historical Society (NYHS) Collections*. Ed. G.I. Scull (New York, 1881).

Moore, Frank, comp. *The Diary of the American Revolution* (New York, 1967).

Muenchhausen, Friedrich von. *At General Howe's Side: The Diary of General William Howe's aide-de-camp, Captain Friedrich von Muenchhausen*, Trans.Ernst Kipping, Anno. Samuel Smith (Monmouth Beach, NJ, Philip Freneau Press, 1974).

The 3rd English-Waldeck Regiment

Muhlenberg, Henry M.. *The Journals of Henry Melchior Muhlenberg.* Trans. Theodore G. Tappert and John W. Doberstein, 3 vols..(Philadelphia, The Muhlenberg Press, 1942-1955).

Pausch, Georg.. *Georg Pausch's Journal and Reports of the Campaign in America.* Trans. Bruce E. Burgoyne (Bowie, MD, Heritage Press Inc. 1996).

Rainsford, Charles. "Commissary Rainsford's Journal of Transactions, Etc., 1776-1778", *NYHS Collections* (New York, 1879).

Ritchie, Carson I. A., ed.. "A New York Diary of the Revolutionary War", *Narratives of the Revolution in New York; A Collection of Articles from the NYHS Quarterly* (New York, 1975).

Riedesel, Friedrich Adolph. *Memoirs and Letters and Journals of Major General Riedesel,* Trans. William L. Stone, 2 vols., reprint edition (New York, The New York Times & Arno Press, 1969).

Robertson, Archibald. *Archibald Robertson, His Diaries and Sketches in America, 1762-1780.* Trans. Harry W. Leydenberg,. (New York, The New Yorkk Public Library, 1930).

Serle, Ambrose. *The American Journal of Ambrose Serle, Secretary of Lord Howe, 1776-1778.* Trans. Edward H. Tatum.(San Marino, CA, The Huntington Library,1940).

Seume.Johann Gottfried. "Adventures of a Hessian Recruit", *Proceedings of the Massachusetts Historical Society* (Boston, 1889).

Smith, William. *Historical Memoirs from 26 June 1778 to 12 November 1783 of William Smith.* Ed. William H.W. Sabine, reprint edition (New York, Arno Press, 1971).

Waldeck, Philipp. *Eighteenth Century America; As Noted in the Diary of Chaplain Philipp Waldeck, 1776-1780.* Trans. Bruce E. Burgoyne (Bowie, MD, Heritage Press Inc., 1994).

The 3rd English-Waldeck Regiment

Young, William. "Journal of Sergeant William Young, Written during the Jersey Campaign in the Winter of 1776-7", *Pennsylania Magazine of History and Biography* (Philadelphia, 1884).

The 3rd English-Waldeck Regiment
General Works

Anon. "The Capture of Colonel Moses Rawlings", *Maryland Historical Magazine* (Baltimore, 1976).

Anon (A Society of Gentlemen). *The History of the British Empire from the Year 1765 to the Year 1783*, 2 vols., reprint edition (Boston, Gregg Press, 1972).

Anon. "Lee Papers," *NYHS Collections* (New York, 1872).

Anon. "Mount Washington and its Capture," *Magazine of American History* (New York, February 1877).

Anon. "Note from 'An Account of the Surveys of Florida,' London 1790, page 3," *The Historical Magazine* (New York, 1860).

Anon. "Proceedings of a Board of General Officers of the British Army at New York, 1781," *NYHS Collections* (New York, 1916).

Anon. "Revolutionary Letters," *The Historical Magazine* (New York, November 1858).

Anon. "Unpublished Letters of Edmund Pendleton," *Massachusetts Historical Society Proceedings*, 2nd Series (Boston, 1906).

Anon. "West Florida, The Capture of Baton Rouge by Galvez, September 21st, 1779," *The Florida Historical Quarterly* (Gainesville, FL, October 1960).

Auerbach, Inge and Froehlich, Otto (Eds.). *Waldeck Truppen im amerikanischen Unabhaengigkeitskrieg, (HETRINA)*. 5 vols. (Marburg, Germany, Der Archivschule Marburg, 1972-1976).

Bill, Albert H. *The Campaign of Princeton, 1776-1777* (Princeton, NJ, Princeton University Press, 1948).

Burnett, Edmund C. (Ed.). *Letters of Members of the Continental Congress*, 8 vols., reprint edition (Glouster, MA, Peter Smith, 1963).

Carrington, Henry B, *Battles of the American Revolution* (New York, A.B. Barnes & Co., 1877).

The 3rd English-Waldeck Regiment

Clark, William B., ed. *Naval Documents of the American Revolution*, 8 vols. (Washington, D.C., US Naval Department, 1969).

Clinton, George. *Public Papers of George Clinton, First Governor of New York, 1777-1795 and 1801-1804*, 10 vols, reprint edition (New York, The State of New York, 1973).

Condit, William W. "Christopher Ludwig, Patriotic Gingerbread Baker," *Pennsylvania Magaziine of History and Biography* (Philadelphia, 1957).

Dalwigk, Freiherr von.. *Geschichte der Waldeckischen und kurhessiscche Stammtruppen der Infantrie Regiment Witisch, (3rd Kurhessischen)* (Oldenburg, Germany, 1909).

Davies, K.G. ed.. *Documents of the American Revolution, 1770-1783*, 21 vols. (County Dublin, Ireland, Irish University Press, 1981),

Demandt, Karl B. *Geschichte des Landes Hessen* (Cassel, Germany, Baumeister Verlag. 1972).

Dippel, Horst. *Germany and the American Revolution, 1776-1800, A Sociohistorical Investigation of Eighteenth Century Political Thinking*, Trans. Bernhard A. Uhlendorf (Wiesbaden, Germany, Franz Steuer Verlag, GMBH, 1978).

Eelking, Max von.. *Die deutschen Huelfstruppen im Nordamerikanischen Befreiungskrieg, 1776-1783 (Leipzig, Germany, Verlag von Otto Wigand,* 1856).

Eelking, Max von. *The German Allied Troops in the North American War of Independence, 1776-1783*, Trans. Joseph G. Rosengarten, reprint edition (Baltimore, Genealogical Publishing Co., 1969).

Faye, Stanley. *The Spanish and British Fortifications of Pensacola, 1698-1821* (Pensacola, FL, Pensacola Historical Society, 1977).

Flexner, James T. *States Tyckmann, American Loyalist* (Boston, Little, Brown & Co., 1980).

The 3rd English-Waldeck Regiment

Force, Peter (Ed.). *American Archives, Fifth Series, July 4, 1776 - September 3, 1783,* 3 vols. (Washington, D.C., 1848-1853).

Haarmann, Albert H. "The Spanish Conquest of British West Florida, 1779-1781", *The Florida Historical Quarterly* (Gainesville, FL, October 1960).

Haarmann, Albert W. "The 3rd Waldeck Regiment in British Service, 1776-1783", *Army Historical Research Journal* (n.p., Autumn 1970)

Haynes, Robert V. *The Natchez District and the American Revolution* (Jackson, MS, University of Mississippi Press, 1976).

Hazard, Samuel, comp. *Pennsylvania Archives,* 1st Series (Philadelphia, 1853).

Hazard, Samuel, comp. *Pennsylvania Collected Records,* Colonial Records (Harrisburg, PA, 1852)..

Holmes, Jack P.L. "German Troops in Alabama During the American Revolution, The Battle of January 7, 1781," *The Alabama Quarterly Review* (Montgomery, Spring 1974).

Honeyman, A. Van Doren, ed.. *History of Union County, New Jersey, 1664-1923),* 2 vols. (New York, Lewis Historical Publishing Co. Inc., 1923).

Horn, D.B., ed. *British Diplomatic Representatives, 1689-1789,* Camden Third Series (London, Office of the Society, 1932).

Johnston, Henry P. *The Battle of Harlem Heights, September 16, 1776,* reprint edition (New York, AMS Press, 1970).

Jones, Thomas. *History of New York during the Revolutionary War,* Ed. T. Delancey , 2 vols., reprint edition (New York, The New York Times & Arno Press, 1968).

Kapp, Friedrich. "The Hessians of the Revolution," *The Historical Magazine,* (New York, Jan. 1866).

The 3rd English-Waldeck Regiment

Kemble, Stephen. "Order Books of Lieutenant Colonel Stephen Kemble, Adjutant General of the British Forces in America, 1775-1783," *NYHS Collections* (New York, 1883).

Ketchum, Richard M. *The Winter Soldiers* (Garden City, NJ, Doubleday & Co., 1973).

Kinnaird, Lawrence ed.. "Spain in the Mississippi Valley, 1765-1794", *Annual Report of the American Historical Association*, (Washington, DC, 1949).

Krupp, Louis trans. *German Mercenaries in Pensacola during the American Revolution, 1779-1781* (Pensacola, FL, Pensacola Historical Society, 1977).

Learned, Marion D. *Guide to the Manuscript Materials Relating to American History in the German State Archives* (Washington, D.C., Carnegie Institution of Washington, 1912)

Lee, Francis B. ed.. *Documents Relating to the Revolutionary History of the State of New Jersey*, 2nd Series (Trenton, NJ, The Publishing Society of New Jersey, 1903). .

Lefferts, Charles M. *Uniforms of the American, British, French, and German Armies in the War of the American Revolution, 1775-1783* (Old Greenwich, CT, WE, Inc., 1971).

Lossing, B.J. *Field Book of the Revolution*, 2 vols. (New Yoirk, 1851).

Lowell, Edward J. *The Hessians and the other German Auxiliaries of Great Britain in the Revolutionary War* (New York, Harper & Brothers, 1884).

Lundin, Leonhard. *Cockpit of the Revolution; The War for Independence in New Jersey* (New York, Octagon Books, 1972).

Marshall, Douglas W. and Peckham, Howard H. *Campaigns of the American Revolution; an Atlas of Manuscript Maps* (Ann Arbor, MI, University of Michigan Press, 1976).

Medding, Wolfgang. "Waldecker Soldaten kaempten im amerikanischen Unabhaengigkeitskrieg", in "Mein Waldeck", Nr. 5, Supplement to the *Waldeckischen Landeszeitung* (Korbach, Germany, March 1964).

Mollo, John and McGregor, Malcolm. *Uniforms of the American Revolution* (New York, Macmillian Publishing Co., 1975).

Osborn, George S. "Major General John Campbell in British West Florida," *The Florida Historical Quarterly* (Gainesville, FL, April 1924).

Roberts, Robert B. *New York Forts in the American Revolution* (Cronburg, NJ, Associated University Press, Inc., 1950).

Rosengarten, Joseph G. "A Defense of the Hessians," *Pennsylvania Magazine of History and Biography* (Philadelphia, July 1890).

Rosengarten, Joseph G. *The German Soldier in Wars of the United States* (Trenton, J. B. Lippincott, 1901).

Schwab, John C. *The Revolutionary History of Fort Number Eight on Morris Heights* (New Haven, CT, Privately Printed, 1897.

Scott, Kenneth, comp. "Rivington's New York Newspaper; Excerpts from a Loyalist Press, 1773-1783," *NYHS Collections*, (New York, 1973).

Sears, Robert. *The Pictorial History of the American Revolution with a Sketch of the Early History of the Country* (New York, Robert Sears, 1847).

Service, James A., ed. *The Log of HMS Mentor, 1780-1781*, (Pensacola, FL, The John C. Pace Library, 1982).

Slagle, Robert O. *The von Lossberg Regiment; a Chronicle of Hessian Participation in the American Revolution*, unpublished, The American University (Washington, DC, 1965).

Sparks, Jared, ed. *The Writings of George Washington*, 12 vols. (Boston, Little, Brown & Co., 1858).

Staedtler, Erhard. *Die Ansbach-Bayreuth Truppen im Amerikanischen Unabhaengigkeitskrieg, 1773-1783* (Nuernberg, Germany, Gesellschaft fuer Familienforschungen Franken, 1956).

The 3rd English-Waldeck Regiment

Steiner, Bernard C., ed. *Archives of Maryland, Journal and Correspondence of the Council of Maryland* (Baltimore, 1921).

Stevens, Benjamin F., ed. *Clinton-Cornwallis Controversy* (London, 1888).

Stevens, Benjamin F. *Facsimilies of Manuscripts in European Archives Relating to America*, 24 vols. (London, 1891).

Stryker, William S. *The Battles of Trenton and Princeton*, reprint edition (Spartansburg, SC, The Reprint Co., 1967).

Stryker, William S. ed. "Extracts from American Newspapers, 1776-1777", *Documents Relating to the Revolutionary History of the State of New Jersey* (Trenton, 1901).

Trevelyan, George Otto. *The American Revolution*, 3 vols. (New York, Longmans, Green & Co., 1905).

Uhlendorf, Bernhard A. and Wosper, Edna, eds. *Letters from Major Baurmeister to Colonel von Jungkenn; Written during the Philadelphia Campaign, 1777-1778* (Philadelphia, The Historical Society of Pennsylvania, 1937).

Ward, Christopher L. *The Delaware Continentals, 1776-1783* (Wilmington, DE, The Historical Society of Delaware, 1941).

Whinyates, Francis A. *The Services of Lieut. Colonel Francis Downman, R.A. in France, North America, and the West Indies, Between the Years 1758 and 1784* (Woolwich, England, Royal Artillery Institution. 1808).

Willcox, William B. *Portrait of a General, Sir Henry Clinton, in the War of Independence* (New York, Alfred A. Knopf, 1964).

Winsor, Justi, ed. *Narrative and Critical History of America* (Boston, Houghton Mifflin Co., 1888).

Wright, J. Leitch, Jr. *Florida in the American Revolution* (Gainesville, FL, University Press of Florida, 75).

FULLNAME INDEX

ADAMSON, James 67
ADLUN, John 50
ALBERTI, 150 August 188 Augustin
    120 149 162 207 209 215 240 243
    Augustin Christian 5 Capt 98 109
    Christoph 11 112 188 192 194 245
    Franz Christian 23 164 Franz Chrn
    204
ALBRACHT, Friedrich 15 107
    Johannes 15 196 230
ALBRECHT, Christian 60 85 229 243
    Peter 6
ALEX, Friedrich 89 93
ALLEN, 97
ALMOND, John 4
ALT, Joh Nikolaus 91 205 Nikolaus
    231
ALTNER, Christoph 217 238
ALTVATER, Karl 24 59
AMELUNG, Christian 16 62
AMMENHAEUSER, Karl 68 164 204
    231
AMPFURT, G A 34
ANDRE, Christoph 6 52 117
ANDREAS, Ernst 217 238 Georg 82
    106
ARBUTHNOT, Marriot 88
AREND, Christoph 16 119 132 190
    208 214 Henrich 6 198 235
ASCHAUER, Adam 14
ASCHENHAUER, Josef 177 181
ASSMANN, Johannes 24 121 146
ATLEE, 86 William 73

ATLEE (cont.)
    William Augustus 83
BACHMANN, Georg 185 194 234
BACHSTAEDTER, Ignatius 6 165 198
    212 230
BACKES, Johannes 217 223
BACKHAUS, Georg 6 51
BAILEY, Richard 144
BANGERT, Jakob 110 Jakob Joh 6
    Johannes 177 213
BANSE, Dietmar 20 61 79
BARTH, Adam 177 200 213 236
BASCH, 220
BASTE, Henrich 63
BATISTER, Henrich 79 Joh Henr 61
    Joh Henrich 20
BAUER, Adam 89 93 Andreas (Adam)
    217 237 Christian 89 129 Friedrich
    16 107 Georg 24 121 145 Karl 177
    199 212 233 238 Philipp 91 101
BAUERSCHMIDT, Ludwig 6 60 87
    118 188 210
BAUMBACH, 191 Capt 151
BAUMGARTEN, Georg 177 200 235
BAUMMUELLER, Andreas 124
BAUMUELLER, Andreas 24 121
BAURMEISTER, 47-48 66 86 94 100
    152 160 174 175 221 222 244
BAUS, Adam 233 Andreas 70 197
BAYLOR, Col 94
BEAUMARCHAIS, Pier Augustin
    Caron De 34
BECK, Christoph 70 81

The 3rd English-Waldeck Regiment

BECK (cont.)
　Daniel 117 119 190 192 214
　Daniel Henrich 132 Franz Karl 70
　129 Henrich 207 231 Henrich Dan
　15
BECKER, 102 Christian 68 197 231
　Jakob 16 112 124 127 197 235
　Johannes 12 24 60 84 121 130 190
　205 208 211 Lorenz 177 199 212
　234 Lt 31 68 89 Matthias 12 130
　205 211 Wilhelm 29-30
BECKES, Johannes 213
BECKMANN, Dietrich Henr 20 204
　Dietrich Henrich 163 Henr 236
BEHR, Johannes 89 107
BEISENHERTZ, Daniel 12 112 190
　195
BELCHER, 53
BELSS, Georg 165
BENDER, Georg 68 George 77
BERCKEN, Konrad 77
BERCKENHAUSER, Christian 196
　Friedrich 12
BERGER, Justinus 70 163 203 236
　Ludwig 20 52 61 81 84
BERGES, Bernhard 24 120 190 207
　Henrich 12 112 169 Johannes 24
　121 190 208 Ludwig 9 118 188
BERGHENN, Peter 200
BERGHOEVER, Wilhelm 118 188
BERGHUEVER, Wilhelm 234
BERGLASS, Joh Konrad 22
BERGMANN, Christian 16 197
　Henrich 92 121 Hermann 124
BERINGER, Michael 177 200 213 236
BERLIN, Christian 89 129
BERNIGHAUSEN, Andreas 29
BERTHOLD, Henrich 20 163 203
BERTRAM, Matthias 217 228
BESSELBACH, Johannes 68 148
BESSERLING, G F 33
BEST, Henrich 11
BESTELMEIER, Wilhelm 177 199
　210 233

BETHE, Henrich 217
BETHUNE, 141 Farquhar 157
BETTE, Joh Ewilhelm 204 Joh
　Wilhelm 20 Johann Wilhelm 163
BETZ, Michael 92 106
BEUSCH, Philipp 68 77
BEVER, Friedrich 28 82
BEYER, Benhard 211 Bernhard 12 60
　84 130 165 205
BICKMANN, Christian 24 121 145
BIEBER, 171 Ignatius 68 130 171
BIEG, Jakob 68 197 235
BIGGE, Christian 222 Franz 60 80 84
　Franz Christian 196 Franz Chrn
　Adam 177 182 Otto 24 121 124
BIGGS, Franz 12
BILL, Albert H 56
BILLERBECK, Christian 217
BIRCK, Adam 91 101
BIRCKENFELD, Andreas 29
BIRCKENHAUER, Friedrich 152
BIRCKMANN, Johannes 16 63
BLANC, Sgt De 220
BLANK, 220
BLAUFUS, Jakob 12 112 145
BLESS, Georg 91 205 Georg Joh 236
　Johannes 90 130 Paul 89 117
BLOCK, Col 67 Philipp 90 130 172
　221 233
BOCK, Georg 61 145 Georg Andreas 6
　118 Henrich 20 46 Joh Georg 24
　189 230 243 Johann Georg 118
　Konrad 177 199 212
BODDINGTON, John 126
BOEHLE, Friedrich 134 165 205 236
　Wilhelm 213 Wilhelm Henrich
　134
BOEHME, Cadet 144 192 Friedrich
　144 185 196 201 231
BOEHMER, Philipp 68 172
BOEHNE, Wilhelm 70 130 203 211
BOEPEL, Wilhelm 132
BOESAM, Georg 217
BOETTGER, Philipp 12 112 124

The 3rd English-Waldeck Regiment

BOLTZE, Henrich 134 198 230
BOP, Joh 207 John 185 211
BORN, Johannes 92
BORNEMANN, Henrich 29 Ludwig 70 121 147
BOUDINOT, Elias 83
BOURG, Cromat De 174
BRABENDER, Henrich 82 130 205 211 235
BRAND, Christian 24 55 74 117 121 190 208 224 234 Wilhelm 16 51
BRANDENSTEIN, Dan Christian 24 Daniel 190 208
BRANDES, Ludwig 217
BRANDSTEIN, Daniel 121
BRASSER, Ludwig 217 232
BRAUN, Johannes 6 80 89 129 Konrad 29 Peter 90 101
BRAUNS, Adam 147 Adams 134 Karl 28 184 237
BREMER, Ludwig 198 Ludwig (Lewis) 177 Wilhelm 30
BRESSLER, Georg 217 238
BREUNINGER, Anton 217 232 Friedrich 6 60
BREY, Christian 228 Christoph 217 Joh Henr 77 Joh Henr Daniel 70
BREYER, Anton 232
BRIANT, Charles 74
BRISCOE, Dep Qm Gen 32
BROCK, Konrad 177 200 213 237
BROWN, Alexander 44 Thomas 66 105 138 140
BRUCKHAUSER, Hermann 24
BRUECKHAUSER, Henrich 81
BRUEHNE, Karl 11 60 87 130 149 203 210 Karl Friedrich 87 Otto 12 147
BRUEMANN, Christian 29
BRUENINGER, Friedrich 80
BRUME, Gottfried 217
BRUMHARD, 191 Andreas 117 128 188 Andreas Geo 24 Lt 185
BUBENLEBER, Friedrich 217

BUCHHOLTZ, Ludwig 177 200 213
BUCHHOLZ, Ludwig 236
BUCKERT, Franz Konrad 31
BUDDE, 192 Christian 196 Christoph 15 149 Friedrich 12 112 123 Johannes 185 201 214
BUDDECKER, Bernhard Henr 24
BUDELBACH, Johannes 70
BUECHER, Adam 68 204 231
BUECKER, Adam 164
BUECKING, Wilhelm 20 61 82
BUEDDECKER, Bernhard 51
BUEHLER, Johannes 177 200 213 234 Sebastian 177 233
BUENAU, 50 Lt 221
BULLE, Karl 217 232
BUNSE, Konrad 20 61 87 164 167 205 236 Theodor 198 235 Theodor Geo 90
BUNTROCK, Friedrich 16 82
BUREHNE, Otto 112
BURGHANN, Peter 178
BURGHARD, Johannes 24 121 144 Michael 90 130 205 211 235
BURGHENN, Peter 213 234
BURGOYNE, 95 Gen 83
BURR, Johannes 92 121 147
BUSECK, Peter 68 129
BUTTERWECK, Jakob 20 72
BYRON, 94 John 108
CADWALADER, John 58
CAESAR, 207 Servant 185
CAMERON, 141-142 151-152 158 Alexander 105 138 Indian Commissioner 109
CAMPBELL, 106 127 136 138 142-143 155 157 167 174 Archibald 99 Brig 71 Brig Gen 99-100 104 Capt 126 Gen 105 107-109 113-114 137 139 141 151 154 158-159 161-162 165 174 205 James 155 160 John 66 221
CANON, Winter Lacount 170
CANTZLER, George 77 Joh Georg 20

The 3rd English-Waldeck Regiment

CARL AUGUST FRIEDRICH, Prince 2
CARLETON, 227 239-240 Gen 41 244 Guy 39 Sir Guy 226
CARLSON, R 13
CARNISCH, Josef 145
CARNISH, Josef 68 112
CARRINGTON, 175
CASPAR, Henrich 106
CASTNER, Georg 244
CHALMER, 97 157
CHELEIERMACHER, Johannes 8
CHESTER, 152 Gov 136 Peter 104 109 159 Pitre 159
CHINMAN, Henry 74
CHRISTENAU, Friedrich 178 199 212
CHRISTIE, Mr 156
CLARK, John 58 227 Lt Col 139
CLEEMANN, Christian 181 Christoph 70 164
CLEMENS, Jakob 20 163 203
CLINTON, 96 99 138 140 143 166-167 183 186 Gen 72-73 97 105 110 114 139 244 George 56 73 240 Gov 174 Henry 95
COETTE, Christian 90
COLBERT, 158
COLDSTREAM, William 66
COLLIG, Nikolaus 178 196
CONET, Johannes 68 121 146
CONRADI, Daniel 9
CORNWALLIS, 139 157 Gen 184
CRAMER, Franz 7 60 87 118 189 224
CREWE, Richard 56
CROLLPATH, Josef 91 165 205 234
CUMMERO, Friedrich 92 132
D'ESTAING, 95 Jean Baptiste Comte 93
DAENTZER, Martin Wilhelm 92
DALLING, Gov 127 143 John 104
DANNEMANN, 220
DANTZ, Joh Jost 12 243 Johann Jost 118 Johannes 61 Jost 125 Thomas 7 118

DANTZER, Martin 132 198 214 237
DAUDENBERG, Georg 217
DAWES, Mr 157
DE LIOR, Jean 145
DE SILVE, Master Of The Hunt 242
DEAN, 169 Capt 154-155 157 166-167 Robert 139
DEBORRE, Prudhomme 71
DECKER, Johannes 68 81 Philipp 68 112 145
DEEGE, Johannes 178 200 212
DEHM, Georg 68 130 172
DEIERLAIN, Friedrich 121
DEIERLEIN, Friedrich 68 145
DEILINGER, Josef 130 205 211 230
DELIOR, Jean 122 Jean (Johannes) 92
DEMMER, Joh Hermann 21 204 Johann Henrich 163
DEMUTH, Valentin 25 63
DENDER, Salomon 91 Solomon 169
DENGEL, Friedrich 217 238
DEPMEIER, Henrich 71 185 201 237
DETTENDALER, Georg 91 165 205 234
DIAMOR, Leonhard 16 147
DICKE, Henrich 16 61 117 Jakob 218 239
DICKSON, 126 Alexander 109 Lt 114 Lt Col 111 114-116
DIEDRICH, Friedrich 200 212
DIETRICH, Friedrich 178 230 Sebastian 218 228 Theo Frede 13
DIETZ, Christian 12 130 158 Daniel 12 112 147 Stefan 12 72
DIGBY, Adm 227 239 Martin 39 Robert 226
DILLINGER, Josef 12
DIOR, Jakob (Jean) De La 178 Jakob De La 213 Jean De La 199
DISTE, Christian 12 112 146
DITMAR, Johann Stefan 31
DOEDECKE, Friedrich 164 204 225
DOENIG, Konrad 74
DOETIKE, Friedrich 23

The 3rd English-Waldeck Regiment

DOWNMAN, Francis 98
DRECHSLER, Johannes 218 238
DREWES, Joh Jost 12 224 Johann Jost 190 Jost 195 Jost Johann 112
DRUBE, Adam 7 60 80
DRUMMEL, 220
DUCKENBERG, Henrich 12 130 172
DUESSE, Philipp 25 121 190 209 224
DULLMANN, Christian 16 198
DURNFORD, Elias 104 136
DURST, Johannes 25 121 146
EBE, Philipp 198 214 Phillip 6
EBERHARD, Christian 29
EBERSBACH, Henrich 7 118 189
ECKHARD, Georg 68 164 204 231
EFFE, Kaspar 71 185 201 231
EGERDING, Gottfried 30
EICHENGER, Andreas 68
EICHINGER, Andreas 118 189
EISEN, Franz 21 129
EISENBERG, Christian 12 189 Christoph 118 Henrich 11-12 130 153 203 205 210-211 Joh Christian 12 211 235 Joh Chrn 205 Johann Christian 131 Qm Sgt Henrich 130
EMBDE, Christian 203 Christoph 11 131 152 Henrich 30 Johannes 7 118 189
EMDE, Christoph 27 Friedrich 144 181
EMMERICH, Andreas 184
ENGELBRECHT, Andreas 30
ENGELHARD, Christian Jakob 190 Henrich 178 182 Jakob 121 208 Jakob Christoph 25 Johann Georg 147
ENGLAND, King Of 95
ENGLEHARD, Joh Georg 21
ENSLIN, Johann Ludwig 93 Ludwig 91
ERB, Christian 178 181
ERHARD, Peter 25 61 80 85
ERLE, Michael 68 120 124
ERNST, Peter 68 118 189 210

EULER, Franz 31
FAHNIE, Konrad 208
FARMAR, 152 156-158 162 167 Robert 168
FASS, Alisius 91 198 231
FASSHAUER, Johannes 218 238
FAUCITT, 4 35 143 Col 66 87-88 William 3 38
FAUSER, Jakob 68 197 235
FAUST, Johannes 7 117
FAX, Georg 30
FERST, Joh Adam 25 Johann Adam 48
FICHTNER, Gottlieb 89 118 147
FIEBERLING, Jakob 178 199 214 237
FIEGER, Johannes 178 199 210 233
FIELDING, Capt 43 Charles 41 Richard 42
FIESLER, Karl 29
FIGE, Wilhelm 197 235
FIGGE, Bernhard 21 163 203 Christian 16 120 132 190 209 224 Daniel 29 Henrich 12 131 147 Wilhelm 16
FINGERHUT, Friedrich 12 131 205 211
FISCHEER, Friedrich 129
FISCHER, Adam 90 131 205 211 230 Fried Anton 25 Friedrich 89 Henrich 12 112 178 190 195 199 214 224 237 Johannes 68 77 John 186 Jost 7 118 124 Konrad 7 110 Ludwig 178 200 214
FLAME, Henrich 113
FLAMME, Henrich 127 134 198 205 211 230 235 Johannes 7 20 110 165 230 Matthias 16 61 84 86 132 190 208 215 230 Matthies 120
FLAMMES, Henrich 214
FLECK, Paul 25 51
FLEISCHHUT, Wilhelm 19
FLEISCHHUTH, Wilhelm 53
FLEXNER, James 32
FLINSCHBACH, Jakob 218 238
FOCKESEN, Henrich 221

The 3rd English-Waldeck Regiment

FORD, John 42
FORSTER, Capt 116
FOX, William 37
FOXEN, William 66
FRANCKE, Christeian 20 Christian 16 149 165 196 205 230 Henrich 25 121 190 208 224 237 Johannes 89 106 Sebastian 178 199 210 233
FRANTZ, Georg 92 121 Johannes 16 110
FRANZTER, Jakob 220
FRASER, William 37
FREDE, Barthold 63 Berthold 7 Dietrich 52 131 211 Dietrich Theo 205
FREESE, Christoph 89 106
FRENSDORF, Count 160
FRESE, Christian 21 148 Christoph 24 120 124 Friedrich 25 61 121 124 243 Johann Philipp 98 132 Philipp 24 102
FREYSE, August 178 181
FRICKE, 220 Anton 178 210
FRIEDEBORN, Georg 13 112 190 195 224
FRIEDINGER, Sebastian 91 171
FRIEDRICH, Prince 2 3 31 34 39
FUEHRER, Georg 68 197 235
FUSER, Lt Col 126
GABELAENDER, Peter 81 91
GALLE, Konrad 18 29
GALVEZ, 114-115 123 127 138 142 152 160 173 175 Bernardo De 109 111 161 165 169 Don 136 153-155 159 Don Josef De 110 Joseph De 170
GANS, Philipp 25 121 124
GATELL, Pedro 162
GAUCITT, 176
GAULD, Mr 161
GEICHER, Franz 81
GEISSEL, Christian 213
GEITZ, Adam 16 197

GEITZ (cont.)
 Georg 25 61 84 121 190 208
GELDBACH, 220
GENUIT, Franz 163 204 Franz Henr 21 Henrich 13 131 147
GEORCKE, Georg 196
GEORGE, King Of England 39
GEORGE III, King Of England 3
GERGER, Johannes 178 198 212 230
GERGHOEVER, Wilhelm 6
GERHARD, Georg 16 62 Henrich 13 61 131 205 211 Karl 178 199 233
GERLA, Sgt 31
GERLACH, Moritz 16 197 225
GERMAIN, 39-41 54 60 64 74 88 95-96 99 110 126-127 133 137 140-143 151-154 159 165-167 176 186 Georg 45
GIEBEL, Johannes 178 201 222
GIEDE, David 163 204 David Danl 21
GIER, Geo Ludwig 61 Georg Ludwig 25 234 Ludwig 80 Ludwig Georg 221
GIESEL, Christian 231
GIESENSCHLAGER, Georg 21 85
GIESING, Henrich 7 52
GIESSEL, Christian 178 199
GIESSENSCHLAEGER, Geo 61
GIESSENSCHLAGER, Georg 146
GLAENTZER, 192 Christian 4 196 Konrad 4 107 149
GLEICHER, Franz 21
GOCKEL, Henrich 11 112 190 194 211 Johannes 13 112
GOEBEL, Christian 7 60 84 131 205 235 Christoph 211 Henrich 13 62 Johaannes 25 Johannes 16 21 76 120-121 132 164 190 194 204 224 Johannes Jr 209 Johannes Sr 208 Michael 91 149 152 198 236 Sgt 31
GOEBERL, Johannes 224
GOEBERT, Lorenz 7 118 124

The 3rd English-Waldeck Regiment

GOECKE, Henrich 28 77
GOEDECKE, Christian 25 121 190 208 225
GOEDELING, Wilhelm 68 110
GOERCKE, Georg 178 214
GOETTE, Christian 107 Friedrich 21 77 Ludwig 20 163 203
GORDON, Lt 152 165-167
GOSE, Joachim 121 Joachim Joh 70 Johann Joachim 147
GOSMANN, Philipp 13 131 158
GOTHARD, Ulrich 30
GOTTLIEB, Georg 218 Goerg 230
GOTTMANN, Georg 30
GRAEBE, Friedrich 16 197 230 Jakob 15 167 185 196 237 Johannes 21 61 87 164 204
GRAEBER, Georg 218 228
GRAEBES, Christoph 89 129
GRAEBING, Henrich 61 229 243 Joh Henrich 16
GRAEVE, Jakob 71
GRANT, Gen 99
GREENE, Nathaniel 157
GREIF, Henrich 218
GREISER, August 20 149 203 231
GRIESHEIM, Georg 91 171
GRIMES, Peter 74
GRIMM, David 95 Philipp 13 131 172
GROB, Johannes 7 62
GRUBB, Curtis 75
GRUBERT, Georg 9 60 63 Johannes 178 199 233
GUDE, Johannes 31
GUENTHER, Ernst Christian 148 Ernst Chrn 91 Konrad 218 238
GUERGEL, Andreas 16 63
GUMMERO, Friedrich 170
GUNSTMANN, Joh Friedrich 21 203 236 Johann Friedrich 163
GUTHMANN, Konrad 69 76
GUTTERMILCH, Erdmann 230 Joh Erdmann 21 204 Johann Erdmann 164

HAACKE, 209 Capt 73 Friedrich 28 62 Simon 28 76
HAAG, Christian 199 Christoph 178 212 Henrich 178 202 223
HAARMANN, 32 111 116 137 151-152 Albert 4
HAASE, Christian 15 Jakob 25 117
HAGEL(N), Jakob 178 181
HAGEMEYER, Joh Franz 29 Kaspar 25 59
HAGENER, Jakob 69 170
HAHNE, Ernst 13 112 172 Georg 7 117 Karl Fried 91 Karl Friedrich 146
HAHNEFELD, Andreas 218
HALDIMAND, Frederick 176
HAMEL, Philipp 7 118 189 Wilhelm 218 237
HAMM, Peter 178 200 214 231
HAMMERSDORF, Johannes 13 106
HANCKE, Ludwig 21
HANCKER, Ludwig 172
HANDEL, Konrad 191
HANSMANN, Christian 25 121 144
HANSTEIN, Johann Friedrich 46 Johannes 6
HANXLEDEN, 153
HAPPE, Peter 7 46
HAPPEL, Daniel 218 239
HARGOOD, William 161
HAROLD, Konrad 129
HARTEL, Alexander 91
HARTIG, Albrecht 178 199 212 234
HARTMANN, Adam 25 121 147 Anton 178 200 231 Daniel 7 118 189 244 Johannes 25 124 Lt 222 Thomas 218 Ulrich 178 200 212 234
HAUSCHILD, Matthias 13 77 Philipp 178 182
HAUSER, Peter 178 199 237
HAUSMANN, Christian 117
HAYNES, 111
HEATH, Gen 58 William 48

The 3rd English-Waldeck Regiment

HEBERLEIN, Leonhad 201 Leonhard 178 222
HECK, Jakob 179 200 210 232
HECKENROTH, Andreas 91 106
HECKMANN, Joh Henrich 20 Johann Henrich 163 203
HEIDORN, Martin 28 184 201 237
HEILIG, Johannes 91 149 170
HEINECKE, Gottlieb 218 Henrich 25 121 190 208
HEINEMANN, Jak 61 Jakob 20 85 149 Joh Konrad 205 Philipp 16 197 235
HEINSCHEL, Balthasar 16 197 235
HEINTZ, Christian 238 Christoph 218
HELDRING, 191 Capt Lt 155 Gerhard 188 Gerhard Henr 20 Gerhard Henrich 128 148 Henrich 195 Lt 73 75 85 108 167 186
HELFRING, Gerhard Henrich 60
HELLER, Daniel 21 164 204
HEMMELING, Andreas 182
HEMMERLING, Amandus 70 192 196 Anton 30
HEMPELMANN, Johannes 177
HENCKELER, Franz 191 207 210
HENCKELMANN, Henrich 21 61 84 86 164 205 236
HENDEL, Konrad 25 121 208 210
HENKELER, Franz 24 120
HENRICH, Philipp 16 118 189
HENTZE, Gottfried 28 77 Phil Henrich 215 Philipp 61 84 131 Philipp Hen 13 Philipp Henr 205 211
HEPDEN, William 66
HERBERT, Andreas 13 Jakob 30
HERBOLD, Henrich 7 118 189
HERBST, Andreas 131 205 211 230
HERDES, Jost 25 121 Justus 124
HERING, Henrich 16 197
HERMANN, 220 Georg 69 164 204 234
HEROLD, Konrad 89

HERTEL, Alexander 169
HERTER, Andreas 7 63
HERTZIG, Peter 218
HERTZOG, Friedrich 179 199 212 Stefan 16 196 210
HESSE, Georg 186 Johannes 16 197 Kaspar 91 146
HEUSTER, Andreas 218
HIILLEBRAND, Christian 29
HILLEBRAND, Johann Jost 179 181
HIMMELMANN, Wilhelm 134 205 211
HINTERBERGER, Franz 134 149 169
HINTERTHUER, Dietrich 69 112 145
HOEHLE, Georg 13 205 211 George 131 Michael 25 110
HOEHNE, 28 Wilhelm 25 45
HOELSCHER, Henrich 17 120 132 191 208 215
HOFFMANN, Daniel 217 228 Georg 218 239 Henr Konrad 90 Henrich 21 131 164 204-205 211 215 231 Johannes 218 Konrad 215 Wolfath 218
HOFFMEISTER, 192 Henrich 93 236 Joh Henrich 20 203 Johann Henrich 163
HOFMANN, Christoph 70 101
HOFMEISTER, Henrich 89
HOHMANN, 191 207 Adam 13 131 205 211 235 August 24 120 128 Christoph 91 Karl 163 188 203 Karl Christian 20 148 Kaspar 91 107 Konrad 13 131 205 211 235
HOLMES, H D 153
HOLTZAPPEL, Johannes 17 119 124
HOLTZMANN, Nickolaus 69 Nikolaus 82
HOMBERGER, Andreas 91
HOMBURGER, Andreas 107
HOPPE, Henrich 218 Johannes 179 198 214
HORN, 191 Stefan Christoph 17
HORNSBERGER, Henrich 25 133 172

The 3rd English-Waldeck Regiment

HORSCHLER, Friedrich 29
HOWE, 58 64 Gen 41-45 47 50 52-55 72 75 95 100 Lord 94 Richard Lord 43 66 William 40
HUEBSCH, Wilhelm 28 185 201 237
HUFEISEN, 192 Henrich 89 129 196 234
HUGEN, Peter 13 81 131 181
HUMBRACHT, Franz 13 131 205 211
HUNDERTMARCK, Hermann 91 107
HUNECKE, Joh Henr Bern 21 147 Johann Bernhard 128
HUNOLD, Peter 179 199 210 233
HUNTINGTON, Samuel 173
HUTH, Herman 81 Hermann 27 121 145
HUTHMANN, 61 Christian 24 229 243 David 89 118 145 Wilhelm 182 Wilhelm 179
HUYN, 50
INDENKAUF, Jakob 232
INDENKAUFF, Jakob 218
INGENTRON, Josef 218
ITZMANN, Karl Wilhelm 25 121 147 Wilhelm 81
JACKSON, Henry 67
JACOBS, Maximilian 41
JAEGER, Barthold 25 121 191 Bathold 208 Friedrich 13 131 207 223 Johannes 21 163 203
JAKOB, Joh Adam 21 63
JEWEL, Robert 73
JOHANNES, Michael 26
JOHNSON, Guy 105
JOHNSTONE, William 156
JONAS, Martin 179 200 233
JONES, Thomas 40
JORDAN, Lt 73
JOST, Georg 85 152 Joh Georg 196 Johann Geo 17 Johannes 231
JUNCKER, Ludwig 69 76
JUNCKERMANN, Karl 25 122 147
JUNG, Ernst 6 62
JUST, Joh Georg 61
JUTLEIN, Johannes 228 Josef 218
KABEL, Henrich 90 106 Leonhard 112 147
KAESEMEYER, Georg 16 George 82
KAHLER, Jakob 92 121 124
KALTWASSER, Balthasar 12 112 146
KAMM, Christoph 29
KAMPF, Ernst De La 217 238 Karl 178 199 213 237
KANN, Adam 6 118 189 224 Henrich 30 Johannes 6 118 189 Wilhelm 6 48 229
KAPP, Friedrich 2
KASPAR, Henrich 90
KAUFFMANN, Henrich 60 87 118
KAUFMANN, Henrich 6 189 Jost 217 232
KAUS, Peter 16 196
KEINEMANN, Johann Konrad 165
KEIPEL, Bernhard 178 199 213 236
KEISER, Joh Henrich 29
KEITEL, Joh Henrich 20 204 Johann Henrich 52 164
KELFS, Henrich 217
KELLY, Timothy 138
KELTER, Joh Friedrich 20 204 Johann Friedrich 164
KEMBLE, 59 99
KEMPFERT, Dietrich 29
KENTHANS, Johannes 9
KEPPEL, 191 207 Wilhelm 11 130 188 203 215
KERN, Bernhard 92 121 124
KESPAR, Johannes 30
KESSLER, Gottlieb 178 199 213
KESTHANS, Johannes 52 118 189 Theodor 31
KESTING, Andreas 91 101 Emanuel 6 Moritz 77
KESTINGS, Emanuel 118 Moritz 20
KETCHUM, Richard 51 Robert M 56
KIEPE, Anton 217 238
KING, Cunrod 74
KINHOLD, Henrich 74 81

The 3rd English-Waldeck Regiment

KINOLD, Henrich 16 61 84 196 225
KINTZER, Valentin 217
KIRCHNER, Georg 211
KIRSCHNER, Georg 68 130 152 205 232 Johannes 68 170
KLAAUS, Henrich 12
KLAHOLD, Jaspar 197 Kaspar 16 231
KLAPP, Daniel 20 61 87 101 Joh Henrich 16 Johannes 61 229 243
KLAUS, Henrich 60 84 112 190 194 Phil Peter 16 Philipp 196
KLEE, Christian 89 130 196 212 Henrich 91 198 235
KLEIMENHAGEN, Henrich 200-201 235 Joh Henr 63
KLEINE, Karl 16 119 132 190 209 224 Konrad 7 118 124
KLEINEISEN, Josef 92 101
KLEINENHAGEN, Joh Henr 20
KLEINHORST, Friedrich 27
KLEMEN, Justus 217
KLEUCKER, Jost 210 Jost Stefan 7 118 189
KLOPFER, Philipp 91 101
KLUCKER, Anton 217 232
KLUECKE, Friedrich 112 145
KLUECKS, Friedrich 90
KLUNCK, Adam 217 238
KLUSS, Georg 7 110
KNEES, Georg 178 181
KNEILE, Daniel 217 238
KNEUPPEL, Peter 181
KNIES, Henrich 90 130 181
KNIGHT, George 39
KNIPP, Christian Dan 12 Daniel 77
KNIPSCHILD, 191-192 Friedrich 165 205 Henr Jakob 188 Henrich 245 Henrich Jakob 15 128 195 Jakob 184 Joh Jakob 20 Johannes 163 203 230
KNOCKE, Joh Henrich 25 Johann Henrich 51
KNOECHEL, Barthold 12 118 189 224 Christian 16 61 167

KNOECHEL (cont.)
Christoph 86 Joh 61 Johannes 15 196 223
KNOECKEL, Christoph 85
KNOX, Henry 57 William 126 142 144 158
KNUEPPEL, Adam 6 76 Johannes 20 82 Peter 21 61 84 164
KNUST, Philipp 59 Philipp Andreas 7
KNYPHAUSEN, 50 Gen 244
KOBER, Friedrich 7 117
KOBERL, Leonhard 12
KOBERT, Ernst 11 130 203 211
KOCH, Friedrich 7 60 80 Georg 27 Henrich 7 24 60 76 145 Jakob 86 Johann Henrich 120 132 Johannes 16 46 48 Konrad 7 62
KOEHLER, 50 65 Henrich 198 Joh Henrich 25 213 Johann Henrich 132 Wilhelm 7 121 147
KOENIG, Karl 110 Konrad 7
KOHL, Lorenz 178 199 213 Nikolaus 21 61 80
KOHLBOERSCH, Ludwig 68 77
KOHLBREI, Franz 23
KOPPE, Christian 7 60 84 110
KOPPENHOEFFER, Adam (Kaspar) 217 Adam Kaspar 237
KOPPENRATH, Henrich 30
KORAL, Georg 90 101
KRAEMER, Georg 217
KRAFFT, 222 Johann Karl Philipp 173 Johannes 68 118 145
KRAMER, Georg 31 239 Peter 29 Philipp 197 Siegfried 92 121 145
KRATZ, Joh Jakob 7 Johannes 118 125
KRAUS, Georg 231
KRAUSE, Dave 76
KRAUSS, Georg 178 200 213
KRELL, Bernhard 217
KREMER, Peter 16 119 132 177 190 208 215 Phil David 16
KREUTZER, Adam 12 82

The 3rd English-Waldeck Regiment

KREUTZER (cont.)
  Balthasar 119 124 Balthasar Henr 91 Valentin 90 112 123
KREYEER, Karl 178
KREYER, Karl 199 213 236
KRIEGMANN, Christian 178
KRIEGSMANN, Christian 15 119 181 Friedrich 178 213
KROLL, Christian 25 82
KRUHM, Georg 7 60 84 129
KRUSE, Konrad 121
KUECHER, Johannes 217 239
KUEHN, Christian 177
KUEHNE, Wilhelm 185 207
KUEMPEL, Henrich 68 107
KUESTER, Franz Henr 21 204 Franz Henrich 163 Gottfried 130 205 211 Gottfried Jak 12 Ludwig 12 112 146
KUETHE, Franz 29 Henrich 12 112 134 146 198
KUHLEMANN, Joh Josef 7
KUHLMANN, Johannes 63
KUHN, Johannes 178 198 214 231
KUNCKEL, Johannes 16 61 80
KUNSTMANN, Konrad 77
KUNTZE, Christoph 10
KUNTZMANN, Christoph 68
KURSE, Konrad 25 124
KURTZ, Christoph 45
KURTZE, Christoph 7
KUSSENBAUER, Christoph 68 130 152
LACOUR, Friedrich 13 63
LAHM, Johannes 6
LAHME, Fifer 9 Johannes 27 122 147
LAHR, Nikolaus 25 77
LANDBERGER, Henrich 118
LANDESBERGER, Henrich 70
LANDSBERGER, Henrich 147
LANGE, Gottfried (Georg) 218 Gottfried Georg 238 Henrich 17 63 79 197 236 Phil Henr 60 Philipp Henr 13

LAUBACH, Philipp 179 199 212
LAUE, Christian 179 199 214 234
LEE, Charles 53 Col 173 Gen 64
LEESER, Johannes 17 120 124
LEIDNER, Kaspar 92 101
LEIMBACH, Bernhard 21 149 163 203 225
LEMMERING, Henrich 9 17-18 27 62
LENDE, Christoph 70 106
LENGEL, Andreas 218 232
LENTZ, Johann Christoph 221
LENTZER, Adam 179 200 214 237
LEONHARDI, Joh Wilhelm 24 Johann Wilhelm 124 Lt 113 116 Wilhelm 120
LERCHER, Friedrich 218 223
LESLIE, Alexander 157
LESMANN, Bernhard 218 238
LESUIRE, Ens 31 Lt 31
LEUGLING, Friedrich 218 237
LEUTMANN, Friedrich 179 181
LEVERINGHAUSEN, Johannes 31
LEYDENBERG, 107 Eberhard 7
LICHT, Peter 70 129
LICHTNER, Johannes 91 198 235
LIMPERT, Henrich 25 59
LINCKER, Ludwig 171 Ludwig Wilhelm 17
LINDAUER, Michael 179 200 237
LINDE, Valentin 7 117-118 146
LINDEBORN, Henrich 218
LINDEMEIER, Friedrich 200
LINDEMEYER, Franz 179 212 233
LINDIG, Henrich 168 Joh Henrich 21 Johann Henrich 149
LINDNER, Konrad 21 163 204 Wilhelm 17 21 163 197 204 236
LINNEKUGEL, Jost Henrich 31
LITTLET, Wilhelm 13 80 149 205 211 235
LITZAU, Henrich 28 168
LOCK, Konrad 17 52
LOEBLEIN, Jakob 217 238
LOECKEL, Henrich 131 211

The 3rd English-Waldeck Regiment

LOEFFLER, Johannes 69 145
LOEFLER, Johannes 112
LOHRMANN, David 17 19 23 David Friedrich 164 Michael Fried 234
LOOS, 65
LORHMANN, David 204
LORIMER, John 104
LORRING, Joshua 83
LOSSBERG, 50
LOWELL, 116 Edward J 3
LUDWIG, Christopher 74
LUDWIG IX, Landgrave Of Hesse Darmstadt 32
LUECKEL, 220 Henrich 13 205 235
LUENART, Philipp 25
LUENERT, Philipp 122 148
LUTZ, Johannes 12 112 145
MAAB, William 66
MACARTNEY, John 42
MACKENZIE, 72 97 173-176 182-184 Frederick 245
MADISON, James 222
MAETSCH, Gottfried 90 Gottlieb 101
MALCHES, Valentin 17 197 Walentin 231
MANGEL, Franz 25 61 133 149 201
MANN, Daniel 29 218
MARC, 192 Jakob 33 Philipp 4 33 188 195 245
MARCKERT, Friedrich 91 107
MARIONILKE, Cpl 220
MARKHOLT, Peter 30
MARSHALL, 151-152 162
MARTIN, Daniel 17 197 231 Peter 17 197 236
MATERNS, Henrich 220 234
MATTE, Drummer Jakob 189 Jakob 6 117
MATTERN, 192 Christian 4 196 Ludwig Christian 188
MATTHIAS, Kaspar 90 131 147
MAUER, Peter 7 77
MAURER, Valentin 17 76
MAUSER, Bartholomaeus Joh 17

MAUSKE, Jakob 29
MAXWELL, Gen 57-58 William 54
MAY, Henrich 17 61 80 236 245
MCDONALD, John 157 Maj 167
MCDOUGALL, Alexander 54 Gen 55
MCINTOSH, 141 John 138
MCMICHAEL, James 48
MCNAMARA, James 138 Lt 139
MCPHERSON, Donald 155
MECHEL, Daniel 17 60 Kaspar 122
MECKEL, Daniel 76 Georg 25 61 84 122 124 Jost 211 Kaspar 92 144
MECKELER, Joh Friedrich 212
MECKLER, Friedrich Joh 179 Johannes 233
MEIBON, Maj 95
MEIDR, Johannes 236
MEIDT, Johannes 91 165 205
MEIER, Christian 172 Christoph 17 120 132 Zacharias 25 122 146
MEINBERG, Henrich 31
MEINHARD, Wolrath 218
MEISNER, Christian 134 198 214 237 Joh 60 Johannes 6 84 118 146
MEISTER, Philipp 17 149 167 196
MELCHER, Isaac 73 Wilhelm 196 244 Wilhelm Phil 17
MELTZER, Ludwig 92 117
MENCKEL, Josef 131 Jost 13 Jost Josef 165 205
MENENIR, J 81
MENGER, Adam 218 232
MENGERINGHAUSEN, Bernhard 25 122 191 208 237
MERCKER, Friedrich 69 129
MERTZ, Johannes 7 60 84 164 207 223 Ludwig 179 199 214 237
MESNARD, Lt 56
METTE, Jakob 7 77
METZER, Friederich 56
MEUSER, Barthold 197 Joh Barth 61 Joh Bartholameus 87
MEUSKE, Adam 17 Johannes 17 120 132 209 224

The 3rd English-Waldeck Regiment

MEYBAUM, Johannes 13 60 112 190 195 243
MEYER, Christoph 7 107 Eberhard 24 129 Franz 92 129 Georg 60 91 101 Henrich 13 25 61 85 131 205 211 229 243 Jakob 26 122 191 208 225 Joh Georg 8 84 Joh Henrich 21 Johann Georg 107 Johann Henrich 23 Johannes 185 205 211 235 Konrad 17 61 84 120 132 179 191 199 208 223 233 Thomas 218 238
MICHAEL, Daniel 21 163 203 Georg 179 200 213 233 Johannes 189 224
MICHEL, Jakob 177 Johannes 118
MICHLAER, Johannes 198
MIELIG, Wilhelm 69 129
MIETING, Johannes 10 17-19 27 122 145
MILLER, Lt 73 155
MINCKE, Georg Henrich 84 86 Henrich 26 117
MIRANDA, 156-157 159 161 169-170 Gen 158
MIRO, Don Estaban 123
MISCO, Johannes 134 181
MITZE, Johannes 17 120 125
MOEHLEN, Philipp 21 106
MOER, Christoph 21 61 80
MOERING, Joh Wilhelm 21 204 Johann Wilhelm 164
MOLLE, Friedrich 13 131 205 211 215
MOLLO, 46
MONTRESOR, 86 93
MOOCK, Johannes 8 119 189
MOORE, Mr 104
MORGAN, John 53
MUELER, Alexander 134 Christian 122 Daniel 17 Johannes 70 Karl 6
MUELLER, 191 207 Alexander 171 Andreas 218 August 216 Barthold 179 200 214 237 Christian 26 70 119 179 189 244

MUELLER (cont.)
Christian Karl 53 Christoph 8 17 77 110 237 Daniel 13 60 85 120 131-132 191 205 208 215 Daniel Christian 225 Franz 26 122 145 179 196 198 202 212 244 Friedrich 26 145 217 244 Georg 179 198 236 Henrich 13 21 52 63 131 205 211 Joh Peter 21 203 Johannes 13 80 87 169 Karl 9 20 60 119 147 163 188 Kaspar 17 119 146 Konrad 8 119 146 Ludwig 70 164 205 236 Nikolaus 89 124 131 205 211 235 Peter 163 231 Philipp 8 23 118 189 210
MUENCH, Philipp 197 230 Philipp Friedrich 70
MUENCHHAUSEN, Adj 58 Capt 65 67
MUENCHMEIER, Henrich 201
MUENCHMEYER, Henrich 179 222
MUENDER, Johannes 218
MUENSTER, Andreas 69 164 204 234
MUESKE, Adam 77 Johannes 191
MUHLENBERG, 95 Henry Melchior 83 94
MULLIN, Robert 74
MUNDHENCK, Bernhard 13 190
MUNDHENCKE, Henrich 26 122 124
MUNTERBACH, Jost (Justus) 218
MUNTHENCK, Bernhard 112 195
MUUS, Georg 15 61 149 196 Henrich 61 85 149 196 Hernich 15 Jakob 26 72 Philipp 6 120 125
NAHM, Friedrich 218 228
NASEMANN, Barthold 13 113
NASER, Bernhard 218 237
NASSLER, Andreas 70 122 124
NASSMANN, Barthold 147
NAVARRO, 111 171 Diego Josef 110 Gen 170 Martin 154
NELLE, Christian 20 149 163 203
NETTER, Johannes 171
NEUBAUER, Franz 218

The 3rd English-Waldeck Regiment

NEUBAUER (cont.)
  Wilhelm 92 122 191 208 232
NEUENDORF, Gottfried Joh 21
  Gottfried Joh Fried 236 Joh
  Gottfried 204 Johann Gottfried 164
NEUMANN, Ferdinand 119 146
  Johannes 221
NEUMEIER, Ernst 179 199 213
NEUMEYER, Johannes 8 119
  Wilhelm 26 48 84 229
NEUSCHAEFER, Friedrich 201
NEUSCHAEFFER, Bernhard 218 239
  Henrich 8
NEUSCHAFER, Henrich 110
NIEL, Arthur 104 Mr 156
NIEMEYER, Konrad 29
NIKOLAUS, Gottfried 69 197 233
NOELTING, Ens 111 116 Henrich
  Fried 11
NOEZEL, Lt 31
NOLL, Anton 8 60 87 119 189 224 244
NOLLE, Paulus 8 62
NOLT, Jakob Wilhelm 122 Jokob
  Wilhelm 26 Wilhelm 145
NOLTE, Christian 107 Friedrich 26
  122 145 Henrich 92 165 205 233
  Joh Arendt 30 Johannes 21 168
  Philipp 8
NORTH, Lord 226-227 239-240
NUEMANN, Ferdinand 9
OBACHER, Johannes 219
OBERLAENDER, Paul 89 117
OBERMANN, Henrich 179 214
  Melchior 171
OBKIRCHER, Thomas 179
OBKIRCKER, Thomas 200 233
OCHSE, Matthias 26 62
OEHL, Henrich 92 122 125
OHLHABER, Matthias 70 198 235
OHM, Henrich 29
OHMS, Hermann 8 106
OHNGEFOCHTEN, Daniel 219 239
OLDENBRUCK, David 76

OLDENBURG, David 76
OPP, Michale 84
OPPENDAHL, 119 Friedrich 89 146
OPPENHAEUSER, Peter 69 129
OPPENHEIMER, Nikolaus 219 238
OSBORN, Muster Master 64 Sir
  George 49 60 67 74
OSCHMANN, Konrad 26 122 125
OSTEN, Capt 32
OSTERHOLD, Konrad 17 62
OSTMEIER, Henrich 219 223
OSTWALD, Anton 29
OTTO, Friedrich 17 196
OURRY, George 66
PACKE, Wilhelm 26 122 124
PAER, Emanuel 21 76
PAIS, 220
PAPE, Kaspar 30 Konrad 134 165 205
  236 Rudolph 9 21 23 63
PARKER, Adm 136 138 143 153 Pater 126
PARR, John 239
PATERMANN, Friedrich 179 213
PATERSON, J 72
PATTON, Joseph 88
PAUSCH, Capt 3 41-42 Georg 2-3 40
PAUSTER, Pewter 204
PEARSON, Richard 42
PECKHAM, 151-152 162
PELSHAENGER, Joh Wilh 147
PELTZ, Reinhard 197
PELZ, Lorenz 219
PELZHAENGER, Joh Wilhelm 70
PENDLETON, Edmund 222
PENTZEL, 191 194 Capt 98 143
  Christian Fried 20 Christian
  Friedrich 128 148 162 Friedrich
  188 195 Maj 167 229
PERLE, Josef 70 113 190 194 223
PETER, 220 Friedrich 127 196 236
  Georg 90 131 205 211 235 Jakob
  90 131 203 211 235 Samuel 21
  171
PETERMANN, Friedrich 198

The 3rd English-Waldeck Regiment

PETERS, Christian 179 181
PETERSON, Paul Samuel 179 181
PEUSTER, Peter 22 164
PFEIFFER, Johannes 179 199 234
PFEIL, Henrich 13 113 145
PFENNIG, Jost 69 110 Karl 68 76
PFISTER, 192 Karl 131 203 211 Karl Fried 11
PFITZER, Michael 91 198 231
PFLADO, Adam 200 214 237
PFLANTZER, Johannes 70 106
PICKEL, Kaspar 17 19 27 133 198 214 231
PICKENS, Gen 173
PIEPER, Henrich 26 52 122 191 208
PILGER, Konrad 22 168 203 225
PINCK, Thomas 185 201
PIPHARD, Henrich 60 Joh Henrich 22 62
PIQUE, Wilhelm 8 119 145
PISTER, Thomas Wilhelm 33
PITTIUS, Daniel 217 Friedrich 219
PLADO, Adam 179
PLETZ, Reinhard 17
PLEUGER, Fried Joh Phil 8 60 Philipp 80
POHLMANN, Anton 15 48
PORTER, W 93
POTTER, William 194-195 202 207 209
POTTS, Richard 173
PREISS, Henrich 214 219 223 Michael 179 200 232
PRENTZEL, Konrad 30
PRICK, Georg 30
PRIEUR, Claude 26 133 182
PROBST, Georg 200 212 234 Georg Joh 179 Johannes 238
PROPPER, Christoph 31
PUETTMANN, Philipp 8 46
PULASKI, 83
PUOLL, Anton Andreas 91 146
QUANDE, Philip 165
QUANDS, Philipp 92 205 234

RAAB, Anton 24 244
RAABE, Christoph 17 62 Friedrich 17 197 Henrich 17 197
RABANAUSE, Johannes 26
RABANUS, Johannes 122 125
RABENSPRIOCK, Philipp 195
RABENSPROCK, Jost 179 214 237 Just 199 Philipp 13 113 190
RAINSFORD, 3 Capt 104 Charles 2
RALL, 50 55 Col 53-54 Johann 51
RAMSPOTH, Henrich 29
RANDOLPH, Edmond 173
RANGE, Wilhelm 26 107
RAUCH, Henrich 13 82
RAUSCH, 220
RAWLINGS, Moses 50
REED, James 63
REESE, Georg 179 202 223
REHROHR, Johannes 179 199 210 235
REICHARD, 220
REICHERT, Vice-Corporal 240
REICHHARD, 179 Johannes 199 210 233
REINECK, Andreas 8 63
REINHARD, Georg 219 Henrich 13 113 169 Sebastian 82 90
REINHARDF, Georg 232
REISMANN, Philipp 24 84 110
REISS, Michael 179 199 213 223
RENCKE, Joh Wilhelm 22 79 Wilhelm 61
RENNE, Friedrich 179 196 214 234
RENNERT, Jakob 22 163 203
RENNO, Gustav 24 120 125
REPCKE, Friedrich 219 238
REPP, Alan 217 Theodor 6 118 189
REUTER, 192 Bernhard 179 196 201 244 Christian 76 Friedrich 219 239 Jakob 22 146
RHODE, Joh Georg 30
RIEMENSCHNEIDER, Arnold Franz 77 Franz 6
RIESE, Henrich 8 119 145

The 3rd English-Waldeck Regiment

RIPP, Adam 238
RISCH, Johannes 69 122 191 209 224
RISCHEBUSCH, Christian 179 200 212 234
RISCHER, Josef 26 122 145
RITTER, Friedrich 89 129 Johannes 22 164 204
RITTMEYER, Aubust 26 August 76
ROBERTSON, Archibald 56 65
ROCHAMBEAU, Jean Baptiste Donatien De Vimeaur Comte De 222
RODE, Johannes 17 77
RODEN, Wals 10
RODEWALD, Friedrich 26 61 84 119 189 224
ROEDER, Johannes 177
ROEGEL, Johannes 17 76
ROEHLING, Philipp 22 163 231
ROEHRIG, Friedrich 69 131 205 212 235
ROELCKE, Christian 113 Christoph 13 124
ROEMER, Christian 230 Christoph 6 118 189 224 Friedrich 17 61 84 197
ROESTER, Valentin 29
ROHDE, 220 Christian 15 217 219 235 Daniel 17 128 185 198 201 Georg 219
ROLL, Joh Philipp 22 Johann Philipp 48 51
ROMRODT, Capt 31
ROOSE, Konrad 179 199 214 237
ROQUETTE, Karl 180 200 213 236
ROSE, Johannes 92 122 144
ROSENBERG, Joh Peter 79 Peter 61
ROSENBURG, Joh Peter 22
ROSENGARTEN, Joseph 34 Jos G 1
RUDD, Joseph 62
RUDELBACH, Johannes 15 196
RUESEL, Christian 4 46
RUETE, Christian 15
RUMMEL, Georg 180 199 213

RUMPELHARD, Michael 219 232
RUNTE, August (Justus) 172 Johannes 22 119 189 Justus 13 131
RUPP, Georg 90 119 132 145
RUPPERT, Ludwig 92 122 146
RUSALL, Wilhelm 15
SACHS, Michael 92 107
SAENGER, Henrich 201 Joh Henrich 20 Ludwig 219
SAHLMEYER, Andreas 79
SALMEYER, Andreas 69
SALTZMANN, August 90 110
SALZMANN, Johannes 26 61 85 122 124
SANDER, Karl 13 60 131 149 203 212
SANDWICH, Lord 39
SASSMANNSHAUSEN, Johannes 201 223
SASSMANSHAUSEN, Johannes 180
SAUNDERS, James 66
SAURE, Bernhard 20 63
SCHAACKE, Adolf 90 Johannes 92
SCHAAKE, Adolf 113 124 Joh 122
SCHADE, Jakob 69 77 Peter 22 163 203 Wilhelm 107 Willibald 91
SCHAEFER, Thomas 61
SCHAEFFER, Andreas 22 62 Christian 92 165 205 Christoph 31 Henrich 30 219 Joh Adam 204 Joh Georg 26 Johann Adam 164 Johann Georg 117 Johannes 6 8 26 110 119 133 189 198 214 230 Konrad 219 Philipp 20 107 Thomas 26 229 243 Wilhelm 24 90 119-120 124 145
SCHAPER, Bernhard 14 113 190 194 Georg 180 196 213 235
SCHAPPE, Lorenz 171
SCHARSCHMID, Jakob 26 122 191 208 225
SCHART, Michael 92 107
SCHEER, Lorenz 182 185
SCHEIDELER, Daniel 8 52

The 3rd English-Waldeck Regiment

SCHELE, Friedrich 26 133 198 214 231
SCHELP, Friedrich 18
SCHEMMING, Goerg 18
SCHENCKEL, Konrad 180
SCHENKEL, Konrad 181
SCHEPP, Jakob 131 205 212 233 Jakob Josef 14
SCHETZ, Wilhelm 123
SCHEUERMANN, Christian 110 Christoph Kon 8
SCHILLING, Johannes 219 228
SCHIMANECK, Gottfried 219 228
SCHIMMEL, Anton 165 205 Anton Jost 92 236 Joh Georg 26 191 209 224 Johann Georg 122 Jost 14 77
SCHIRR, Franz 17 120 132 191 208 215
SCHLAUDERBACH, Michael 69
SCHLAUDERBECK, Michael 197 231
SCHLEIERMACHER, Henrich 18 149 196 Johannes 110
SCHLOSSMUELLER, Henrich 62 Joh Henr 22
SCHLUCKEBIER, Henrich 6 117 169 186
SCHLUESSLER, Christian 212
SCHLUND, 220
SCHMECK, Georg 14 60 131 205 212 Jakob 14 131 212 Johann Georg 165 Johannes 14 77 205
SCHMID, Adam 18 197 Georg Henrich 30 Maj Gen 51
SCHMIDT, 191 207 Adam 52 Christian 128 Christian Lud 15 Christian Ludwig 148 203 Felix 69 164 204 Franz 22 62 Friedrich 26 61 122 145 219 Friedrich Jr 69 Friedrich Sr 70 85 122 124 Georg 18 55 Henrich 8 62 90 129 131 180 198 205 214-215 237 Jakob 22 76 Johannes 8 18 55 107 119 124 185 208 215

SCHMIDT (cont.) Konrad 18-19 26-27 62 90 122 131 172 191 208 212 221 Ludwig 92 131 165 188 205 209 234 Martin 49 Peter 91 144 Philipp 26 101
SCHMIDTMANN, Christian 180 199 213 223 Konrad 20 Sgt 23 45 Wilhelm 219 239
SCHMOECKELL, Georg Konrad 34
SCHNABEL, Karl 14 131 149 185 203 212 223
SCHNEIDER, David 127 129 231 David Sr 91 197 Franz 31 92 107 Henrich 14 30 63 Phil Geo 8 Philipp 59 219 239 Thomas 180 199 214 231
SCHNELL, Georg 31
SCHNEPPER, Friedrich 219 Henrich 134 198
SCHNETTLER, Otto 31
SCHNITZIUS, Ludwig 14 113 145
SCHOENBERGER, Johannes 70
SCHOENEBERGER, Johannes 171
SCHOENEFELD, Christian 91 129
SCHOPER, 220
SCHOTTE, Dietrich 11 112 190 194 235
SCHRAGE, Friedrich 90 120 124 128
SCHRAMM, Johann Zacharias 181 Zacharias 180
SCHRANTZ, Josef 14 61 84 113 146
SCHRAUFF, Georg 8 119 148 Konrad 8 119 125
SCHREIBER, Bernhard 90 112 190 194 209 Ulrich 8 60 119 189 234 243
SCHREIER, Johannes 180 185 200 233
SCHREYER, Franz 164 204 Franz Fried 22 236 Johannes 213 Leonard 92 Leonhard 146
SCHROEDER, Friedrich 18 117 Konrad 30
SCHUESSLER, Christian 205 235

303

The 3rd English-Waldeck Regiment

SCHUESSLER (cont.)
  Christoph 90 132
SCHUETLER, Geo David 26 Georg
  David 122 124
SCHUETTE, Henrich 219
SCHUETTLER, Adam 110 David 52
SCHUETZ, Anton 134 198 214 237
  Henrich 134 165 205 236 Wilhelm
  26 122
SCHULTZE, 192 Andreas 22 81 163
  207 223 Christoph 14 132 205 212
  Friedrich 29 Joh Stefan 22 236 Joh
  Stefanstiehl Johannes 204 Johann
  Stefan 164 Karl 217 232 Martin 70
  77 Michael 180 201 223 Wilhelm
  28 184 201 237
SCHUM, Friedrich 90 112 123
SCHUMACHER, Andreas 219 238
  Arnold 134 146 Henrich 15 77
  Philipp 180-181
SCHUMANN, Peter 69 172 207
SCHURCK, Ludwig 219 228
SCHUTLER, Justus 23
SCHWALBACH, Wilhelm 24 106
SCHWARTZ, Jakob 219 239
SCHWENCKE, Friedrich 14 61 119
  146 243
SCHWENDER, Wilhelm 219
SCHWERD, Henrich 181 Joh Henrich
  22 Johann Henrich 164
SCRIBA, Wilhelm 70 120 191 207
  210
SEBISCH, 102 Capt 89 Maj 88-89 240
  245
SECK, Friedrich 132 205 232
  Friedrich Josef 90 Josef Friedrich
  212
SEIBEL, Dietrich 197 Franz Adolf 204
SEIL, Hermann 18 120 124
SELTSAM, Geo Wm Joh 22 Georg
  204 Georg Wilhelm 225
SEMPER, Adam 92 165 205 234
SENFF, Hermann 29
SENFT, Georg 219 239

SERLE, Ambrose 45 53 67
SEUME, Johann Gottfried 1
SHARPE, William 173
SHAW, Charles 140 158
SHELBURNE, Earl Of 221
SIEBEL, Adolf 52 Dietrich 18 230
  Franz Adolf 22 164
SIEBERT, Friedrich 29 92 146 Jakob
  61 80 Joh Jakob 22
SIEGELER, Alexander 147
SIEGLER, Alexander 8 117
SIEMON, Christian 180 199 214
  Christian Johann 199 Friedrich
  217 219 Joh Christian 213 223
  Johannes 180 234
SIEVERS, Henr Hermann 18 Hermann
  152
SIMSHAEUSER, August 120 210
  Justus 191
SIMSHAUSER, August 207 Julius 24
SINEMUS, Christian 180 200 214
  Johannes 180 200
SINN, Konrad 180 213 228
SIX, Georg 14 132 205 212 235
SKINNER, 222 Maj Gen 66
SMALLWOOD, William 71
SMITH, Henry 155 John 32 Judge 222
  Robert 66 Rodney 42 William 174
SOELTZER, Friedrich 18 197
SOMMER, Josef 219 Thomas 219 228
SONDERMANN, Daniel 69 110
SONNENSCHEIN, Friedrich 14 113
  124
SORG, Andreas 91 146
SPAIN, King Of 110
SPARHAWK, Col 56
SPERLING, Georg 14 132 205 212
SPUDEL, 220
STABROTH, Gottfried 71 185 201
  237
STAEDTER, Ignatius Bach 130
STALLMAN, Wilhelm 189
STALLMANN, Henr Wilhelm 224
  Henrich 18 77 90

The 3rd English-Waldeck Regiment

STALLMANN (cont.)
   Henrich Wilhelm 119
STARCKE, Konrad 180 196 213
STAUDINGER, Karl 219 232
STEIGER, Emanuel 219 232
STEIN, Valentin 69 82
STEINBACH, Friedrich 219 228
   Henrich 8 46
STEINCK, Konrad 197
STEINECK, Konrad 18
STEINHARD, Johannes 31
STEINMETZ, Albrecht 180-181
STEINMEYER, Christoph 6 117 189
   Philipp 14 47
STEMPEL, Stefan 22 164 204
STEMPFLER, Kaspar 120 132 145
STEMPLER, Kaspar 71
STEPHANSON, Stephen 87
STERLING, Lord 97 99
STERNER, Henrich 219 230
STESSEL, Eberhard 146
STEUERNAGEL, 2 93 Carl Philipp 1
   Karl 163 203 Karl Philipp 20
STEVENS, Philipp 43
STIEGLER, Michael 8 122 145
STIEGLITZ, 33
STIEHL, Joh Henrich 22 236
   Johanrich 164
STIEL, William 104
STIERLEIN, Ens 97 184 Joh Henrich
   4 Lt 151-152
STIESING, Henrich 14 113 190 224
STINECK, Konrad 231
STOECKER, Johannes 14 113 190
   195 224
STOESING, Georg 195
STOESSEL, Eberhard 69 113
STOLTS, Jakob 232
STOLTZ, Jakob 219 Wilhelm 18 61
   85 152
STORMONT, Viscount 176
STRACKE, Johannes 9 110
STREHLE, Johannes 71 198 235
STREMME, Johannes 22 62

STREMME (cont.)
   Jost 18 120 125
STREMMEL, Ludwig 180 199 213
   234
STRIEPECKE, Henrich 8 119 189
STROSSER, Johannes 177
STRUBBERG, 191 Karl 188 Karl
   Henrich 6 117 245 Lt 185
STRUCK, Karl 180 200 213 234
STRUEBE, Stefan 14 113 194
STUART, 105 Charles 105 138 Col
   108 John 104 138 Mr 140
STUCKENBROCK, Henrich 18
   Ludwig 14 Mortiz 216
STUCKENBRUCK, Ludwig 113
STUECKENBROCK, Ludwig 148
STUHLDREHER, Friedrich 14 77
STUHLMANN, Karl 9
STUKENBRUK, Henrich 29
SUDE, Friedrich 163 203 236
   Friedrich Philipp 134 Wilhelm 14
   77
SUFFOLK, Earl Of 66 87 133 Lord 3
SUISS, Johannes 18 76
SULLIVAN, John 71
SUNDAHL, Chretien Louis Philipps
   De 50
SUNNAHL, Chretien Louis Philipps
   De 50
SYMONDS, Thomas 100
TABROTH, Wilhelm 180 198 210 233
TANNER, Fifer 15 Martin 9 12 62
TAUBERT, Wilhelm 8 60 85 165 197
   236
TEICHLER, Johannes 180 199 213
   234
TEIGTMEYER, Friedrich 14-15 45
TENT, Georg 26 122 191 208 210
TENTE, Christian 14 113 147
TEONGES, Henrich 165 205
TESCHEL, Georg 180-181
TEWES, Johannes 18 197 Philipp 69
   132 205 212
THALER, Lorenz 69 169

The 3rd English-Waldeck Regiment

THEILE, Johannes 238
THIELE, Friedrich 171 Johannes 219
THIELEMANN, 220 Georg 8 60 229 243
THIEMANN, Friedrich 181 Henr Fried 71 Henrich Friedrich 164
THIERLE, Konrad 6
THIETKE, Christian 89 168 185 201 237
THOMAS, Christoph 81 90 106
THOMSON, Mr 159
THOR, Johannes 26 122 144
THUMERICH, Peter 18 62
TILGHMAN, Tench 48
TISCH, Martin 86
TODT, Christian 134 165 205 Henrich 20 107 Jakob 11 132 203 212 225
TOENGES, Henrich 92
TONYN, Gov 154 173 Patrick 153
TOWNSHEND, Thomas 226
TRAINER, Marcus 22 164 204 236
TRAITLING, Christian 22
TRAND, Konrad 15
TREIER, Philipp 30
TREITLING, Christian 61 82
TREVELYAN, 48 52 58 Otto 3
TROLL, Friedrich 219 232 Joh Philipp 22 Joh Phillipp 101
TROST, Friedrich 219 Konrad 11 113 123 128
TRUEBENDDOERFER, Leonhard 92
TRUEBENDORFER, Leonhard 107
TUCH(SCHEER), Georg 231
TUCHSCHEER, Georg 180 200 210
TUITEL, Jean 92 120 191 207 Johannes 224
TUSCHOF, Bernhard 27
UELLER, Karl 203 Nikolaus 13 119
UHLE, Philipp 26 122 145
UHLMANN, Friedrich 91 235 Rriedrich 198
ULBRICHT, Gottlob 177
ULENBRUCH, Henrich 6 120
ULENBRUCK, Henrich 146

ULM, Jakob 219 238
ULMER, Kaspar (Adam) 219 232
ULNER, Georg 15 148 196
ULRICH, Andreas 180 Christian 92 122 124 Joh Peter 22 Johann Peter 48 Johannes 18 197 Lorenz 128 185 198 201 Peter 229
ULRICXH, Lorenz 18
UNGER, Johannes 12 112 190 195 224 Ludwig 30
URBACH, Andreas 213 235 Josef 180 200 213 234
URSALL, Ens 151 Theodor 168 Wilhelm Theodor 148
URSPRUCH, Henrich 132
URSPRUND, Georg 205
URSPRUNG, Geo Henrich 14 Georg 212
V AXLEBEN, Friedrich 6
V CANSTEIN, Bernhard 6
V DALWIGK, Ludwig 4
V HANXLEDEN, Joh Lud Wm 4 Wilhelm 15
V HORN, Konrad Albrecht 5
V NEHM, 60 Daniel 26 Kaspar 6
V RHENA, Karl 6
V SPIEGEL, Schoenberg 11
VAHLE, Johannes 24 120 145
VALAND, Johannes 22 163 204
VALENTIN, Joh Jost 22 205 Johann 61 Johann Jost 164 Johannes 85 231
VAN DER HOOVEN, Col 2
VAN HANXLEDEN, Col 38
VANLIER, William 87
VAUGHAN, Gen 58-59 72
VENTURINI, 34 242
VERCKEN, Konrad 71
VERGLASS, Joh Konrad 63
VERST, Adam 229
VESPER, Johannes 217
VOEPEL, Christoph 14 113 124 Henrich 26 61 85-86 117 Wilhelm 14 205 212

The 3rd English-Waldeck Regiment

VOGEL, Friedrich 29 Kaspar Anton 81-82 93
VOLAND, Friedrich 220
VOLCKE, Philipp 182 Philipp Henr 22
VOLKE, Johannes 27
VOLLMAR, Johannes 26 123 191 208 225
VOLLMUELLER, Georg 71 George 77
VOLMAR, Friedrich 123
VOLMER, Friedrich 93
VON AXELBEN, Friedrich 61
VON AXLEBEN, Ens 108 Friedrich 128
VON BAUMBACH, Alexander 15 188 195 209
VON CANSTEIN, Bernhard 118 128 148 243
VON CLOSEN, Baron 174
VON DALWIGK, Freiherr 2 Ludwig 62
VON EELKING, 3-4 34 37 47 109 116 151 170 174 242
VON EYB, Friedrich Ludwig Albrecht 65
VON HAACKE, Baron 165 Capt 75 85 192 195 Georg 24 60 117 188 209 243
VON HANXLEDEN, 152 Col 39-41 74 86 89 93 98 108-109 151 165 182 Lt Col 49 Wilhelm 182
VON HEISTER, Gen 49 65 67
VON HORN, Albrecht 188 195 Capt 39 Col 184 Karl 128 134 148 Konrad 81 243 Konrad Albert 133 Lt Col 134 150 157 160 166-167 194 202 207 245 Maj 82 98 102 108-109 Stefan 120 132
VON KNYPHAUSEN, Gen 49-50 Lt Gen 51 Wilhelm 41
VON LOEWENFELS, Georg Wilhelm 51
VON LOSSBERG, Lt Gen 240

VON MIRBACH, Gen 67
VON MUENCHHAUSEN, 71
VON NEHM, Daniel 122 191 208 Joh Kaspar 189 Kaspar 117 128 243
VON RHENA, Karl 77
VON RIEDESEL, Friedrich 41
VON SALZBURG, August Valentin Von Voit 66
VON SPIEGEL, Schoenberg 77
VON WALZOGEN, Capt 221
VON WILMOWSKY, Friedrich 15 188 195
VON WUTIGINAU, Mandern Capt 51
WAGENER, Ciriacus 86 Daniel 4 Georg 220 232 Jaspar 48 Johann Adam 31 Johannes 14 22 61 85 113 146 164 204 236 Kaspar 22 229 Nikolaus 180 200 210 232 Werner 22 163 203
WAGENSTAHL, Johannes 180 200 214 237
WAGES, Andreas 220
WAGNER, Johan Christoph 71
WAHL, Karl 22 61 87 164 205
WALDECK, 192 Chaplain 93 182 Friedrich 2 Philipp 2 4 188 195 Prince Of 143 186
WALKER, Josias 43 William 66
WALTER, Anton 220 223 Jacob 119 Jakob 8 189 224 Leonhard 9 63 Wilhelm 233
WARE, Richard 66
WARLICH, Jeremias 12 112 190 195 224
WASHINGTON, 53-55 58 96-97 99 173 226 Gen 47 57
WASSERFELD, Henrich 22 62
WATERSON, John 39
WATSON, James 67
WAY, Joh Tom 207 Johannes 185 Tom 215
WEBER, Andreas 220 233 Franz 18 196 Joh Henrich 90 119 189 224 Johannes 8 110

The 3rd English-Waldeck Regiment

WEICHSEL, Matthias 144 170
WEICHSELFELDER, Wilhelm 177
WEIDENHAGEN, Johannes 26 52 123 191 208
WEIL, Jost 220 238 Wilhelm 220 228
WEINECK, Henrich 82 Hermann 22
WEINEKE, Konrad 31
WEINHOLD, Anton 18 61 197 235 243
WEINKAUF, Adam 205 212
WEINKAUFF, Adam 90 132
WEIRAUCH, Adam 18 52 172
WEISENBORN, Johannes 91
WEISER, Thomas 61
WEISHAUPT, Christoph 6 118 189 210
WEISMANN, Philipp 61
WEISS, Adam 180 210 233 Christian 220 Gottlob 69 119 146 Johannes 180 200 213 228
WEISSENBORN, Johannes 198 231
WEITENKAMP, Christoph 14 77
WEITNER, Johannes 90 119 124 Leonhard 90 107
WEITZEL, Nikolaus 180-181
WELCKER, Ludwig 26 123 145
WELLNER, Johannes 23 170
WENDOLPH, Jakob 92 171
WENTHE, Christian 28 168
WERBEIN, Karl 110 Karl Geo 8
WERKE, Johannes 14
WERLE, Johannes 52
WERNER, Henrich 22 Jakob 8 132 172 Werner Henrich 110
WERSINGER, Wilhelm 69 164 204 236
WERTZ, Johannes 169
WESSERLEIM, August 180
WESSERLEIN, August 201 222
WESTE, Henrich 180 198 213 233
WESTMEIER, August 198
WESTMEYER, August 230 August (Justus) 134
WETHERDEN, Robert 67

WETTERHACKE, Johannes 14 63
WETTERSWALD, Martin 123
WETTERWALD, Martin 69 145
WEYBRENNER, Georg 69 119 169
WEYMOUTH, Viscount 67
WIBBECKE, Henrich 23 203
WICHARD, Stefan 8 117 189 Stfan 119
WIEBER, Jakob 171
WIEDERHOLD, Andreas 51 Joseph 50
WIEDESHALAT, Joseph 50
WIEDLAACKE, Otto 12
WIEDLAAKE, Otto 52 82
WIEGAND, 192 Gottfried 27 118 146 Karl 195 Karl Theodor 4 Philipp 120 145 Theodor 188
WIEGMANN, Christian 231 Christoph 69 197
WIEGOLD, Daniel 134 212 Dnaiel 205 235
WIENAND, Christian 15 76
WIESER, Henrich 168 Joseph Thomas 87 Thomas 27 133 168
WIETH, Samuel 180 198 214 237
WIGAND, Philipp 24
WILDSTACH, Franz Theo 191 Theodor 120 207 223
WILHELM, Christian 81 Jakob 18 197 Joh 8
WILKE, Henrich 23 61 85 164 205
WILMOWSKY, 191 Lt 151
WILSTACH, Theodor 24
WINCKE, Henrich 61
WINCKELMANN, Karl 18 171
WINTER, Peter 63 69
WINTERBERG, Johannes 14 62
WIRTH, Christian 180 202 223
WIRTHS, Franz Phil 20 Franz Philipp 163 203 209
WISSELER, Johannes 217
WISSEMANN, Georg 8 60 129 243
WISSLER, Johannes 238-239
WOLFF, Anton 14 82 92 170

The 3rd English-Waldeck Regiment

WOLFF (cont.)
    Jakob 30 Veit 180-181
WOLLENHAUPT, Johannes 23 163 204 229
WUERTZ, Johannes 69 119
WUTGINAU, 50
YORKE, Sir Joseph 2
ZAHNER, Johannes 92 165 205 236
ZANGE, Gottlieb 27 59
ZEIGER, Kaspar 27 123 165 191 208 210
ZENCKE, Erdmann 185
ZENECKE, Erdmann 71 201 231
ZENTLER, Michael 18 46
ZICK, Ludwig 6 117
ZIEGENHAINER, Peter 69 170
ZIEGLER, Franz 27 133 198 214 231
ZIMMERMANN, Christoph 30
    Friedrich 8 119 Heinrich 209
    Henrich 27 61 85 123 191 224
    Konrad 23 163 203 225
ZIPP, Peter 69 129
ZOELLNER, Friedrich 14 48 62
ZURMUEHLEN, Henrich 12
ZWICK, Karl 8 62

THE AUTHOR

Bruce E. Burgoyne was born 25 October 1924 in Benton Harbor, Michigan, and is married with three grown sons. His wife Marie, a Doctor of Education from the University of Southern California, is a helpful research companion and source of encouragement. Mr. Burgoyne's education includes a Master of Arts in Social Science (History, Economics, and Government) from Trinity University in San Antonio, Texas, plus course work at half a dozen other colleges and universities in America and overseas. He has also completed numerous military courses in such subjects as German language, Counterintelligence, and Public Information.

His employment, in addition to recently teaching a seminar course on the Hessians at Delaware State University, has included twenty years of military service in the Navy, Army, and Air Force, and six years as a civilian intelligence officer with the Army. During his military and civilian service he lived six years in Germany during which time he attended German language school in Oberammergau and two months of in-depth study, living in German households and undergoing Berlitz-type training. His daily duties required interviewing and interrogating in German, which further developed his knowledge of the language.

His forty years of research on the role of the Hessians in the American Revolutionary War have taken him and his wife to archives in England and Holland, as well as those in Germany and the United States, and resulted in the translation of more than 35 major Hessian documents.

www.ingramcontent.com/pod-product-compliance
Lightning Source LLC
Chambersburg PA
CBHW070231230426
43664CB00014B/2265